COMPUTATIONAL INTELLIGENCE

IEEE Press
445 Hoes Lane
Piscataway, NJ 08854

Books of Related Interest from the IEEE Press

Evolutionary Computation: The Fossil Record
David Fogel
2000 Hardcover 640 pp ISBN 0-7803-5379-X

Intelligent Signal Processing
Simon Haykin and Bart Kosko
2001 Hardcover 576 pp ISBN 0-7803-6010-9

Understanding Neural Networks and Fuzzy Logic: Basic Concepts and Applications
Stamatios Kartalopoulos
1996 Paperback 232 pp ISBN 0-7803-1128-0

COMPUTATIONAL INTELLIGENCE

The Experts Speak

Edited by

DAVID B. FOGEL
CHARLES J. ROBINSON

IEEE PRESS

A JOHN WILEY & SONS, INC., PUBLICATION

Published simultaneously in Canada.

Library of Congress Cataloging-in-Publication Data is available:

ISBN: 0-471-27454-2

10 9 8 7 6 5 4 3 2 1

CONTENTS

CONTRIBUTORS

Kenneth Bauer, Department of Operational Sciences, Air Force Institute of Technology, Wright Patterson Air Force Base, Ohio

James C. Bezdek, Computer Science Department, University of Western Florida, Pensacola, Florida

Rui J. P. de Figueiredo, Laboratory for Machine Intelligence and Neural and Soft Computing, University of California, Irvine, California

Gang Feng, Department of Manufacturing Engineering and Engineering Management, City University of Hong Kong, Tat Chee Avenue, Kowloon, Hong Kong

David B. Fogel, Natural Selection, Inc., La Jolla, California

Toshio Fukuda, Department of Micro Systems, Nagoya University, Nagoya, Japan

Pablo Funes, Computer Science Department, Brandeis University, Waltham, Massachusetts

Jennifer Hallinan, Institute of Molecular Bioscience, The University of Queensland, Queensland, Australia

Richard J. Hathaway, Math and Computer Science Department, Georgia Southern University, Statesboro, Georgia

T. Higuchi, National Institute of Advanced Industrial Science and Technology Tsukuba, Ibaraki, Japan

Gregory Hornby, Computer Science Department, Brandeis University, Waltham, Massachusetts

T. Itatani, National Institute of Advanced Industrial Science and Technology Tsukuba, Ibaraki, Japan

M. Iwata, National Institute of Advanced Industrial Science and Technology Tsukuba, Ibaraki, Japan

Matthew Kabrisky, CADx Systems, Inc., Beavercreek, Ohio

I. KAJITANI, National Institute of Advanced Industrial Science and Technology Tsukuba, Ibaraki, Japan

Y. KASAI, National Institute of Advanced Industrial Science and Technology Tsukuba, Ibaraki, Japan

JAMES M. KELLER, Computer Engineering and Computer Science Department University of Missouri-Columbia, Columbia, Missouri

NAOYUKI KUBOTA, Department of Human and Artificial Intelligent Systems Fukui University, Fukui, Japan

HOD LIPSON, Computer Science Department, Brandeis University, Waltham, Massachusetts

PASCAL MATSAKIS, Computer Engineering and Computer Science Department University of Missouri-Columbia, Columbia, Missouri

JAMES F. MCEACHERN, Office of Naval Research, Ocean Atmosphere and Space Department, Sensors, Sources and Array Program, Arlington, Virginia

ROBERT T. MIYAMOTO, Applied Physics Laboratory, University of Washington Seattle, Washington

M. MURAKAWA, National Institute of Advanced Industrial Science and Technology, Tsukuba, Ibaraki, Japan

H. NOSATO, Department of Information Sciences, Toho University, Funabashi, Chiba, Japan

MARK E. OXLEY, Department of Mathematics and Statistics, Air Force Institute of Technology, Wright Patterson Air Force Base, Ohio

JORDAN B. POLLACK, Computer Science Department, Brandeis University, Waltham, Massachusetts

CHARLES J. ROBINSON, CyBERS, Louisiana Tech University, Ruston, Louisiana; Overton Brooks VA Medical Center, Shreveport, Louisiana; Orthopaedic Surgery Department, LSU Health Science Center, Shreveport, Louisiana

STEVEN K. ROGERS, Qualia Computing, Inc., Beavercreek, Ohio

H. SAKANASHI, National Institute of Advanced Industrial Science and Technology Tsukuba, Ibaraki, Japan

RUDY SETIONO, National University of Singapore, Singapore

MARJORIE SKUBIC, Computer Engineering and Computer Science Department University of Missouri-Columbia, Columbia, Missouri

DONG SUN, Department of Manufacturing Engineering & Engineering Management, City University of Hong Kong, Tat Chee Avenue, Kowloon, Hong Kong

HAROLD SZU, Office of Naval Research, Arlington, Virginia

HIDEYUKI TAKAGI, Kyushu Institute of Design, Fukuoka, Japan

E. Takahashi, National Institute of Advanced Industrial Science and Technology Tsukuba, Ibaraki, Japan

Louis Wang, School of Electrical Engineering and Telecommunications University of New South Wales, Sydney, Australia

Lloyd Watts, Audience, Inc., Los Altos, California

Paul J. Werbos, National Science Foundation, Arlington, Virginia

Janet Wiles, ITEE and Psychology, The University of Queensland, Queensland, Australia

David H. Wolpert, NASA Ames Research Center, Moffet Field, California

Hans-Jürgen Zimmermann, Aachen Institute of Technology, Aachen, Germany

PREFACE

The 2002 IEEE World Congress on Computational Intelligence (WCCI 2002), held May 12–17, 2002 in Honolulu, Hawaii, marked important milestones in the development of intelligent machines. The congress represented the collective current state of research in neural networks, fuzzy systems, and evolutionary computation, three synergistic areas of computational intelligence that promise to have a significant impact on machine intelligence. About 1300 people attended this important meeting—the first meeting sponsored by the new IEEE Neural Networks Society following its transition from an IEEE Council. One highlight of the congress was a series of invited plenary and special lectures from the leading experts in the field of computational intelligence. This book provides an expanded, peer-reviewed record of many of these outstanding presentations, which were both a summary of current technology as well as a look to the future and a forecast of what problems and discoveries await us in computational intelligence. Thus, the book looks beyond the horizons of this rapidly expanding field just as the IEEE Press book *Computational Intelligence: Imitating Life*—from the 1994 WorldCongress (WCCI 1994)—captured the nascent beginnings of the field.

The papers presented here not only identify diverse aspects of groundbreaking research in self-organizing systems, situation awareness, human-machine interaction, gleaning insight from data, automatic control, supplementing human intelligence, and many other areas, they also indicate the challenges that we face and place the efforts of the computational intelligence community in perspective, without hype or undue pessimism. The result is a balanced, fair assessment of where our community stands now, still at the dawn of the new millennium, and a map to guide future efforts. Moreover, some of the results presented in this book represent novel contributions to the field of computational intelligence, and thus the book serves both as primary reference literature and as a tutorial and survey.

We thank all of the plenary and special lecturers at WCCI 2002 for lending us their time and expertise. Special thanks are owed to those who have contributed their expertise to us in this book. We sincerely hope and expect this volume to be of lasting value to the computational intelligence community. We look forward to the next IEEE World Congress on Computational Intelligence to be held in 2006, when we may learn of the progress that will have been made by building on the framework laid out in this book. That progress, no doubt, will come as a result of the efforts of people such as you, the reader, and we thank you in advance for what that future progress might bring to our community.

The editors thank Estevan Garcia, senior media specialist at Louisiana Tech's CyBERS, and Rosemary Robinson, past managing editor, *IEEE Trans. Rehab. Engr.*, for their help in assembling, producing a draft pdf version, proof-editing, and final compiling of the book. Without their help, and the diligence of all of our authors, this book would not have been possible.

DAVID B. FOGEL
General Chairman, WCCI2002

CHARLES J. ROBINSON
Plenary Chairman, WCCI2002

La Jolla, California
Ruston, Louisianna
March 2003

CHAPTER 1

THREE GENERATIONS OF COEVOLUTIONARY ROBOTICS

JORDAN B. POLLACK, HOD LIPSON, PABLO FUNES, and GREGORY HORNBY

1.1 ROBOECONOMICS

The field of robotics today faces a practical economic problem: flexible machines with minds cost so much more than manual machines and their humans operators. Few would spend $2000 on a vacuum cleaner when a manual one is $200, or half a million dollars on a driverless car when a regular car is $20,000, plus $6 per hour for its driver. The high costs associated with designing, building, and controlling robots have led to a stasis [1], and robots in industry are only applied to simple and highly repetitive manufacturing tasks. Even though sophisticated teleoperated machines with sensors and actuators have found important applications (exploration of inaccessible environments, for example), they leave very little decision, if at all, to the on-board software [2].

The central issue addressed by our work is a low-cost way to get a higher level of complex physicality under control. We seek more controlled and moving mechanical parts, more sensors, more nonlinear interacting degrees of freedom, without entailing both the huge fixed costs of human design and programming, and the variable costs in manufacture and operation. We suggest that this can be achieved only when robot design and construction are fully automatic, and the results are inexpensive enough to be disposable.

Traditionally, robots are designed on a disciplinary basis: mechanical engineers design complex articulated bodies, with state-of-the-art sensors, actuators, and multiple degrees of freedom. These elaborate machines are then thrown over the wall to the control department, where software programmers and control engineers struggle to design a suitable controller. Even if an intelligent human can learn to control such a device, it does not follow that automatic autonomous control can be had at any price. Humans drastically underestimate animal brains: looking into nature, we

Computational Intelligence: The Experts Speak. Edited by D. B. Fogel and C. J. Robinson
ISBN 0-471-27454-2

see animal brains of very high complexity, brains more complex than the bodies they inhabit, controlling bodies that have been selected by evolution precisely because they were controllable by those brains. In nature, the body and brain of a horse are coupled tightly, the fruit of a long series of small mutual adaptations; like chicken and egg, neither one was designed first. There is never a situation in which the hardware has no software, or where a growth or mutation—beyond the adaptive ability of the brain—survives. The key is thus to evolve both the brain and the body, simultaneously and continuously, from a simple controllable mechanism to one of sufficient complexity for a particular specialized task.

The focus of our research is how to automate the integrated design of bodies and brains using a coevolutionary learning approach. The key is to evolve both the brain and the body simultaneously from a simple controllable mechanism to one of sufficient complexity for a task. Within a decade we see three technologies that are maturing past the threshold to make this possible. One is the increasing fidelity of advanced mechanical design simulation, stimulated by profits from successful software competition [3]. The second is rapid, one-off prototyping and manufacture, which is proceeding from three-dimensional (3D) plastic layering to stronger composite and metal (sintering) technology [4]. The third is our understanding of coevolutionary machine learning in the design and intelligent control of complex systems [5–7].

1.2 COEVOLUTION

Coevolution, when successful, dynamically creates a series of learning environments each slightly more complex than the last, and a series of learners that are tuned to adapt in those environments. Sims' work [8] on body–brain coevolution and the more recent Framsticks simulator [9] demonstrated that the neural controllers and simulated bodies could be coevolved. The goal of our research in coevolutionary robotics is to replicate and extend results from virtual simulations such as these to the reality of computer-designed and constructed special-purpose machines that can adapt to real environments. We are working on coevolutionary algorithms to develop control programs that operate realistic physical-device simulators, both commercial-off-the-shelf and our own custom simulators, where we finish the evolution inside real embodied robots. We are interested ultimately in mechanical structures that have complex physicality of more degrees of freedom than anything that has ever been controlled by human-designed algorithms, with lower engineering costs than currently possible because of minimal human-design involvement in the product.

It is not feasible that controllers for complete structures could be evolved (in simulation or otherwise) without first evolving controllers for simpler constructions. Compared to the traditional form of evolutionary robotics [10–14], which serially downloads controllers into a piece of hardware, it is relatively easy to explore the space of body constructions in simulation. Realistic simulation is also crucial for providing a rich and nonlinear universe. However, while simulation creates the ability to explore the space of constructions far faster than real-world building and evaluation could, there remains the problem of transfer to real constructions and scaling to the high complexities used for real-world designs.

1.3 RESEARCH THRUSTS

We describe three major thrusts in achieving fully automated design (FAD) and manufacture of high-part-count autonomous robots. The first is evolution inside simulation, but in simulations more and more realistic, so the results are not simply visually believable, as in Sims' work [8], but also buildable. We investigated transferring evolved high part-count, static structures from simulation to the real world. The second thrust is to evolve automatically buildable dynamic machines that are nearly autonomous in both their design and manufacture. The third thrust, and perhaps hardest, addresses scaling to more complex tasks: handling complex, high part-count structures through modularity. We have preliminary and promising results in each of these areas, which we outline below.

1.3.1 Buildable Simulation

Commercial computer-aided design (CAD) models are in fact not constrained enough to be buildable, because they assume a human provides numerous constraints to describe reality. In order to evolve both the morphology and behavior of autonomous mechanical devices that can be built, one must have a simulator that operates under many constraints, and a resultant controller that is adaptive enough to cover the gap between the simulated and real world. Features of a simulator for evolving morphology are:

- Representation: should cover a universal space of mechanisms.
- Conservative: because simulation is never perfect, it should preserve a margin of safety.
- Efficient: it should be quicker to test in simulation than through physical production and test.
- Buildable: results should be convertible from a simulation to a real object.

One approach is to custom build a simulator for modular robotic components, and then evolve either centralized or distributed controllers for them. In advance of a modular simulator with dynamics, we recently built a simulator for (static) Lego bricks, and used very simple evolutionary algorithms to create complex Lego structures, which were then constructed manually [15–17]. Our model considers the union between two bricks as a rigid joint between the centers of mass of each one, located at the center of the actual area of contact between them. This joint has a measurable torque capacity. That is, more than a certain amount of force applied at a certain distance from the joint will break the two bricks apart. The fundamental assumption of our model is this idealization of the union of two Lego

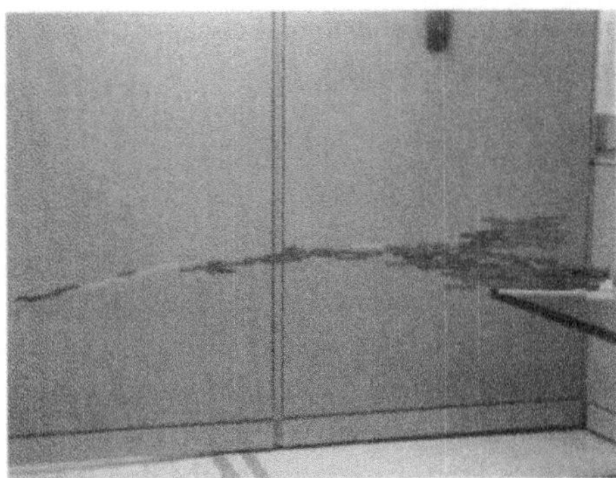

Figure 1.1 The FAD Lego bridge (cantilever) and crane (triangle). (See http://demo.cs.brandeis.edu/lego)

bricks. The genetic algorithm reliably builds structures that meet simple fitness goals, exploiting physical properties implicit in the simulation. Building the results of the evolutionary simulation (by hand) demonstrated the power and possibility of fully automated design. The long bridge of Figure 1.1 shows that our simple system discovered the cantilever, while the weight-carrying crane shows it discovered the basic triangular support.

1.3.2 Evolution and Construction of Electromechanical Systems

The next step is to add dynamics to modular buildable physical components, and to insert their manufacturing constraints into the evolutionary process. We are experimenting with a new process in which both robot morphology and control evolve in simulation and then replicate automatically into reality [18]. The robots comprise only linear actuators and sigmoidal control neurons embodied in an arbitrary thermoplastic body. The entire configuration is evolved for a particular task and selected individuals are printed preassembled (except motors) using 3D solid printing (rapid prototyping) technology, later to be recycled into different forms. In doing so, we establish for the first time a complete physical evolution cycle. In this project, the evolutionary design approach assumes two main principles: (1) to minimize inductive bias, we must strive to use the lowest-level building blocks possible, and (2) we coevolve the body and the control, so that they stimulate and constrain each other. We use arbitrary networks of linear actuators and bars for the morphology, and arbitrary networks of sigmoidal neurons for the control. Evolution is simulated starting with a soup of disconnected elements and continues over hundreds of generations of hundreds of machines, until creatures that are sufficiently proficient at the given task emerge. The simulator used in this research is based on quasi-static motion. The basic principle is that motion is broken down into a series of statically stable frames solved independently. While quasi-static motion cannot describe high-momentum

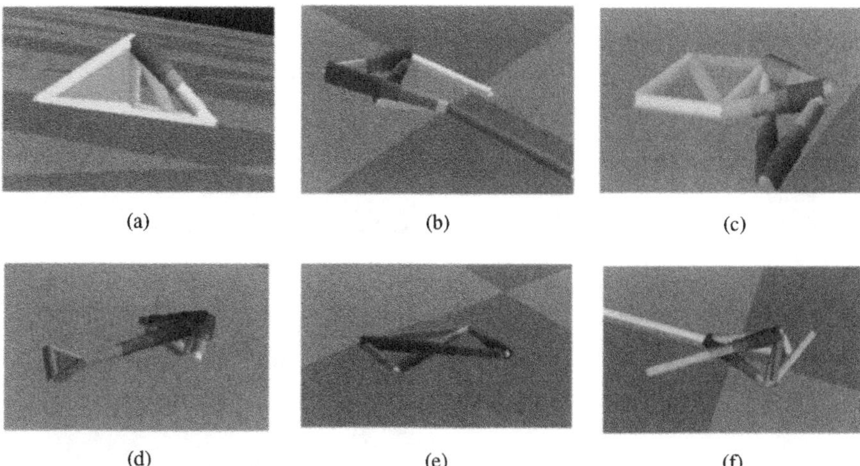

Figure 1.2 (a) A tetrahedral mechanism that produces hingelike motion and advances by pushing the central bar against the floor. (b) Bipedalism: the left and right limbs are advanced in alternating thrusts. (c) Moves its two articulated components to produce crablike sideways motion. (d) While the upper two limbs push, the central body is retracted, and vice versa. (e) This simple mechanism uses the top bar to delicately shift balance from side to side, shifting the friction point to either side as it creates oscillatory motion and advances. (f) This mechanism has an elevated body, from which it pushes an actuator down directly onto the floor to create ratcheting motion. It has a few redundant bars dragged on the floor. (See http://demo.cs.brandeis.edu/golem)

behavior such as jumping, it can accurately and rapidly simulate low-momentum motion. This kind of motion is sufficiently rich for the purpose of the experiment and, moreover, it is simple to induce in reality since all real-time control issues are eliminated. Several evolution runs were carried out for the task of locomotion. Fitness was awarded to machines according to the absolute average distance traveled over a specified period of neural activation. The evolved robots exhibited various methods of locomotion, including crawling, ratcheting, and some forms of pedalism (Fig. 1.2). Selected robots are then replicated into reality: their bodies are first fleshed to accommodate motors and joints, and then copied into material using rapid prototyping technology. A temperature-controlled print head extrudes thermoplastic material layer by layer, so that the arbitrarily evolved morphology emerges preassembled as a solid 3D structure without tooling or human intervention. Motors are then snapped in, and the evolved neural network is activated (Fig. 1.3). The robots then perform in reality as they did in simulation.

1.3.3 Modularity Through Generative Encodings

The main difficulty for the use of evolutionary computation for design is that it is doubtful whether it will reach the high complexities necessary for practical

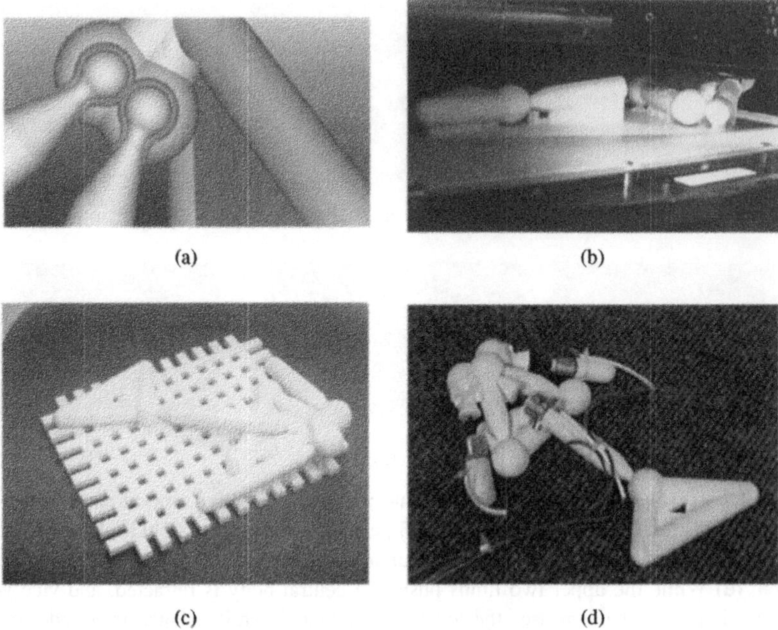

(a) (b) (c) (d)

Figure 1.3 (a) Fleshed joints, (b) replication progress, (c) preassembled robot, (d) final robot with assembled motor. (See http://demo.cs.brandeis.edu/golem)

engineering. Since the search space grows exponentially with the size of the problem, search algorithms that use a direct encoding for designs will not scale to large designs. An alternative to a direct encoding is a generative specification, which is a grammatical encoding that specifies how to construct a design [19,20]. Similar to a computer program, a generative specification can allow the definition of reusable subprocedures allowing the design system to scale to more complex designs than can be achieved with a direct encoding. Ideally, an automated design system would start with a library of basic parts and would iteratively create new, more complex modules from ones already in its library. The principle of modularity is well accepted as a general characteristic of design, as it typically promotes decoupling and reduces complexity [21]. In contrast to a design in which every component is unique, a design built with a library of standard modules is more robust and more adaptable [22]. Our system for automated modular design uses Lindenmayer systems (L-systems) as the genotype evolved by the evolutionary algorithm. L-systems are a grammatical rewriting system introduced to model the biological development of multicellular organisms. Rules are applied in parallel to all characters in the string, just as cell divisions happen in parallel in multicellular organisms. Complex objects are created by successively replacing parts of a simple object by using the set of rewriting rules. Using this system we have evolved 3D static structures [23], and

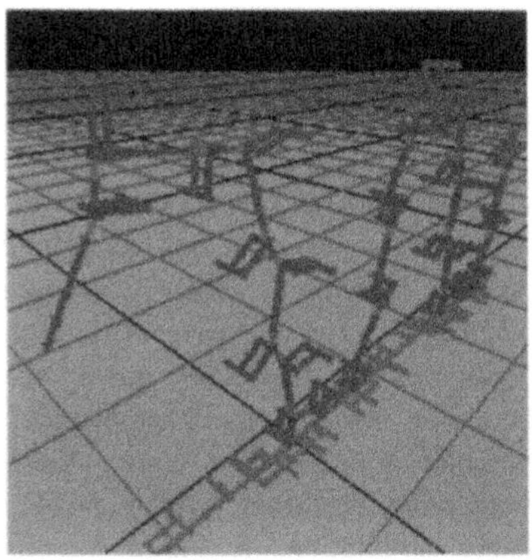
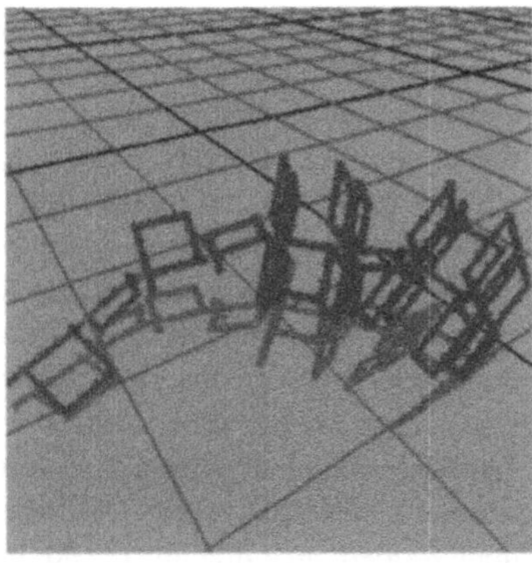

Figure 1.4 Examples of evolved, modular creatures. (See http://demo.cs.brandeis.edu/tinkerbots)

locomoting mechanisms [24], some of which are shown in Figure 1.4, and transferred successfully into reality, as seen in Figure 1.5 [25].

1.4 CONCLUSION

Can evolutionary and coevolutionary techniques be applied to real physical systems? In this chapter we have presented a selection of our work, each of which addresses a physical evolutionary substrate in one or more dimensions. We have

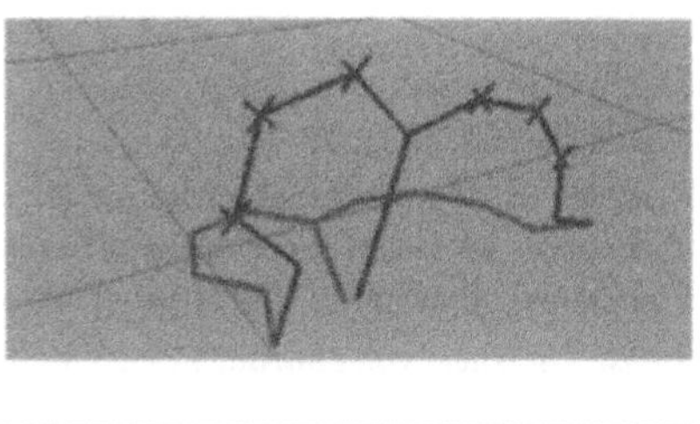
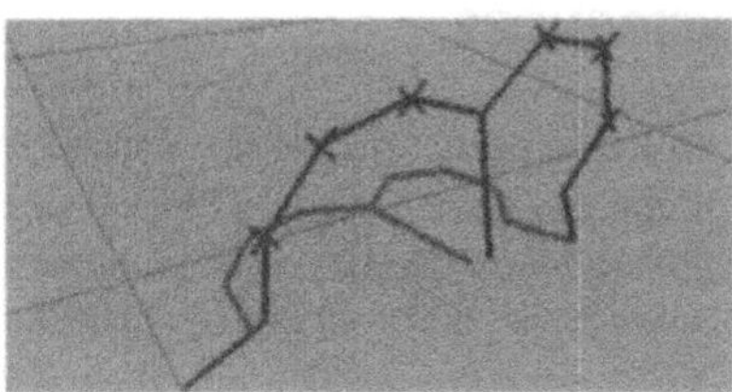
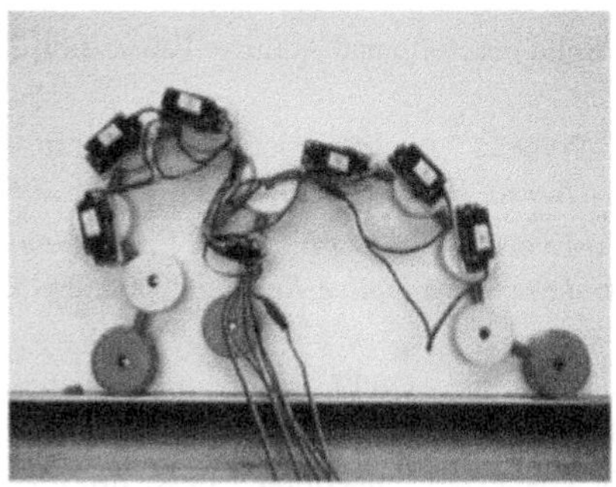
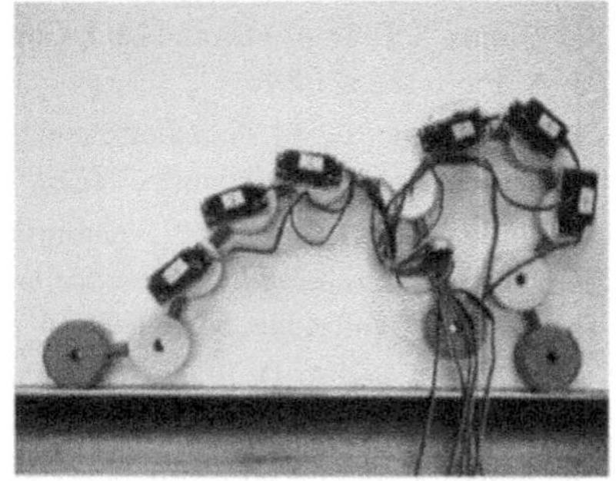

Figure 1.5 Two parts of the locomotion cycle of a 2D, modular locomoting creature in both simulation and reality. (See http://demo.cs.brandeis.edu/tinkerbots)

overviewed research in the use of simulations for handling high-part-count static structures that are buildable, dynamic electromechanical systems with complex morphology that can be built automatically, and generative encodings as a means for scaling to complex structures. Our long-term vision is that both the morphology and control programs for robots arise directly through morphology and control-software coevolution: starting from primitive controllers attached to primitive bodies, the evolutionary system scales to complex, modular creatures by increasing the dictionary of components as stored in the creature encoding. Our current research moves toward the overall goal down multiple interacting paths, where what we learn in one thrust aids the others. We envision the improvement of our hardware-based evolution structures, expanding focus from static buildable structures to buildable robots. We see a path from evolution inside CAD/CAM (computer-aided manufacture) and buildable simulation, to rapid automatic construction of novel controlled mechanisms, and finally the use of generative encodings to achieve highly complex, modular individuals. We believe such a broad program is the best way to ultimately construct complex autonomous robots whose corporate assemblages consist of simpler, automatically manufactured parts.

ACKNOWLEDGMENTS

This research was supported in part by the National Science Foundation (NSF), the office of Naval Research (ONR), and the Defense Advanced Research Projects Agency (DARPA).

REFERENCES

1. H. P. Moravec. "Rise of the Robots." *Sci. Am.*, 124–135, Dec. 1999.
2. K. Morrison and T. Nguyen. "On-Board Software for the Mars Pathfinder Microrover." In *Proceedings of the Second IAA International Conference on Low-Cost Planetary Missions*, Johns Hopkins University Applied Physics Laboratory, Baltimore, MD, April 1996.
3. M. Sincell. "Physics Meets the Hideous Bog Beast." *Science*, vol. 286, no. 5439, 398–399, Oct. 1999.
4. D. Dimos, S. C. Danforth, and M. J. Cima. "Solid Freeform and Additive Fabrication." In J. A. Floro (ed.), 1998.
5. P. J. Angeline, G. M. Saunders, and J. B. Pollack. "An Evolutionary Algorithm that Constructs Recurrent Networks." *IEEE Trans. Neural Networks*, vol. 5, no. 1, 54–65, 1994.
6. H. Juillé and J. B. Pollack. "Dynamics of Co-Evolutionary Learning." In *Proceedings of the Fourth International Conference on Simulation of Adaptive Behavior*, pp. 526–534, MIT Press, Cambridge, MA, 1996.
7. J. B. Pollack and A. D. Blair. "Coevolution in the Successful Learning of Backgammon Strategy." *Mach. Learn.*, vol. 32, 225–240, 1998.
8. K. Sims. "Evolving 3d Morphology and Behavior by Competition." In R. Brooks and P. Maes (eds.), *Proceedings 4th Artificial Life Conference*, pp. 28–39, MIT Press, Cambridge, MA, 1994.

9. M. Komosinski and S. Ulatowski. "Framsticks: Towards a Simulation of a Nature-Like World, Creatures and Evolution." In J.-D. N. D. Floreano and F. Mondada (eds.), *Proceedings of 5th European Conference on Artificial Life (ECAL99)*, vol. 1674 of *Lecture Notes in Artificial Intelligence*, pp. 261–265, Springer-Verlag, New York, 1999.

10. D. Cliff, I. Harvey, and P. Husbands. "Evolution of Visual Control Systems for Robot." In M. Srinivisan and S. Venkatesh (eds.), *From Living Eyes to Seeing Machines*, Oxford University Press, Oxford, 1996.

11. D. Floreano and F. Mondada. "Evolution of Homing Navigation in a Real Mobile Robot." *IEEE Trans. Syst., Man, Cybern.*, 1996.

12. J. C. Gallagher, R. D. Beer, K. S. Espenschield, and R. D. Quinn. "Application of Evolved Locomotion Controllers to a Hexapod Robot." *Robotics Auton. Syst.*, vol. 19, 95–103, 1996.

13. Y. Kawauchi, M. Inaba, and T. Fukuda. "Genetic Evolution and Self-Organization of Cellular Robotic System." *JSME Int. J. Ser. C. (Dyn. Control, Robotics, Des. Manuf.)*, vol. 38, no. 3, 501–509, 1999.

14. H. Lund. "Evolving Robot Control Systems. In Alexander (ed.), *Proceedings of 1NWGA*. University of Vaasa, Vaasa, Finland, 1995.

15. P. Funes and J. B. Pollack. "Computer Evolution of Buildable Objects." In P. Bentley (ed.), *Evolutionary Design by Computers*, pp. 387–403. Morgan-Kaufmann, San Francisco, 1999.

16. P. Funes and J. B. Pollack. "Computer Evolution of Buildable Objects." In P. Husbands and I. Harvey (eds.), *Fourth European Conference on Artificial Life*, pp. 358–367, MIT Press, Cambridge, MA, 1997.

17. P. Funes and J. B. Pollack. "Evolutionary Body Building: Adaptive Physical Designs for Robots." *Artif. Life*, vol. 4, no. 4, 337–357, 1998.

18. H. Lipson and J. B. Pollack. "Automatic Design and Manufacture of Robotic Lifeforms." *Nature*, vol. 406, no. 6799, 974–978, 2000.

19. M. Schoenauer. "Shape Representations and Evolution Schemes." In L. J. Fogel, P. J. Angeline, and T. Bäck (eds.), *Proceedings of the 5th Annual Conference on Evolutionary Programming*, MIT Press, Cambridge, MA, 1996.

20. P. Bentley and S. Kumar. "Three Ways to Grow Designs: A Comparison of Embryogenies of an Evolutionary Design Problem." In Banzhaf, Daida, Eiben, Garzon, Honavar, Jakiel, and Smith (eds.), *Genetic and Evolutionary Computation Conference*, pp. 35–43, 1999.

21. N. P. Suh. *The Principles of Design*. Oxford University Press, Oxford, 1990.

22. H. Lipson, J. B. Pollack, and N. P. Suh, "Promoting Modularity in Evolutionary Design." In *Proceedings of DETC'01 2001 ASME Design Engineering Technical Conferences*, Pittsburgh, PA, Sept. 9–12, 2001.

23. G. S. Hornby and J. B. Pollack. "Body-Brain Coevolution Using l-Systems as a Generative Encoding." In *Genetic and Evolutionary Computation Conference*, 2001.

24. G. S. Hornby and J. B. Pollack. "The Advantages of Generative Grammatical Encodings for Physical Design." In *Congress on Evolutionary Computation*, 2001.

25. G. S. Hornby, H. Lipson, and J. B. Pollack. "Evolution of Generative Design Systems for Modular Physical Robots." In *IEEE International Conference on Robotics and Automation*, 2001.

26. P. J. Bentley. "Generic Evolutionary Design of Solid Objects using a Genetic Algorithm." Ph.D. Thesis, Division of Computing and Control Systems, School of Engineering, The University of Huddersfield, Huddersfield, Yorks., UK, 1996.

27. P. Bentley, ed. *Evolutionary Design by Computers*. Morgan-Kaufmann, San Francisco, 1999.
28. R. Brooks. "Intelligence Without Representation." *Artif. Intell.*, vol. 47, no. 1–3, 139–160, 1991.
29. D. Cliff, and J. Noble. "Knowledge-Based Vision and Simple Visual Machines." *Philos. Trans. R. Soc. London: Ser. B*, vol. 352, 1165–1175, 1997.
30. P. Husbands, G. Germy, M. McIlhagga, and R. Ives. "Two Applications of Genetic Algorithms to Component Design." In T. Fogarty, (ed.), *Evolutionary Computing. LNCS 1143*, pp. 50–61, Springer-Verlag, New York, 1996.
31. N. Jakobi. "Evolutionary Robotics and the Radical Envelope of Noise Hypothesis." *Adapt. Behav.*, vol. 6, no. 1, 131–174, 1997.
32. C. Kane and M. Schoenauer. "Genetic Operators for Two-Dimentional Shape Optimization." In J.-M. Alliot, E. Lutton, E. Ronald, M. Schoenauer, and D. Snyers (eds.), *Artificial Evolution—EA95*, Springer-Verlag, New York, 1995.
33. W. Lee, J. Hallam, and H. Lund. "A Hybrid gp/ga Approach for Co-Evolving Controllers and Robot Bodies to Achieve Fitness-Specified Tasks." In *Proceedings of IEEE 3rd International Conference on Evolutionary Computation*, pp. 384–389, IEEE Press, New York, 1996.
34. H. Lund, J. Hallam, and W. Lee. "Evolving Robot Morphology." In *Proceedings of IEEE Fourth International Conference on Evolutionary Computation*, pp. 197–202, IEEE Press, New York, 1997.
35. M. J. Mataric and D. Cliff. "Challenges in Evolving Controllers for Physical Robots." *Robotics Auton. Syst.*, vol. 19, no. 1, 67–83, 1996.
36. N. J. Nilsson. "A Mobile Automaton: An Application of Artificial Intelligence Techniques." In *Proceedings of the International Joint Conference on Artificial Intelligence*, pp. 509–520, 1969.

CHAPTER 2

BEYOND 2001: THE LINGUISTIC SPATIAL ODYSSEY

JAMES M. KELLER, PASCAL MATSAKIS, and MARJORIE SKUBIC

2.1 INTRODUCTION

Consider the really great computational personalities of science fiction: Robby the Robot, HAL, The Terminator, Commander Data, Andrew the Bicentennial Man, to name but a few. Even though R2D2 is smarter, C-3PO's actions are easier to interpret. Why can we relate more to them than, say, to the computer on the *Enterprise* or the robot from *The Day the Earth Stood Still*? In our opinion, a large part of the reason lies in the (imagined) ability of these machines not only to reason about their environment but to discuss this reasoning with humans in a natural language or through other human-based media. In this chapter, we discuss efforts at the University of Missouri to move toward this goal of efficient linguistic communication between a computer (or a robot) and humans. We will not produce a survey of all research in this field (and apologize apriori), but provide our insights into solutions to particular subproblems and to speculate on the future utility of linguistic communication.

Determination and utilization of spatial relationships among objects in an image has been an active area of research for many years [1–11]. In earlier work, Keller and Wang [10,12] used a fuzzy rule-base to generate linguistic description of relative position between two image objects, and ultimately, to produce a complete description of the scene. The fuzzy rule-base received confidence values of the four main directional relations (LEFT, ABOVE, RIGHT, BELOW) and SURROUND based on the histogram of angles [7,8]. Subsequently, Matsakis and Wendling [11] and Matsakis et al. [13] designed a system for spatial relationship estimation through an axiomatic framework for functions from which "histograms of forces" were generated to represent the relative position between a pair of two-dimensional (2D) image objects. By selecting particular functions, we can construct various

Computational Intelligence: The Experts Speak. Edited by D. B. Fogel and C. J. Robinson
ISBN 0-471-27454-2

histograms, ranging from the histogram of angles to a histogram of gravitational forces. In [13], we utilized the histogram of forces to generate numeric features from multiple-force histograms that were then used to generate a linguistic description of a scene using a fuzzy rule-base. This approach encompassed the earlier paradigm and led to a richer language for scene description. Due to the complementary nature of the histograms of forces, it was even possible to construct a self-assessment measure for each linguistic description between a pair of image objects. Next, we used the properties of these histograms along with fuzzy similarity measures to match scenes while recovering the camera pose parameters [14,15].

2.2 FORCE HISTOGRAMS AND LINGUISTIC SCENE DESCRIPTION

The fuzzy relative position between 2D objects is often represented by a histogram of angles [7,8,10]. The histogram of angles associated with any pair (A,B) of crisp and digitized objects is a function Ang^{AB} from $\mathbf{R}$ into $\mathbf{N}$. For any direction, θ, the value $\mathrm{Ang}^{AB}(\theta)$ is the number of pixel pairs (p,q) belonging to $A \times B$ such that p is in direction θ of q. In [11], Matsakis and Wendling introduced the notion of the histogram of forces. It generalizes and supersedes that of the histogram of angles. It ensures rapid processing of raster data as well as of vector data, and of crisp objects as well as of fuzzy objects. It also offers solid theoretical guarantees, and allows explicit accounting of metric information. The histogram of forces associated with (A,B) via F, or the F-histogram associated with (A,B), is a function F^{AB} from $\mathbf{R}$ into $\mathbf{R}_+$. Like Ang^{AB}, this function represents the relative position of A with regard to B. For any direction, θ, the value $F^{AB}(\theta)$ is the total weight of the arguments that can be found in order to support the proposition "A is in direction θ of B." More precisely, it is the scalar resultant of elementary forces. These forces are exerted by the A points on those of B, and each tends to move B in direction θ, as depicted in Figure 2.1. Actually, the letter F denotes a numerical function. Let r be a real. If the

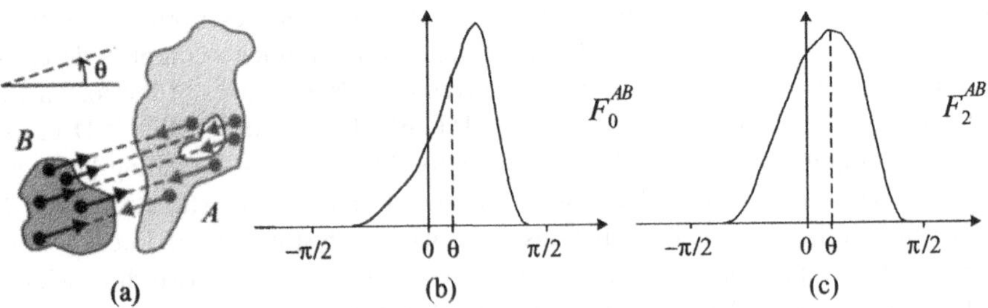

Figure 2.1 Force histograms. (a) $F^{AB}(\theta)$ is the scalar resultant of forces (black arrows). Each one tends to move B in direction θ. (b) The histogram of constant forces associated with (A,B). It represents the position of A relative to B. (c) The histogram of gravitational forces associated with (A,B). It is another representation of the relative position between A and B.

elementary forces are in inverse ratio to d^r, where d represents the distance between the points considered, then F is denoted F_r. For instance, the F function associated with the universal law of gravitation is F_2. The F_2-histogram and F_0-histogram (histogram of constant forces) have very different and very interesting characteristics. The latter, very similar to the histogram of angles, gives a global view of the situation. It considers the closest parts and the farthest parts of the objects equally, whereas the F_2-histogram focuses on the closest parts.

Force histograms are naturally not sensitive to translations, but they are sensitive to scale changes. A simple normalization (such that the forces sum to 1) allows this issue to be handled. Then, the forces are classified in different types. Consider, for instance, the proposition "*A* is in direction 0 of *B*" (which will be read "*A* is to the *RIGHT* of *B*"). First, the set of directions is divided into four quadrants, as shown in Figure 2.2. The forces $F_r^{AB}(\theta)$ of the outer quadrants ($\theta \in [-\pi, -\pi/2] \cup [\pi/2, \pi]$) are elements that, to various degrees, weaken the proposition "*A* is to the *RIGHT* of *B*;" the forces of the inner quadrants ($\theta \in [-\pi/2, 0] \cup [0, \pi/2]$) are elements that support the proposition. Some forces of the third quadrant are used to compensate—as much as possible—the contradictory forces of the fourth one. The proportion of these compensatory forces is defined by some angle α_+. Forces of the second quadrant are used in a similar way to compensate the contradictory forces of the first one. The amount of these compensatory forces is defined by α_-. The remaining forces are called the effective forces. A threshold, τ, divides them into optimal and suboptimal components. The optimal components support the idea that *A* is "perfectly" to the right of *B*: whatever their direction, they are regarded as horizontal and pointing to the right. The "average" direction α_0 of the effective forces is then computed, in conformity with this agreement.

In [13], we produce a linguistic description of the relative position between any 2D objects *A* and *B* based on the sole primitive directional relationships: "to the right of," "above," "to the left of," and "below." First, eight values are extracted from the analysis of each histogram F_0^{AB} and F_2^{AB}. These values are a_r(RIGHT), b_r(RIGHT), a_r(ABOVE), b_r(ABOVE), a_r(LEFT), b_r(LEFT), a_r(BELOW), and b_r(BELOW). They represent the "opinion" given by the histogram considered. For instance, according to F_2^{AB}, the degree of truth attached to the proposition

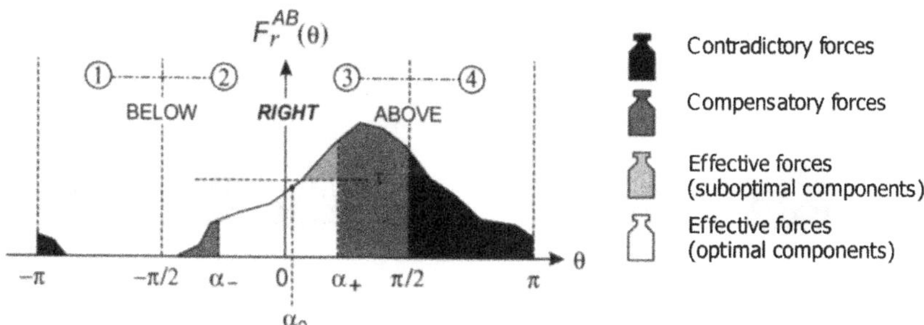

Figure 2.2 Force typology associated with the proposition "*A* is to the *RIGHT* of *B*."

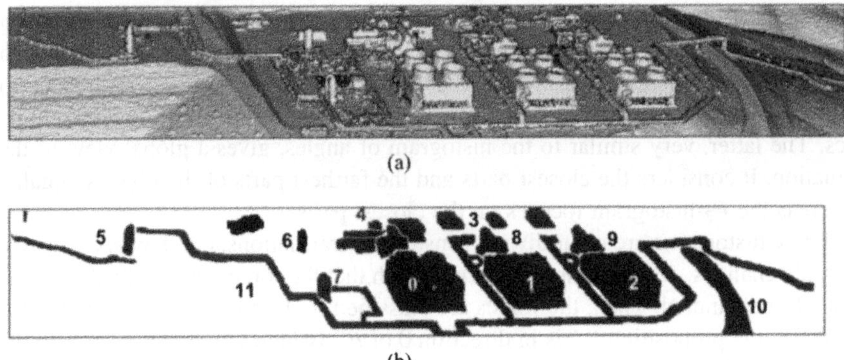

Figure 2.3 LADAR range image NAWC 20675: (a) after pseudointensity filtering; (b) after hand-segmentation and labeling.

"*A* is to the right of *B*" belongs to the interval [a_2(RIGHT),b_2(RIGHT)]. Then, the two opinions—16 values—are combined using a heuristic scheme. We work on the principle that F_0^{AB} is never too optimistic, but is often too cautious. We attribute the previous drawback to the fact that F_0^{AB} only has a global view of the situation, and we correct it considering F_2^{AB}, which focuses on the closest parts of the objects. However, just because of this characteristic, the opinion of F_2^{AB} may be excessive: sometimes excessively pessimistic, and sometimes excessively optimistic. Four numeric and two symbolic features result from the heuristic combination. They feed a system of fuzzy rules that finally outputs the expected description.

In [13], we used laser radar (LADAR) range images of a power plant at China Lake, CA, provided by the Naval Air Warfare Center. These images were processed by first applying a median filter, and then the pseudointensity filter $1/\sqrt{1+G_x^2+G_y^2}$, where G_x and G_y are the Sobel gradient magnitudes in a 3×3 window. Finally, the filtered images were segmented and labeled manually. Wang and Keller used the same real data to test a fuzzy rule-based approach for linguistic scene description [12]. Figure 2.3 shows a typical LADAR scene after preprocessing, followed by the results of segmentation and labeling.

As a simple representative example, consider the two configurations in Figure 2.4. The resultant linguistic description of part (a) is: "The stackbuilding 1 is *perfectly to*

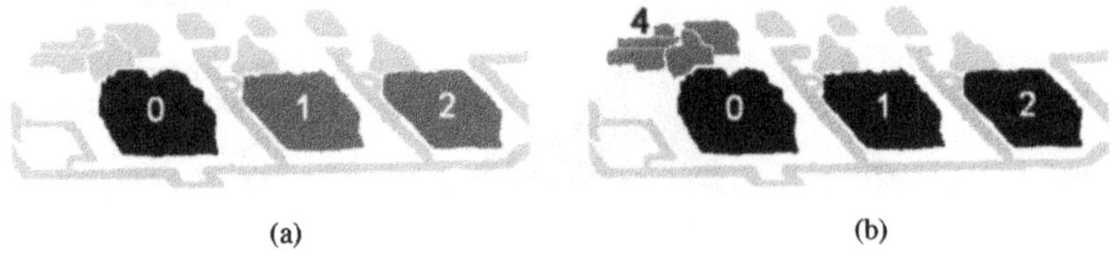

Figure 2.4 Two configurations from Figure 2.3. For each image, the reference object is in black, and the argument(s) in dark gray. The light-gray objects are ignored.

the right of the reference stackbuilding 0, but *slightly shifted upward*. The description is *satisfactory*." and "The stackbuilding 2 is *perfectly to the right of* the reference stackbuilding 0. The description is *satisfactory*," whereas that of part (b) is: "The group 4 of storehouses is *loosely above-left of* the group of stackbuildings. The description is *satisfactory*." System details and many other cases are shown in [13].

2.3 SCENE MATCHING

In [14, 15] we considered the problem of matching two views of the same scene from the information contained in the force histograms and LADAR range data. In this case, the views were reconstructed so that they were independent of the third dimension and the tilt (or declination) of the camera. In other words, the 3D information contained in the range data was used to determine the declination angle, and to transform the segmented scene to a position as viewed from above. Matching was then performed by comparing the relationships between the objects in the transformed scenes. The force histograms were treated as fuzzy sets, and similarity measures were employed to determine rotation and scale for each object pair match and to provide a ranking of the matches.

Figure 2.5 depicts an example of this matching. Only the four labeled objects were considered. The shapes of the objects and the distance between a given pair in these scenes vary greatly. By "eliminating" the declination, these factors are ameliorated. The similarity measures from [15] are shown in Table 2.1. In that table, the symbol *a_b* corresponds to the force histogram of the object pair (*a*,*b*) in the top image (rows) and in the bottom image (columns).

These results are not sufficient to match object pairs, let alone the entire scene. In every row, except for 0_3, the highest similarity measure does not correspond to the true matching. Thus, it is necessary to use additional information, such as the

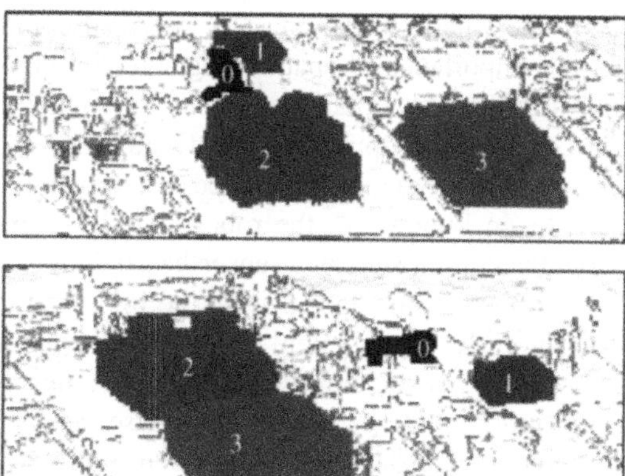

Figure 2.5 These two images are from the same scene shown from two different viewpoints.

TABLE 2.1 Similarity Measures of Object Pairs in Figure 5

	0_1	0_2	0_3	1_2	1_3	2_3
0_1	0.484	0.484	0.925	0.736	0.928	0.363
0_2	0.52	0.525	0.808	0.817	0.824	0.386
0_3	0.457	0.451	0.896	0.689	0.86	0.345
1_2	0.329	0.322	0.699	0.514	0.665	0.255
1_3	0.308	0.3	0.644	0.479	0.613	0.242
2_3	0.733	0.701	0.384	0.491	0.407	0.696

rotational differences and the scaling ratios calculated from the histograms. There are 720 possible ways to assign object-pair labels between the two images. Using all the information available (histogram similarity, recovered rotation angle similarity, and estimated scale consistency), an overall matching degree is computed for each case. The highest degree was found to be the true matching, with a value of 0.997. The next closest matching swaps the relationships of objects 0 and 3 with objects 1 and 3, and only earns a matching degree of 0.976. The high value is because objects 0 and 1 are both about the same size, and the relationships between them and object 3 only differ by a few degrees. Only 8 of the 720 matching possibilities achieved a matching degree above 0.9.

2.4 HUMAN–ROBOT DIALOG

We now move from external views of scenes to an ego-centered perspective. People often use spatial relationships in conversation to describe their environment, e.g., "there is a pillar in front of me and a doorway behind it," and to give instructions such as, "go around the pillar and through the doorway." Recent cognitive models suggest that people use these types of relative spatial concepts to perform day-to-day navigation tasks and other spatial reasoning [16; personal communication, 2001], which may explain the importance of spatial language and how it developed. We have initiated work, using the histograms of forces, to embed this capability into a mobile robot. Ego-centered descriptions are produced based on both direct sensor readings [17–19] and on sensor readings integrated over time into an occupancy grid map [20]. For example, in Figure 2.6, the robot and six segmented and labeled objects extracted from the current state of a sensor-based digital grid map are shown for scene 1. Note the robot heading specified by the line from the center (looking "toward" object 5). The fuzzy logic system using force histogram inputs produces the detailed and high-level linguistic descriptions shown in the textbox. The linguistic nature of this description could be used as a concise means of communication with a person in an interactive fashion. In fact, as demonstrated in [21], the robots seem human-like because we can interact with them in the same way we would interact with another person.

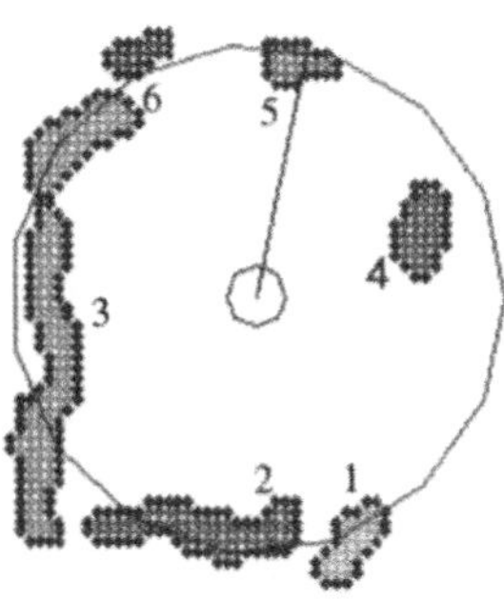

Scene 1

DETAILED SPATIAL DESCRIPTIONS for 6 OBJECTS IN SCENE 1:

Object number 1 is mostly behind me but somewhat to the right (the description is satisfactory). The object is very close.

Object number 2 is behind me (the description is satisfactory). The object is very close.

Object number 3 is to the left of me but extends to the rear relative to me (the description is satisfactory). The object is very close.

Object number 4 is mostly to the right of me but somewhat forward (the description is satisfactory). The object is very close.

Object number 5 is in front of me (the description is satisfactory). The object is very close.

Object number 6 is to the left-front of me (the description is satisfactory). The object is close.

HIGH-LEVEL DESCRIPTION

There are objects in front of me and behind me.

Object number 3 is to the left of me.

Object number 4 is mostly to the right of me.

Figure 2.6 Robot scene 1. Objects were extracted from an actual robot-sensed grid map and the detailed and high-level descriptions were produced by the fuzzy logic system.

Figure 2.7 contains a second example of the descriptive power of this robot language. The environment is the same as in scene 1, but the robot is headed in a different direction. Note in particular that the high-level description is very concise. From it, the robot or a person controlling the robot could easily deduce that there is an opening to the rear.

Of course, it is difficult to get a real feeling for where the robot is from this information alone since the objects can have an arbitrary numeric labeling. Since the goal of this particular project is to have the robot interact with a person within a given environment over time, some objects in the grid map will always be present and could be labeled by the robot or the human. Figure 2.8 shows an example where on one time snapshot, the pillar was identified and labeled by a human. On the current frame, the robot sensor-based grid map generates object 3 that overlaps the pillar object. From a simple algorithm that matches linguistic spatial descriptions and the distance values, the final merged explanation equates the pillar and object 3. This capability enhances the information content of a two-way communication. Much more work is needed to allow the robot to perform object recognition. Here, though, the advantage is that the environment is reasonably stable, and so, the number and type of objects can be restricted. Additionally, the ability for the human to interact easily with the robot to specify names for particular objects lessens

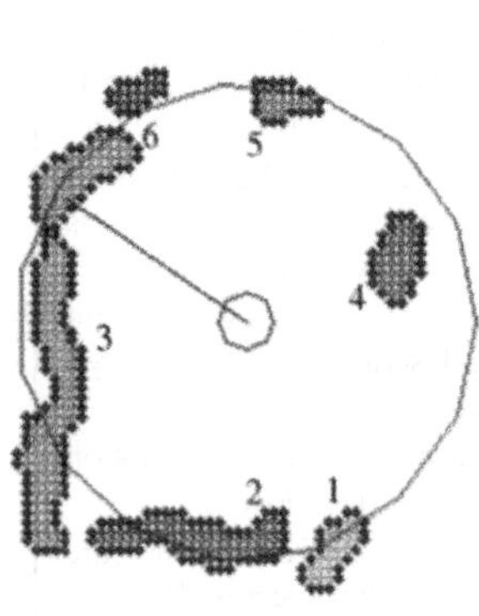

Scene 2

DETAILED SPATIAL DESCRIPTIONS for 6 OBJECTS IN SCENE 2:

Object number 1 is mostly behind me but somewhat to the left (the description is satisfactory). The object is very close.

Object number 2 is mostly to the left of me but extends to the rear relative to me (the description is satisfactory). The object is very close.

Object number 3 is in front of me but extends to the left relative to me (the description is satisfactory). The object is very close.

Object number 4 is mostly to the right of me but somewhat to the rear (the description is satisfactory). The object is very close.

Object number 5 is mostly to the right of me but somewhat forward (the description is satisfactory). The object is very close.

Object number 6 is mostly in front of me but somewhat to the right (the description is satisfactory). The object is close.

HIGH-LEVEL DESCRIPTION:

There are objects in front of me, on my rear left, and on my right.

Figure 2.7 Robot scene 2. The basic scene is the same as in Figure 2.6. The robot heading, and hence, the generated detailed and high-level descriptions are different.

the burden on fully autonomous recognition in uncertain environments. Recognition is difficult for robots, but usually easy for humans, so the human provides the difficult recognition for the robot and names landmarks that can be used later as references in the dialog.

With this spatial information and these linguistic descriptions, in [21] a dialog using a spatial language was established with the robot. As an example, consider the scene in Figure 2.7 for the dialog below. This figure is similar to those shown in [21] and utilizes the multimodal robot interface developed at the Naval Research Laboratory [22]. The robot responds using synthesized speech output.

User: "How many objects do you see?"
Robot: "I am sensing 6 objects."
User: "What objects do you see?"
Robot: "There are objects in front of me, on my rear left, and on my right."
User: "Where is the nearest object on your right?"
Robot: "Object number 4 is mostly to the right of me but somewhat to the rear. It is very close."

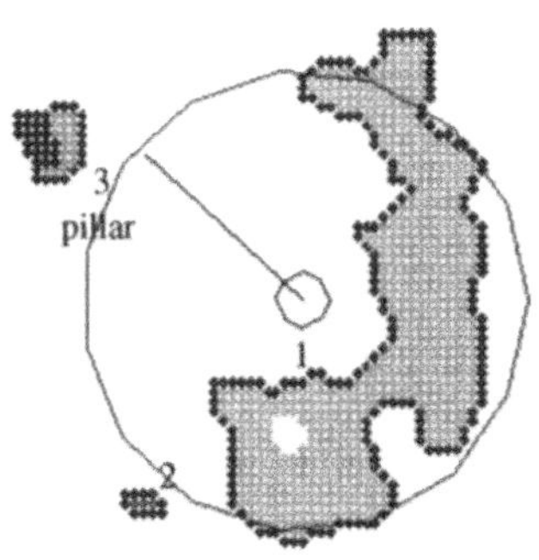

Scene 3

DETAILED SPATIAL DESCRIPTIONS for 3 OBJECTS IN SCENE 3:

I am surrounded from the rear (surrounded by object number 1). The object is very close.

Object number 2 is to the left of me (the description is satisfactory). The object is close.

Object number 3 is mostly in front of me but somewhat to the left (the description is satisfactory). The object is close.

HIGH-LEVEL DESCRIPTION:

I am surrounded from the rear. Object number 2 is to the left of me. Object number 3 is mostly in front of me.

Persistent Objects:

The pillar is mostly in front of me but somewhat to the left (the description is satisfactory). The object is close.

MERGED HIGH-LEVEL DESCRIPTION:

I am surrounded from the rear. Object number 2 is to the left of me. The pillar is mostly in front of me

Figure 2.8 Demonstration of a merged high-level description when a "persistent" object is given a label by a human.

Motion directives can also be given using spatial language, as shown below:

User: "Go to the nearest object in front of you."
Robot: "Looking for the nearest object in front of me." "I found it. Going to the object."

2.5 SKETCHED ROUTE MAP UNDERSTANDING

When someone invites you to their house and you are not quite sure where it is, often times you ask your friend to draw a map. Certainly these maps are not precise and to scale, but if there are sufficient landmarks, we normally do not have too much trouble navigating to the destination. A human-friendly method to communicate qualitative route information to a robot would be the same: hand-drawn route maps in which the user sketches an approximate representation of the environment and then draws the desired robot path within that scene. The communication medium can be a personal digital assistant (PDA), such as a PalmPilot, as in [20], and the information extracted from a sketch includes spatial information about the map and

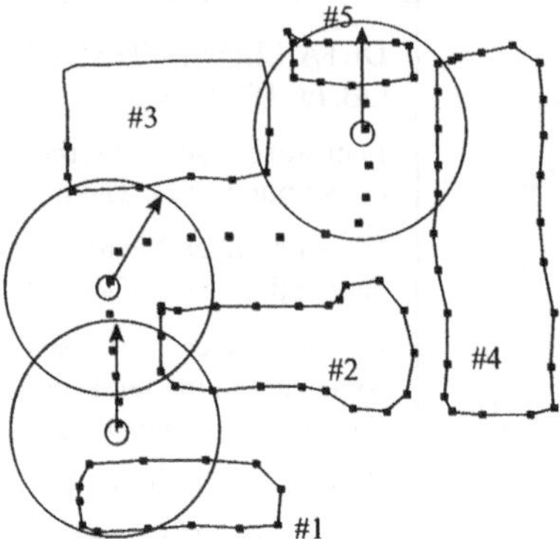

Figure 2.9 The PDA sketch. The original sketch with an overlay of the robot's sensory radius for several points along the route.

a qualitative path through the indicated landmarks. The stylus interface of the PDA allows the person to sketch a map much as he or she would on paper for a friend. The PDA captures the string of (x,y) coordinates sketched on the screen, which forms a digital representation suitable for processing. This information is used to build a task representation for the robot, which operates as a semiautonomous vehicle. In this approach, all information and the resultant representation are based on robot sensing and *relative* instead of *absolute* position.

Figure 2.9 displays three particular locations on a path that was drawn by a user along with the representation of the principal landmarks. In addition to extracting

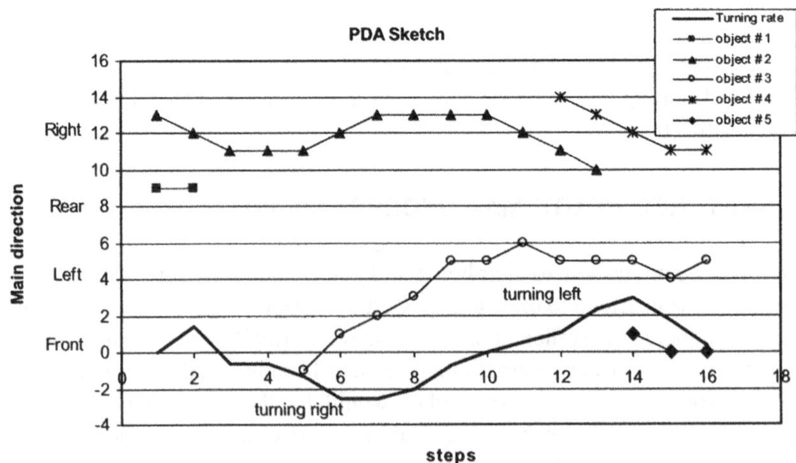

Figure 2.10 Normalized turning rate of the robot along the sketched route with the corresponding discrete main directions of the objects.

spatial information with respect to the labeled objects as before, we also extract the movement of the robot along the sketched path. The computation of the robot heading provides an instantaneous orientation. However, we also want to track the change in orientation over time and compute what would correspond to robot commands, e.g., move forward, turn right, make a "hard" left. The turning rate is determined by computing the change in instantaneous heading between two adjacent route points and normalizing by the distance between the points. A positive rate means a turn to the left, and a negative rate means a turn to the right.

In Figure 2.10, the main direction of each object is plotted for the route steps in which the object is "in view;" labels of the corresponding directions are displayed on the graph to show the symbolic connection. The normalized turning rate that tracks the robot movement along the trajectory is also shown. The turning rate, although not translated into discrete robot commands, shows the general trend in the robot movement along the route and the correlation with relative positions of the environment landmarks. At the beginning of the route, when object #1 is behind the robot, the robot's movement is generally straight ahead (slightly to the left). When object #3 is in view, the robot turns to the right until the object is mostly on the left. When object #4 is in view to the front, the robot turns left and stops when object #5 is in front and very close. In this way, we can extract the key points along the route where a change in direction is made.

2.6 THE FUTURE

The ability to interact with computers and particularly with robots in natural human ways will make these devices immeasurably more useful. We think the research toward that goal presented in this chapter is pretty impressive. But we have just scratched the surface, and much more work needs to be done to realize the goal. Let us speculate for a while. One of the tools that will make a major impact on getting robots to behave in a more human-like fashion is *recognition technology*. Recognition technology, as defined by L. Zadeh [23], refers to current or future systems that have the potential to provide a "quantum jump in the capabilities of today's recognition systems." Zadeh claims that this can occur as a result of three converging developments: (1) major advances in sensor technology; (2) major advances in sensor data-processing technology; and (3) the use of soft computing techniques to infer a conclusion from observed data. Exploring new soft computing recognition techniques coupled closely with advances in sensors and signal/image processing will significantly enhance the ability of robots to become increasingly autonomous. Handling the uncertainty and ambiguity in object recognition is a requirement to intelligent-like behavior. From the current trends, we see a steady improvement in this aspect of the bigger problem.

The key ingredient, though, in any application is the ability of the robot or the computer system to interact with people. So, what is coming down the road? In the short term, we think that significant near-term advances will be made in fairly (though not completely) structured environments. Besides getting better with the

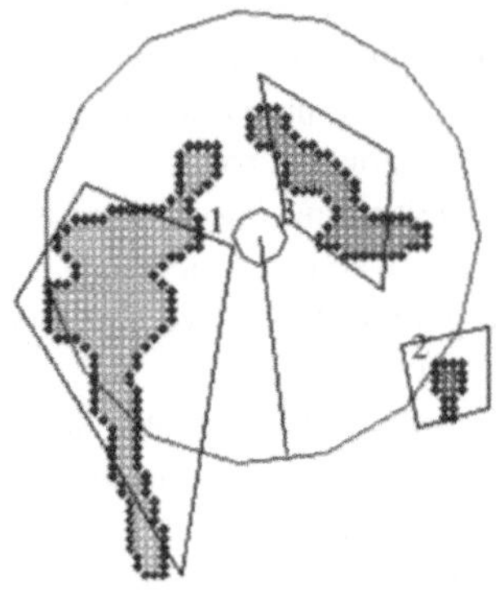

DETAILED SPATIAL DESCRIPTIONS for 3 OBJECTS IN SCENE 4:

Object number 1 is to the right of me (the description is satisfactory). The object is very close.

Object number 2 is to the left-front of me (the description is satisfactory). The object is close.

Object number 3 is loosely behind-left of me (the description is satisfactory). The object is very close.

Figure 2.11 Robot scene depicting potential places for the robot to move right of, left of, in front of, and behind each object. Places were determined by the relative-position information.

communication as indicated in this chapter, robots will be able to interpret dynamic behavioral commands, such as "Go to the right of object #2," or "Continue moving generally to the south until you pass behind object #3." Figure 2.11 shows some preliminary work using histograms of forces on defining positions that could be considered right of, left of, in front of, and behind the three objects in scene 4.

In the realm of automated surveillance, we see big advances coming in the way of temporal processing. For example, systems that can report activities like "Object 1 is moving mostly north but a little east" or "The car is executing a left turn" are currently being investigated. In this case, we are envisioning systems that can perform such an analysis based only on the relative linguistic positions of objects on a sequence of frames while resorting directly to the image data. These applications will expand both in scope and complexity. Full 3D spatial reasoning is also on the near horizon. Besides the obvious use in medical and biological imagery, coupling (almost) 3D reasoning to range images will provide better static and temporal descriptions of natural scenes.

Down the road a bit, we foresee greater application of robotics to the increasingly important task of search and rescue. Here, the environment is very uncertain and perhaps dynamically changing. It will be essential for our machines not only to be able to react to the environment, but to communicate with people and to receive and interpret possibly complicated linguistic commands. Flexibility and robustness will be at a premium. Not only research, but intense engineering development will be required to make the machines reliable enough to bet human life on. On the lighter side, personal-assistant robots that can recognize particular people and interact with them would be a great benefit to, say, bed-ridden children.

Is the Bicentennial Man on the horizon? Probably not, but the future of linguistic human/machine interaction is bright. Let us communicate.

ACKNOWLEDGMENTS

The authors thank Clifford Lau and Behzad Kamgar-Parsi at the Office of Naval Research for their support of this research through ONR Grant N00014-96-0439. We also thank Alan Schultz, Dennis Perzanowski, Bill Adams, and Magda Bugajska of the Naval Research Laboratory for their assistance and contributions to human/robot interaction.

REFERENCES

1. P. Winston. "Learning Structural Descriptions from Examples." In P. Winston (ed.), *The Psychology of Computer Vision*, McGraw-Hill, New York, 1975.
2. J. Freeman. "The Modeling of Spatial Relations." *Comput. Graphics Image Process.*, vol. 4, 156–171, 1975.
3. R. Brooks. "Symbolic Reasoning Among 3-D Models and 2-D Images." *Artif. Intell.*, vol. 17, 285–348, 1981.
4. S. Dutta. "Approximate Spatial Reasoning: Integrating Qualitative and Quantitative Constraints." *Int. J. Approximate Reasoning*, vol. 5, 307–331, 1991.
5. E. Walker, M. Herman, and T. Kanade. "A Framework for Representing and Reasoning about Three-Dimensional Objects in Vision." *Artif. Intell.*, vol. 9, no. 2, 47–58, 1988.
6. R. Antony. "A Hybrid Spatial/Object-Oriented DBMS to Support Automated Spatial, Hierarchical, and Temporal Reasoning." In S. Chen (ed.), *Advances in Spatial Reasoning*, vol. 1, pp. 63–132, Ablex Publishing, Norwood, NJ, 1990.
7. R. Krishnapuram, J. M. Keller, and Y. Ma. "Quantitative Analysis of Properties and Spatial Relations of Fuzzy Image Regions." *IEEE Trans. Fuzzy Syst.*, vol. 1, no. 3, 222–233, 1993.
8. K. Miyajima and A. Ralescu, "Spatial Organization in 2D Segmented Images: Representation and Recognition of Primitive Spatial Relations." *Fuzzy Sets Syst.*, vol. 65, no. 2/3, 225–236, 1994.
9. J. M. Keller and X. Wang. "Comparison of Spatial Relation Definitions in Computer Vision." In *ISUMA-NAFIPS'95*, College Park, MD, 1995, pp. 679–684.
10. X. Wang and J. M. Keller. "Human-Based Spatial Relationship Generalization Through Neural/Fuzzy Approaches." *Fuzzy Sets Syst.*, vol. 101, no. 1, 5–20, 1999.
11. P. Matsakis and L. Wendling. "A New Way to Represent the Relative Position between Areal Objects." *IEEE Trans. Pattern Anal. Mach. Intell.*, vol. 21, no. 7, 634–643, 1999.
12. J. M. Keller and X. Wang. "A Fuzzy Rule-based Approach for Scene Description Involving Spatial Relationships." *Comput. Vision Image Understanding*, vol. 80, 21–41, 2000.
13. P. Matsakis, J. Keller, L. Wendling, J. Marjamaa, and O. Sjahputera. "Linguistic Description of Relative Positions of Objects in Images." *IEEE Trans. Syst., Man, Cybern.*, vol. 31, no. 4, 573–588, 2001.
14. O. Sjahputera, J.M. Keller, P. Matsakis, P. Gader, and J. Marjamaa. "Histogram-Based Scene Matching Measures." *Proceedings of NAFIPS'2000*, Atlanta, GA, July 2000, pp. 392–396.
15. J. Marjamaa, O. Sjahputera, J. Keller, and P. Matsakis. "Fuzzy Scene Matching in LADAR Imagery." In *Proceedings of the Tenth IEEE International Conference on Fuzzy Systems*, Melbourne, Australia, December, 2001.

16. F. H. Previc. "The Neuropsychology of 3-D Space." Psychological Rev., vol. 124, no. 2, 123–164, 1998.
17. M. Skubic, G. Chronis, P. Matsakis, and J. Keller. "Generating Linguistic Spatial Descriptions from Sonar Readings Using the Histogram of Forces." In *Proceedings of the IEEE 2001 International Conference on Robotics and Automation*, vol. 1, Seoul, Korea, May 2001, pp. 485–490.
18. M. Skubic, P. Matsakis, and J. Keller. "Spatial Relations for Tactical Robot Navigation." In *Proceedings of the SPIE Conference Unmanned Ground Vehicle Technology III*, Orlando, FL, April 2001.
19. M. Skubic, P. Matsakis, B. Forrester, and G. Chronis. "Extracting Navigation States from a Hand-Drawn Map." In *Proceedings of the IEEE 2001 International Conference on Robotics and Automation*, vol. 1, Seoul, Korea, May 2001, pp. 259–264.
20. M. Skubic, S. Blisard, A. Carle, and P. Matsakis. "Hand-Drawn Maps for Robot Navigation." Accepted for the AAAI Spring Symposium, Sketch Understanding Session, March 2002.
21. M. Skubic, D. Perzanowski, A. Schultz, and W. Adams. "Using Spatial Language in a Human-Robot Dialog." Accepted for the IEEE 2002 International Conference on Robotics and Automation, Washington, DC, May 2002.
22. D. Perzanowski, A. C. Schultz, W. Adams, E. Marsh, and M. Bugajska. "Building a Multimodal Human-Robot Interface." *IEEE Intelligent Systems*, 16–20, Jan./Feb. 2001.
23. L. Zadeh. "Soft Computing, Fuzzy Logic and Recognition Technology." In *Proceedings of the IEEE International Conference on Fuzzy Systems*, Anchorage, AK, May 1998, pp. 1678–1679.

CHAPTER 3

COMPUTING MACHINERY AND INTELLIGENCE AMPLIFICATION

STEVEN K. ROGERS, MATTHEW KABRISKY, KENNETH BAUER, and MARK E. OXLEY

3.1 INTRODUCTION

Understanding intelligence is a classic problem that both engineers and philosophers have considered [2]. The chapter begins by considering issues associated with defining and measuring intelligence. Examples are presented that are associated with attempts at estimating the intelligence of animals by observing the complexity of the tasks they can accomplish. The self-awareness calculation is discussed and the relevance to intelligence is presented. By restricting our attention to intelligence associated with accomplishment of an observable task or sets of tasks, we reduce the intelligence estimation problem and make it more manageable. A list of tasks is generated that require intelligence. The list of tasks requiring intelligence is shown to have changed over time. Next, definitions and historical tests associated with measuring intelligence are presented, culminating with the work of A.M. Turing and his well-known imitation game [2]. Some of the deficiencies of the Turing Test are presented, including the issue of self-awareness and qualia [3]. The focus of the Turing Test is the interaction of a computer and a human. Using that basis we offer intelligence amplification (IA) as opposed to artificial intelligence as the real attainable goal of the "computational intelligence" community [4, 5]. A working definition of IA is presented and examples analyzed. A variety of the application examples is used to introduce the concept of problem diversity space. IA applications can be categorized based on their characteristics, that is, their location in problem diversity space. The No Free Lunch Theorem is used to make the point that when going into a particular application, there is no way to know which soft-computing or conventional-engineering approach is best or if the task is even doable [7]. Appropriate measures of success for IA applications are shown to be different from

Computational Intelligence: The Experts Speak. Edited by D. B. Fogel and C. J. Robinson
ISBN 0-471-27454-2

common engineering measures employed in pattern recognition. A general methodology for the calculation of the amount of IA for a given application is presented from the perspective of a design of experiment. The methodology allows the determination of the most appropriate pattern-recognition technique for a given problem. IA can be explained by examining solutions formed from a set of common processing modules, in effect, an IA platform. The amount of IA of the platform is shown in general to be greater than a single-application IA solution. The presentation concludes with a vision of the future of IA. Example futuristic IA applications are used to illuminate the differences with current applications and to define the many challenges researchers face. That future is cast in terms of interactive intelligence, and is suspiciously very similar to the original premise of the imitation game.

3.2 ESTIMATING INTELLIGENCE

Portia, the Australian jumping spider (Fig. 3.1), is an interesting animal with very complex predatory behavior [1]. It has the genetic advantage of an appearance that can easily be confused as debris by its prey, other spiders. As Portia walks out on the web of its prey, it must use deception to keep its prey unaware of its approach. Portia will wait for a gust of wind or use an irregular gait to mask its vibrations on the web. If the prey detects Portia approaching, it will fling itself off the web to escape. If there is no wind, Portia will flex its legs to set up an artificial masking vibration—an artificial wind—on the web. Portia will also attempt to imitate the prey's characteristic web vibration to fool its prey into believing it is a spider of the same species approaching. Portia will drum on the web with a variety of sequences until it gets a response, implying that it has sent out a signal that is characteristic of its prey [1]. When it receives a response, it continues that species-specific input to the web so the prey does not flee. One of Portia's prey is the Orb web spider (Fig. 3.2). If the Orb

Figure 3.1 Portia, Australian jumping spider.

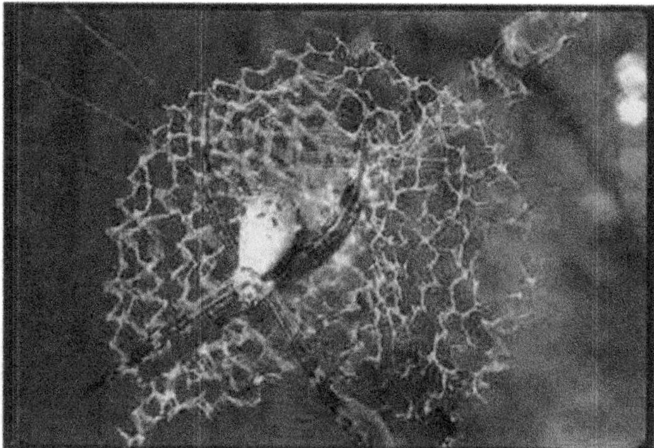

Figure 3.2 Orb web spider.

web spider senses an intruder on its web, it flexes its legs so violently that it flings the invader off the web. Portia goes to great lengths to thwart this defense. It will sometimes take over an hour to approach the Orb web spider, taking routes that sometimes take it out of sight of the prey. Portia's goal is to get to a vantage point that will allow it to drop a silk line so that it can descend to a point on the web next to the prey. The calculation of the location of the prey in relation to Portia's current position in three-dimensional (3D) space even when the prey is out of sight is quite impressive. This does not appear to be the behavior of a simple animal with rigid predatory rules of engagement. Portia is an animal with a poppy-seed-sized brain that learns, by trial and error, successful predatory behavior. It matches its predatory behavior to the prey that is currently its target. Observing any natural behavior, no matter how complex, can be a dangerous method for estimating intelligence. It is important to realize that virtually all of this behavior could be accounted for by a Terminator-like drop-down menu of preexisting subroutines.

Pigeons have also been studied to find the limits of their abilities. B. F. Skinner even proposed using pigeons as the intelligence in terminal guidance for "smart bombs" during Word War II (Fig. 3.3) [14,25]. Each pigeon is trained to peck on a small translucent screen on which the target's image was projected through a lens in the missile's nose. The pecking is used as guidance commands to the missile. Marijuana seed was used for the reward, having the side effect of keeping the pigeons calm in the dark noisy environment of a missile. This shape-recognition ability, with all the distortions of scale and rotation and noise in the images, is very impressive. The authors, having spent many years trying to make computer vision systems for visually guided smart bombs, admit inferiority to these bird brains. They seem to have the ability to recognize and remember examples of virtually any object or scene and to remember them for more than a year. But there appears to be a limit to the concept-level discrimination ability of pigeons. Tests that attempt to train the pigeons to recognize the classic odd stimulus (see below) seem to fail. Showing

Figure 3.3 Pigeon-guided bomb [14].

pigeons three letters at a time where the correct answer is always the letter that is different seemed to be solved by memorizing all the patterns that are correct and incorrect rather than abstracting to the generalizing concept that the correct answer is always the odd letter [10]. Pigeons have also been trained to recognize whether the hands of a clock are moving at constant speed, even when the hands temporarily go out of sight of the bird [11]. Pigeons are not even considered to be the smartest bird.

The cache recovery ability of birds is also very impressive [12]. Without using olfactory cues or random search, a single nutcracker stores from 22 K to 33 K seeds that they later harvest. They store these seeds at specific sites, 1–3 cm deep, on south-facing wind-blown ridges or ledges. The mechanism they use for this is unknown. As Darwin pointed out in his *Descent of Man*, in 1871, the mental faculties of men and lower animals don't differ in kind, only in degree.

Observing behavior and using those observations to estimate intelligence is very risky. There is remarkable complexity even in plant behavior [26]. The work of Braitenberg clearly shows some of the difficulties in this approach. A simple vehicle, his Type 3, with inhibitory influence by the sensors on the drive motors appears to exhibit characteristics that are similar to what we call "love" [8] and even a system of values (Fig. 3.4). Unlike observing animals, we can "pop the top off" these vehicles and see the simplicity of the computations that are controlling this apparently complex behavior.

So if observing uncontrolled behavior is a risky idea for deducing the intelligence of an animal or plant, what is our alternative? One approach might be to generate a list of tasks that require intelligence to accomplish. What would such a list contain? The ability to write a poem that can "pucker your parts" when you read it. Take that poem that you wrote and set it to music that brings you to tears. Perform speech recognition such that the meaning of "cutchuzall" when used in a sentence can be deduced. A vision machine that can find any significant object in a scene once its semantic attributes are given. Match scenes according to some semantic description, i.e., "having fun in the summertime." Lists like this must change over time.

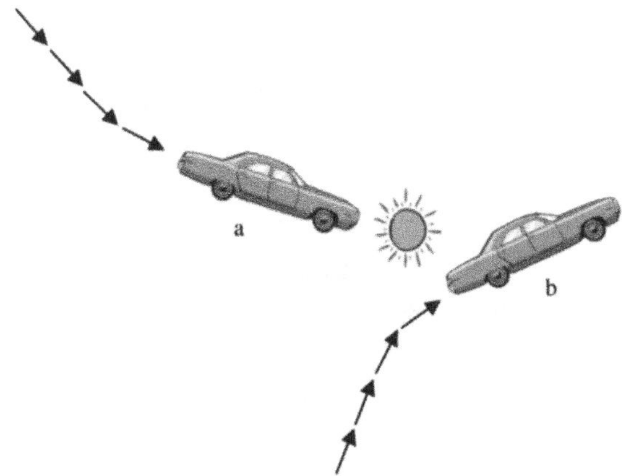

Figure 3.4 "Love" vehicles [8], a vehicle of Type 3, with inhibitory influence of the sensors on the motors.

Clearly, previous versions of our list of tasks that require intelligence included the ability to beat a grandmaster at chess. We used to say this! Now it is clear that playing chess does not require intelligence.

A dictionary definition of intelligence is the ability to acquire and apply knowledge. We would supplement this definition to include the appropriate application of knowledge. Yoerg defines intelligence as the ability to figure things out, to adapt quickly and appropriately, and to use past experience and current information to get the mental job done right [1]. Any measure of intelligence, when defined on a single axis, is very risky. Nobody should think you can measure intelligence in a half-hour written test. The most intelligent being will have intellectual blind spots that result in poor performance on some tasks. Recall that Mozart clearly was not very intelligent with respect to social interactions. Idiot savants provide case studies of islands of performance. If we took all the axes, where each task used to measure intelligence is an axis, then there is a maximum volume in this space that constitutes the limitation of the human brain. Any definition of intelligence will certainly change as we learn more and more about biological and *in silico* information processing. However intelligence is defined, we all have the feeling that we can recognize it when we see it.

Clearly, any measures of intelligence associated with an anatomical or physiological measure of the brain of the animal that is being tested have also been controversial. In birds, corvids and parrots have larger brains than pigeons or chickens [9] (Fig. 3.5). Even sharks have much larger brains for their size than other fish. Note the size of the animal has to be considered when doing such calculations or we would make the assumption that animals like the whale (Fig. 3.6) are the most intelligent. We are forced to conclude that any physiological brain measures of intelligence are too far removed to be explanatory of intelligence.

How do qualia, memory, emotion, self-awareness, consciousness, and thinking relate to intelligence? One necessary inclusion on any list of tasks that require

Figure 3.5 Corvid.

intelligence would be the ability to think about yourself, self-awareness. This ability to think about oneself can be nested within itself. That is, you can think about thinking about yourself. If we were to write the computer code for this activity, it would look something like: while thinking about yourself, do think about yourself until something distracts you. Personal recursion (self-awareness), however, seems to be so personal that it may be impossible to ever decide whether any machine you have built is really doing it no matter what the machine claims it is doing. How does self-awareness add to intelligence? How are all these concepts related to each other?

Both pit vipers and humans respond to heat. We call our internal perception of heat a quale to describe what it is like to feel anything. We are willing to assume

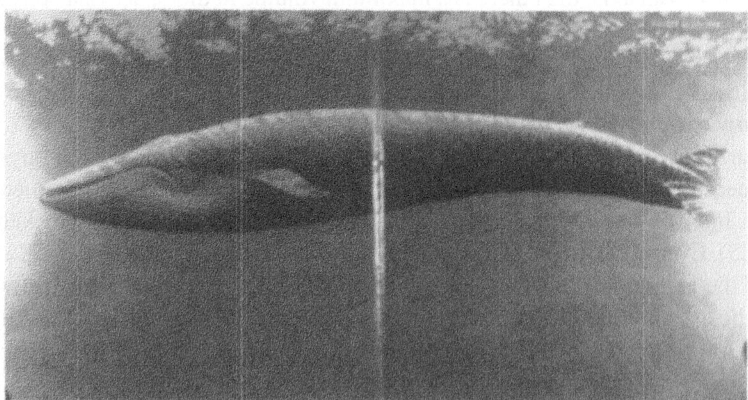

Figure 3.6 Blue whale.

that all humans form a quale for heat. What does quale formation add to the ability to represent the stimulus and the ability to more intelligently respond to it? Why is there a quale for pain, instead of a notification to the animal of the stimuli by ringing a bell inside their brain? Why does a dog yelp when you accidentally step on its foot? This reaction is not unlike a child crying when it falls down. At some point in evolution, quale was chosen as a mechanism to augment the processing of information, most probably to increase variability in stimuli that could be responded to appropriately and to limit the number of events that have to be memorized. One of the simplest explanations of qualia is that they are our internal perception of the basis set we use to represent the variety of stimuli we encounter.

Qualia function as our basis set upon which we construct our world model. This basis set allows the representation of the infinite variety of stimuli we sense into a small number of clusters, qualia, of relevant things. Redness is a word we use to describe a specific electromagnetic spectral component and jealousy is the quale of a specific social situation. The more qualia (clusters) that an information processor can generate and meaningfully manipulate, the more intelligent it will be perceived to be. As a basis-set axis, pain is a very efficient representation that allows common responses to lots of variable stimuli that do not have to be remembered individually and specifically. Note that the basis-set representation is not meant for reconstruction of the stimuli but an intelligent response to the stimuli. The dog, not unlike a young child, cries out in response to pain because both are seeking the assistance of other members of the pack. An octopus would have no reason to yelp. Unfortunately, humans relate to the yelp and for that reason are far more distressed when subjecting an animal like a dog to an experiment that would result in yelping than they would to that same experiment on an octopus. Our ethical treatment of animals is unfortunately tied to how similar we are willing to attribute their responses to human responses. To say that the qualia of one animal are similar to the qualia of another animal would be a big leap and possibly irrelevant in addition to being surely unmeasurable. Measuring the similarity or even the existence of the qualia can be very tricky and the results depend on the test and the tester and the set of stimuli that the information processor has been exposed to prior to the test.

Self-awareness is the quale resulting from the activity in the do-loop of thinking about oneself. Since it is a quale, it will always be inaccessible and fundamentally inexplicable. This explanation of the intrinsic inexplicability is all we can ever hope for in understanding self-awareness. Self-awareness is a feeling, a quale. Nobody worries about the fact that their personal quale of redness is inexplicable. Similarly, we should not worry about the inexplicable nature of self-awareness.

What does thinking have to do with intelligence? Without thinking one would have to respond to a given stimuli with fixed rules. Thinking is therefore necessary to adaptively acquire and apply knowledge, intelligence. Therefore thinking increases intelligence by increasing an animal's ability to acquire and apply knowledge in response to variations in the environment. Thinking allows animals the ability to manipulate their internal representation, to improve the predicted quality of the response to the stimulus as judged by memory. Memory stores the representation and the observed quality of the response to stimuli.

How about the quale of consciousness? You can acquire and apply knowledge without having the quale that you are conscious of it. Things that you do not know you know can be responded to appropriately via the conditioned response. Intelligent behavior does not always take place where you are aware of it. This same disconnect occurs on the other end of the response spectrum, the expert response. As one becomes an expert in some activity, the activity is accomplished without the necessity of awareness of the details of the actions. In fact, the work of Libet [13] shows that thoughts that seem to the human to activate action really occur after the initiation of the action. That leads us to conclude that consciousness is a quale that the brain creates as a cover story to aide in the formation of the consistent and useful world model. Consciousness is the quale resulting from observing our manipulation of our qualia basis set. We adopt a view of consciousness that is similar to Darwin's view of animal information processing. All animals are conscious to some level. We are only arguing to what degree and how we would measure it. The pull-down Terminator lists, which we are willing to assume Portia has to control its processing options, are generated before she becomes conscious of them. When humans think of their options of responses to a given stimuli, they have the quale that the alternatives are available (the pull-down lists) before they become conscious of needing them, preconscious. The processing thus feels instantaneous. Where are the preconscious and conscious computations taking place? Are they orthogonal like the electric and magnetic fields of Maxwell's equations?

Consciousness is just an emergent property that accomplishes the analysis of the processing of stimuli as represented by quale. With this explanation, we can conclude that a colony of ants can be conscious. That is, collectively they have a unifying consciousness hovering between them that analyzes and as a result modifies the representation of stimuli to achieve a more intelligent response. No neuron knows it is part of a sentient being and in that is no different than a single ant. Consciousness is a holistic property of the entity.

Emotion is another quale axis. The projection on this axis allows the prioritization and often measures the appropriateness of our responses. This position allows us to associate emotion with all animal behavior independent of the amount of consciousness attributable to the animal. Emotion has often been quoted as something that will never be achievable by a machine. As with every other quale, we will not worry about the inexplicable nature of emotion.

Figure 3.7 shows the relationships between these concepts. In summary, intelligent responses are achieved by projecting the stimuli on the qualia basis set. Let Q be a set of qualia. A stimulus presented to a human can be represented internally by a quale $q \in Q$. A problem or task presented to a human is a stimulus, and hence can be represented by a quale. Assume the set Q can be approximated by a finite-dimensional linear space. Consequently, there exists an ordered basis set for Q, say $\Theta = \{\mathbf{q_1}, \mathbf{q_2}, \ldots, \mathbf{q_N}\}$. Now each stimulus $\mathbf{s}$ can be represented by an N-tuple in Q with respect to the basis Θ, that is, $\mathbf{s} = s_1\mathbf{q_1} + s_2\mathbf{q_2} + \mathrm{T} + s_N\mathbf{q_N}$ or just by its coordinates $\mathbf{s} = (s_1, s_2, \ldots, s_N)$. Thus, a task presented to human h has a representation in qualia space with respect to the basis Θ.

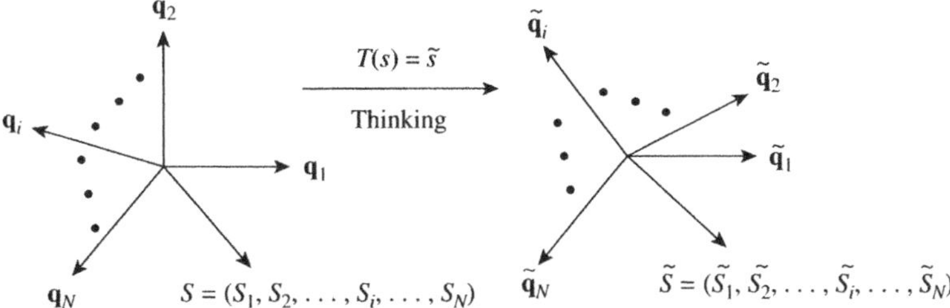

Figure 3.7 Qualia basis set, where all stimuli (s) are represented. Thinking is a manipulation of that qualia basis set, and thus a manipulation of the representation of a stimulus (internal or external).

Qualia make it unnecessary to remember specific events to enable an animal to use its memory to react to a new stimulus quickly and intelligently. Thinking is the manipulation of that representation optimized by memory for evaluation of the quality of the new representation. Consciousness is the quale resulting from observing this activity.

3.3 TURING TEST AND INTELLIGENCE AMPLIFICATION

All of these discussions about various abilities or disabilities that are associated with intelligence have been discussed by many of the great philosophers and brain scientists. The problems in devising a test that would allow the determination of the existence of intelligence within a computer were taken to a new level by the work of Alan Turing [2].

To understand the greatness of Alan Turing you must understand the perspective of the state of computing in 1950 when he wrote his famous paper [2]. Many people believed at that time that computers would soon put them out of business. That is, the amount of planning and coding required to do problems of significance would completely overwhelm the value of the computations. Not everyone agreed with this idea. In his 1949 address to the IBM seminar on Scientific Computation, John von Neumann voiced the opposite opinion. In his view the problems would stay in equilibrium with the computing power [15]. One really interesting problem that the visionaries of the time were interested in was how far computing could go in approximating human intelligence. If a machine were intelligent, how would you know?

Turing's 1950 work proposed a test to determine whether a machine was intelligent. In many respects this paper represents the beginning of artificial intelligence, a term coined by John McCarthy in 1956 at Dartmouth College, and its ultimate goal. His test, the imitation game, consists of a man, a woman, and an interrogator. The interrogator questions the man and the woman from a remote location through a computer connection and tries to determine which is the woman. The man tries to convince the interrogator that he is a woman while the woman tries to help the interrogator correctly choose her. If a machine can perform in the imitation game as well as the man, then the machine passes the Turing test. Is the deception aspect of the imitation game an integral part of the test? More current versions of the imitation game do not include this aspect of the game and only requires the machine to fool the interrogator into believing that it is human. Certainly if any machine could pass the imitation game, then the programmer of the machine might not be able to explain its actions. This is contrary to the opinion of Lady Ada Lovelace, the first programmer, who believed that machines could never originate anything and thus could never surprise their creators. Turing himself believed that by now, 2002, machines would be able to play the imitation game so well that after 5 minutes of interaction the human interrogator would only have a 70% chance of correctly determining that it is a computer. Since 1991, there have been competitions, the Loebner Prize Competitions, sponsored by a New York philanthropist, to determine if any computer program can pass the Turing test. Although no computer has ever passed the test, their average scores have edged closer to 5 on a 1 to 10 scale. An important part of the imitation game is that the human interrogator is forced to anthropomorphize the computer being interacted with [16].

It is interesting that Kasparov stated at times during his match against Deep Blue that he doubted that he was playing against a computer. Deep Blue therefore passed the Turing test in this limited application. If you accept the Turing test as a measure of intelligence, then Deep Blue plays chess intelligently. Note that there have been similar breakthroughs in computers performing at the Turing level in musical composition, understanding continuous speech, the processing of medical information, and even aircraft guidance. Turing did not specify whether a machine that can pass the Imitation Game would be conscious [17].

Not everyone believes that the Turing Test is relevant to current work in intelligent computing [18,19]. Artificial intelligence could take the path of human flight in the sense that in some respects airplanes are very different from birds. Perhaps a better goal is to come up with a measure of how much value a computer brings in a given application as opposed to the Turing illusion of intelligence. This is the idea of IA.

The concept of IA is credited to Vannevar Bush in 1945. He described a hypothetical machine called the Memex that used microfilm technology, which allowed vast storage with cross references and quick accurate retrieval. Bush built the first well-integrated, large computing machine, the differential analyzer. This device did its computing with rotating disks instead of electrical components [5]. The fundamental idea behind IA is the use of a machine to boost the intelligence of the human user. Although measuring intelligence is difficult if not impossible, measuring IA may be easier and more relevant. By restricting our attention to the quality of decisions associated with observable tasks, we can observe humans perform the task with and without the aid of the machine. We can measure the performance of the human in both cases and contrast them. Using long-accepted methods of experimental design, we can then decide if the device has indeed improved the performance of the human for the task at hand. There is always a risk involved with the designed experiments, so we will never know with certitude, but we can enjoy a high level of confidence. In the next section we examine some example tasks that lend themselves to this

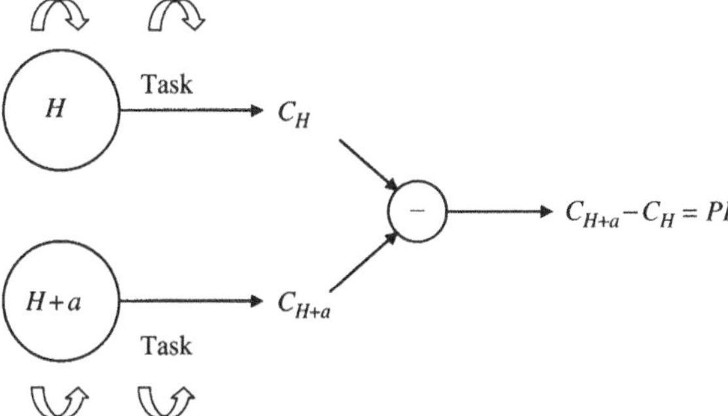

Figure 3.8 Performance assessment—the human performs the task with and without the use of aid. C measures the performance of the task. PI is the performance improvement.

approach to measuring the amount of IA a particular computer program achieves (Fig. 3.8).

3.4 MEASURING INTELLIGENCE AMPLIFICATION

Although it can be debated whether current computer programs are intelligent or not, it is somewhat easier to demonstrate that current computer programs achieve IA. Most software companies [20] have concluded that it is necessary to employ innovative techniques to make their products provide more value when assisting humans in tasks. The Microsoft paperclip that keeps coming up as we write this chapter is an example. The authors have spent many years developing computer applications to assist our war fighters to make more intelligent decisions [22] (Fig. 3.9). There are recent examples where this same technology has been applied to improve health care [21,23] (Fig. 3.10). Products such as Second Look® currently provide a second

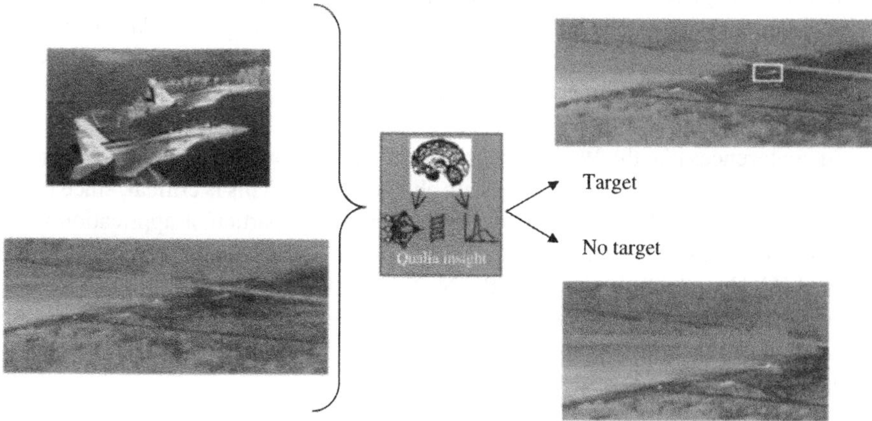

Figure 3.9 IA for ATR.

Figure 3.10 Second Look® machine—43% of cancers missed would be found with the use of Second Look.

opinion for the first reading of screening or diagnostic mammograms. A second human reading has been demonstrated to increase sensitivity by 5–15%. In clinical trials designed to measure IA, it was proved that 43% of cancers currently missed would have been found if the radiologist used Second Look. There have also been great breakthroughs in financial applications as relevance filters, in video monitoring (e.g., wildlife crossing alarms, antiterrorism) and more efficient drug/vaccine design. Drug design is an extremely expensive process (averaging \$500–\$800 million per drug) because of the high failure rates in testing of compounds both in the laboratory and in clinical trials. The use of IA technology to make early decisions on which compounds have the highest probability of having the necessary druglike characteristics (potency, selectivity, toxicity, metabolism properties) has great promise (Fig. 3.11).

At conferences like the World Congress on Computational Intelligence, researchers in many soft computing disciplines are able to interact. This is critical, since from the No Free Lunch Theorem we know that, going into a particular application with an unknown measure of success, there is no way to know which technique will be optimal [6]. How do the concepts of the No Free Lunch Theorem apply to IA? What is the best soft computing algorithm for achieving IA that will always outperform all other choices regardless of the problem? To answer these questions we introduce some new concepts.

We propose an experiment that consists of three basic elements: a problem (or task), p, a human, h, and an aid (or device), a. Each of these elements contributes

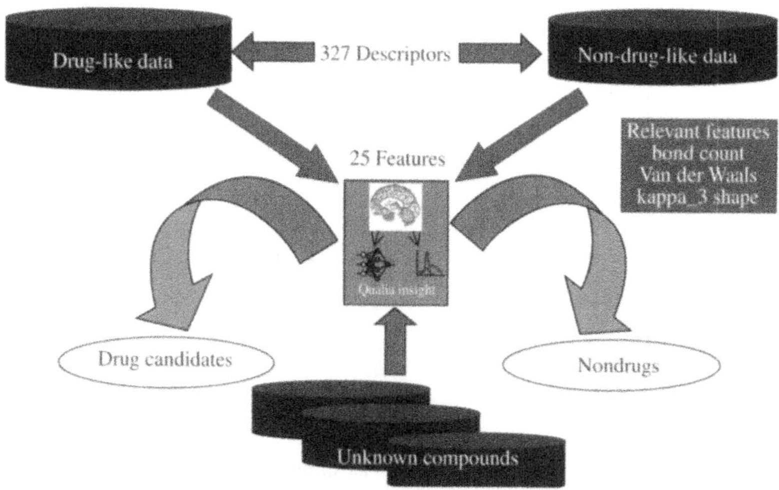

Figure 3.11 Computer-aided drug design.

to the variation we observe in a performance function, f, calculated during the conduct of an experiment. Our goal is to decide whether or not IA has occurred and, even if we are not conscious of the following, we will do so across some population of humans, H, subject to the inherent variability of both the device and the task. This process is shown in Figure 3.8.

Let Π be a set of problems or tasks. (We will use problem and task interchangeably.) An individual problem $p \in \Pi$ is presented to an algorithm, a. We take an abstract view of an algorithm. An algorithm could be a human, an aid/device (e.g., a computer with special programs), or a human with an aid. Each problem presented to a human is a stimulus that is represented in qualia space. As we vary the input problem, then the representation varies in qualia space; thus, one gets a "picture" of the diversity of the problems in Π by viewing their corresponding representations.

Assume we have a metric ρ defined on problems Π so that (Π, ρ) is a metric space. Thus, for two problems $p, q \in \Pi$ the real number $\rho(p,q)$ denotes the "distance" between p and q (Fig. 3.12). Thus, an open ball of problems centered at p with radius r is the set in Π denoted by

$$B(p, r) = \{q \in \Pi : \rho(p, q) < r\}$$

With this concept we can talk about clusters of problems in problem/task space (Fig. 3.12). Problems that are diverse mean that they are far apart with respect to the metric.

We would like to define an intelligence function on problems and algorithms, but as discussed earlier, this is an elusive quantity, so we seek an IA function. If an intelligence function, I, did exist, then the IA function IA should look like

$$IA(p, a, b) = I(p, a \wedge b) - I(p, a)$$

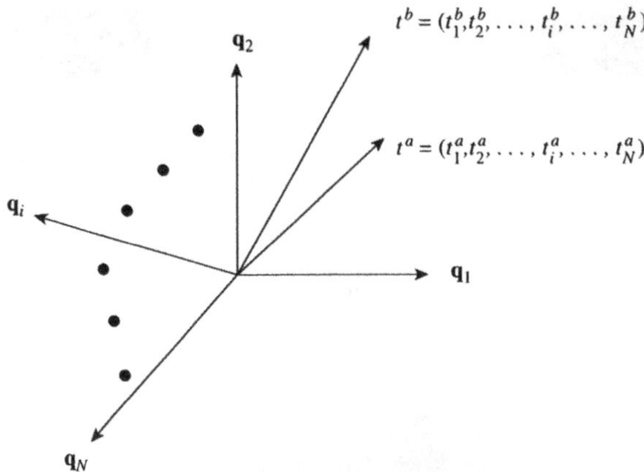

Figure 3.12 Task as represented to the human as stimuli by their qualia bases projections; $\rho(t^a, t^b)$ denotes the "distance" between the two problems/tasks.

for problem, p, and algorithms a and b. Since function I is difficult to define, we focus on defining IA alone. In particular, for human, h, and aid, a, we are interested in the function $IA(p, h, a)$. Algorithms that provide large IA at some problem p in problem space (Fig. 3.12) might not provide much IA at another problem q. Let a and b be two different aids to assist the human h with the task of solving problem p. Let $h \wedge a$ denote the human using the aid a (that is, h and a) and $h \wedge b$ the human using aid b. We want to quantify how well $h \wedge a$ and $h \wedge b$ performed. In fact, one is interested in knowing which aid helped more. Of course, this begs the question "how do you define 'better'?" Let f be a particular assessment (or performance) function that measures the quality of how well human h performed problem p. This quality is the measure of intelligence along that problem or task "axis;" see Figure 3.13. We use this assessment function to quantify the intelligence amplification for each problem (Fig. 3.8). Let $P_m = \{p_1, p_2, \ldots, p_m\} \subset \Pi$ be a finite subset of problems/

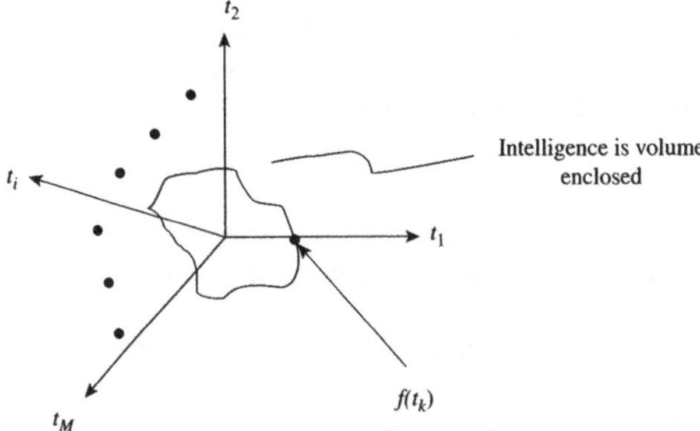

Figure 3.13 Intelligence as volume enclosed where the distances down each task axis represents the quality of accomplishment of that task or problem, $f(t_k)$.

tasks, and let human, h, using an aid, a, solve these problems. We use the assessment function, f, to measure the quality of performance for each problem, that is, $f(p_k, h \wedge a)$. As k varies from $1, 2, \ldots, m$, then we get an ordered set of real numbers $\vec{c} = (c_1, c_2, \ldots, c_m)$, where $c_k = f(p_k, h \wedge a)$. Using $\vec{c}$, we can assess the quality of the human, h, with the aid, a, on the set of problems, P_m. Suppose the problems are chosen randomly. What is the conditional probability that a given histogram $\vec{c}$ will be obtained? Thus, we seek $\Pr(\vec{c}\,|f, P, h \wedge a)$, where P is a random set of problems. The following theorem results from the No Free Lunch Theorem [7].

THEOREM 3.1 (No Free Lunch for performance functions) Let human, h, be aided by a and b working on a subset of problems, P, then

$$\sum_f \Pr\left(\vec{c}\,\middle|\, f, P, h \wedge a\right) = \sum_f \Pr\left(\vec{c}\,\middle|\, f, P, h \wedge b\right)$$

This theorem asserts that no aid yields better performance over all performance functions. On the other hand, given a few problems and constraints on the performance function (that is, we have a priori knowledge), then an aid a could perform better than aid b. This approach gives engineers criteria to decide when new products improve human performance.

Part of the reason that we cannot have a best IA algorithm is that we have not chosen a single measure of goodness. Let us choose a single performance function, $\hat{f}$, then one can compare the goodness of each aid on a problem or subset of problems. If we have several humans $H = \{h_1, h_2, \ldots, h_n\}$ using the same aid, a, then we can assess their performance by using $c_i = \hat{f}(p, h_i \wedge a)$ for $i = 1, 2, \ldots, n$. Suppose we choose the humans randomly from some population. What is the conditional probability that a given histogram $\vec{c}$ will be obtained? Thus, we seek $\Pr(\vec{c}\,|f, p, H \wedge a)$, where H is a random set of humans. We formalize this with another No Free Lunch Theorem.

THEOREM 3.2 (No Free Lunch for problems) Let a set of humans, H, be aided by a and b working on the set of problems, Π, assessed by the cost function, $\hat{f}$, then

$$\sum_p \Pr\left(\vec{c}\,\middle|\, \hat{f}, p, H \wedge a\right) = \sum_p \Pr\left(\vec{c}\,\middle|\, \hat{f}, p, H \wedge b\right)$$

This theorem implies that no aid performs better than another aid on all problems. Hence, we have to limit the number and/or type of problems we consider (again, a priori knowledge) before this comparison can be possible. These two theorems warn us to be careful when defining a measure of IA.

Let $\hat{f}$ be a fixed assessment function. We define the measure of IA of human h using aid a to solve a set of problems $P \subset \Pi$ to be

$$\mu(IA(P, h, a)) = \sum_{p \in P} \hat{f}(p, h \wedge a) - \hat{f}(p, h)$$

The term $\hat{f}(p,h \wedge a) - \hat{f}(p,h)$ is called the performance improvement (PI) (Fig. 3.8). Similarly, we define the measure of *IA* of the collection of humans, *H*, using aid *a* to solve a set of problems $P \subset \Pi$ to be

$$\mu(IA(P,H,a)) = \frac{1}{n}\sum_{h \in H}\sum_{p \in P}\hat{f}(p,h \wedge a) - \hat{f}(p,h)$$

In this equation, *n* is the number of humans. Of course, if $P = \{p\}$, singleton set, then this becomes a measure of *IA* of the collection of *n* humans, *H*, using aid *a* to solve the problem, *p*

$$\mu(IA(P,H,a)) = \frac{1}{n}\sum_{h \in H}\hat{f}(p,h \wedge a) - \hat{f}(p,h)$$

As an example of this process we look at some recent experiments in the area of computer-aided detection (CAD) in mammography. The conventional engineering technique for measuring the performance of a CAD device is to assess its sensitivity and the number of false marks per image or case (thus, a choice of $\hat{f}$). Unfortunately, these measures give no insight into how much value the device will provide a human radiologist in finding cancers and improving health care. Here we refer to the essence of a method found in Burhenne et al. [24]. In our related study using Second Look (Fig. 3.10), we determined the potential reduction in false negatives due to the introduction of CAD into a screening mammography environment. We had panels of 3 radiologists each examine 374 prior mammograms with visible lesions out of 906 current biopsy-proven cancers. It is important to note that the radiologists in the previous reading missed these lesions. Each mammogram was given a score corresponding to the number of radiologists on the panel who identified the lesion correctly. The score was also taken to be proportional to the probability of a radiologist detecting the lesion correctly. The number of actionable mammograms was calculated as $\sum_{i=0}^{3} N_{T_i} \times P_i$, where N_{T_i} is the number of type *i* mammograms. A type *i* mammogram is a mammogram in which *i* of 3 radiologists correctly detected the lesion and $P_i = i/3$. The CAD system was able to identify the proportion P_i^{CAD} of the type *i* actionable mammograms. The estimated total number of CAD-identified actionable mammograms was $\sum_{i=0}^{3} N_{T_i} \times P_i \times P_i^{CAD}$, a number called the "potential CAD benefit." It was taken as the number of missed lesions a radiologist using the CAD device would have detected. Since the baseline human performance is zero by definition (all lesions were missed), then the "potential CAD benefit" becomes an estimate of PI (our choice of $\hat{f}$). The newest version of Second Look 4.0 software was released as a product because it demonstrated a clinically significant IA (potential CAD benefit) increase from 27% to 43% with a 60% reduction in false positives. This IA measure is more relevant than the common engineering measure of sensitivity.

The IA examples we presented work on single applications. A device like Second Look does not help a human design a new drug or vaccine. By our definition of the measure of IA, we need to design computer programs that provide value across

Qualia Insight™

Qualia Insight: Proprietary
Fully Integrated Feature Selection, Classifier Creation and Context-based Decisions

- Representation of Data

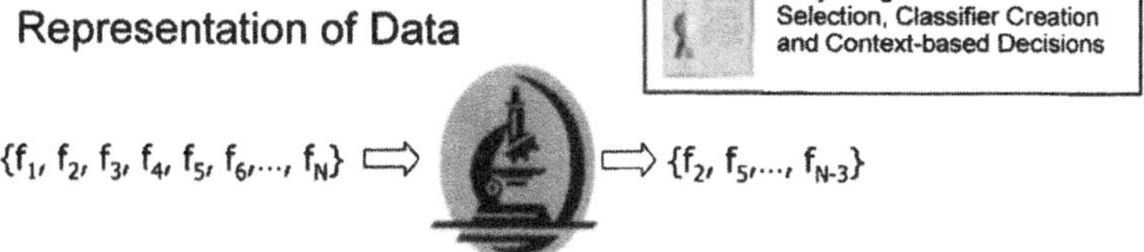

- Representation of Knowledge

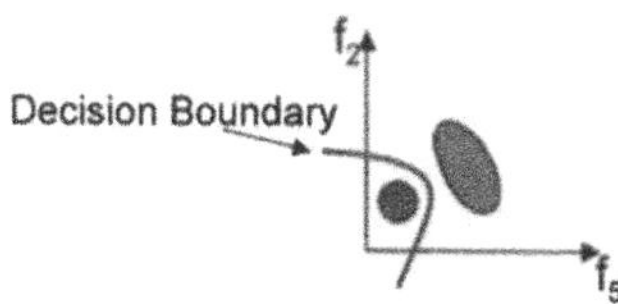

- Application of Knowledge to Particular Problem

Figure 3.14 Qualia Insight™ platform.

multiple tasks. PI is seen to be a measure of IA for any specific task. Devices might some day be able to aid in more than one task.

One approach to building a device that can assist humans in multiple tasks is to build a platform that consists of the necessary components of all IA applications. Figure 3.14 shows the essential steps that make up all IA applications. In each application, the aid changes the qualia representation of the stimulus/tasks (Fig. 3.15). The platform can provide IA across multiple tasks. It is interesting to note the similarity of the platform components and the concept of the qualia basis set, thinking, memory, and consciousness. This platform is the core of the medical, financial, video, and drug/vaccine applications we presented. The future of IA will be dominated by these multiple-application solutions.

3.5 THE FUTURE OF INTELLIGENCE AMPLIFICATION

The authors, being professors, often fantasize about an IA program that performs like the perfect graduate student. The graduate student program works around the clock searching for data relevant to the professor's current interest, thereby saving him time while providing the assurance that something very important in the literature has not been overlooked. Whenever the professor accesses the program, it adjusts to his current prioritizing topics and therefore changes its internal representation. This implicit change in the program is not something the professor needs to think about, and in fact, is something that he expects. The results of the program's activity may well change the content of the professor's mind and alter the professor's activities; that is what the professor had in mind when deciding to interact with the program. The program helps the professor and changes the qualia in his or her mind

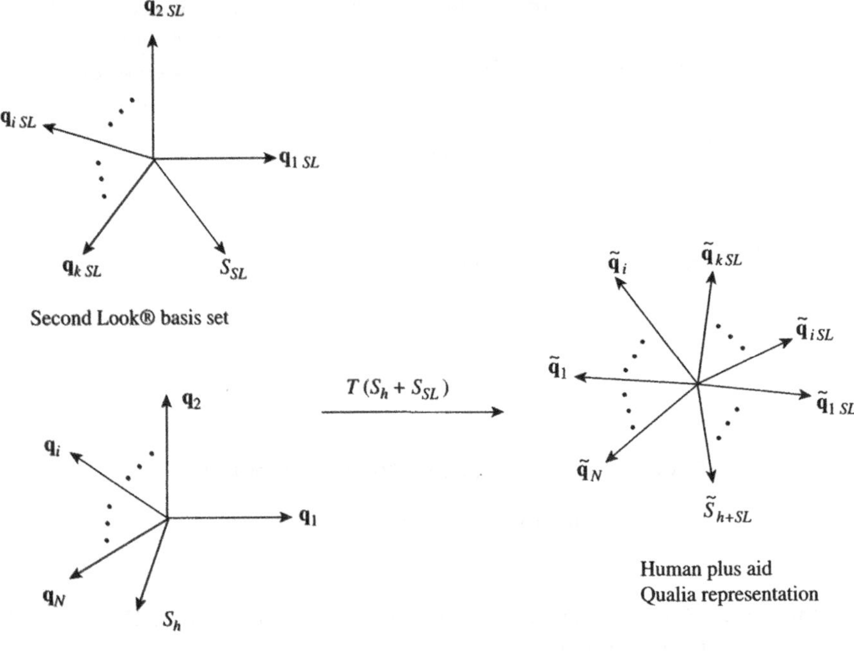

Figure 3.15 IA as qualia manipulation.

just as surely as his or her responses change the program's internal basis set. This human–machine relationship, with its interacting qualia manipulation, fits the diagrams in Figures 3.8 and 3.15, and upon reflection, the human–machine interplay proposed by Turing.

It is easy for us to imagine other examples of interactions with an IA program. Such a program could provide personalized instruction for children, sensing the child's interests, educational needs, level of achievement, and current level of interest. The child need never take a test, since the IA machine is continuously modeling the totality of its exhibited qualia. If the program is written well, the child will see learning as an exciting and friendly interlude in life.

An IA CAD program could interact with a physician and present its own novel quale to represent the patient's state derived from physiological data, patient history, and the program's model of the qualia used by a particular physician. If the physician responds, the qualia in the IA program as well as the qualia in the physician will modify each other, each perhaps learning and creating by taking advantage of the strengths and capabilities of the other.

Unlike Deep Blue, which demonstrates a great breakthrough in the use of algorithms to process vast quantities of information efficiently at a rate of 100 million positions/second, interactive intelligence will require elegant algorithms to process more limited information effectively. Interactive intelligent systems must deduce the context of the questions and the responses to correctly apply knowledge. To

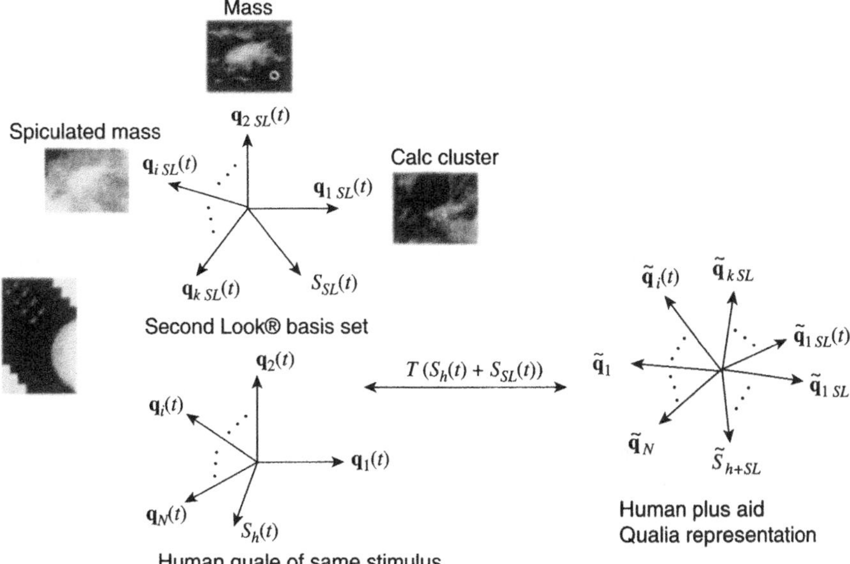

Figure 3.16 Closing the loop on IA manipulation.

maximize the amount of IA achieved these interactive intelligent systems must have access to the results (performance) of the observable task being aided. From that information, the interactive intelligent system will modify its qualia basis set to increase the probability of increasing the amount of IA achieved (Fig. 3.16).

It is interesting that the future of computing ends up with a goal that is very reminiscent of the original goals of the Turing Test. Whether the aid in Figure 3.8 is a computer or another human, the measure of the amount of IA can be accomplished similarly. Increasing the amount of IA achieved by our programs is the attainable and useful goal of computational intelligence, in contradistinction to the Imitation Game's illusion of intelligence.

REFERENCES

1. S. I. Yoerg. *Clever As A Fox*. Bloomsbury Publishing, New York, 2001.
2. A. M. Turing. "Computing Machinery and Intelligence." *Mind*, vol. 59, 433–460, 1950.
3. P. Millican and A. Clark. *Machines and Thought: The Legacy of Alan Turing*, vol. I. Oxford University Press, Oxford, 1999.
4. F. Brooks. *Proceedings of the SIGGRAPH 94 Annual Conference*, June 1994 – July 1995.
5. V. Bush. "As We May Think." *The Atlantic Monthly,* vol. 176, no. 1, 101–108, 1945.
6. D. H. Wolpert and W. G. Macready. "No Free Lunch Theorems for Optimization." *IEEE Trans. Evol. Comput.*, vol. 1, no. 1, 67–82, April 1997.
7. D. H. Wolpert and W. G. Macready. "No Free Lunch Theorems for Search." *Tech. Rep. SFI-TR-95-02-010*, Santa Fe Institute, Santa Fe, NM, 1995.

8. V. Braitenberg. *Vehicles: Experiments in Synthetic Psychology.* MIT Press, Cambridge, MA, 1986.
9. A. Portman. "Etudes sur la Cerebralisation des Oiseaux. II. Les Indices Intracerebraux." *Aluada*, vol. 15, 1–25, 1947.
10. D. S. Blough. "Discrimination of Letters and Random Dot Patterns by Pigeons and Humans." *J. Exp. Psychol.: Anim. Behav. Processes*, vol. 11, 261–280, 1985.
11. J. J. Neiworth and M. E. Rilling. "A Method for Studying Imagery in Animals." *J. Exp. Psychol.: Anim. Behav. Processes*, vol. 13, 203–214, 1987.
12. S. B. Vander Wall and R. P. Balda. "Ecology and Evolution of Food-Storage Behavior in Conifer-Seed-Caching Corvids." *Z. Tierpsychol.*, vol. 56, 217–242, 1981.
13. B. Libet. "Unconscous Cerebral Initiative and the Role of Conscious Will in Voluntary Action." *Behav. Brain Sci.*, vol. 8, 529–566, 1985.
14. D. Christensen. "Pigeon-Guided Missiles That Bombed Out." *IEEE Spectrum*, 46, Aug. 1987.
15. J. von Neumann. "The General and Logical Theory of Automata." Paper presented at the Hixon Symposium, Pasadena, CA, Sept. 29, 1948.
16. P. H. Millar. "On the Point of the Imitation Game." *Mind*, vol. 82, 595–597, 1973.
17. D. Michie. "Turing Test and Conscious Thought." In P. Millican and A. Clark (eds.), *Machines and Thought: The Legacy of Alan Turing*, pp. 27–51. Oxford University Press, Oxford, 1996. (Originally printed in *Artificial Intelligence*, vol. 60, 1–22, 1993.)
18. P. Hayes and K. Ford. Turing Test Considered Harmful. In *Proceedings of the Fourteenth International Joint Conference on Artificial Intelligence*, vol. 1, 1995, pp. 972–977.
19. B. Whitby. "The Turing Test: AI's Biggest Blind Alley?" In P. Millican and A. Clark, (eds.), *Machines and Thought: The Legacy of Alan Turing*, pp. 53–63. Oxford University Press, Oxford, 1996.
20. S. Hedberg."Is AI Going Mainstream at Last? A Look Inside Microsoft Research." *IEEE Intel. Syst.*, Mar./Apr. 1998.
21. S. K. Rogers, D. W. Ruck, and M. Kabrisky. "Artificial Neural Networks for Early Detection and Diagnosis of Cancer." *Cancer Lett.*, vol. 77, nos. 2, 3, 79–83, 1994.
22. S. K. Rogers, J. M. Colombi, C. E. Martin, J. Gainey, K. H. Fielding, T. Burns, D. W. Ruck, M. Kabrisky, and M. E. Oxley. "Neural Networks for Automatic Target Recognition," *Neural Networks* (*Special Issue on Neural Networks and Automatic Target Recognition*). vol. 8, no. 7/8, 1153–1184, 1995.
23. R. Mitchell. "Second Generation Computer-Aided Detection (CAD): Exploiting Context used by Radiologists for Mammography," Paper presented at RSNA 2001, Chicago, IL, Nov. 28, 2001.
24. L. J. Warren-Burhenne. "Potential Contribution of Computer-Aided Detection to the Sensitivity of Screening Mammography." *Radiology*, 554–562, 2000.
25. B. F. Skinner. *The Shaping of a Behaviorist: Part Two of an Autobiography.* Knopf, New York, 1979.
26. A. Trewavas."Mindless Mastery." *Nature*, vol. 415, 841, 2002.

CHAPTER 4

VISUALIZING COMPLEXITY IN THE BRAIN

LLOYD WATTS

4.1 INTRODUCTION

How does the human brain work? The challenge presented by this question has motivated countless philosophers and scientists throughout history to study the brain and the nature of intelligence, in search of the organizing principles of human thought and perception. Yet, despite the enormous funding of the neurosciences and tremendous advances in technology in the latter half of the twentieth century, it appears that there is not yet a meaningful consensus on the organizing principles of brain function.

There are good reasons to believe that we are at a turning point, and that it will be possible within the next two decades to formulate a meaningful understanding of brain function. This optimistic view is based on several measurable trends, and a simple observation that has been proven repeatedly in the history of science:

> Scientific advances are enabled by a technology advance that allows us to see what we have not been able to see before.

Examples of enabling technologies include the invention of the compound microscope in the 1860s, the invention of neural staining techniques by Golgi in the 1880s, the invention of stroboscopic illumination, each of which enabled new scientific discoveries. In these cases, the technology breakthroughs that enabled something new to be seen had to do with seeing something *smaller*, *more translucent*, or *faster-vibrating* than could be seen before. But for understanding the brain in the early twenty-first century, we need to be able to see something *more complex* than we have been able to see before, which is a fundamentally different kind of

Computational Intelligence: The Experts Speak. Edited by D. B. Fogel and C. J. Robinson
ISBN 0-471-27454-2

problem. We already have a good understanding of the behavior of individual synapses, neurons, axons, and dendrites. The interesting question is now: How do we understand and visualize the complexity of the brain?

The technology advance that allows us to see the complexity we could not see before is provided by the recent strong advances in computing and graphics technology. The availability of inexpensive computers with multigigahertz processors, gigabytes of on-board memory, hundreds of gigabytes of disk storage, and powerful graphics rendering chips provide an unprecedented platform for real-time brain modeling and visualization that simply did not exist even a few years ago. Kurzweil [1] has projected Moore's Law out to 2020 and beyond, and has concluded that we will have computers with sufficient memory and computing capacity to simulate major brain functions within the next 20 years. The question is: Will we have the right algorithms to run on these phenomenal machines to simulate brain function and achieve brainlike performance?

I believe that the way to create a brainlike intelligence is to build a real-time working model system, accurate in sufficient detail to express the essence of each computation that is being performed, and verify its correct operation against measurements of the real system. The model must run in real time so that we will be forced to deal with inconvenient and complex real-world inputs that we might not otherwise think to present to it. The model must operate at sufficient resolution to be comparable to the real system, so that we build the right intuitions about what information is represented at each stage. Following Mead [2], the model development begins necessarily at the boundaries of the system (i.e., the sensors) where the real system is well understood, and then can advance into the less-understood regions. The model of the independent or well-understood parts of the system can be used to gain insights into dependent or less-understood parts of the system, since in many cases the well-understood parts provide inputs to the less-understood parts. In this way, the model can contribute fundamentally to our advancing understanding of the system, rather than simply mirroring the existing understanding. In the context of such great complexity, it is possible that the only practical way to understand the real system is to build a working model, from the sensors inward, building on our newly enabled ability to *visualize the complexity of the system* as we advance into it. Such an approach could be called *reverse engineering the brain.*

Note that I am not advocating a blind copying of structures whose purpose we do not understand, like the legendary Icarus who naïvely attempted to build wings out of feathers and wax. Rather, I am advocating that we respect the complexity and richness that is already well understood at low levels, before proceeding to higher levels. Once information is thrown away, it can never be recovered. One of the powerful principles that is emerging about the operation of the brain is that it extracts and makes use of all the information in the signal.

Mead [2] has pointed out that the constraints we impose on a problem have a powerful influence on our approach and the form of the solution that will result. Therefore, it is very important at the beginning of a project of this magnitude to be clear about the choice and prioritization of those constraints. I have had success so far using the following prioritization of constraints:

1. High-resolution representations, verifiable against the biology.
2. Real-time operation and visualization of the results.
3. Fast design turnaround time.

A notable and perhaps surprising omission in this approach is any constraint on implementation technology. Allen (personal communication, 1999) advised an early focus on the algorithms, while remaining flexible on the implementation technology, since the project was likely to take many years and the implementation technology changes so quickly. Since this work began in 1989, the algorithms have been implemented in several different technologies, appropriate for the questions under investigation and resources available at the time: analog very large-scale integration (VLSI), field-programmable gate arrays (FPGAs), batch-mode software on desktop machines displayed in real-time as QuickTime movies, and real-time software on a networked supercomputer. Other implementation technologies are imminent as the project verges on commercial deployment. The only constant is the need to get the algorithms right, in real time, as soon as possible.

The ambition of reverse engineering the brain in verifiable detail may appear overwhelming and unrealizable, but it is possible to make a sound argument that the goal is attainable within 20 years. Substantial progress has already been demonstrated on a significant subsystem with this approach. The issues to be addressed are:

1. *Neuroscience Knowledge* Do we know enough about the brain to begin building an artificial one?
2. *Computing Technology* Do we have a computational medium in which to prototype a design that can express the richness of the computations done in a real brain, such that the model could really inform the study of the real system?
3. *Nontechnical Issues* Many experts will be required to contribute to the effort. Why should they help? Who will pay for the monumental effort? What is the economic model for funding the work?

As in all major endeavors, timing is everything. The approach can only succeed if all necessary ingredients are present and can contribute synergistically. Since 1950, advances in neuroscience knowledge and computing technology have led many workers to speculate that brainlike intelligence and performance was just around the corner, only to discover that the system was more complex, interconnected, and robust than had been previously appreciated, and that far more computing horsepower was required than was available at the time. The bold attempts and subsequent disappointments in each decade since 1950 have all led to a well-justified skepticism in both the scientific and investment community as to whether it will be possible to build a working intelligent machine. In fact, the previous attempts were based on overly simple models implemented on the inadequate machines of the day, which, in hindsight, did not have the necessary ingredients for success. I believe that the lesson to be learned from the previous disappointments was that the brain is much more complex than we would like to admit, and we need correspondingly complex models and serious computing horsepower, properly utilized, to build a robust, working system.

Fortunately, neuroscience knowledge and computing technology have both advanced dramatically in the last decade, as has our respect for the required complexity. Unusually favorable conditions exist for the period 2000–2020, whereas they most certainly have not existed in any previous time in history. For the remainder of this chapter, I will discuss the reasons for this optimistic view.

4.2 NEUROSCIENCE KNOWLEDGE

Does anyone know enough about the brain, in 2002, to be able to build an artificial one? No. There are still many unanswered questions about brain function, and there is no single individual who understands the brain in its entirety to the level that he or she could build a working model. But does the neuroscience community, in 2002, *collectively* know enough that we could *begin* modeling the brain in the well-understood regions? Absolutely. I will describe ongoing modeling efforts in the auditory pathway, shown in Figure 4.1, as an example brain subsystem in which significant progress has already been made, and as an example of the kind of complexity that is evident in the real brain.

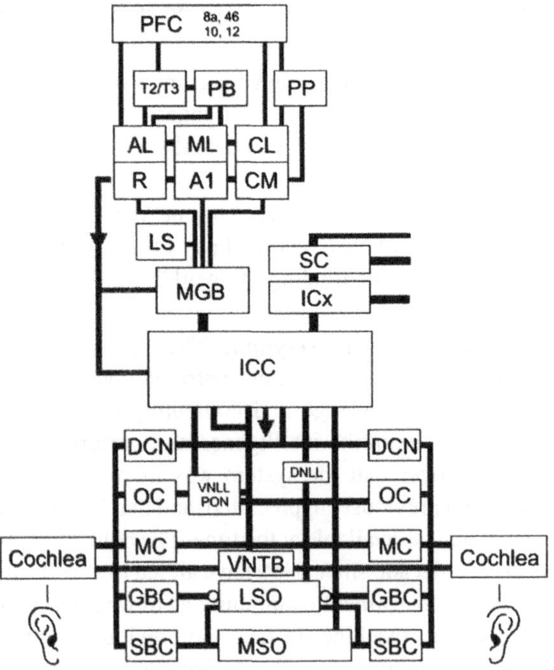

Figure 4.1 Auditory pathway (highly simplified). (Adapted from Young [3], Oertel [4], Casseday et al. [5], LeDoux [6], and Rauschecker and Tian [7].)

In the auditory system, the middle ear and cochlea are now well understood, after about 100 years of research (the cochlea could not have been called well understood even 10 years ago, due to controversy over the role played by the outer hair cells). It is now possible to build a real-time, high-resolution working model of the cochlea that accounts for its spectral sensitivity, temporal responses, nonlinear frequency-dependent amplitude compression and gain control, masking, and other subtle features, directly verifiable against biological and psychophysical data. This model can then be used in our investigation and modeling of the next layer in the system: the cochlear nucleus, which Shepherd has described as one of the "best understood regions of the brain" [8]. The basic circuit of the cochlear nucleus is given by Young [3], describing in detail the essential cell types responsible for detecting spectral energy, broadband transients, fine-timing in spectral channels, enhancing sensitivity to the temporal envelope in spectral channels, and spectral edges and notches, all while adjusting gain for optimum sensitivity within the limited dynamic range of the spiking neural code. Again, it is possible to build a real-time, high-resolution working model of the cochlear nucleus that receives its inputs from the working model of the cochlea, and can be verified against real measurements from cochlear nucleus neurons.

An output of such an auditory model is shown in Figure 4.2, for a complex speech input. This shows the output of the ensemble of T-multipolar cells (labeled MC in

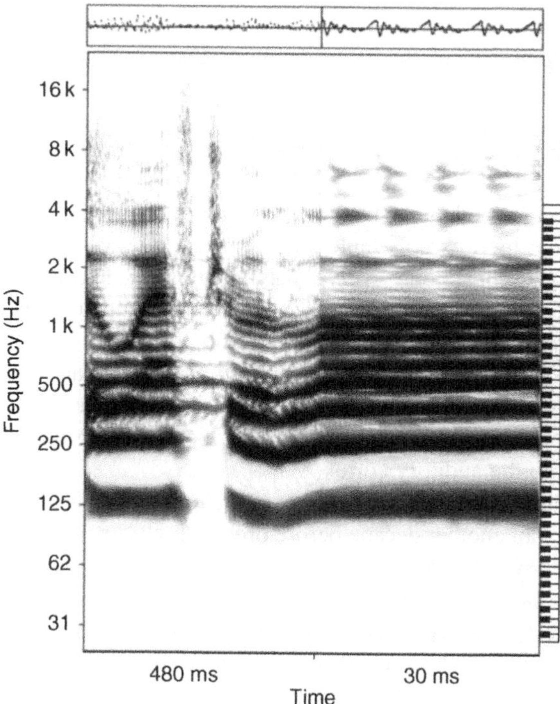

Figure 4.2 Multipolar cell response to speech (male speaker in the middle of the utterance "so after a lot of thought").

Fig. 4.1), which receive inputs from the cochlea/auditory nerve, and extract and encode the spectral energy in a way that is stable as sound level changes [3]. In Figure 4.2, the fundamental frequency of the speaker's voice can be seen at approximately 125 Hz, along with many harmonics at the integer multiples of the fundamental frequency. Strong bands of resonant energy can also be seen at around 500 Hz, 1 kHz, 2 kHz, and 4 kHz—these are the formant frequencies (resonances of the vocal tract)—that correspond to and encode the different vowel qualities. The figure includes two time scales to allow fine response detail to be seen in the right half of the display, with context over a longer period shown in the left half of the display. The four strong pulses at 4 kHz in the right half of the display correspond to the glottal pulse periods at about 8 ms, giving a periodicity cue that corresponds to the pitch frequency at 125 Hz. Also evident in the display are two short bursts of high-frequency noise, corresponding to the letters *f* and *t* in the word "after." Figure 4.2 represents a snapshot of a working, high-resolution, real-time system—it is not possible on a printed page to convey the complexity of the animated output that responds in real time, synchronized with the input sounds.

Figure 4.3 shows a snapshot of the dynamic output of the auditory model for a moving sound source, showing the spectral energy representation computed by the multipolar cells in the cochlear nucleus, interaural time difference (ITD) representation computed by the medial superior olive (MSO) [9] and the interaural level difference (ILD) representation computed by the lateral superior olive (LSO) and further normalized and refined by the inferior colliculus (IC) [5]. These images indicate the complexity of the representations that are computed in the auditory brainstem, organized by the inferior colliculus, and conveyed to the cortex via the thalamus. If we are to have any hope of understanding what is happening in the cortex, we must first have a good model of all of the low-level representations that serve as its inputs.

In 2002, there is good understanding of the representations up to the inferior colliculus. However, there is no simple answer to the question "What is the inferior colliculus doing?"—it is doing everything! It aggregates, normalizes, and organizes all the ascending representations from lower centers, computes new representations, and modifies them all with descending information from the cortex [5]. This does not mean that we will be unable to answer the question, it just means that the answer will be necessarily very complex, and we will need a way to express that complexity and verify that our understanding of it is correct, before being able to advance in a detailed way into the auditory cortex.

In 2002, in the absence of a conclusive model of the inferior colliculus, does this mean we must wait another decade before proceeding? Not at all. Bregman [10] has elucidated the psychoacoustic principles by which sounds are grouped to form perceptions of objects in auditory scenes. Many research groups around the world, including Sheffield and MIT, have been building models that account for various parts of the scene-analysis machinery. What is important is that we link the high-level psychoacoustic model to the low-level neurophysiological model, so as to reap the benefit of all the information that is extracted by the lower levels of the real brain.

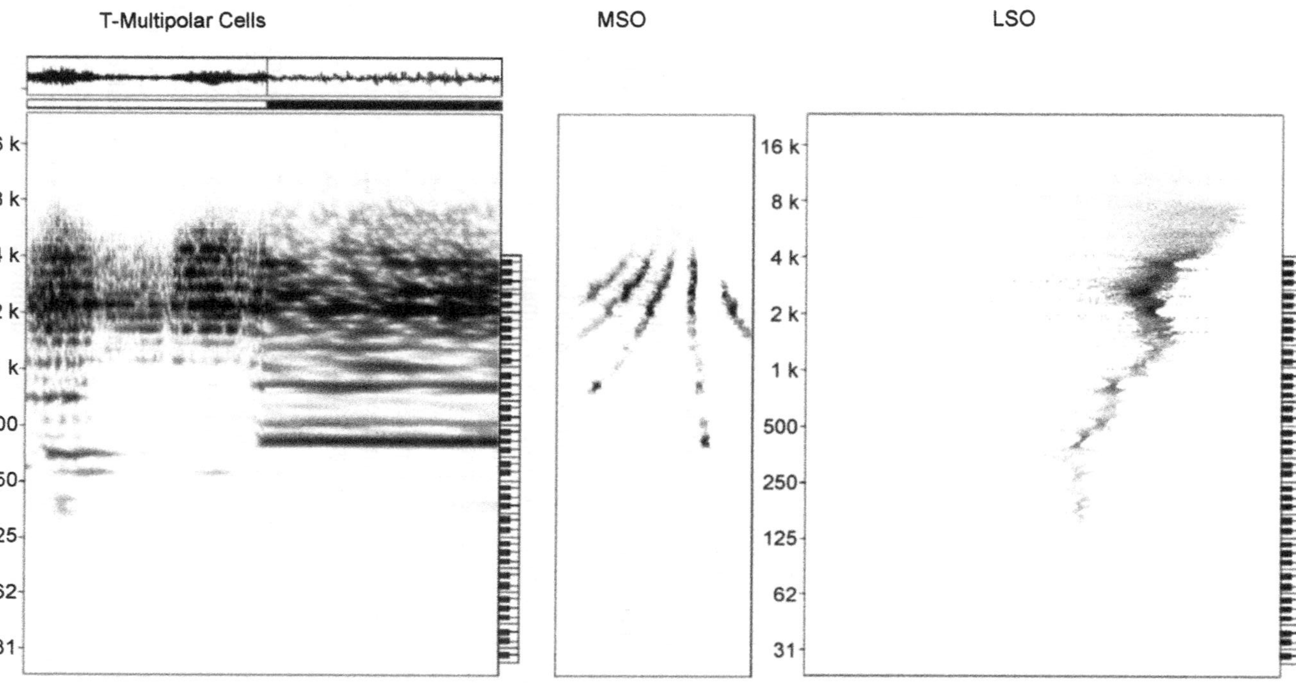

Figure 4.3 Multipolar cell, MSO, and LSO response to a moving sound source coming from the right side.

One example of the opportunity that exists is in the area of speech recognition. Present-day speech recognizers are capable of 90–98% word recognition accuracy, depending on vocabulary size, number of users, noise levels, and other factors. It has taken 40 years and thousands of talented engineers to build speech-recognition systems this good. And yet, these systems still perform very poorly compared to humans [11]. These systems use a kind of engineered psychoacoustic model (phoneme classification and Viterbi search through a space defined by a hidden Markov model) to account for the human cortical recognition process, while relying on a very low-resolution front end (128-point fast Fourier transform (FFT), smoothed and orthogonalized to create a 13-point cepstrum, updated every 10 ms) to provide the spectral information to the phoneme classifier [12].

At the level of the FFT, the amount of information represented is 64 spectral coefficients, 100 times/s, or 6400 values/s. By comparison, the human cochlea represents the spectrum with 30,000 auditory nerve fibers, representing the outputs of approximately 3000 inner hair cells (10:1 for better signal representation). The cochlea produces outputs with 6-μs temporal resolution [9], with 3000 unique outputs represented, organized on an (approximately) logarithmic frequency scale. Accounting for the fact that low-frequency channels do not carry as much information as high-frequency channels, we estimate the bandwidth on the auditory nerve to be about 10 million values/s, approximately 1500 times as much information as the frame-based FFT, as used in a conventional speech recognizer. (The expansion in bandwidth from the raw audio waveform at, say, 44,100 samples/s, to the auditory nerve representation at 10 million values/s may seem surprising: the auditory nerve representation is a high-bandwidth redundant version of the signal from which the higher centers can extract the necessary information.) The higher temporal and spectral resolution is vital for performing auditory stream analysis to extract speech from background sounds and to detect fine timing distinctions used in distinguishing confusable consonants, precisely the two areas in which existing speech recognizers fail. Speech recognition is a prime example of a relatively powerful psychoacoustic model of a cortical process (hidden Markov models and Viterbi search) being starved by a poor model of a subcortical process, to the detriment of overall system performance.

The preceding argument suggests that it should be possible to improve speech recognition with an auditory model front end that replaces the FFT/filterbank/cepstral front end. To date, all such attempts have failed to produce any significant improvement, so that, again, there is great skepticism in both the scientific and investment community about the potential for progress in this area. Hermansky [13] has surveyed the previous attempts and offered several possible explanations for the disappointing results, including a wise warning of the dangers of blindly copying what is known about the brain without understanding the underlying principles. I agree that it would be pointless to simply bolt a cochlear model onto a hidden Markov model. The biological system does a tremendous amount of feature extraction between the cochlea and the cortex, and within the cortex, as shown in Figure 4.1. It is not surprising that early naïve attempts to connect a cochlea to the cortex have failed. Success will be achieved when we extract all the robust features used by the human system to process speech, and feed them correctly into an appropriate cortical model. It is not possible to extract the necessary features if vital information is thrown away at the first processing step. The cues for distinguishing the confusable consonants are well known [14,15], and the high-resolution cochlea model supports the extraction of all of those cues, whereas the frame-based FFT method fundamentally does not. In addition, the cochlea model provides all the information used by the human system to separate the speech from other sounds, whereas the frame-based FFT method again does not. I expect to see improved speech recognizers, based on powerful auditory models, deployed commercially by 2005–2006, with vastly better performance than present-day systems, both in quiet conditions and in noisy, reverberant environments.

The previous discussion has focused on the auditory system, and built the case that the neuroscience community already knows an overwhelming amount about how it works. Everything we know about the auditory system suggests that it is far more complex than any present-day engineering model. The same case can be made for the visual system. The visual system has been mapped out in detail in the macaque monkey [16], resulting in a convenient high-level block diagram from the retina up to complex cortical areas responsible for recognizing faces, supported by hundreds of studies of the various cell types and their connectivity. Douglas and Martin [17] have studied the neural structure of the neocortex, and provided a canonical microcircuit diagram for conceptualizing its operation. Calvin [18] has offered a rather speculative theory of how the cortex might work, useful at least in encouraging us to begin thinking about a connection between the cellular connectivity of the cortex and its high-level functions. Churchland and Sejnowski [19] have examined many aspects of neurobiology, including learning and memory. The problem is not that we know too little about the brain. The problem is that what we do know is overwhelming, and we need a fundamentally new way to think about it, visualize it, collaborate on it, and consolidate it into a working engineering model.

4.3 COMPUTING TECHNOLOGY

Do we have computers powerful enough in 2002 to be able to build an artificial brain? No—at least most of us do not; there are some research labs that are making impressive progress, however. In 2002, IBM is the current recordholder with a 7.2×10^{12} operations/second machine (Top 500 Web site [21]). Present-day desktop computers are capable of performing about 4×10^9 operations/s. Kurzweil [1] has estimated that we will need a computer capable of performing 10^{16} operations/s, and that these machines will not be available, at reasonable cost, until about 2020. But that is the estimated computing performance needed to simulate the *entire* human brain. As described in the previous section, we do not need to do that yet; we only need to simulate the well-understood parts well enough to let us branch into a new less-understood part. The available computing power has recently become adequate for that purpose. In my own work, I have found that a modest amount of computing hardware is sufficient to simulate the major functions of the auditory pathway up to the inferior colliculus, with efficient algorithms. Rodney Brooks stated in a 1999 colloquium at Stanford University that, in his work on building anthropomorphic motor systems, "a paradigm shift has recently occurred—computer performance is no longer a limiting factor. We are limited by our knowledge of what to build" (personal communication).

Prior to 1999, we knew enough about the brain to have been able to build a little of it, but the necessary computing power was not available. In practice, this meant that researchers struggled with feeble computers to painstakingly simulate the operation of a few neurons, and did not really learn anything they did not already know. Now, the computing power is great enough that we can implement a detailed model of a subsystem that we understand, and learn something *new* about it by watching it run in response to a complex, real-world stimulus. This new ability is related to Kurzweil's Law of Accelerating Returns [20], and it will add an important new element to neuroscience research. The only requirement will be that the model be realistic, that is, verifiable against the neurobiology. Otherwise, we will get a fast answer about some system we made up, not a fast answer about the brain. This is why priority #1 must be high-resolution representations, verifiable against the biology.

Computing power, in operations/s, is not the only factor in the paradigm shift. How will we verify our high-resolution representations? The only way I can see is to make high-resolution animated images of them. In addition to requiring a lot of computing power, this also requires fast, high-resolution graphics-rendering capability. Even as recently as 1998, real-time graphics rendering of high-resolution brain simulations was simply not possible on affordable machines. In 2002, it is not only possible, it is inexpensive.

4.4 NONTECHNICAL ISSUES

With a wealth of neuroscience knowledge available with which to begin, and all the computing power we can really use, what else do we need to undertake the program of reverse engineering the brain?

The first major issue is the need for direct collaboration with qualified neuroscientists. In the first section of this chapter, I stated that the neuroscience community *collectively* knows enough about the brain that we could begin a detailed modeling process. But their collective knowledge will not help us build a working model. Someone has to distill their knowledge into a concise form that can be implemented efficiently in a machine. This requires an active, long-term collaboration between the modeler and many neuroscientists—it is simply not possible to learn what the system is doing by reading their papers. There are just too many papers. And the only way to verify that the model is right is to show it to the neuroscientists who measured the real system, and keep changing it until the neuroscientists agree that it is right.

The other major issues relate to funding. Who will pay for this effort? What is the economic model for funding the work? Are there commercial applications that can justify an investment model?

There are several ways that this kind of project can be funded. The choice of funding model and funding source depends on the particular characteristics of the problems being addressed and the people involved, and could range anywhere from an academic lab funded by a government agency, a corporate research lab, or a start-up funded by angel investors or venture capitalists, if commercial applications can be developed on the appropriate time scale. I have found that the single biggest obstacle in funding this kind of project is the widespread skepticism in both the scientific and investment communities, after so many decades of high hopes and deep disappointments. I have been very fortunate to find scientific advisors and visionary investors who have taken the time to understand the promise of the approach, and by contributing to the effort, are causing it to succeed.

4.5 CONCLUSIONS

At about the turn of the twenty-first century, we passed a detectable turning point in both neuroscience knowledge and computing power. For the first time in history, we (collectively) know enough about our own brains, and have developed such advanced computing technology, that we can now seriously undertake the construction of a verifiable, real-time, high-resolution model of significant parts of our own intelligence. The ability to visualize the staggering complexity as we develop and verify the working model will be a necessary element in this ongoing program.

REFERENCES

1. R. Kurzweil. *The Age of Spiritual Machines*. Penguin, New York, 1999.
2. C. Mead. *Analog VLSI and Neural Systems*. Addison-Wesley, Reading, MA, 1989.
3. E. Young. In G. Shepherd, (ed.), *The Synaptic Organization of the Brain*, 4th ed., Oxford University Press, Oxford, 1998.
4. D. Oertel. In D. Oertel, R. Fay, and A. Popper, (eds.), *Integrative Functions in the Mammalian Auditory Pathway*, pp. 1–5. Springer-Verlag, New York, 2002.
5. J. Casseday, T. Fremouw, E. Covey. In D. Oertel, R. Fay, and A. Popper, (eds.), *Integrative Functions in the Mammalian Auditory Pathway*, pp. 238–318. Springer-Verlag, New York, 2002.
6. J. LeDoux. *The Emotional Brain*, Simon and Schuster, New York, 1997.
7. J. Rauschecker and B. Tian. "Mechanisms and Streams for Processing of "What" and "Where" in Auditory Cortex." *Proceedings of the National Academy of Sciences*, vol. 97, no. 22, 2000, 11800–11806.
8. G. Shepherd. *The Synaptic Organization of the Brain*, 4th ed., p. vi. Oxford University Press, Oxford, 1998.
9. T. Yin. In D. Oertel, R. Fay, and A. Popper, (eds.), *Integrative Functions in the Mammalian Auditory Pathway*, pp. 99–159. Springer-Verlag, New York, 2002.
10. A. Bregman. *Auditory Scene Analysis*. MIT Press, Cambridge, MA, 1990.

11. R. P. Lippman. "Speech Recognition by Machines and Humans." *Speech Commun.*, vol. 22, no. 1, 1–15, 1997.
12. L. Rabiner and B. Juang. *Fundamentals of Speech Recognition.* Prentice Hall, Englewood Cliffs, New Jersey, 1993.
13. H. Hermansky. "Should Recognizers have Ears?" *Speech Commun.*, vol. 25, 3–27, 1998.
14. G. Miller, and P. Nicely. "An Analysis of Perceptual Confusions Among Some English Consonants." *J. Acoust. Soc. Am.*, vol. 27, no. 2, 1955.
15. P. Ladefoged. *A Course in Phonetics.* 4th ed. Harcourt Brace, New York, 2001.
16. D. van Essen, and J. Gallant. "Neural Mechanisms of Form and Motion Processing in the Primate Visual System." *Neuron*, vol. 13, 1–10, 1994.
17. R. Douglas, and K. Martin. In G. Shepherd (ed.), *The Synaptic Organization of the Brain*, 4th ed., pp. 459–510. Oxford University Press, Oxford, 1998.
18. W. Calvin. *The Cerebral Code.* MIT Press, Cambridge, MA, 1998.
19. P. Churchland, and T. Sejnowski. *The Computational Brain.* MIT Press, Cambridge, MA, 1992.
20. R. Kurzweil. *The Singularity Is Near,* book precis, 2000.
21. Top 500 supercomputers website (2002), *http://www.top500.org/.*

CHAPTER 5

EMERGING TECHNOLOGIES: ONR'S NEED FOR INTELLIGENT COMPUTATION IN UNDERWATER SENSORS

JAMES F. McEACHERN and ROBERT T. MIYAMOTO

5.1 INTRODUCTION

This paper explores the Office of Naval Research's (ONR) need for intelligent computation in the development of underwater sensors. It is instructive to begin with a review of ONR's overall mission and research areas that provide the context for the specific need addressed here for underwater sensor research. Following this is an overview of current systems and needs. Examples of computationally intelligent applications (i.e., neural nets, fuzzy systems, and evolutionary computation) are then discussed, followed by a brief review of specific needs for the future.

ONR [1] is focused on the development and demonstration of a new generation of technologies to support national defense. ONR's mission is to inspire and guide innovation that will provide technology-based options for future Navy and Marine Corps capabilities. Founded in 1946, ONR provided the first U.S. federal government sponsorship of basic research, which was later followed by the National Science Foundation, established in 1950. Over the years, ONR has worked to support a mixture of basic and applied research that satisfies its major constituencies: the U.S. Congress, the Fleet, the Department of Defense, industry, and universities. ONR sponsors a wide range of development, including fundamental research, which transitions to technology development, and finally technology demonstration. Recently, ONR has reinvented itself, integrating basic science with applied development and technology demonstrations to support prioritized future naval capabilities. These prioritized capabilities result in an improved investment that reacts to the Navy's needs.

Computational Intelligence: The Experts Speak. Edited by D. B. Fogel and C. J. Robinson
ISBN 0-471-27454-2

ONR assigns departments to create programs that address specific capabilities. The major departments within ONR are Information, Electronics & Surveillance; Ocean, Atmosphere & Space; Engineering, Materials & Physical Science; Human Systems; Naval Expeditionary Warfare; and, finally, Industrial and Corporate Programs. Divisions of these departments partition the effort into functional managerial units led by program managers in a specific area. Program managers create research-and-development teams of government laboratories, universities, and industry that work together to develop new capabilities.

While many ONR departments could benefit from research and development in computational intelligence, the Ocean, Atmosphere, and Space (OAS) Department has a specific need for applications in undersea sensor technologies. The OAS Department is interested generally in science and technology in battlespace environments (BSE); antisubmarine warfare (ASW); mine warfare (MIW); and maritime intelligence, surveillance, and reconnaissance (ISR) and space exploitation. Within these areas, the OAS Department is interested in the understanding and synthesis of ocean and atmosphere processes along with innovative ways to evaluate the performance of assimilation, model, and simulation methods; real-time environmentally adaptive sensors, processing, systems, and strategies; development and use of distributed and autonomous ocean systems; exploitation of multispectral sensor information; innovative approaches to model building that do not require perfect or complete knowledge; automated target recognition in highly cluttered undersea environments; and space technologies for remote sensing of the ocean and atmosphere.

The OAS Department consists of two divisions, Sensing and Systems, and Processes and Prediction. The department also includes the Naval Space Science and Technology program office, the focus for the Department of the Navy's space science and technology activities.

A major thrust of the OAS Sensing and Systems division is to develop undersea warfare concepts to deal with threats that may attempt to restrict sea-based transportation that is vital to the world economy, and to protect naval combatants supporting operations ashore that protect the peace. The United States is not unique in this concern. Naval forces around the world continue to see submarines, torpedoes, and mines hiding beneath the surface as significant threats to a nation's independence and prosperity. The key elements to success are in the sensors. This is the primary research topic of the Sensors, Sources, and Arrays team in the Sensing and Systems division.

The Sensors, Sources, and Arrays team conducts multidisciplinary science and technology development in all aspects of acoustic source and sensor systems for Navy surface ship, submarine, aircraft, or fixed-ocean applications, such as a moored acoustic array. These systems can be carried as on-board equipment or deployed and operated autonomously or remotely as mobile or moored (i.e., stationary) equipment.

5.2 BACKGROUND

Building sensors that see through the water is a difficult task. Most underwater naval sensors in existence today were built for the open ocean to combat global nuclear war. To combat the far-ranging, deep water, global threat the Navy has developed sensors that could be deployed from long-endurance aircraft. These expendable sensors, termed *sonobuoys*, have a small surface float with a radio antenna that suspends a hydrophone at some depth below the surface of the water. The cost of such a sensor is on the order of hundreds of dollars. The sonobuoys can be listening devices in a passive mode, or have active acoustic sources that transmit (ping) into the ocean while the hydrophone listens for echoes from man-made objects. A field of many sonobuoys is launched from an aircraft to conduct a search over a wide area while sensor operators in the aircraft monitor the buoys and make detections. The operator must separate the man-made objects from the natural environmental noise arising from wind, rain, and reverberation from the surface and bottom of the ocean. Operators are faced with streams of analog traces from which to identify true targets of interest from among the many false targets.

The operator of today is highly motivated, but has minimal training. Much of the training is received on the job. Today's Navy has many new missions in support of regional conflicts, but without the same level of operational experience as it had in the past. The pace of operations is such that an operator may only see a real threat once or twice during a two-year tour of duty. While it is remarkable what operators can adapt to, there are limits to what can be expected.

Existing sensor systems are therefore severely challenged to perform at a reasonable level and at a time when the loss of a single ship, or the inability to transport critical supplies, can have a negative impact on national policies. The technology that drove the sensor design was based on analog systems that contained limited processing power and restricted communication capabilities. Today's conflicts are regional in nature, far from land bases from which forces can be supported. Naval forces are required to maneuver over shallow seas near the conflict to support operations ashore. In general, these shallow seas have yet to be surveyed and are subject to local weather and tides. The bottom may be convoluted and consist of rocks, sand, and mud. The water is nearly opaque to light and other forms of electromagnetic propagation. Sound travels effectively through the ocean, but in shallow water sound loses energy to the boundaries. The sound that does not propagate forward, scatters back toward a listening device causing a fog of reverberation that is difficult to penetrate. Noise from ships, fishing vessels, whales, shrimp, wind, and rain create a din through which a quiet submarine cannot be heard. To reliably find something in these harsh environments requires smarter sensors than we have today.

5.3 THE CHALLENGE

The solution to the more complex acoustic environments is to build arrays of sensors with greater frequency response, and to put more transmissions in the water. More sensors in the water provide more search coverage and greater spatial discrimination using modern techniques to form acoustic beams. Greater frequency response provides robustness in changing environmental conditions, but also higher temporal and spatial resolution of echoes. More transmissions in the water provide more echoes that can result in better tracking and classification. To provide long-term monitoring of a large search area that does not require many ships or aircraft, it is desirable to have long-lasting autonomous sensors with over-the-horizon communication capabilities. Longer life requires more power-efficiency combined with cheap, higher-energy density acoustic sources that still fit into a small buoy.

The ability to put more sensors, frequencies, and transmissions into the water can also result in the ability to better characterize the environmental conditions. A network of sensors can map out the acoustic medium and identify the propagation and scattering conditions that govern the acoustic environment. With this knowledge of the acoustic environment, sensor systems can be optimized to ensure complete coverage of an area with minimal assets and not leave gaps in the search coverage.

These techniques result in much more data and an associated increase in signal and information processing, which in turn can result in more power and communication requirements. Communication for naval applications will be restricted for the foreseeable future. While line-of-sight radio-frequency communications can provide large amounts of bandwidth, the number of sensors and the sampling rate can result in data rates of over 8 Mb/s. On a good day, a data transfer rate of 10 Mb/s might be achievable from the buoy to a monitoring aircraft. However, power requirements restrict the use of communication to a duty cycle of approximately 1%. Fields of buoys can number 50 to 100. Moreover, satellite communication links do not support these data rates. Therefore, the amount of data being generated by a sonobuoy's field can quickly overwhelm the communication capabilities available.

On the other hand, processors are becoming cheaper, faster, and require less power. Field-programmable gate arrays can achieve performance of many giga-operations per second. Techniques that turn data into information and provide for greater content, but less bandwidth, are highly desirable. However, processing still translates into power needs that may not be met because of size and cost of autonomous ocean sensors.

Even with data compression, the operator will need to perform at superhuman levels, or be provided with techniques to process the combined sensor data sets automatically and reduce the amount of false contact data to a manageable level. Sensors must be automated to adapt to the current environmental conditions so that optimal performance can be maintained. The cognitive load of evaluating the changing environmental conditions and then identifying the impact on the sensor is much too great. Sonar systems developed for deep ocean operations had to deal with an acoustic environment with a time constant on the order of hours or days. The time constant for shallow-water operations is on the order of minutes.

Therefore, from the sensor to the operator there are many opportunities for improvement in the current systems and in new requirements for future systems. ONR seeks innovative concepts and technologies to transform current systems into future systems that will enable the Navy to complete its missions successfully.

5.4 CURRENT APPLICATIONS

Computationally intelligent processing can provide new approaches to the large number of challenges ahead. The application of computational intelligent applications (e.g., fuzzy systems, neural nets, evolutionary computation) has proven itself both in research applications and in commercial markets. The main advantages of such algorithms are simplicity and performance. Complex nonlinear mapping of system dynamics can be obtained without the need for structured models. The superior noise-rejection capability and the tolerance to system fluctuations are two key advantages over more classic adaptation. The performance tends to be fast, simple, and straightforward.

An example of such an application is an automated sonar controller being developed by a multidisciplinary research team at the University of Washington. A sonar controller evaluates the current oceanographic and weather conditions and chooses the optimal sonar settings that maximize the detection range. One of the key challenges to the control of a sonar is an acoustic model that translates oceanographic and weather conditions to the acoustic conditions that the sonar hears. The acoustic model is extremely complex and computationally intensive. While modern processors can reduce calculation time, the increased physics required to model the complex shallow-water regional environments can increase the calculation time even more.

A layered-perceptron neural net is being used to solve this problem [2]. The slow acoustic model is used to produce the training and testing data for the neural net. Unlike some applications where neural nets have had difficulties, the acoustic model serves as an oracle that can generate the complex, nonlinear mapping between the acoustic model inputs and the outputs. New training data can be generated by simply running the acoustic model for the inputs that result in large output changes.

University of Washington researchers created probability density functions of a representative environment, e.g., wind speeds, sound speed, ocean depth, and ocean sediment composition, and calculated the distributions of the sonar operating parameters, e.g., transmit waveform type, frequency, and transmit power level. These distributions of the sonar operating parameters are used to produce the training data for the neural net. The input vector is about 28 elements, depending on the type of sonar system and the degree of fidelity of the acoustic model. The output is a matrix in depth and range (from the transmitter) of calculated signal-to-interference ratios. This matrix has a depth scale of 20–400 m and a range scale of 500 m to 20 km, resulting in 800 output values. Each model run is a realization of a specific environment and a specific sonar operating point. An example training set of 20,000 acoustic-model runs takes several days. Runs are made on five dual-processor 1.2-GHz Pentium computers. It takes about one week to train the neural net. Some of the data are held back for testing and evaluation. Special techniques have been developed to overcome specific features of the acoustic outputs such as near-bottom acoustic accuracy and acoustic channels. While the amount of time taken to create the training set combined with the training and testing time is substantial, the result is a relatively highly accurate emulation of the acoustic model. An individual acoustic model run might take several minutes, but the neural net can reproduce the same results on the order of milliseconds. This is a tremendous reduction in computation time.

The neural net therefore allows for many more calculations than the acoustic model and provides for greater flexibility in sonar optimization. In addition, the properties of the neural net allow for the calculation of the sensitivity of the sonar to the input parameters. Thus, once the operating parameters of the sonar are chosen, the user can also learn whether or not changing a specific aspect of the sonar, such as the frequency, will impact the operational capability of the sonar. Another desirable aspect of the neural net is that it can be implemented quickly and simply, with the coefficients of the neural-net nodes as a simple set of parameters. This reduces the cost substantially, since there is no need to implement and maintain an acoustic model. If a new acoustic model is desired or a specific attribute of a regional environment is emphasized, the development of the neural net can occur off-line and be downloaded easily to the system without software modification. This is attractive to acoustic modelers and system developers alike. Finally, the reduction in processing can result in lower power requirements, thus providing improved capability at reduced cost and with increased flexibility.

Algorithms are being developed using neural nets to estimate geoacoustic conditions in the ocean bottom [3]. The geoacoustic conditions govern the acoustic propagation and scattering in shallow water that limit acoustic sensor performance. Geoacoustic models are computationally intensive, so once again a neural net has been shown to have considerable advantage in reducing the processing load, thus reducing power, reducing software development, and thereby reducing costs, with minimal loss in accuracy.

With the ability of a sensor to infer the geoacoustic conditions, and the reduction in time to map the environment to the output detection map, it becomes possible to provide a feedback control to the sonar system. Computationally intelligent techniques [4] have been developed to invert the detection map so that a sonar operator can choose a specific geometric area of the ocean, then focus the sonar on that area. The sonar controller alters the controllable parameters (e.g., depth of the sonar, beam directions, transmit waveform) without operator intervention even if the environmental conditions change.

An autonomous intelligent agent based on a self-learning fuzzy system has also shown may advantages over current techniques [5,6]. Currently, extensive manual labor and considerable computer time are required to plan for a ship's track through the ocean in order to locate possible threats. The capability to provide a much simpler robust system is highly desirable. An unsupervised learning system, instilled with task-specific instincts and the ability to learn and speculate, is implemented as a simulated autonomous agent. The agent, dubbed the ORG, employs fuzzy logic and clustering techniques to efficiently represent and retrieve knowledge, and the ORG uses innovative sensor modeling and attention to process a large number of stimuli. Simple initial fuzzy rules (instincts) are used to influence behavior and communicate intent to the agent. Self-reflection is utilized so the agent can learn from its environmental constraints and modify its own state. Speculation is utilized in the simulated environment to produce new environmental and interaction rules and fine-tune performance and internal operational parameters. The ORG is released in a simulated shallow-water environment where its mission is to effectively cover a specified region in minimal time while simultaneously learning and modifying its own behavior.

5.5 FUTURE

There are many more potential opportunities for computationally intelligent techniques. Successful concepts will provide reduced operating costs, increased system life, and improved networked sensor capabilities. Reducing power requirements and reducing software complexity are two possible ways to reduce costs.

Power management and security are fields in which computational intelligence has played a major role [7,8]. Power management within a deployed sonobuoy is a highly dynamic process that must be optimized. Sonobuoy lifetimes can be maximized through the intelligent use of sensor and processing resources. Communication resources also require optimization, since networked information management is certain to be a key factor.

The range of computational intelligent capabilities needed to improve networked sensor performance is broad. Techniques that improve the signal and information processing by allowing for full-spectrum processing of the information are desirable. Also needed are improved algorithms for adaptive beam forming that are more robust and can eliminate interfering sources such as surface ships and biological organisms. Additionally, we need improved classification techniques that increase the probability of detection, yet reduce false alarms. We must conduct new research

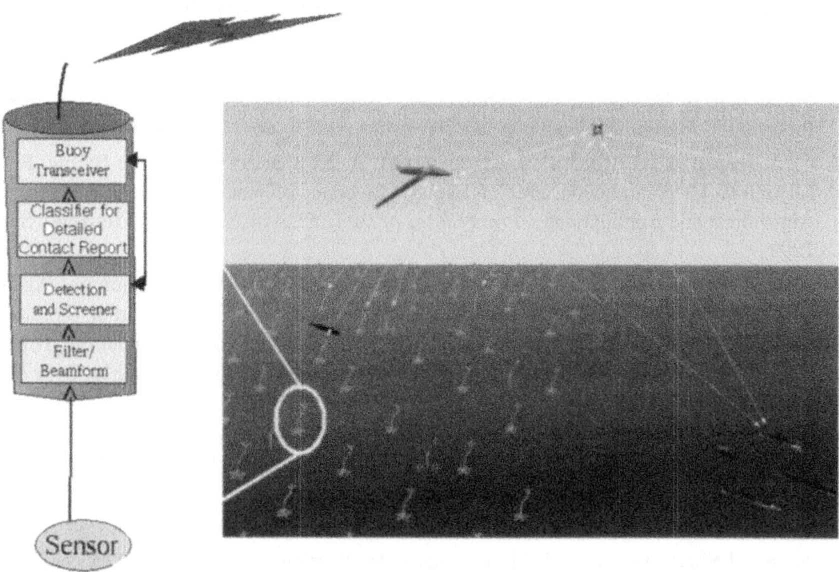

Figure 5.1 A distributed field of sensors with in-buoy signal processing. The processor in the sensor detects and classifies information in the data stream to reduce the data rate out of the buoy to a rate that can be accommodated by the over-the-horizon radio network. Typically, this requires a reduction in throughput of three to four orders of magnitude, without rejecting target information.

in algorithms that are data driven and robust to a wide range of signal-to-noise conditions and noise statistics. Improved capabilities are needed to determine what the current environmental conditions are and how to exploit them. Methods must be developed for future Navy personnel that facilitate the human decision process such that the human performance requirements are attained more easily.

5.6 SUMMARY

Office of Naval Research (ONR) is supporting research and development in new underwater sensor technologies. Tremendous challenges are ahead in the development of new sensor systems that enable the Navy to support national goals in regional conflicts. Initial applications of computational intelligence show much promise and indicate considerable potential for further applications.

REFERENCES

1. ONR, http://www.onr.navy.mil/, 2002.
2. Jae-Byung Jung, Mohamed A. El-Sharkawi, Robert J. Marks II, Robert T. Miyamoto, Warren L. J. Fox, G. M. Anderson, and C. J. Eggen, "Neural Network Training for Varying Output Node dimension." *Proc. Int. Joint Conf. Neural Networks*, Washington D.C., 1733–1738, 2001.
3. Y. Stephan, X. Demoulin, and O. Sarzeaud, "Neural Direct Approaches for geoacoustic Inversion," *Journal of Computational Acoustics*, vol. 6, nos. 1,2, 151–166, 1998.
4. C. A. Jensen, R. D. Reed, R. J. Marks, II, M. A. El-Sharkawi, Jung, Jae-Byung, R. T. Miyamoto, G. M. Anderson, and C. J. Eggen, "Inversion of Feedforward Neural Networks: Algorithms and Applications." *Proceedings of the IEEE*, vol. 87, no. 9, 1536–1549, Sept. 1999.
5. George Chrysanthakopoulos and Robert J. Marks II, "Simulated Autonomous Agents Utilizing Self-Reflection, Instincts and External Behavior Learning in a Simulated Environment: Orgs in Orgland," *Proc. Int. Conf. Evolutionary Computation (ICEC)*, IEEE World Congress on Computational Intelligence, Anchorage, Alaska, May 5–9, 727–734, 1998.
6. George Chrysanthakopoulos, Warren L. J. Fox, Robert T. Miyamoto, Gregory M. Anderson, Christian J. Eggen, Robert J. Marks II, and Mohamed A. El-Sharkawi, "Active Sonar Search for Underwater Targets Utilizing an Autonomous Agent as the Supervisory Controller" *IEEE Transactions on Fuzzy Systems* in preparation.
7. M. A. El-Sharkawi and R. J. Marks, (eds.), *Applications of Neural Networks to Power Systems.* IEEE Press, Piscataway, NJ, Catalog Number 91TH0374-9, 1991.
8. M. A. El-Sharkawi and Dagmar Niebur, (eds.), *Application of Artificial Neural Networks to Power Systems*, IEEE Press, Piscataway, NJ, 96 TP 112-0, 1996.

CHAPTER 6

BEYOND VOLTERRA AND WIENER: OPTIMAL MODELING OF NONLINEAR DYNAMICAL SYSTEMS IN A NEURAL SPACE FOR APPLICATIONS IN COMPUTATIONAL INTELLIGENCE

RUI J. P. DE FIGUEIREDO

6.1 INTRODUCTION

Nonlinear dynamical systems are playing a major role in a number of applications of computational intelligence. In order to maintain the current growth of the technologies supporting these applications into this new century, it is essential to develop rigorous, accurate, efficient, and insightful models for describing nonlinear dynamical systems' behavior, including *adaptation*, *learning*, and *evolution*, based on input–output observations or input–output specifications. If based on observations, the modeling process is called *system identification*, and if based on specifications, it is called *system realization* or *design*.

In this chapter, we present optimal solutions to both of the preceding problems in the setting of a *Neural Space* $\mathcal{N}$ introduced by the author in 1990 [1,2]. $\mathcal{N}$ is a separable Hilbert space of nonlinear[1] maps, f, that map a given vector x from a data space, X, which itself is a separable Hilbert or Euclidean space, to an m-vector y of m scalar outputs $y_j = f_j(x), j = 1, \ldots, m$, and f_j are bounded analytic functionals on X expressible as Volterra functional series on X [3]. The f_j belong to an appropriately constructed reproducing kernel Hilbert space, F, also introduced by de Figueiredo et al. in [4] in 1980, as a generalization of the symmetric Fock space. Details on this formulation as well as applications have been presented and discussed elsewhere [5–24].

[1]Throughout this chapter, by "nonlinear" we mean "not necessarily linear."

Computational Intelligence: The Experts Speak. Edited by D. B. Fogel and C. J. Robinson
ISBN 0-471-27454-2

Our objective here is to provide an overview and a further extension, oriented toward *computational intelligence*, of the underlying concepts and methodology for a mixed engineering/mathematical audience. The presentation will be from an approximation-theoretic rather than random-field viewpoint. The latter will be presented separately [24].

First and foremost, it is worthwhile pointing out the following two special features of our formulation.

First, our approach is *nonparametric* and leads to a simultaneous determination of an optimal structure as well as optimal values of parameters for the model of the system to be identified or realized. This is done by minimizing the maximum error (with respect to (w.r.t.) a metric in $\mathcal{N}$) between a desired but unknown nonlinear map, f, to be identified or realized, and its best estimate (model), $\hat{f}$, under prescribed prior uncertainty conditions on f and subject to the input–output observed or specified data constraints on f. This type of estimation embodies the notion of a *best robust approximation* of f by $\hat{f}$.

Second, even though no a priori structure is assumed for the model, the optimal solution appears in the form of a neural system. Thus an additional feature of our formulation is that it provides a mathematical justification for why biological systems, like the human brain, that perform tasks requiring computational intelligence have a neural system structure; and it points a way to model artificial and natural neural systems rigorously under a common framework.

Despite the power and richness in their description, prior works in the area of Volterra series [3,28–32] and its variants, such as Wiener–Bose series [25–32], had the following shortcomings, which we have attempted to overcome.

6.1.1 Shortcomings of the Previous Volterra and Wiener Formulations

The Volterra functional series (VS) representation of a nonlinear map, f, from a function space, X, to the complex plane, C, is an abstract power series in the input $x \in X$ of the form

$$y(t) = f(t;x) = \sum_{n=0} \frac{1}{n!} f_n(t;x) \tag{6.1}$$

where t is an indexing time variable for the scalar output variable $y(t)$, and if $X = L^2(I)$, I being an interval of the real line,

$$f_n(t;x) = \int_I \cdots \int_I h_n(t;t_1,\ldots,t_n)x(t_1)\cdots x(t_n)\ dt_1\cdots dt_n \tag{6.2}$$

where the kernels $h_n(t;\cdots)$ belong to an appropriate space like $L^2(I^n)$.

An expression for f_n when $x \in E^N = X$, where E^N is an N-dimensional complex Euclidean space, is given in a later section (6.31).

The VS representation (6.1)–(6.2), which has been used widely as a feedforward model for continuous time-parameter nonlinear dynamical systems [3,28–32], has some serious limitations. The multiple integrals in (6.2) are difficult to implement computationally. If, in order to mitigate this difficulty the series is truncated except for a few terms, (1) the resulting truncation errors are significant except when the amplitude of the input x is small, and (2) any least-squares approximation of the model, to satisfy the input–output data constraints, takes place in a finite dimensional space spanned by the truncated series rather than in an infinite-dimensional space to which the series may belong. This difficulty does not occur in our formulation.

To mitigate these difficulties, Wiener and Bose [25,26] proposed a Gram–Schmidt orthogonalization of the VS in the space of the output random variable $y(t)$, with the input as white Gaussian noise (WGN).

Specifically, the Wiener–Bose model is expressed in the form [25–28]

$$y(t) = H(Lx(t)) \tag{6.3}$$

where L is a linear differential dynamical system that enables the expansion of the input signal into Laguerre functions $l_i(\cdot)$, and $H(\cdot)$ represents a zero-memory nonlinear system that expands the range of L (i.e., in terms of the scalar variable $z = Lx(t)$) into orthogonal Hermite functions[2] $\varphi_k(z)$ (see Fig. 6.1). This leads to an expansion in the form (6.1) and (6.2), where the functionals $f_n(t;x)$ are expressed in terms of the Laguerre and Hermite basis functions appearing in the representation (6.3). The coefficients associated with the kernels in such a parametric representation are obtained by using WGN as the test input x and performing a Gram–Schmidt

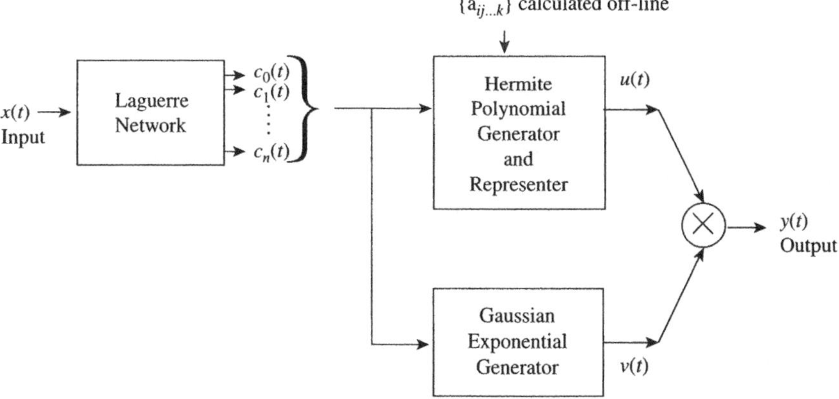

Figure 6.1 The Wiener–Bose nonlinear functional series model. In this model, the functional expansion is $y(t) = \sum_{k_0=0}^{\infty} \cdots \sum_{k_n=0}^{\infty} a_{k_0 \cdots k_n} \eta_{k_0}(c_0(t)) \eta_{k_1}(c_1(t)) \cdots \eta_{k_n}(c_n(t)) \exp\left[-\frac{1}{2}\sum_{i=0}^{n} c_i^2(t)\right]$, where $c_i(t) = \int_{-\infty}^{t} l_i(t-\tau)x(\tau)\,d\tau$.

[2] Orthogonal Hermite functions $\varphi_k(z)$ are of the form $\varphi_k(z) = \eta_k(z)\exp\left(-\frac{1}{2}z^2\right)$, where $\eta_k(z)$ is a Hermite polynomial in z of degree k.

orthogonalization of the output random variable $y(t)$ with respect to the random variable output of each kernel.

Thus the parameters in the model are determined so that, when $x(t)$ is WGN, the following (known as Wiener G-functional decomposition) holds:

$$E[y(t)] = f_0(t;x) \tag{6.4}$$

$$E[f_0(t;x)f_1(t;x)] = 0 \tag{6.5}$$

$$E[f_0(t;x)f_2(t;x)] = E[f_1(t;x)f_2(t;x)] = 0 \tag{6.6}$$

$$E[f_0(t;x)f_3(t;x)] = E[f_1(t;x)f_3(t;x)] = E[f_2(t;x)f_3(t;x)] = 0 \tag{6.7}$$

etc . . .

This orthogonalization guarantees that, when the input is WGN, truncation gives the minimum mean-square estimate of the output using the untruncated terms.

Despite this property, the Wiener–Bose model also has some fundamental limitations.

First, the model presents a conceptual difficulty posed by its use of WGN as a test signal. While WGN is an ideal test signal for probing linear time-invariant (LTI) systems, because different frequency components pass through an LTI system without mutual interference, WGN appears the least desirable one for testing nonlinear dynamical systems because of the effects of this interference.

Second, a truncation of the series optimized w.r.t. WGN input need not be optimal with respect to any nonwhite or/and non-Gaussian input. Of course, the Wiener–Bose procedure could be repeated for a given nonwhite or/and non-Gaussian input signal, but then the model would not be optimal w.r.t any other type of input statistics.

These considerations and the computational effort in the implementation of the model mentioned previously point to the need of looking for other approaches.

Numerous papers and treatises have appeared on the analysis and control of nonlinear dynamical systems (see, e.g., [28–51]) that in one way or another relate to the approach presented here. Limitations in space do not permit us to review them here.

6.1.2 Summary of This Chapter

In Section 6.2 we briefiy describe the three basic types of nonlinear dynamical system models grouped according to their configuration and description. They are *feedforward*, *recurrent*, and *state-space models*. In these models we indicate the generic nonlinear maps that appear in their description. These are in general m-tuples f_j, $j = 1, \ldots, m$, of nonlinear maps from a complex separable Hilbert space X (which could be the N-dimensional Euclidean space E^N) to the complex plane C.

In Section 6.3 we make the fundamental and very general assumption that the maps f_j are bounded analytic functionals on X expressible as an abstract power series (VS) in $x \in X$. We construct a reproducing kernel Hilbert space (RKHS), F, to which the maps f_j can be made to belong, and study the properties of this space, F, needed in the modeling of the nonlinear dynamical systems described in Section 1.2.

In Section 6.4 we show how these properties provide a rationale for the derivation/design of sigmoid functions as elements in the nonlinear dynamical-system modeling process.

In Section 6.5 we formally introduce the neural space $\mathcal{N}$ and present, as mentioned earlier, an explicit expression for the best robust approximation $\hat{f}$ of f in $\mathcal{N}$. We show that such an $\hat{f}$ appears as an abstract two-hidden-layer artificial neural network, called by us an *optimal interpolating (OI) neural network*, so obtained without prior assumption that $\hat{f}$ have a neural structure. This motivates our calling $\mathcal{N}$ a neural space. These theoretical developments also provide new rationales for representation of neural systems as linear combinations of shifted sigmoid functions and as linear combinations of radial basis functions (RBF). Also in that section, an optimal solution, $\hat{f}$, for the case in which the data are corrupted by WGN is given, with a two-layer *optimal smoothing (OS) neural network* as a special case.

In section 6.6, we port the developments of the preceding section to feedforward, recurrent and state-space models of nonlinear dynamical systems in the neural space $\mathcal{N}$. Extensions to complex models, such as OMNI (optimal multilayer neural interpolating) net and OSMAN (optimal smoothing multilayer artificial neural) net, which may include feedback, are also presented.

Section 6.7 provides a framework for porting the technology developed in the present chapter to computationally intelligent systems by modeling these systems as *mixed* (continuous/discrete) *systems*. The synthesis of these systems is achieved through appropriate application-specific combinations of MOI (mixed OI) and MOS (mixed OS) nets. Finally, in this section, a framework is presented for modeling what we call *intelligent learning* by CI systems as a combined adaptation and evolution process, and discovery as a consequence of augmentation of a higher-level neuronal layer in the system.

We end, in Section 6.8, with concluding remarks on some current and potential applications of this technology.

6.2 CLASSES OF NONLINEAR DYNAMICAL SYSTEM MODELS

There are in general three categories of basic models of nonlinear dynamical systems, namely *feedforward*, *recurrent*, and *state-space* models. Furthermore, by interconnection of such models (see, e.g., [51]), more complex models with any appropriate degree of complexity can be obtained.

In this section we discuss descriptions of the basic models just listed at the block-diagram level, both for the discrete-time-parameter (DTP) and continuous-time-parameter (CTP) cases. For simplicity in presentation, we restrict discussion to single-input/multiple-output systems in the feedforward case, to single-input/single-output systems in the recurrent case, and to multiple-input/multiple-output systems in the state-variable case. For the descriptions of the three basic models we will show in Section 6.6 how the nonlinear maps that appear in the various blocks

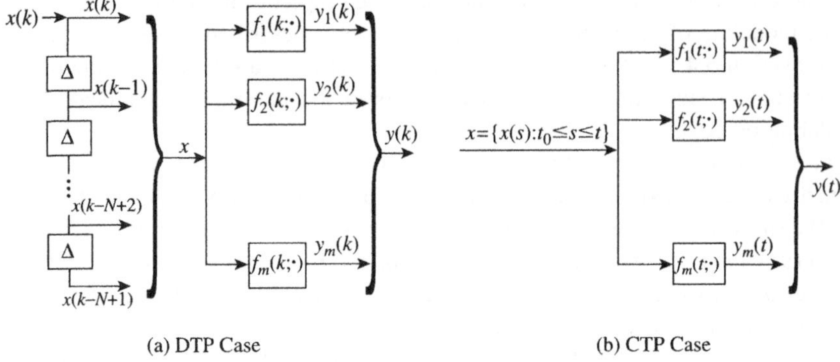

Figure 6.2 Feedforward models for single-input/multiple-output dynamical systems.

in the diagrams of this section can be optimally approximated and realized using our approach. *A Note Regarding Notation*: Even though we will call X the input data space, it will stand for the domain of the functionals that appear in various blocks. However, the meaning of X will be clear from the context.

6.2.1 Feedforward Models

For the single-input/multiple-output feedforward model we have the following descriptions, as depicted in Figure 6.2.

DTP Case

$$\begin{aligned} y(k) &= f(k;x) \\ &= (f_1(k;x),\ldots,f_m(k;x))^T \end{aligned} \tag{6.8}$$

where the superscript T denotes the transpose, $x(k) \in E^1$ and $y(k) \in E^m$ are scalar input and vector output samples at the instant k, and we use the notation

$$x = (x(k), x(k-1), \ldots, x(k-N+1))^T \tag{6.9}$$

for the input data string of length N up to and including k, and $f_j(k;\cdot)$, $j = 1, \ldots, m$, are bounded analytic functionals (VS) on E^N. Thus the input data space, X, for this case is the space E^N of strings x. If the strings, x, are square summable and of infinite length, X is l^2.

CTP Case

$$\begin{aligned} y(t) &= f(t;x) \\ &= (f_1(t;x),\ldots,f_m(t;x))^T \end{aligned} \tag{6.10}$$

where the input signal (data) x on an interval $I = [t_0, t]$ belongs to a complex-valued function Hilbert space X such as $L^2(I)$ or[3] $W_N^2(I)$, and $f_j(t, \cdot)$ are bounded analytic functionals (VS) on X.

Note that (6.8) and (6.10) can be viewed as discrete- and continuous-time parameter nonlinear convolutions with the input x.

6.2.2 Recurrent Models

The general description for a recurrent single-input/single-output nonlinear dynamical system in Direct Form I, as depicted in Figure 6.3, is as follows.

DTP Case

$$y(k) + f(k; y) = g(k; x) \tag{6.11}$$

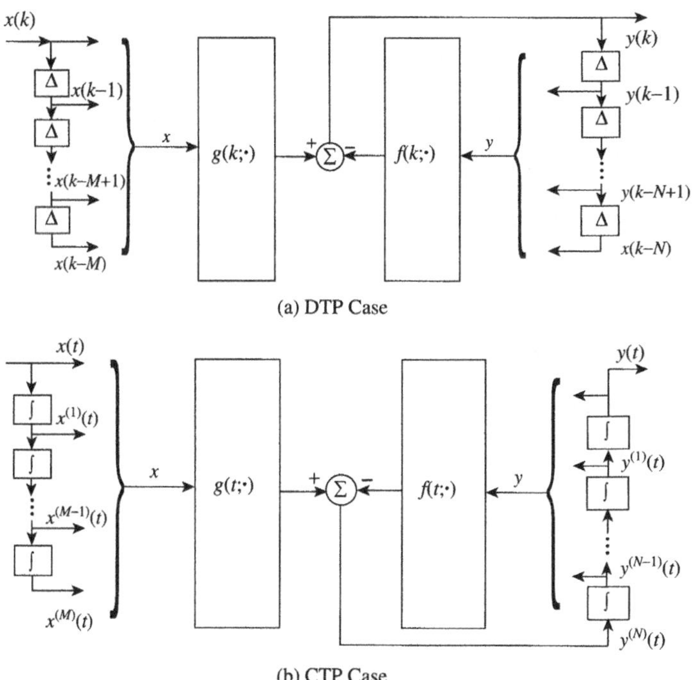

Figure 6.3 Recurrent models for single-input/single-output dynamical systems.

[3] W_N^2 is the Sobolev space of complex-valued functions, f, on I such that $f^{(i)}$, $i = 1, 2, \ldots, N-1$ are absolutely continuous and $f^{(N)} \in L^2(I)$.

where $x(k)$ and $y(k)$ denote the scalar input and output samples at instant k, and x and y are given by

$$x = (x(k), \ldots, x(k-M))^T \in E^{M+1} \tag{6.12}$$

$$y = (y(k-1), \ldots, y(k-N))^T \in E^N \tag{6.13}$$

Thus, for this case, the input data space, X, to which x belongs, is E^{M+1}, and $g(k; \cdot) : E^{M+1} \to C$ is a bounded analytic functional on X. Similarly, y is the string of previous output samples from $k-1$ to $k-N$, and $f(k; \cdot) : E^N \to C$ is a bounded analytic functional (VS) on E^N.

CTP Case

$$y^{(N)}(t) + f(t; y) = g(t; x), \qquad (\cdot)^{(j)} = \frac{d^j}{dt^j} \tag{6.14}$$

where $x(\cdot)$ and $y(\cdot)$ are appropriate scalar input and output functions of the continuous, t, variable, and, for convenience we use the abbreviated notation[4]

$$x = (x(t), x^{(1)}(t), \ldots, x^{(M)}(t))^T \in E^{M+1} \tag{6.15}$$

$$y = (y(t), y^{(1)}(t), \ldots, y^{(N-1)}(t))^T \in E^N \tag{6.16}$$

where $f(t; \cdot)$ and $g(t; \cdot)$ are defined as in the DTP case. Thus the space, X, to which x belongs is E^{M+1}, the set of values at time, t, of the input $x(\cdot)$ and its derivatives up to order M, together constituting the space E^{M+1}. Note also that in (6.14), $f(t; \cdot)$ is a nonlinear analytic function of the values $y^{(1)}(t), \ldots, y^{(N)}(t)$ constituting the space E^N, while in (6.10) $f_j(t; \cdot)$ represents a nonlinear convolution with the input function $x(\cdot)$.

6.2.3 State-Space Models

For a general M-input/N-output state-space model, we have, as indicated below.

DTP Case

As depicted in Figure 6.4a,

$$x(k+1) = f(k; x(k), u(k)) \tag{6.17}$$

$$y(k) = g(k; x(k), u(k)) \tag{6.18}$$

where $x(k) \in E^s$, $u(k) \in E^M$, and $y(k) \in E^N$ denote the state, input, and output vectors at time k, and $f(k; \cdot, \cdot)$ and $g(k; \cdot, \cdot)$ are, respectively, s-tuples and N-tuples

[4] Note that $x(\cdot)$ needs to be sufficiently smooth by belonging to a function space such as $W_M^2(I)$ in order for the representation (6.15) to be possible.

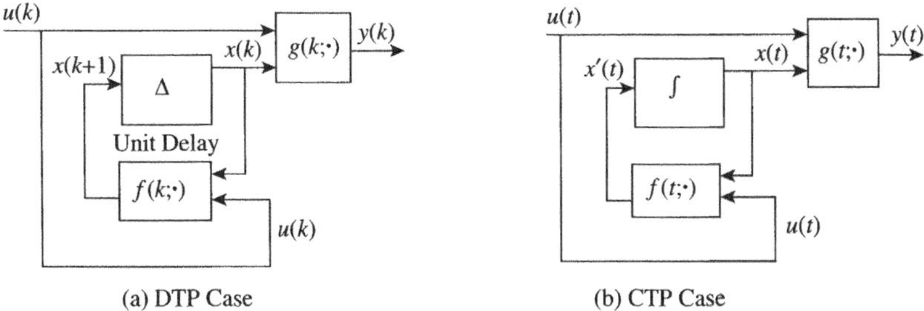

(a) DTP Case (b) CTP Case

Figure 6.4 State-space models for multiple-input/multiple-output dynamical systems.

of bounded analytic functionals on E^{s+M}. We can label this space X for the purpose of modeling f and g.

CTP Case

As shown in Figure 6.4b,

$$\frac{dx(t)}{dt} = f(t; x(t), u(t)) \tag{6.19}$$

$$y(t) = g(t; x(t), u(t)) \tag{6.20}$$

where $f(t; \cdot, \cdot)$ and $g(t; \cdot, \cdot)$ are the same mappings as in the DTP case.

In each of the preceding cases our detailed modeling depends on the best approximation of a generic bounded analytic functional on a separable Hilbert space, X, different notations and interpretations being given for such functionals in the descriptions of the three categories of models just presented.

On this basis we now proceed to construct and study the properties of an RKHS, F, to which such functionals are made to belong and which will aid in achieving our objectives.

6.3 THE DE FIGUEIREDO–DWYER–ZYLA SPACE *F*

6.3.1 Definition of the Space

Let X denote an abstract separable Hilbert space over C, with the scalar product and norm in X being denoted by $\langle x; z \rangle$ and $\|x\| = \langle x, x \rangle^{1/2}$ for any x and z in X. For example, depending on the model under consideration, X could be a finite dimensional Euclidean E^N, l^2, $L^2(I)$, or $W_N^2(I)$ for some positive integer N.

Let there be given a bounded set Ω in X defined by

$$\Omega = \{x \in X : \|x\|^2 \leq \mu^2\} \tag{6.21}$$

for some positive μ, as well as a sequence of positive weights, expressing prior uncertainty in the model

$$\lambda = \{\lambda_0, \lambda_1, \ldots\} \tag{6.22}$$

satisfying

$$\sum_{n=0}^{\infty} \lambda_n \frac{\mu^{2n}}{n!} < \infty \tag{6.23}$$

Also, let $\eta_i : i = 0, 1, \ldots$ denote an orthonormal basis in X. Then a homogenous Hilbert–Schmidt (H-S) polynomial f_n of degree n in elements of X is defined by the tensor product

$$\begin{aligned} f_n &= \sum_{i_1=0}^{\infty} \cdots \sum_{i_n=0}^{\infty} c_{i_1 \cdots i_n} \eta_{i_1} \otimes \eta_{i_2} \otimes \cdots \otimes \eta_{i_n} \\ &= \sum_{i_1=0}^{\infty} \cdots \sum_{i_n=0}^{\infty} c_{i_1 \cdots i_n} \langle \eta_{i_1}, \cdot \rangle \langle \eta_{i_2}, \cdot \rangle \cdots \langle \eta_{i_n}, \cdot \rangle \end{aligned} \tag{6.24}$$

where $c_{i_1 \cdots i_n}$ are complex constants, symmetric in the indices, satisfying

$$\|f_n\|_n \triangleq \left[\sum_{i_1=0}^{\infty} \cdots \sum_{i_n=0}^{\infty} |c_{i_1 \cdots i_n}|^2 \right]^{1/2} < \infty \tag{6.25}$$

The completion X^n, under (6.25), of all homogeneous H-S polynomials of degree n in elements of X is a Hilbert space under the inner product

$$\langle f_n, g_n \rangle_n \triangleq \sum_{i_1=0}^{\infty} \cdots \sum_{i_n=0}^{\infty} c^*_{i_1 \cdots i_n} d_{i_1 \cdots i_n} \tag{6.26}$$

where $*$ denotes complex conjugation, and $d_{i_1 \cdots i_n}$ are the coefficients associated with the H-S representation of g_n.

In terms of the element of X^n

we can define
$$x^n = x, x \otimes x, \ldots, x \otimes \cdots \otimes x \tag{6.27}$$

$$f_n(x) \triangleq \langle f_n, x^n \rangle_n \tag{6.28}$$

This leads to the following [4].

Definition 1 Under (6.21)–(6.23), the de Figueiredo–Dwyer–Zyla (dFDZ) space,[5] denoted by $F_\lambda(\Omega)$ or simply F, is the completion, under the norm (6.29), of the space spanned by the sequence $f = \{f_n \in X^n : n = 0, 1, \ldots\}$, satisfying

$$\|f\|_F \triangleq \left(\sum_{n=0}^{\infty} \frac{1}{n!\lambda_n} \|f_n\|_n^2\right)^{1/2} < \infty \tag{6.29}$$

Remark 1 Clearly, the following developments hold if F stands for a closed subspace of the space F defined earlier with some of the terms in the power series missing. This may occur in some applications.

Remark 2 Belonging to F are the bounded analytic functionals on Ω expressed as VS in the form

$$f(x) = \sum_{n=0}^{\infty} \frac{1}{n!} f_n(x) \tag{6.30}$$

For the case in which $X = L^2(I)$, $f(\cdot)$, the form of $f(t, \cdot)$, was expressed previously by (6.1), with t as an indexing variable.

If $X = E^N$, the functional $f_n(x)$, where $x = (x_1, \ldots, x_N)^T$ takes the form

$$f_n(x) = \sum_{|k|=n} c_k \frac{|k|!}{k!} x^k \tag{6.31}$$

where

$$\begin{aligned}
k &= (k_1 \cdots k_N), \\
|k| &= k_1 + k_2 + \cdots + k_N, \\
k! &= k_1! \cdots k_N! \\
c_k &= c_{k_1 \cdots k_N}, \\
x^k &= x_1^{k_1} \cdots x_N^{k_N}.
\end{aligned}$$

Remark 3 F constitutes a generalization of the symmetric Fock space used in the representation of non-self-interacting Boson fields in quantum field theory [52–54]. Also, Hilbert spaces of analytic functions on C^n have been investigated extensively (see, e.g., [55–57]). Our approach considers the more general case of functionals

[5] Previously, we called this space *generalized Fock space*.

(rather than functions) on a Hilbert space. It is based on the work of Dwyer on differential operators of infinite order [58].

Finally, F has a unique reproducing kernel that often is available in closed form, as stated in the following theorem the proof of which is given elsewhere [4,5,7].

THEOREM 1 Under the scalar product

$$\langle f, g \rangle_F = \sum_{n=0}^{\infty} \frac{1}{n!} \frac{1}{\lambda_n} \langle f_n, g_n \rangle_n \tag{6.32}$$

where F is an RKHS with the reproducing kernel

$$K(u, v) = \varphi(\langle u, v \rangle) = \sum_{n=0}^{\infty} \frac{\lambda_n}{n!} \langle u, v \rangle^n \tag{6.33}$$

that is,

$$\varphi(s) = \sum_{n=0}^{\infty} \frac{\lambda_n s^n}{n!} \tag{6.34}$$

In the special case in which

$$\lambda_n = \lambda_0^n \tag{6.35}$$

the reproducing kernel takes the form

$$K(u, v) = \exp(\lambda_0 \langle u, v \rangle) \tag{6.36}$$

and so

$$\varphi(s) = \exp(\lambda_0 s) \tag{6.37}$$

6.3.2 Properties of *F*

The following three propositions follow from the theory of reproducing kernels [61]. We will use them in the solution of the modeling problem.

PROPOSITION 1 As a function of x, $\varphi(\langle v, x \rangle)$, and in particular $\exp(\lambda_0 \langle v, x \rangle)$, are members of F. We express this as

$$\varphi(\langle v, \cdot \rangle) \in F \tag{6.38}$$

and in particular,

$$\exp(\lambda_0 \langle v, \cdot \rangle) \in F \tag{6.39}$$

PROPOSITION 2 $\varphi(\langle v, \cdot \rangle)$ is the representer (in the sense of the Riesz representation theorem) in F of the point evaluation functional on F, i.e.,

$$\langle \varphi(\langle v, \cdot \rangle), f(\cdot) \rangle_F = f(v) \tag{6.40}$$

$\forall f \in F$.

PROPOSITION 3 Let ξ be a continuous linear functional on F. Then a representer $\xi(\langle v, \cdot \rangle) \in F$ of ξ is obtained by the action of ξ on φ with φ as a function of its adjoint argument, this being denoted by a respective subscript on ξ, that is,

$$\xi(\langle v, \cdot \rangle) = \xi_v(\varphi(\langle v, \cdot \rangle)) \tag{6.41}$$

Remark 4 For the purpose of this chapter it will be sufficient to consider the class of linear functionals on F defined in terms of bounded sequences of constants $(\alpha_0, \alpha_1, \ldots)$ by

$$\xi_v(f) = \sum_{n=0}^{\infty} \frac{\alpha_n}{n!} f_n(v) \tag{6.42}$$

where f_n is as in (6.28) and (6.30).

By considering $\varphi(\langle v, x \rangle)$ as an element of F in terms of v, with x a fixed parameter, we have, according to (6.42), and (6.33),

$$\xi_v(\varphi(\langle v, x \rangle)) = \sum_{n=0}^{\infty} \frac{\alpha_n}{n!} \lambda_n \langle v, x \rangle^n \tag{6.43}$$

and hence, according to (6.33) and (6.42), (6.43) gives (6.41) explicitly, i.e.,

$$\langle \xi_v(\varphi(\langle v, \cdot \rangle)), f(\cdot) \rangle_F = \sum_{n=0}^{\infty} \frac{\alpha_n}{n!} f_n(v) \tag{6.44}$$

6.4 DERIVATION OF SIGMOID FUNCTIONALS

Sigmoid functions[6] [37] play an important role in computationally intelligent systems. In our formulation, they are *representers* of linear observation or specification

[6] A sigmoid functional is a composition of two maps: a nonlinear function and a scalar product in X. The first map is called a *sigmoid function*.

functionals on F. Hence their modeling is application specific. We derive expressions for such representers ((6.47), (6.50), (6.51), (6.54), (6.55)) for five important cases. We denote by superscripts the labels of the corresponding sigmoids and illustrate their well-known characteristics for some of them in Figure 6.5. In these expressions, the parameter λ_0 determines the reproducing kernel (RK) of F and hence the metric of F. So in a given application, by adjusting λ_0 one may make this metric match the prior mode uncertainty expressed by the RK.

6.4.1 Exponential Activation Functional

The exponential activation functional is the point evaluation functional ξ_v^p on F, i.e.,

$$\xi_v^p(f) = f(v) \tag{6.45}$$

and according to Proposition 1, its representer is

$$\xi^p(\langle v, \cdot\rangle) = \varphi(\langle v, \cdot\rangle) \tag{6.46}$$

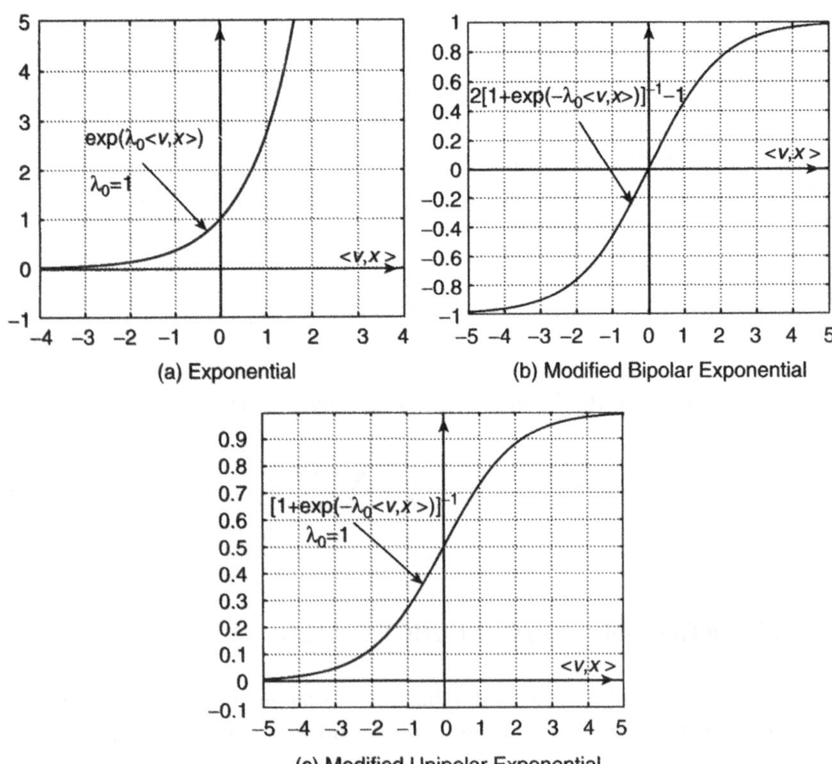

Figure 6.5 Examples of sigmoid functions.

and in the case of (6.37)

$$\xi^{p}(v, \cdot) = \exp(\lambda_0 \langle v, \cdot \rangle) \tag{6.47}$$

Note that the constants α_n in (6.42) are equal to 1 for this functional.

6.4.2 Modified Exponential Sigmoid Functional

This functional corresponds to the unipolar activation functional

$$g_{eu}(x) = \frac{1}{1 + \exp(-\rho\langle v, x \rangle)} \tag{6.48}$$

where ρ is a scaling parameter and v is an appropriate element of X.

This functional corresponds to the one defined by (6.42) with the constants α_n:

$$\alpha_n = \frac{1}{2}(-1)^n E_n(0) \tag{6.49}$$

where $E_n(0)$ denotes the coefficient of the zeroth-order term of the nth-degree Euler polynomial, i.e., α_n is the zeroth-order nth-degree Euler number.

With this agreement, the representer in F for this functional is as in (6.42) with the α_n as in (6.49), and in the special case of the exponential reproducing kernel (6.37),

$$\xi^{eu}(\langle v, \cdot \rangle) = \frac{1}{1 + \exp(-\lambda_0 \langle v, \cdot \rangle)} \tag{6.50}$$

where the a priori uncertainty weight λ_0 in F corresponds to the scaling parameter ρ in (6.48).

In a similar way, one can derive the expression for the representer of the bipolar-modified exponential sigmoid functional

$$\xi^{eb}(\langle v, \cdot \rangle) = \frac{2}{1 + \exp(-\lambda_0 \langle v, \cdot \rangle)} - 1 \tag{6.51}$$

6.4.3 Hyperbolic Tangent Sigmoid Functionals

To obtain the representer in F corresponding to the bipolar hyperbolic tangent activation functional

$$g_{tb}(v) = \tanh(\rho\langle v, x \rangle) \tag{6.52}$$

where ρ and ν are the same as defined in connection with (6.48), assume that in (6.42) the even power coefficients are zero. Then the desired representer is obtained by letting the odd power coefficients in (6.42) be

$$\alpha_{2n-1} = \frac{2^{2n}(2n-1)}{n} B_{2n}, \qquad n = 1, 2, \ldots \tag{6.53}$$

where B_{2n} denotes the Bernoulli [62] number of degree $2n$. The corresponding representer, in the special case of the exponential reproducing kernel (6.37), is

$$\begin{aligned} \xi^{tb}(\langle \nu, \cdot \rangle) &= \sum_{n=1}^{\infty} \frac{1}{(2n-1)!} \alpha_{2n-1} (\lambda_0 \langle \nu, \cdot \rangle^{2n-1}) \\ &= \tanh(\lambda_0 \langle \nu, \cdot \rangle) \end{aligned} \tag{6.54}$$

where the scaling weight λ_0 is equal to ρ in (6.52).

In a similar way, we can obtain the representer of the unipolar hyperbolic tangent functional in F:

$$\xi^{tu}(\langle \nu, \cdot \rangle) = \frac{1}{2}[1 + \tanh(\lambda_0 \langle \nu, \cdot \rangle)] \tag{6.55}$$

6.5 BEST ROBUST APPROXIMATION OF f IN THE NEURAL SPACE $\mathcal{N}$

We now introduce the neural space $\mathcal{N}$ by way of the following.

Definition 2 For a given positive integer, m, and space, F, the neural space $\mathcal{N}$ is the Hilbert space of m-tuples $f = (f_1, \ldots, f_m)$, with $f_j \in F, j = 1, \ldots, m$, with scalar product and norm in $\mathcal{N}$ for any f and g in $\mathcal{N}$ defined by

$$\langle f, g \rangle_{\mathcal{N}} = \sum_{j=1}^{m} \langle f_j, g_j \rangle_F \tag{6.56}$$

and

$$\|f\|_{\mathcal{N}} = [\langle f, f \rangle_{\mathcal{N}}]^{1/2} \tag{6.57}$$

Remark 5 The space, $\mathcal{N}$, is the direct product of the spaces F, i.e.,

$$\mathcal{N} = \overbrace{F \times F \times \cdots \times F}^{m}$$

so the members of $\mathcal{N}$ having a common domain X. On this basis, (6.56) and (6.57) make sense. We will show that members of $\mathcal{N}$ are optimally implemented as neural networks. Therefore the scalar product (6.56) measures the similarity between the two neural networks that the maps f and g represent, and the norm (6.57) when used as $\|f - g\|_{\mathcal{N}}$ expresses a metric distance between these two networks.

We now state the following best robust approximation problem of a nonlinear map $f \in \mathcal{N}$ (with the notation $f(x) = y$) based on an ellipsoidal prior uncertainty model in $\mathcal{N}$ and a set of q observations or specifications' constraints on f. Even though f may be a component of a larger dynamical system, such as those described in Section 6.2, we call, for convenience, its domain and range spaces, input and output spaces.

PROBLEM 1 Let there be given the input–output data pairs

$$(x^i \in X, y^i \in E^m), \qquad i = 1, \ldots, q \tag{6.58}$$

where $x^i, i = 1, \ldots, q$ are linearly independent, and a set of q functionals of the type (6.42) with the representers in F of the form (6.43) expressed by

$$\xi_{x^i}(\varphi(\langle x^i, \cdot \rangle)), \qquad i = 1, \ldots, q \tag{6.59}$$

with regard to which f satisfy input–output data constraints that confine f to the set

$$\begin{aligned}\Phi = \{f \in \mathcal{N} : \langle \xi_{x^i}(\varphi(\langle x^i, \cdot \rangle)), f_j \rangle_F = y^i_j,\\ i = 1, \ldots, q,\ j = 1, \ldots, m\}\end{aligned} \tag{6.60}$$

and assume that f lies on a prior uncertainty ellipsoidal set in Ω

$$\Gamma = \{f \in \mathcal{N} : \|f\|_{\mathcal{N}} \leq \gamma\} \tag{6.61}$$

for some $\gamma > 0$ sufficiently large so that the set

$$\chi = \Phi \cap \Gamma \tag{6.62}$$

is nonempty.

Find the *best robust approximation* $\hat{f}$ of f as the solution of the min-max optimization problem

$$\sup_{\tilde{f} \in \chi} \|\hat{f} - \tilde{f}\|_{\mathcal{N}} \leq \sup_{\tilde{f} \in \chi} \|f - \tilde{f}\|_{\mathcal{N}} \qquad \forall f \in \chi \tag{6.63}$$

Remark 6 Figure 6.6 provides a geometrical illustration of the sets ϕ, Γ, and χ in $\mathcal{N}$, where ϕ is a hyperplane, Γ an ellipsoid, and χ a subset of ϕ. It is also clear from this figure that the point in χ for which the maximum distance from all other points in χ is minimum is the centroid of χ, which thus corresponds to the solution, $\hat{f}$, of the minimum norm problem

$$\min_{f \in \chi} \|f\|_{\mathcal{N}} \tag{6.64}$$

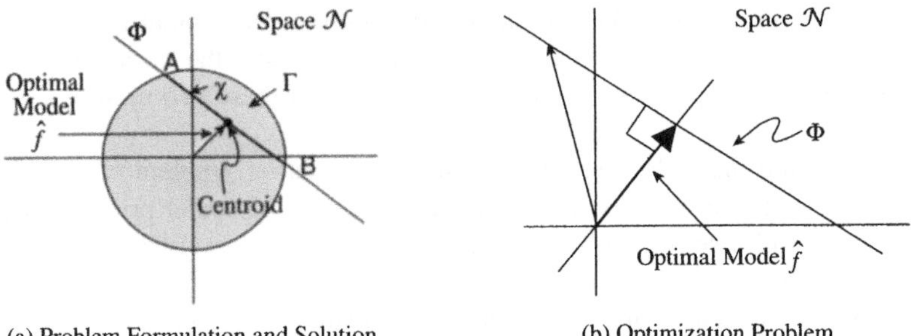

(a) Problem Formulation and Solution

(b) Optimization Problem

Figure 6.6

Remark 7 Since, according to (6.56) and (6.57),

$$\|f\|_{\mathcal{N}} = \left[\sum_{j=1}^{m} \|f_j\|_F^2\right]^{1/2} \tag{6.65}$$

minimization of $\|f\|_{\mathcal{N}}$ is achieved through the minimization of the individual $\|f_j\|_F$, $j = 1, \ldots, m$.

The preceding two remarks explain the validity of the following theorem, a formal proof of which is given elsewhere [1,2,7].

THEOREM 2 Problem 1, expressed by (6.63), has a unique solution, $\hat{f}$, which is the solution of the minimum norm problem

$$\min_{f \in \chi} \|f\|_{\mathcal{N}} \tag{6.66}$$

Each component $\hat{f}_j$ of the solution is the unique vector belonging to the subspace of F spanned by the representers $\xi_{x^i}(\varphi\langle x^i, \cdot\rangle)$ satisfying the interpolating constraints (6.60). This leads to the closed-form expression for $\hat{f}$:

$$\hat{f}(x) = \mathbf{W}^T K(x) \tag{6.67}$$

where $\mathbf{W} = q \times m$ matrix and $K(\cdot)$, a q-dimensional vector, are computed as follows

$$K(x) = (\xi_{x^1}(\varphi(\langle x^1, x\rangle)), \ldots, \xi_{x^q}(\varphi(\langle x^q, x\rangle)))^T \tag{6.68}$$

$$\mathbf{W} = \mathbf{G}^{-1}\mathbf{Y}^T \tag{6.69}$$

where $\mathbf{G}$ is the $q \times q$ matrix with elements

$$\begin{aligned} G_{ij} &= \langle \xi_{x^i}(\varphi(\langle x^i, \cdot\rangle)), \xi_{x^j}(\varphi(\langle x^j, \cdot\rangle))\rangle_F \\ &= \langle \psi(\langle x^i, \cdot\rangle), \psi(\langle x^j, \cdot\rangle)\rangle_F \\ &= \psi(\langle x^i, x^j\rangle) \end{aligned} \tag{6.70}$$

and $\mathbf{Y}$ is the $m \times q$ matrix

$$\mathbf{Y} = (y^1, \ldots, y^q) \tag{6.71}$$

A bound for the residual error ξ is

$$\xi \leq \gamma - YG^{-1}Y^T = \alpha \tag{6.72}$$

Remark 8 Without prior assumption that the solution to the optimization Problem 1 has a neural structure, the optimal solution is in the form of a feedforward two-layer abstract neural network, called by us an *optimal interpolating* (OI) net, depicted in Figure 6.7. In this network the $N \times q$ synaptic weight matrix,[7] X, for the first layer of the network is obtained from the set of input vectors (called *exemplary inputs* or simply *exemplars*)

$$X = (x^1, x^2, \ldots, x^q) \tag{6.73}$$

Therefore, if the input space is E^N, X in (6.73) is an $N \times q$ matrix and X_{ij} is the synaptic weight from the ith input node to the jth node of the first internal layer, as shown in Figure 6.7a. If that space is $L^2(I)$, X_{ij} is a "functional synaptic weight" between the entire x^i signal and the jth node of the first internal layer, as depicted in Figure 6.7b. Functional artificial neural networks, without being called this, were first introduced in [6] and further discussed in [9–10].

Remark 9 The solution provided by Theorem 1 permits one to simultaneously extract optimal structure and the optimal set of parameters that belong to it. The process of this acquisition is called *intelligent learning* vis-a-vis other types of learning based on numerical optimization algorithms like the Amari [36] and Hebbian [37] learning ones. Algorithms for "instantaneous learning" (by obtaining (6.67) with all the exemplars included) and "sequential (adaptive/evolutionary) learning" by (a recursive least-square (RLS) procedure) have been presented and discussed at length by the author in collaboration with Sin [11–13]. Additional comments appear in Section 6.7.3.

Remark 10 The following five comments are of particular relevance:

1. *Point Evaluation Functionals* In the case in which the y^j, $j = 1, \ldots, q$, represent outputs rather than more general observations/specifications described by (6.42), then according to Proposition 2, the representers ξ_x^i are simply

$$\xi_x^i(\varphi(\langle x^i, \cdot\rangle)) = \varphi(\langle x^i, \cdot\rangle) \qquad i = 1, \ldots, q \tag{6.74}$$

[7] Even though we used X to denote the input data space, for convenience we use the same notation for the matrix (6.73), its meaning being clear from the context.

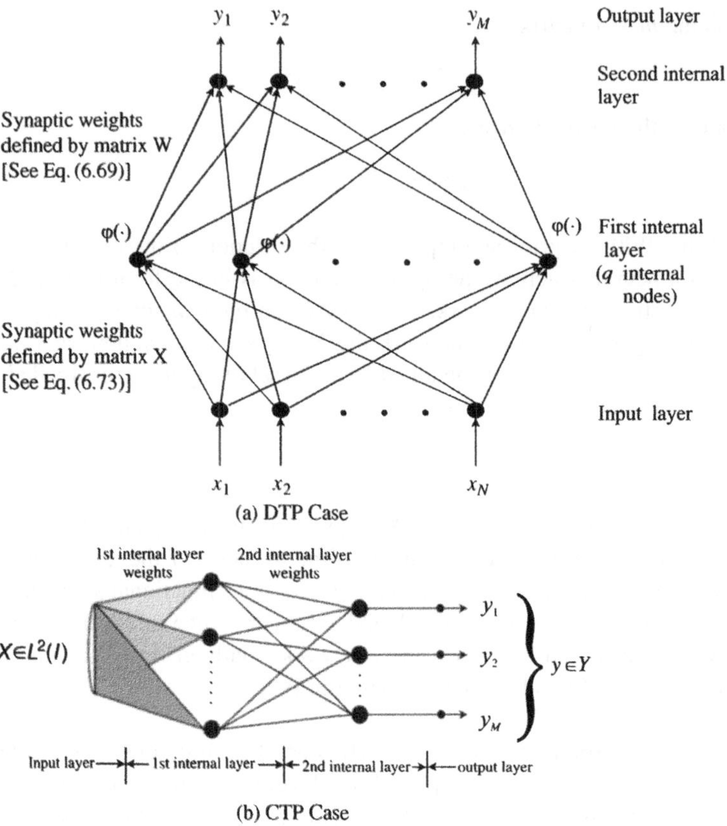

Figure 6.7 Signal-flow graphs for the OI net. (a) DTP case, (b) CTP case.

and (6.68) and (6.70) take the form

$$K(x) = (\varphi(\langle x^1, x\rangle), \ldots, \varphi(\langle x^q, x\rangle))^T \tag{6.75}$$

$$G_{ij} = \varphi\langle x^i, x^j\rangle \tag{6.76}$$

2. *Rationale for Shifted Sigmoids Model Representation* One can interpret the model (6.67) in terms of shifted sigmoids of the type considered in Section (6.4). For simplicity in presentation, we will consider the case in which $m = 1$ (single output), use the abbreviated notation for the representers in (6.59) and (6.68).

$$\xi_{x^i}(\varphi\langle x^i, x\rangle) = \psi(\langle x^i, x\rangle) \tag{6.77}$$

and denote by r_i the shift in the ith sigmoid.

The following cases are of interest:

(a) *Exponential Sigmoid (6.47)* In this case, shifts correspond to the scaling of coefficients of unshifted sigmoids. The shifts are automatically taken into account by our procedure according to:

$$\begin{aligned}\exp(\lambda_0(\langle x^i, x\rangle - r_i)) &= \exp(-\lambda_0 r_i)\exp(\lambda_0\langle x^i, x\rangle) \\ &= A_i\exp(\lambda_0\langle x^i, x\rangle) \qquad i = 1, \ldots, q \end{aligned} \tag{6.78}$$

(b) *Other Sigmoids ((6.50), (6.51), (6.54), (6.55))* In this case, sigmoid shifts can be interpreted and taken into account in one of the following two ways.

(i) They can result from an offset x^0 in the input signal x, i.e.,

$$\psi(\langle x^i, x\rangle - r_i) = \psi(\langle x^i, x - x^0\rangle) \tag{6.79}$$

where

$$r_i = \langle x^i, x^0\rangle, \qquad i = 1, \ldots, q \tag{6.80}$$

(ii) More fundamentally, one would like to represent the model, f, as a sum of abstract power series (Taylor series) around p points $\tilde{x}^k \in X$, $k = 1, \ldots, p$, rather than a single power series around the origin (McLaurin series), as we have done thus far. Typically, the points $\tilde{x}^k$ could be cluster centers of the set of exemplars. One would then construct a new space, F, as a direct sum of spaces, F_k, i.e.,

$$F = F_1 \oplus F_2 \oplus \cdots \oplus F_p \tag{6.81}$$

each F_k being constructed as was F before, except that the space, X, for F_k would be centered at $\tilde{x}^k$.

From such a development it follows that (with $m = 1$)

$$\begin{aligned}\hat{f}(x) &= \sum_{k=1}^{p}\sum_{i=1}^{q}\tilde{w}_{ik}\psi(\langle x^i - \tilde{x}^k, x - \tilde{x}^k\rangle) \\ &= \sum_{k=1}^{p}\sum_{i=1}^{q}\tilde{w}_{ik}\psi(\langle v^{ik}, x\rangle - r_{ik}) \end{aligned} \tag{6.82}$$

where

$$v^{ik} = x^i - \tilde{x}^k \tag{6.83}$$

$$r_{ik} = \langle v^{ik}, \tilde{x}^k\rangle \tag{6.84}$$

Thus, according to our formulation, one would determine $\tilde{x}^k$ from the training data, and obtain the parameters v^{ik} and r^{ik} from (6.83) and (6.84). By arranging the subscripts *ik* lexicographically, we relabel them in terms of a single indexing variable $l = 1, \ldots, L$, where $L = pq$. With this notational agreement, we rewrite (6.82) using the subscript j to cover the case of multiple outputs corresponding to $j = 1, \ldots, m$, in the form

$$\hat{f}_j(x) = \sum_{l=1}^{L} w_{lj} \psi(\langle v^l, x \rangle - r_l) \tag{6.85}$$

Here w_{lj} denotes the weight $\tilde{w}_l = \tilde{w}_{ik}$ for the jth output. By substituting (6.85) in (6.69), taking the preceding notational agreement into account, the desired optimal model (6.67) based on shifted sigmoids can be obtained.

Comment Barron and others (see e.g., [50]) have studied the property of approximation of a known function by a linear combination of shifted sigmoids. Their problem is clearly different from the one we have considered to be best, approximating an unknown function, f, based on the training data, an uncertainty model for f, and an appropriate space where f may reside. Sigmoids appear as a possible consequence rather than a cause according to our formulation.

3. *Rationale for Radial Basis Functions Model Representations* Another popular scheme for modeling artificial neural systems is that based on the RBF [38]. We now show how this scheme fits our model (6.67). Assume that the space, F, consists of VS on $X \times X$, where[8] $X = E^N$. Then using the exponential reproducing kernel (6.37) and the functional (6.42) with $\alpha_n = (-1)^n$, we have for (6.43)

$$\psi(\langle I, x \times x \rangle) = \exp(-\lambda_0 \|x\|^2) \tag{6.86}$$

where I denotes the $N \times N$ diagonal matrix

$$I = \mathrm{Diag}(1, \ldots, 1) \tag{6.87}$$

Constructing now a new space, F, in a way analogous to (6.81), we are led to

$$\hat{f}(x) = \sum_{k=1}^{p} \sum_{i=1}^{q} \tilde{w}_{ik} \exp(-\lambda_0 \|x - \tilde{x}^k\|^2) \tag{6.88}$$

where $\tilde{x}^k$, $k = 1, \ldots, p$, are the vectors around which the VS expansions for F_k, $k = 1, \ldots, p$ occur. The coefficients $\tilde{w}_{ik}$, $k = 1, \ldots, p$, are obtained by interpolating the expression (6.88) at the exemplars using the formulas (6.68)–(6.71) with appropriate interpretation of the notation.

Note that, as indicated under (b)(ii), the $\tilde{x}^k$, $k = 1, \ldots, p$, constitute a set of fiducial points extracted from the training (such as cluster centers or some

[8] X Here denotes the input space.

exemplars themselves) that best represent the structure of the training set for the purpose just explained.

4. *The deF Dimension* The bound α on the residual error (6.72) enables us to define a criterion that we denote by $deF(\alpha)$, which measures an *intrinsic dimensionality* of the OI net, in terms of the minimum number of neurons in its first layer to achieve correct classification of all exemplars. Specifically, we define $deF(\alpha)$ as the minimum number of exemplary pairs (x^i, y^i) needed to keep the uncertainty error in (6.72) below a prescribed α.
5. *Optimal Solution with Noisy Data* If the output data are noisy, i.e.,

$$y_j^i = z_j^i + v_j^i, \qquad i = 1, \ldots, q, \qquad j = 1, \ldots, m$$

where z_j^i, $i = 1, \ldots, q$, constitute the nonnoisy component of the data vector y_j, and v_j^i, $i = 1, \ldots, q$, are the corresponding components of an additive WGN vector v_j with zero-mean and covariance

$$R_j = \text{Diag}(\rho_{1j}, \ldots, \rho_{qj}) \tag{6.89}$$

there are a number of ways one can formulate the approximation problem. One of the simplest ways is to note that the optimal solution lies in the span of $\psi(x^i, \cdot)$, $i = 1, \ldots, q$, i.e.,

$$f_j(x) = \sum_{i=1}^{q} w_{ij}\psi(x^i, x) \tag{6.90}$$

and obtain the desired model as the solution to the penalized optimization problem

$$\min\left\{ \beta\|f_j(\cdot)\|_F^2 + \sum_{i=1}^{q} \rho_{ij}^{-1}(\langle\psi_i(\cdot), f_j(\cdot)\rangle_F - y_j^i)^2 \right\} \tag{6.91}$$

where β is a positive constant to be chosen by the modeler. A small value of β expresses fidelity to the observed data at the expense of smoothness.

Substituting (6.90) and (6.70)–(6.71) in (6.91), we get

$$\beta w_j^T G w_j + \sum_{i=1}^{q} \rho_{ij}^{-1}\left(\sum_{n=1}^{q} G_{in} w_{nj} - y_j^i\right)^2 \tag{6.92}$$

where

$$w_j = (w_{1j}, \ldots, w_{qj})^T \tag{6.93}$$

By differentiating (6.92) partially with respect to each w_{ij} and setting the result equal to zero, we obtain

$$\hat{w}_j = (\beta I + R_j^{-1}G)^{-1}R_j^{-1}y_j \tag{6.94}$$

and

$$\hat{f}_j(x) = y_j^T R_j^{-1}(\beta I + R_j^{-1}G)^{-1}K(x), \qquad j = 1, \ldots, m \tag{6.95}$$

We call the two-layer neural network represented by (6.95) an OS network.

6.6 OPTIMAL COMBINED STRUCTURAL AND PARAMETRIC MODELING OF NONLINEAR DYNAMICAL SYSTEMS IN $\mathcal{N}$

Based on the developments of the preceding section, it is now possible to obtain optimal structural and parametric realizations of the three classes of generic models described in Section 6.2. For this purpose, in each case one picks each block described by a nonlinear functional such as f or g in $\mathcal{N}$ as a feedforward artificial neural system that may constitute the desired solution, or, after combination with other blocks realized in a similar manner, may lead to an overall system that is a recurrent or state-space realization. These procedures are explained graphically for the DTP and CTP cases for feedforward, recurrent, and state-space models in Figures 6.8–6.10, and are clear enough so as not to require further discussion.

Depending on the application, the generic two-layer artificial neural system modules of OI or OS nets can be assembled to produce larger and more complex models. Each module may have an additional Winner–Take–All layer in tandem with it for the purpose of decision as explained in the following section.

A generic feedforward $2n$ layer net called **OMNI** net is shown in Figure 6.11. If the modules are OS nets, the resultant multilayer net is called **OSMAN**. Both OMNI and OSMAN are multilayer perceptrons, the structure and parameters of which are obtained using the framework developed in this chapter. Algorithms extending the procedure (6.67)–(6.71) to this case are described in [8].

Through various interconnections of OI and/or OS modules, a nonlinear dynamical system of any required complexity can be modeled, including, of course, systems with feedback. As an example, Figure 6.12 illustrates a proposed OMNI net implementation of a cortical column of the primary visual cortex of a cat. The connectionist structure was obtained by Bolz, Gilbert, and Wisel [63,64] from pharmacological experiments. Figure 6.12 shows the six OI nets that are used to implement the six layers (regions) in the column and the interconnections.

For the Wiener–Bose (WB) model, we have proposed a modification [10,65] using an OI net (Fig. 6.13). In this approximation, the linear (Laguerre) part of the WB model is preserved and provides "functional" synaptic weights to the first layer. The activations for this layer are provided by the Hermite part of the WB model, and the second layer of the model is linear and consists of a single neuron.

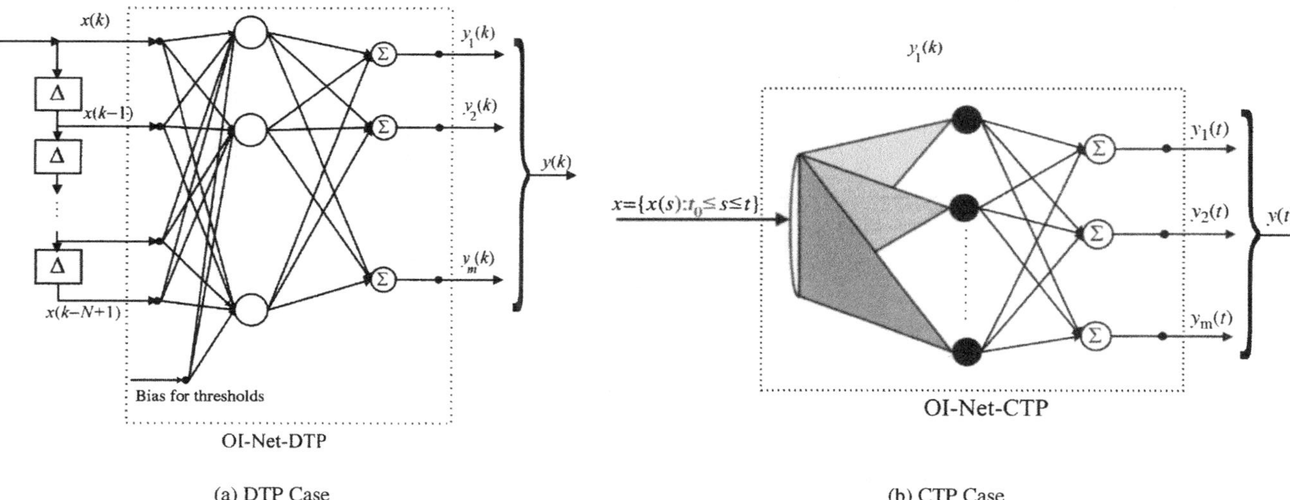

(a) DTP Case

(b) CTP Case

Figure 6.8 Feedforward models for single-input/multiple-output dynamical systems.

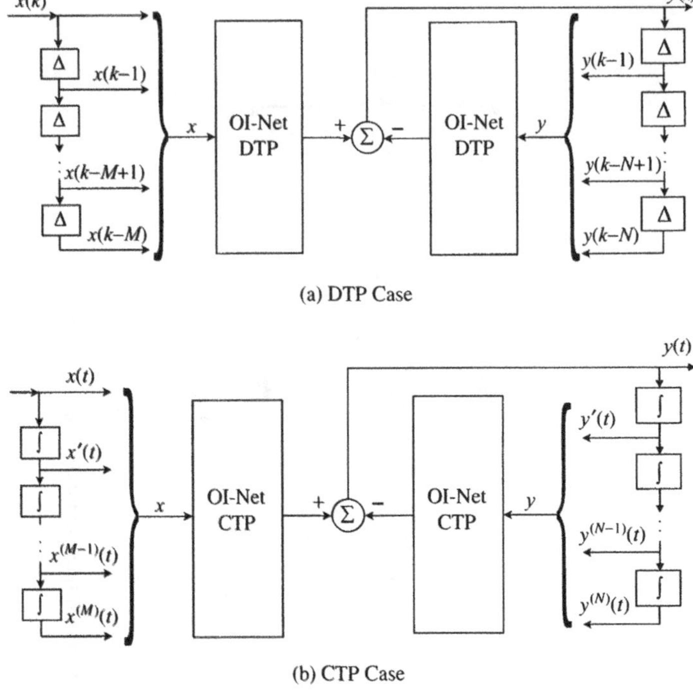

(a) DTP Case

(b) CTP Case

Figure 6.9 Recurrent models for single-input/single-output dynamical systems.

6.7 COMPUTATIONALLY INTELLIGENT (CI) SYSTEMS

The concepts and methodology developed thus far in the present chapter can be of value in the identification and realization of computationally intelligent (CI) systems. In what follows, we present a characterization and follow-up to the previous developments oriented toward this goal.

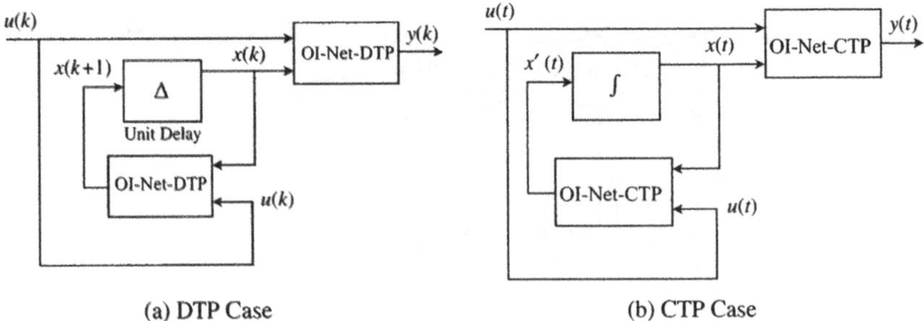

(a) DTP Case (b) CTP Case

Figure 6.10 State-space models for multiple-input/multiple-output dynamical systems.

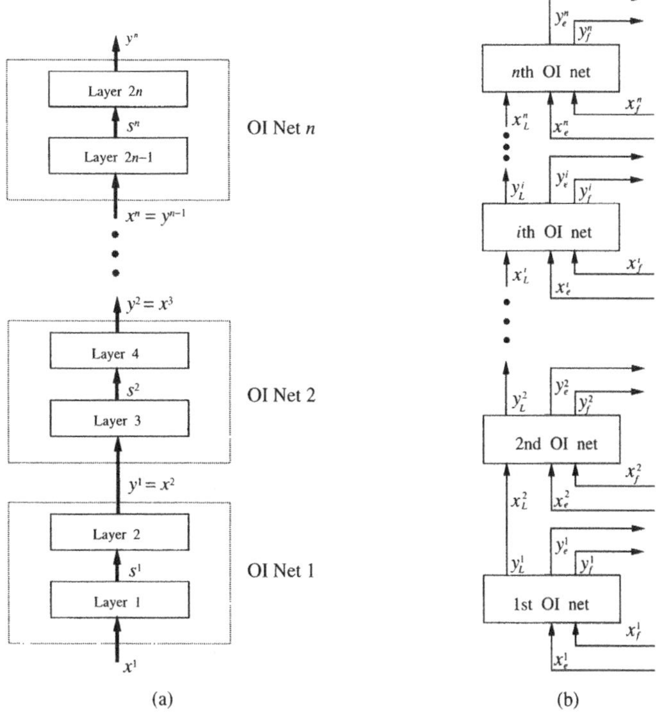

Figure 6.11 A diagram of a general 2n-layer OMNI net with feedforward, feedback, and external connections at every two-layer level (the figure depicts the most general situation).

6.7.1 CI Systems as Mixed Systems

Computationally intelligence usually involves functions that perform decisions regarding simple or complex events present in the data acquired by some sensing system. For this reason, CI systems are best modeled as *mixed continuous/discrete systems*: *continuous* with regard to the computation of a score (or event membership value in the case of a fuzzy CI system[9] [66–68]) on the basis of which a decision is made; and *discrete* in the representation of the event that needs to be detected, classified, or interpreted.

In the case of detection/classification, that is, of mapping a sensed vector x into one of m hypotheses $H_1, \ldots, H_m$ of the occurrence of m possible events, the jth output, $j = 1, \ldots, m$ of an m-output, CI system will be 1 or 0, depending on whether H_j is or is not true. In the case of interpretation, the outputs will be appropriate arrays of 1s and 0s, corresponding to graphs expressing the various interpretations in a given language.

[9] Due to space limitations, we do not discuss applications with appropriate modifications and interpretations to fuzzy neural networks and systems.

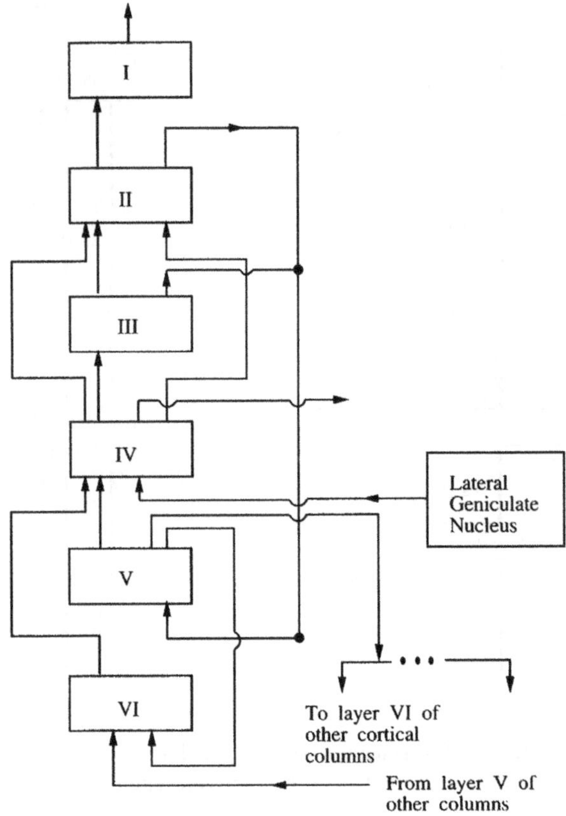

Figure 6.12 Proposed OMNI model for primary visual cortex of a cat.

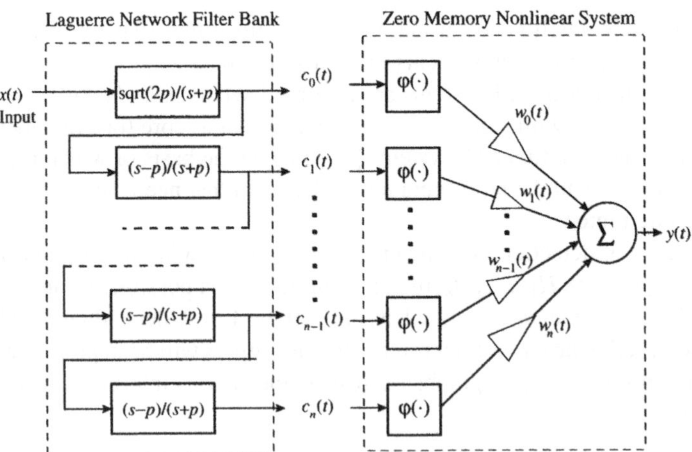

Figure 6.13 Robust best approximation to the Wiener model. Coefficients $w_i(t)$ may be generated recursively using the matrix inversion lemma. (*Note*: sqrt$(\cdot)$ denotes the square root operator, and the blocks on the left side denote transfer functions.)

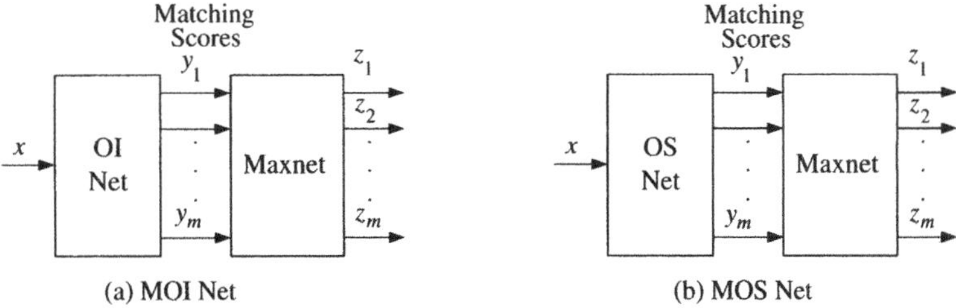

Figure 6.14 Mixed net modules for CI systems.

6.7.2 MOI and MOS Nets

At a basic level, the scheme just described can be incorporated into a MOI net, which is a 3-layer net consisting of an OI net (defined previously) in tandem with a Maxnet that incorporates a Winner-Take-All (WTA) decision based on the scores provided by the OI net. As depicted in Figure 6.14, the OI net maps the input data vector x into the scores y_i, $i = 1, \ldots, m$ provided by its m inputs. These in turn feed into the Maxnet, which selects the output of the OI net with the highest score (see [2]). The Maxnet is a m-input/m-output system, for which the input is a score vector $y = (y_1, \ldots, y_m)^T$, and the output is a binary vector $z = (z_1, \ldots, z_m)^T$, the components of z being all zero, except one, say z_k, corresponding to the component y_k of y having the highest value (score). A (MOS) net may be defined and used in a similar manner (see Fig. 6.14b). Appropriate combinations of MOI and MOS nets can be utilized to identify or simulate complex decision systems or realize new ones.

6.7.3 Intelligent Learning as Combined Adaptation and Evolution

The approach presented here lends itself naturally to a process of *combined adaptation and evolution*. This is what we call *intelligent learning* vis-a-vis conventional learning. Conventional learning is implemented as a strictly numerical optimization algorithm like the error back-propagation algorithm.

The underlying training procedure in our approach is explained for the MOI net shown in Figure 6.15. In this figure, the first layer of the net consists of neurons representative of the exemplars, the properties of which are to be retained by the net. These exemplars are called *prototypes*. Thus the synaptic weights connecting to the ith neuron of this first layer are the components of x^i, assuming that x^i is an exemplar that has been retained as a prototype.

The second-layer neurons correspond to the m hypotheses/events, into one of which the input vector is to be classified and the synaptic weights for this layer are calculated using (6.67)–(6.71).

The training process begins by inserting the first neuron in the first layer of the net with its synaptic weights consisting of the components of x^1 and the second-layer weights being calculated so as to enable its output vector to be the vector, y^1, associated with the first exemplary pair. As this process continues, and a new

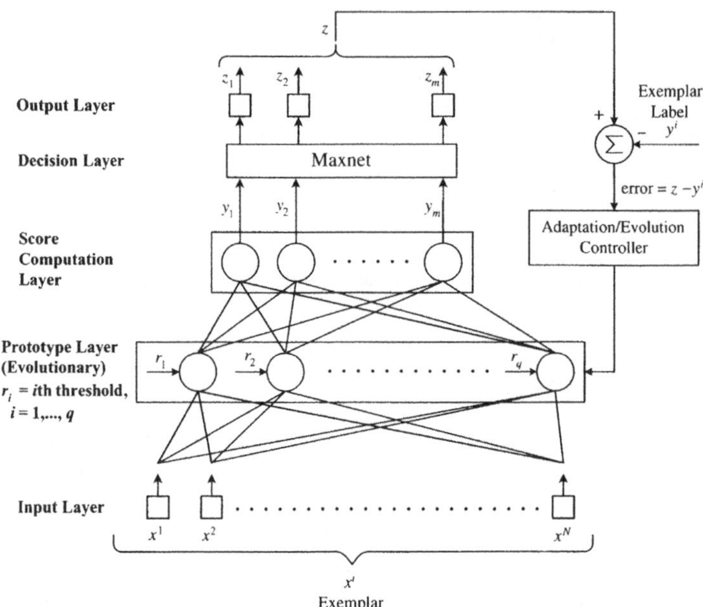

Figure 6.15 Intelligent learning: combined adaptation/evolution process.

exemplar, say x^k, is presented to the net, it gives rise to an output y that the Maxnet maps into a vector, z. This z is then compared to the correct exemplary output vector,[10] y^k. If they agree, the exemplar, x^k, is laid aside and the next exemplar is presented to the net so that the process can continue as before. If z and y^k do not agree, the error signal $z - y^k$ from the subtractor shown in the figure is applied to an adaptation–evolution controller that adds a neuron to the first layer corresponding to x^k as an additional prototype and adjusts the synaptic weights of the second layer accordingly. This process of prototype addition corresponds to evolution, and the one of adjusting the weights of the second layer to adaptation. This entire procedure is based on an algorithm described by Sin and de Figueiredo [13].

The preceding training procedure converges, classifying all exemplars correctly after recycling through the training set a few (typically two or three) times. During this recycling, exemplars that have been laid aside are put back in the training set after each cycle to make sure that all the exemplars have been taken into account.

Note that the number of exemplars retained as prototypes (number of neurons in the first layer) depend on the order in which they have been presented to the net. From the author's experience, a very small number close to $deF(\alpha)$ results when the prototypes are close to the boundaries of the decision region. For a number of examples, see [13] and references therein.

[10] As indicated under 6.7.1, for any given pair $(x^i, y^i), i = 1, \ldots, q$, the components $y^i_j, j = l, \ldots, m$, are binary and $y^i_j = l$ if and only if x^i belongs to H_j.

6.7.4 Discovery

Our formulation allows one to model the process of "discovery" by a neural system, which we will explain, for simplicity, in terms of an MOI net. After the training of a neural system is completed according to the preceding section, some vectors in the new data being received may not classify properly. If a significant number of such outliers appear, the cluster-detection-and-labeling (CDL) network recently developed by us [21] can be applied to such a set of outliers. The clusters obtained by the CDL network can then be considered to constitute training sets for corresponding new classes, and additional neurons added to the second layer of the net by training it with the exemplars from these clusters. As a consequence, we can say that the net discovered those new classes from its experience with the new data. This encapsulates the concept of *discovery* by an artificial or natural neural system, according to our formulation.

6.8 CONCLUDING REMARKS

The framework presented here is especially useful in applications where the dynamics of the generation, processing, and/or delivery of data is nonlinear. Applications of this approach have been made to a number of problems, including nonlinear adaptive time-series prediction and nonlinear equalization in communication channels, sonar signal analysis and detection, and neuroscience [6,12,13,15,17, 20–23]. Limitations in space did not permit us to discuss them here. The potential of this technology is enormous for further applications in many fields, including wireline, cable, fiber, and wireless communications, automated manufacturing, and medical diagnostics and treatment.

REFERENCES

1. R. J. P. de Figueiredo. "A New Nonlinear Functional Analytic Framework for Modeling Artificial Neural Networks." In *Proceedings of the IEEE International Symposium on Circuits and Systems*, New Orleans, LA, May 1990, pp. 723–726.
2. R. J. P. de Figueiredo. "An Optimal Matching-Score Net for Pattern Classification." In *Proceedings of 1990 International Joint Conference on Neural Networks, IJCNN-90*, San Diego, CA, June 1990.
3. V. Volterra. *Theory of Functionals and of Integral and Integro-Differential Equations*. Dover, New York, 1959.
4. R. J. P. de Figueiredo and T. A. W. Dwyer III. "A Best Approximation Framework and Implementation for Simulation of Large-Scale Nonlinear Systems." *IEEE Trans. Circuits Syst.*, vol. CAS-27, no. 11, 1005–1014, 1980.
5. R. J. P. de Figueiredo. "A Generalized Fock Space Framework for Nonlinear System and Signal Analysis." *IEEE Trans. Circuits Syst.*, vol. CAS-30, no. 9, 637–647, 1983.
6. L. V. Zyla and R. J. P. de Figueiredo. "Nonlinear System Identification Based on a Fock Space Framework." *SIAM J. Control Optim.*, 931–939, Nov. 1983.

7. R. J. P. de Figueiredo. "Mathematical Foundations of Optimal Interpolative Neural Networks." In E. Houstis and J. R. Rice, (eds.), *Artificial Intelligence, Expert Systems, and Symbolic Computing*, pp. 303–319, Elsevier, Amsterdam, 1992.
8. R. J. P. de Figueiredo. "An Optimal Multilayer Neural Interpolating (OMNI) Net in a Generalized Fock Space Setting." *Proceedings of 1992 International Joint Conference on Neural Networks, IJCNN-92*, vol. 1, Baltimore, MD, 1992, pp. 111–118.
9. R. W. Newcomb and R. J. P. de Figueiredo. "A Multi-Input Multi-Output Functional Artificial Neural Network." *J. Intell. Fuzzy Syst.*, vol. 4, no. 3, 207–213, 1996.
10. R. J. P. de Figueiredo. "Optimal Interpolative and Smoothing Functional Artificial Neural Networks (FANNs) Based on a Generalized Fock Space Framework." *Circuits, Syst., Signal Process.*, vol. 17, no. 2, 271–287, 1998.
11. S. K. Sin and R. J. P. de Figueiredo. "An Incremental Fine Adjustment Algorithm for the Design of Optimal Interpolating Neural Networks." *Int. J. Pattern Recogn. Artif. Intell.*, Nov. 1991.
12. S. K. Sin and R. J. P. de Figueiredo. "An Evolution Oriented Learning Algorithm for the Optimal Interpolative Net." *IEEE Trans. Neural Networks*, vol. 3, no. 2, 315–323, 1992.
13. S. K. Sin and R. J. P. de Figueiredo. "Efficient Learning Procedures for Optimal Interpolating Networks." *Neural Networks*, vol. 6, 99–113, 1993.
14. R. J. P. de Figueiredo and G. Chen. *Nonlinear Feedback Control Systems: An Operator Theory Approach.* Academic Press, New York, 1993.
15. A. Maccato and R. J. P. de Figueiredo. "Structured Neural Network Topologies with Application to Acoustic Transients." *Proceedings of the 1990 IEEE International Conference on Acoustics, Speech, and Signal Processing*, Albuquerque, NM, April 1990, pp. 877–880.
16. A. Maccato and R. J. P. de Figueiredo. "A Neural Network Based Framework for Classification of Oceanic Acoustic Signals." *Proceedings of the 1989 OCEANS Conference*, Seattle, WA, Sept. 18, 1989.
17. R. J. P. de Figueiredo and T. A. W. Dwyer III. "Approximation-Theoretic Methods for Nonlinear Deconvolution and Inversion." *Inf. Sci.*, vol. 31, 209–220, 1983.
18. R. J. P. de Figueiredo. "Implications and Applications of Kolmogorov's superposition theorem." *IEEE Trans. Automatic Control*, vol. AC-25, no. 5, 1227–1231, 1980.
19. R. J. P. de Figueiredo. "Generalized Nonlinear Functional and Operator Splines in Fock Spaces." In Ward Cheney, (ed.), *Approximation Theory*, pp. 937–944, Academic Press, New York, 1980.
20. T. Eltoft and R. J. P. de Figueiredo. "A DCT-Based D-FANN for Nonlinear Adaptive Time Series Prediction." *IEEE Trans. Circuits Syst.*, Part II, 1131, 2000.
21. T. Eltoft and R. J. P. de Figueiredo. "A New Neural Network for Cluster-Detection and-Labelling." *IEEE Trans. Neural Networks*, vol. 9, 1021–1035, 1998.
22. R. J. P. de Figueiredo and T. Eltoft. "Pattern Classification of Non-Sparse Data Using Optimal Interpolative Nets." *Neurocomputing*, vol. 10, no. 4, 385–403, 1996.
23. R. J. P. de Figueiredo, W. R. Shankle, A. Maccato, M. B. Dick, P. Y. Mundkur, I. Mena, and C. W. Cotman. "Neural-Network-Based Classification of Cognitively Normal, Demented, Alzheimer's Disease and Vascular Dementia from Brain SPECT Image Data." In *Proceedings of the National Academy of Sciences USA*, vol. 92, June 1995, pp. 5530–5534.
24. A. Speis and R. J. P. de Figueiredo. "A Generalized Fock Space Framework for Nonlinear System Identification for Random Input-Output Data." *UCI Int. Rep.*, to be submitted for publication.

25. N. Wiener. *Nonlinear Problems in Random Theory.* MIT Press, Cambridge, MA, 1958.
26. A. G. Bose. "A Theory of Nonlinear Systems." Tech. Rep. No. 309, Research Laboratory of Electronics, MIT, Cambridge, MA, 1956.
27. Y. W. Lee and M. Schetzen. "Measurement of the Wiener Kernels of a Nonlinear System by Cross-Correlation." *Int. J. Control*, vol. 2, 237–254, 1965.
28. P. Z. Marmarelis and V. Z. Marmarelis. *Analysis of Physiological Systems.* Plenum Press, New York, 1978.
29. M. Schetzen. *The Volterra and Wiener Theories on Non-Linear Systems.* Wiley/Interscience, New York, 1980.
30. W. J. Rugh. *Nonlinear System Theory: The Volterra/Wiener Approach.* Johns Hopkins University Press, Baltimore, MD, 1981.
31. L. Ljung and T. Söoderström. *Theory and Practice of Recursive Identification.* MIT Press, Cambridge, MA, 1983.
32. L. Ljung. *System Identification: Theory for the User.* Prentice Hall, Englewood Cliffs, NJ, 1987.
33. D. E. Rumelhart, J. L. McClelland, and the PDP Research Group. *Parallel Distributed Processing: Explorations in the Microstructure of Cognition*, vol. 1, *Foundations.* MIT Press, Cambridge, MA, 1986.
34. B. Widrow and S. D. Stearns. *Adaptive Signal Processing.* Prentice Hall, Englewood Cliffs, NJ, 1985.
35. G. A. Carpenter and S. Grossberg. "Neural Dynamics of Category Learning and Recognition: Attention Memory Consolidation and Amnesia." In J. Davis, R. Newburgh, and E. Wegman (eds.), *Brain Structure, Learning and Memory,* AAAS Symposium Series, Washington, DC, 1986.
36. S. I. Amari. "Mathematical Foundations of Neurocomputing." *Proc. IEEE*, vol. 78, no. 9, 1443–1463, 1990.
37. J. M. Zurada. *Introduction to Artificial Neural Systems.* West, St. Paul, MN, 1992.
38. V. N. Vapnik. *The Nature of Statistical Learning Theory.* Springer-Verlag, New York, 1995.
39. V. N. Vapnik. *Statistical Learning Theory.* Wiley, New York, 1998.
40. A. Dingankar and I. W. Sandberg, "On Error Bounds for Neural Network Approximation." In *Proceedings of the IEEE International Symposium on Circuits and Systems, ISCAS-95*, vol. 1, 1995, pp. 490–492.
41. A. T. Dingankar and I. W. Sandberg. "Tensor Product Neural Networks and Approximation of Dynamical Systems." In *Proceedings of the IEEE International Symposium on Circuits and Systems, ISCAS-96*, vol. 3, 1996, pp. 353–356.
42. J. C. Principe, N. R. Euliano, and W. C. Lefebre. *Neural and Adaptive Systems.* Wiley, New York, 2000.
43. S. Haykin. *Adaptive Filter Theory*, 3rd ed., Prentice Hall, Upper Saddle River, NJ, 1996.
44. W. G. Knecht. "Nonlinear Noise Filtering and Beam-Forming Using the Perception and Its Volterra Approximation." *IEEE Trans. Acoust., Speech, Signal Processing*, vol. 2, no. 1, 55–62, 1994.
45. P. Werbos. "Generalization of Backpropagation with Application to a Recurrent Gas Market Model." *Neural Networks*, vol. 1, 339–356, 1998.
46. A. Weigend, B. Huberman, and D. Rumelhart. "Predicting the Future: A Connectionist Approach." *Int. J. Neural Syst.*, vol. 7, no. 3–4, 403–430, 1990.

47. S. G. Tzafestas. *Computational Intelligence in Systems and Control Design and Applications*. Kluwer, Dordrecht, The Netherlands, 1999.
48. A. Gammerman. *Computational Learning and Probabilistic Reasoning*. Wiley, Chichester, UK, 1996.
49. G. Cybenko, "Approximation by Superpositions of a Sigmoidal Function." *Math. Control, Signals, Syst.*, vol. 2, no. 4, 303–314, 1989.
50. A. R. Barron. "Universal Approximation Bounds for Superpositions of a Sigmoidal Function." *IEEE Trans. Inform. Theory*, vol. 39, issue 3, 930–945, 1993.
51. P. A. Regalia. *Adaptive IIR Filtering in Signal Processing and Control*. Dekker, New York, 1995.
52. V. Fock. *Konfigurationsraum und Zweite Quantelung*. *Z. Phys.*, vol. 75, 622–647, 1932.
53. F. Berezin. *The Method of Second Quantization*. Academic Press, New York, 1966.
54. B. Simon. *The* $P(\Phi)_2$ *Euclidean (Quantum) Field Theory*. Princeton University Press, Princeton, NJ, 1974.
55. V. Bargmann. "On a Hilbert Space of Analytic Functions and on Associated Integral Transform," Part I. *Commun. Pure Appl. Math.*, vol. 14, 187–214, 1961; also Part II. vol. 20, 1–101, 1967.
56. F. Beatrous and J. Burbea. *Dissertations Mathematica*. Warszawa, 1989.
57. M. Beals, C. Fefferman, and R. Grossman. "Strictly Pseudoconvex Domains in C^n." *Bull. (New Ser.) Am. Math. Soc.*, vol. 8, no. 2, 1983.
58. T. W. A. Dwyer III. "Holomorphic Representation of Tempered Distributions and Weighted Fock Spaces." In L. Nachbin, (ed.), *Analyse Fonctionelle et Aplications*, Hermann, Paris, 1975.
59. F. Treves. *Topological Vector Spaces, Distributions and Kernels*. Academic Press, New York, 1967.
60. E. Hille and R. S. Phillips. "Functional Analysis and Semigroups." *Am. Math. Soc. Colloq.*, Publ. 31, New York, 1957.
61. N. Aronsjahn. "Theory of Reproducing Kernels." *Am. Math. Soc. Trans.*, vol. 68, 337–404, 1950.
62. F. B. Hildebrand. *Introduction to Numerical Analysis*. McGraw-Hill, New York, 1974.
63. J. Bolz, C. D. Gilbert, and T. N. Wisel. "Pharmacological Analysis of Cortical Circuitry." *Trends Neurosci.*, vol. 12, no. 8, 292–296, 1989.
64. J. C. Eccles and O. Creutzfeld (eds.). "The Principles of Design and Operation of the Brain." In *Proceedings of the Study Week Organized by the Pontifical Academy of Sciences, Cassia Pius IV, Vatican City*, Springer-Verlag, New York, 1990.
65. R. J. P. de Figueiredo. "Beyond Volterra and Wiener: Some New Results And Open Problems in Nonlinear Circuits and Systems." In *Proceedings of the IEEE Midwest Symposium on Circuits and Systems*, 1998, pp. 124–127.
66. L. A. Zadeh. "Outline of a New Approach to the Analysis of Complex Systems and Decision Processes." *IEEE Trans. Syst., Man Cybern.*, vol. 3, no. 1, 28–44, 1973.
67. L. A. Zadeh. In J. E. Hayes, D. Michie, and L. I. Mikulich, (eds.), *A Theory of Approximate Reasoning, in Machine Intelligence*, vol. 9, pp. 149–194. Elsevier, New York, 1979.
68. G. J. Klir, U. H. St. Clair, and B. Yuan. *Fuzzy Set Theory: Foundations and Applications*. Prentice Hall, Upper Saddle River, NJ, 1997.

CHAPTER 7

TECHNIQUES FOR EXTRACTING CLASSIFICATION AND REGRESSION RULES FROM ARTIFICIAL NEURAL NETWORKS

RUDY SETIONO

7.1 INTRODUCTION

A major drawback often associated with neural networks as tools for predicting is the lack of "explanation" capability of trained networks. Although the predictive accuracy of neural networks is often higher than that of other methods or human experts, it is generally difficult to understand *how* a network arrives at a particular conclusion due to the complexity of its architecture. However, it is often desirable to have a set of concise and meaningful rules that explains the predictions of a trained network. Such rules are a form of knowledge that can be verified by human experts, passed on and expanded. It can also provide a new insight into the problem.

Algorithms that extract rules from neural networks can be divided into two groups according to the problems they solve. The first group consists of algorithms that extract *classification* rules, while the second extracts *regression* rules. Gallant's connectionist expert systems [1] and Saito and Nakano's (RN) method [2] are among the earliest works that attempt to generate classification rules from neural networks. These systems, however, do not actually extract rules from the networks directly; instead, they try to generate an explanation for each particular outcome of the networks.

Thrun [3] describes an algorithm that analyzes the input-output behavior of the network using the validity interval analysis. VI-Analysis divides the activation range of a unit into intervals. The boundaries of these intervals are obtained by solving linear programs. Two approaches of generating rule conjectures, *specific-to-general* and *general-to-specific*, are described.

A simple rule-extraction algorithm is presented in [4]. The rules extracted from neural networks are comparable to those generated by decision trees [5] in terms of

Computational Intelligence: The Experts Speak. Edited by D. B. Fogel and C. J. Robinson
ISBN 0-471-27454-2

their accuracy and comprehensibility. The basic idea behind the algorithm is the fact that it is generally possible to replace the continuous activations of the hidden units by a small number of discrete ones. Rule extraction is realized in two steps. First, rules that describe the network outputs in terms of the discretized activation values of the hidden units are generated. Second, rules that describe the discretized hidden unit activation values in terms of the network inputs are constructed. By merging the rules obtained in these two steps, a set of rules that relates the inputs and outputs of the network is obtained.

While the algorithm can generate symbolic rules that mimic the predicted outcome of the original network, it works only for data with binary inputs. Data with continuous attributes need to be preprocessed before training the network. The preprocessing of the data entails dividing the values of the continuous attributes into intervals. All continuous attribute values that fall in the same subinterval are then represented by a unique discrete value for use as inputs to the neural network. Rules involving the discrete representations of the inputs are generated from the network.

An inherent problem introduced by discretizing the data is that each condition of a rule involving a continuous attribute determines an axis-parallel decision boundary. For some classification problems, it could be more natural to allow oblique hyperplanes to form the boundaries of the decision regions. In other words, instead of imposing the axis-parallel constraint, being able to generate oblique decision hyperplanes makes it possible to let the learning algorithm determine what kind of hyperplane is more suitable for the data in hand. Oblique hyperplanes are more general and they can substantially reduce the number of rule conditions needed to describe the decision region. As a result, a more compact set of rules can be expected.

The algorithm NeuroLinear [6] generates a set of decision rules, where each rule condition is given in the form of the linear inequality

$$\sum_i w_i I_i < \eta \tag{7.1}$$

where w_i is a real coefficient, I_i is the value of the attribute i, and η is a threshold. The neural network used is the standard feedforward neural network with a single hidden layer (Fig. 7.1). In contrast to the tree-growing algorithms that generate the rules in a level-by-level top-down fashion, rules are extracted from a network in two steps: from the hidden layer to the output layer, and from the input layer to the hidden layer. Classification rules are obtained by merging the rules from these two steps. Unlike the decision-tree algorithms [5,7] that consider smaller and smaller subsets of the data to improve the accuracy of the rules, the neural-network approach for rule generation considers the entire training set as a whole.

A similar decompositional approach to rule extraction is also employed in a more recent algorithm that we developed for regression. The algorithm REFANN (rule extraction from function-approximating neural networks) [8] generates rules of the form *if (condition is satisfied), then predict* $y = f(x)$, where $f(x)$ is either a constant or a linear function of x, the attributes of the data. This type of rule is suitable because of its similarity to the statistical approach of parametric regression.

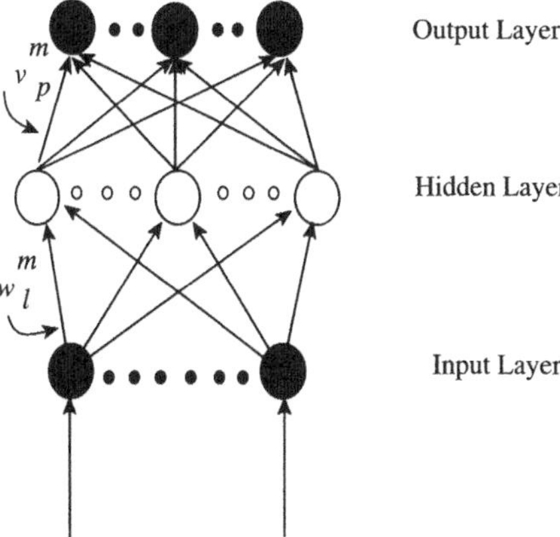

Figure 7.1 A fully connected three-layer feedforward neural network.

The organization of the chapter is as follows. Section 2 describes the rule-extraction algorithms NeuroLinear and REFANN. In Section 3, the steps of the two algorithms are illustrated in detail in two examples. Classification rules are extracted for bankruptcy prediction, while regression rules are extracted for prediction of central processing unit (CPU) performance. Section 4 gives a brief conclusion.

7.2 RULE EXTRACTION

The process of rule extraction from neural networks using the decompositional approach can be summarized as follows:

1. Select and train a network to meet a prespecified accuracy requirement.
2. Remove the redundant connections in the network by pruning while maintaining the accuracy.
3. For a classification problem:
   - Discretize the hidden unit activation values of the network.
   - Extract rules that describe the network outputs in terms of the discretized network activation values.
   - For each discretized hidden unit activation value, generate a rule in terms of the network's inputs.
   - Merge the two sets of rules obtained earlier.

For a regression problem:

- Approximate each hidden unit activation function by a piecewise-linear function.
- Compute the predicted target value as a linear combination of the piecewise hidden unit activation functions.

- Generate the rule conditions that are determined by the domains of the piecewise-linear hidden unit activation functions.

7.2.1 Neural Network Training and Pruning

The basic structure of the neural network is the standard three-layer feedforward network, which consists of an input layer, a hidden layer, and an output layer. The number of input units corresponds to the dimensionality of the data. The number of output units is determined by the number of classes a sample can possibly be classified to or it is usually one for regression problem. The number of hidden units depends on the problem. Two approaches to determine a suitable number of hidden units have been described in the literature. The first approach begins with a minimal number of hidden units, one or two, and more hidden units are added as they are needed to increase the accuracy of the network. The second approach begins with an oversized network and removes redundant connections in the network by pruning. In the process, hidden units that are not connected to any input units and/or output units can be removed as well. We adopt the second approach because we are also interested in removing input units that are irrelevant to the classification/regression. During the pruning phase, irrelevant input units and hidden units can be identified and removed from the network.

Given an n-dimensional sample $I^i, i \in \{1,2,\ldots k\}$ as input, let w_ℓ^m be the weight for the connection from input unit $\ell, \ell \in \{1,2,\ldots,n\}$, to hidden unit m, $m \in \{1,2,\ldots,h\}$, and v_p^m be the weight from hidden unit m to output unit p, $p \in \{1,2,\ldots,o\}$, the pth output of the network for sample I^i is obtained by computing

$$S_p^i = \sigma\left(\sum_{m=1}^{h} \alpha^m v_p^m\right) \tag{7.2}$$

where

$$\sigma(x) = \begin{cases} \text{sigmoid}(x) = 1/(1+e^{-x}) & \text{for classification} \\ x & \text{for regression} \end{cases} \tag{7.3}$$

$$\alpha^m = \delta\left(\sum_{\ell=1}^{n} I_\ell^i w_\ell^m\right) \tag{7.4}$$

$$\delta(x) = \tanh(x) = (e^x - e^{-x})/(e^x + e^{-x}) \tag{7.5}$$

For classification, the target output for a sample I^i that belongs to class C_j is an o-dimensional vector t^i, where $t_p^i = 0$ if $p \neq j$ and $t_j^i = 1$, $j,p = 1,2,\ldots,o$. For regression, the target output t_p^i is usually normalized into the interval $[0,1]$ and $o = 1$. The weights (w,v) are computed such that the following function is minimized:

$$\theta(w,v) = F(w,v) + P(w,v)$$

where $F(w, v)$ is the cross-entropy function:

$$F(w,v) = -\sum_{i=1}^{k}\sum_{p=1}^{o}(t_p^i \log S_p^i + (1 - t_p^i)\log(1 - S_p^i))$$

for classification, or the sum of squared error function

$$F(w,v) = \sum_{i=1}^{k}\sum_{p=1}^{o}(t_p^i - S_p^i)^2$$

for regression P(w, v) is a penalty term used for weight decay [9]:

$$\begin{aligned} \mathrm{P(w,v)} = \varepsilon_1 &\left(\sum_{m=1}^{h}\sum_{\ell=1}^{n}\frac{\beta(w_\ell^m)^2}{1+\beta(w_\ell^m)^2} + \sum_{m=1}^{h}\sum_{p=1}^{o}\frac{\beta(v_p^m)^2}{1+\beta(v_p^m)^2}\right) \\ &+ \varepsilon_2\left(\sum_{m=1}^{h}\sum_{\ell=1}^{n}(w_\ell^m)^2 + \sum_{m=1}^{h}\sum_{p=1}^{o}(v_p^m)^2\right) \end{aligned} \tag{7.6}$$

where $\varepsilon_1, \varepsilon_2$, and β are positive decay parameters.

Connections in the network are removed based on their magnitude. The details of the pruning algorithm and the experimental results on a number of publicly available data sets can be found in [10].

7.2.2 Chi2: Discretization of Hidden Unit Activation Values

The range of the activation values of the network's hidden units is the interval $(-1, 1)$, since they have been computed as the hyperbolic tangent of the weighted inputs (cf. (7.4)). In order to extract classification rules from the network, we group these values into a few clusters while preserving the accuracy of the network. Chi2 [11] is the algorithm employed for this purpose. Given a data set where each sample is described by the values of the continuous attributes $\mathcal{A}_1, \mathcal{A}_2, \ldots$ and the class label of the sample is known, Chi2 finds discrete representations of the data set. Using the χ^2 statistic, Chi2 divides the range of the attributes into subintervals and assigns all values that fall in a subinterval a unique discrete value. The outline of the algorithm is as follows:

The Chi2 Algorithm

1. Let Chi-0 be an initial critical value.
2. For each attribute $\mathcal{A}_i$:
   (a) Sort the data according to the input values of attribute $\mathcal{A}_i$.
   (b) Form an initial set of intervals such that each interval contains only one unique value.

3. Initialize all attributes as "unmarked."
4. For each unmarked attribute A_i:
   (a) For each adjoining pairs of subintervals, compute their χ^2 values:

$$\chi^2 = \sum_{i=1}^{2}\sum_{j=1}^{k}\frac{(A_{ij}-E_{ij})^2}{E_{ij}} \tag{7.7}$$

where

k = the number of classes,
A_{ij} = the number of samples in the ith interval, jth class,
R_i = the number of samples in the ith interval $= \sum_{j=1}^{k} A_{ij}$,
C_j = the number of samples in the jth class $= \sum_{i=1}^{2} A_{ij}$,
E_{ij} = expected frequency of $A_{ij}, E_{ij} = R_i \times C_j/N$. If R_i or $C_j = 0$, E_{ij} is set to 0.05,
N = the total number of samples.

   (b) Find two subintervals with the lowest χ^2 value. If this value is less than Chi-0 and if merging the subintervals does not introduce conflicting data,[1] then merge these subintervals, and repeat from Step 4(a). Else if merging the subintervals will introduce conflicting data, label attribute i as "marked."
5. If there is still an unmarked attribute, then increase Chi-0 and repeat Step 4.

The Chi2 algorithm involves only one parameter, the initial critical value Chi-0. This value is used to determine whether the null hypothesis that the subintervals and the class labels are independent. If the test statistic (7.7) exceeds the critical value Chi-0, H_0 is rejected. Otherwise, H_0 is not rejected and the subintervals are merged. The critical value Chi-0 is determined by the significance level of the test, α. If no inconsistency in the data is introduced after merging of the subintervals with the initial value of Chi-0, the critical value Chi-0 is increased.

7.2.3 Generating Classification Rules

Rules are generated in two steps. First, rules that describe the classification are obtained in terms of the discretized hidden unit activation values. Second, rules that describe each discretized hidden unit activation values are obtained in terms of the original attributes of the data set.

For the first step, we use a rule generator called X2R [12]. It generates a set of rules that covers all the data with an error rate not exceeding the inconsistency rate present in the data. It is particularly suitable for moderate-sized data sets with discrete attribute values.

1. Conflicting data occur when there are two or more samples from different classes with the same discretized attribute values.

The discretized activation values at all the remaining hidden units are not the only output of the Chi2 algorithm. It also provides the boundaries of the subintervals of the activation values after the merging process has stopped. Let N be the number of subintervals found by Chi2 for the activation values of hidden unit H. There are $N+1$ numbers $\mu_0, \mu_1, \mu_2, \ldots, \mu_N$ such that $-1 = \mu_0 < \mu_1 < \mu_2 < \cdots < \mu_{N-1} < \mu_N = 1$, which form these N clusters. An activation value α of an input sample will be discretized into the jth cluster if $\mu_{j-1} \leq \alpha < \mu_j$. The activation value α is obtained by applying the tangent hyperbolic function (7.4) to the weighted inputs. Hence, it is in $[\mu_{j-1}, \mu_j)$ if its weighted inputs satisfy the condition

$$\tanh^{-1}(\mu_{j-1}) \leq \text{weighted inputs} < \tanh^{-1}(\mu_j) \tag{7.8}$$

where $\tanh^{-1}(x)$ is the inverse of the tangent hyperbolic function. The condition (7.8) defines the half-spaces (in the case of $j = 1$ or $j = N$) or the intersection of two half-spaces (in the case of $j = 2, 3, \ldots, N-1$) in the original input space of the data set where a sample will have a discretized hidden unit activation value located in the jth subinterval.

In order to obtain rules that describe the relation between the hidden unit activation values and the class labels, the weights of the connections between the hidden units and the output units are not needed. On the other hand, rule conditions that determine the subintervals of the discretized activation values are specified by the weights of the network connections from the input units to the hidden units. By combining the rules and conditions obtained from the two steps, we find the decision boundaries in terms of the original attributes that classify the samples of the data set.

7.2.4 Approximating Hidden Unit Activation Function

The first step in our rule-extraction method for regression is to approximate the hidden unit activation function $\sigma(x) = \tanh(x)$ by a three-piece linear function.

Since $\tanh(x)$ is antisymmetric, it is sufficient to illustrate the approximation just for values of $x \geq 0$. Suppose that the input x ranges from 0 to x_*. A simple approximation of $\tanh(x)$ is to overestimate it by the piecewise-linear function $L(x)$, as shown in Figure 7.2. To ensure that $L(x)$ is larger than $\tanh(x)$ everywhere between 0 to x_*, the line on the left should intersect the origin with a gradient of $\tanh'(0) = 1$, and the line on the right should intersect the coordinate $(x_*, \tanh(x_*))$ with a gradient of $\tanh'(x_*) = 1 - \tanh^2(x_*)$. Thus, $L(x)$ can be written as

$$L(x) = \begin{cases} x & \text{if } 0 \leq x \leq x_0 \\ \tanh'(x_*)(x - x_*) + \tanh(x_*) & \text{if } x > x_0 \end{cases} \tag{7.9}$$

The point of intersection x_0 of the two line segments is given by

$$x_0 = \frac{\tanh(x_*) - x_* \tanh'(x_*)}{\tanh^2(x_*)} \tag{7.10}$$

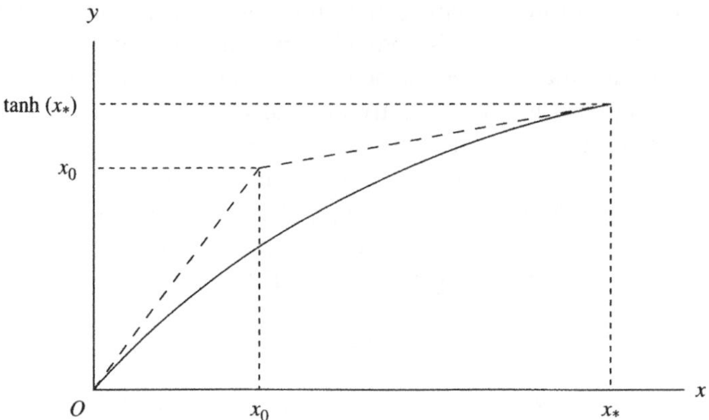

Figure 7.2 The tanh(x) function (solid curve) for $x \in [0, x_*]$ is approximated by a piecewise-linear function (dashed lines).

The total error E_A of estimating tanh (x) by $L(x)$ is given by

$$\begin{aligned} E_A &= \int_0^{x_*} (L(x) - \tanh(x))\, dx \\ &= \frac{1}{2}[x_0^2 + (x_* - x_0)(x_0 + \tanh(x_*))] - \ln\cosh x_* \\ &\to -\frac{1}{2} - \ln 0.5 \quad \text{as} \quad x_* \to \infty \end{aligned} \tag{7.11}$$

That is, the total error is bounded by a constant value.

Another simple linearization method of approximating tanh (x) is to underestimate it by a three-piece linear function. It can be shown that the total error of the underestimation method is unbounded and is larger than that of the overestimation method for $x_* > 2.96$.

7.2.5 Generating Regression Rules

REFANN generates rules from a pruned neural network with H hidden units according to the following steps:

The REFANN Algorithm

Step 1 For each hidden unit $m = 1, 2, \ldots, H$:

1. Determine x_{m*} from the training samples.
2. Approximate the hidden unit activation function as follows:
   - Compute x_{m_0} (7.10).

- Define the function $L_m(x)$:

$$L_m(x) = \begin{cases} (x + x_{m*}) \tanh'(x_{m*}) - \tanh(x_{m*}) & \text{if } x < -x_{m_0} \\ x & \text{if } -x_{m_0} \le x \le x_{m_0} \\ (x - x_{m*}) \tanh'(x_{m*}) + \tanh(x_{m*}) & \text{if } x > x_{m_0} \end{cases}$$

3. Using the pair of points $-x_{m_0}$ and x_{m_0} of function $L_m(x)$, divide the input space into 3^H subregions.

Step 2 For each nonempty subregion, generate a rule as follows:

1. Define a linear equation that approximates the network's output $\hat{y}^i$ for input sample i in this subregion as the *consequent* of the extracted rule:

$$\hat{y}^i = \sum_{m=1}^{H} v_m L_m(s^i_m) \tag{7.12}$$

where

$$s^i_m = \sum_{\ell=1}^{n} w^m_\ell I^i_\ell \tag{7.13}$$

2. Generate the rule *condition*: (C_1 and C_2 and $\cdots$ C_H), where C_m is either $s^i_m < -x_{m_0}$, $-x_{m_0} \le s^i_m \le x_{m_0}$, or $s^i_m > x_{m_0}$.

Step 3 (Optional) Apply C4.5 [5] to simplify the rule conditions.

In general, a rule condition C_m is defined in terms of the weighted sum of the inputs s^i_m (7.13) that corresponds to an oblique hyperplane in the input space. This type of rule condition can be difficult for users to interpret. In some cases, the oblique hyperplanes can be replaced by hyperplanes that are parallel to the axes without affecting the prediction accuracy of the rules on the data set. Consequently, the hyperplanes can be defined in terms of the isolated inputs, and are easier for the users to understand. In some cases of real-life data, this enhanced interpretability would come at a possible cost of reduced accuracy. If the replacement of rule conditions is still desired, it can be achieved by employing a classification method such as C4.5 in the optional Step 3.

7.3 ILLUSTRATIVE EXAMPLES

7.3.1 Bankruptcy Prediction Using NeuroLinear

The first results of a study that looks into the relationship between financial statement data and the financial well-being of a company were reported in the seminal work of Edward Altman [13]. The results show that various financial ratios could be

TABLE 7.1 The Attributes of the Bankruptcy Data Set

Variable	Attributes	Min. Value	Max. Value
X_1	Working capital/total assets	–0.5359	0.6674
X_2	Retained earnings/total assets	–1.6945	0.6970
X_3	Earnings before interest and tax/total assets	–0.4861	0.2994
X_4	Market value of equity/total debt	0.0417	30.6486
X_5	Sales/total assets	0.2216	6.5145

useful discriminators between bankrupt and nonbankrupt companies. Five financial ratios are found to be the attributes that possess discriminating capability. A linear discriminant function partitions the attribute space into two half-spaces, where all input data corresponding to bankrupt companies lie in one side of the hyperplane, and those of nonbankrupt companies on the other side. The coefficients of the linear discriminant function are determined using multivariate discriminant analysis (MDA). Because some of the assumptions required by MDA—such as the multivariate normal distribution within each group—may not be satisfied by the data collected, researchers have looked for alternative methods for classification.

The training input data set consists of 74 samples, 38 are samples that represent bankrupt companies, and 36 represent nonbankrupt companies. The testing data set consists of 27 samples from bankrupt companies and 28 samples from nonbankrupt companies. Each sample is described by the five continuous attributes listed in Table 7.1. The complete data sets can be found in [14] and [15].

We trained 30 fully connected networks to achieve 100% accuracy on the training data set. The attribute values were normalized using the linear transformation:

$$\chi_i = (X_i - X_i^{\min})/(X_i^{\max} - X_i^{\min}) \tag{7.14}$$

where $X_i^{\min}$ and $X_i^{\max}$ are the minimum and maximum values of attributes X_i found among the training samples.

The pruning process was terminated if removing an additional connection caused the accuracy of the network to drop below 100%. The average accuracy rates of the networks on the testing data set before and after pruning are 79.09% and 79.70%, respectively. The average number of connections remaining in the networks was 6.0. We extracted rules from two of the pruned networks.

Network 1 The smallest pruned network that still achieves 100% accuracy rate on the training data set has only one hidden unit left. There are three connections from the input units of X_2, X_3 and the bias to the hidden unit. The weights from inputs X_2 and X_3 are 15.95 and 9.88, respectively. The value of the bias is -19.65. The weight of the connection from the hidden unit to the output unit is -25.20. The activation values of all 74 training samples were discretized using Chi2 and two subintervals were found. Samples with activation values in the interval $(-1, 0)$ are those of bankrupt companies, while samples with activation values in the interval $[0, 1)$ are those of nonbankrupt companies. Since $\tanh^{-1}(0) = 0$, we have the simple rule:

Rule 1 If $15.95\chi_2 + 9.88\chi_3 < 19.65$, then predict **bankrupt**.
Default rule. Predict **nonbankrupt**.

It is easy to obtain an equivalent rule in terms of the original attribute values by noting the transformation (7.14). We have the following rule.

Rule 1-E If $12.53X_2 + 23.64X_3 < 4.18$, then predict **bankrupt**.
Default rule. Predict **nonbankrupt**.

The accuracy rates of the rules are exactly the same as those of the networks from which they are extracted. All samples in the training data set are classified correctly. Ten samples (three nonbankrupt companies and seven bankrupt companies) from the testing data set are misclassified.

Network 2 A network that achieves a higher predictive accuracy than Network 1 has five connections after pruning. Three inputs and the bias unit are connected to the single hidden unit left in the pruned network. A rule involving the transformed attributes is first extracted by NeuroLinear to distinguish between bankrupt and nonbankrupt companies. The equivalent rule involving the original input attributes is as follows.

Rule 2 If $5.96X_2 + 15.64X_3 - 0.13X_5 < 2.21$, then predict **bankrupt**.
Default rule. Predict **nonbankrupt**.

All training samples are classified correctly by this rule, and only nine (four nonbankrupt and five bankrupt companies) of the 55 testing samples are misclassified.

A comparison of the results from other methods as given in [14] and our results are presented in Table 7.2. Note that NeuroLinear correctly classifies more testing samples than the other methods. A hyperplane involving only three of the five input attributes was found by our method. It separates all the bankrupt companies from those nonbankrupt ones in the training data set and it can predict test data samples better than other methods.

7.3.2 CPU Performance Prediction Using REFANN

The data set for this example has six continuous attributes: (1) MYCT: machine cycle time, (2) MMIN: minimum main memory, (3) MMAX: maximum main

TABLE 7.2 Comparison of the Results from Various Methods

	Neurolinear	Ontogenic NN	Discriminant Analysis	Backprop	Perceptron	Athena
Correct	46	42	41	45	45	45
Wrong	9	7	14	10	10	10
Unclassified	—	6	—	—	—	—

memory, (4) CACH: cache memory, (5) CHMIN: minimum channels, and (6) CHMAX: maximum channels. The goal was to predict the CPU's relative performance based on the other computer characteristics [16]. There are 209 samples in the data set. The samples were divided randomly into a training data set (189 samples) and a test set (21 samples). The input values were normalized so that they ranged in the interval $[0, 1]$. A network with eight hidden units is trained. After pruning, only one hidden unit remained. The connections from input MYCT and CHMIN were also removed, indicating that these input attributes are irrelevant. The weighted inputs $\sum_{\ell} w_{\ell}^{1} I_{\ell}^{i}$ for all samples i in the training data set were computed. The largest value among these weighted inputs was assigned as the value of x_* (Step 1.1) and the value of x_0 was computed according to (7.10). Approximation of the hidden unit activation function separated the samples into two groups, those with weighted inputs of less than $x_0 = -0.7354$ and those with weighted inputs greater than or equal to -0.7354. Hence, we approximated the activation function by a piecewise linear function:

$$L_1(s_1^i) = \begin{cases} -0.5693 + 0.2256\, s_1^i & \text{if } s_1^i < -0.7354 \\ s_1^i & \text{if } s_1^i \geq -0.7354 \end{cases}$$

Since there was only one hidden unit, the predicted output for sample i was simply set to $\tilde{y}^i = v_1 L_1(s_1^i)$ (7.12). After rescaling the inputs back to their original values, we obtained the following set of rules:

Rule Set 1

Rule 1 If Region 1, then $\tilde{y} = Y_1$.
Rule 2 If Region 2, then $\tilde{y} = Y_2$.

The division of the input data was as follows:

- Region 1 $s_1^i < -0.7354 \Leftrightarrow 3.00\,\text{MMIN} + 2.69\,\text{MMAX} + 258.10\,\text{CACH} + 281.53\,\text{CHMAX} < 111189.41$
- Region 2 $s_1^i \geq -0.7354 \Leftrightarrow 3.00\,\text{MMIN} + 2.69\,\text{MMAX} + 258.10\,\text{CACH} + 281.53\,\text{CHMAX} \geq 111189.41$

and the rule consequences are linear equations Y_1 and Y_2:

$$\begin{aligned} Y_1 &= 4.966 + 0.0036\,\text{MMIN} + 0.0032\,\text{MMAX} \\ &\quad + 0.3086\,\text{CACH} + 0.3366\,\text{CHMAX} \\ Y_2 &= -453.0270 + 0.0159\,\text{MMIN} + 0.0143\,\text{MMAX} \\ &\quad + 1.3662\,\text{CACH} + 1.4903\,\text{CHMAX} \end{aligned}$$

The boundary between Region 1 and Region 2 can be approximated by rule conditions from C4.5 (Step 3) that do not involve any network weights. All training

TABLE 7.3 Predictive Accuracy for CPU-Performance Data

	RMSE	RRMSE	MAE	RMAE
Pruned network	15.82	15.76	11.52	16.03
Rule set 1	21.52	21.44	13.02	18.11
Rule set 1a	21.52	21.44	13.02	18.11
Linear regression	42.54	42.39	35.44	49.29

samples p with a weighted sum s_{1p} less than -0.7354 are labeled "Region 1," while all others are labeled "Region 2." C4.5 generates the following rules:

Rule Set 1a

Rule 1 If MMAX $\leq$ 24,000 and CACH $\leq$ 142, then "Region 1"
Rule 2 If MMIN $\leq$ 2300 and CHMAX $\leq$ 38, then "Region 2"
Rule 3 If MMAX $>$ 2300, then "Region 2"
Rule 4 If CACH $>$ 142, then "Region 2"
Default Rule: "Region 1"

The error rates of the network and the rule sets are shown in Table 7.3. In addition to the mean absolute error (MAE), the table also shows the errors of each model in terms of the root-mean-square errors (RMSE), relative root-mean-square errors (RRMSE), and relative mean absolute error (RMAE):

$$\text{RMSE} = \sqrt{\sum_{1=1}^{k} \frac{(\tilde{y}^i - y^i)^2}{k}}, \qquad \text{RRMSE} = 100 \times \text{RMSE} \Bigg/ \sqrt{\sum_{i=1}^{k} \frac{(\bar{y} - y^i)^2}{k}}$$

$$\text{MAE} = \frac{1}{k}\sum_{i=1}^{k} |\tilde{y}^i - y^i|, \qquad \text{RMAE} = 100 \times \text{MAE} \Bigg/ \left(\frac{1}{k}\sum_{i=1}^{k} |\bar{y} - y^i|\right)$$

where $\tilde{y}^i$ and $\bar{y}$ are the predicted value for sample i and the average value of all samples, respectively.

We also fit the data using multiple linear regression for comparison. Using the backward regression option of SAS, all attributes except CHMIN are found to contribute significantly to the regression model with the default confidence level of $\alpha = 0.10$. This example illustrates the effectiveness of the neural network approach in generating predicted linear equations. Compared to the linear regression, the RMSE and MAE of the rules extracted by REFANN are 49% and 63% lower, respectively.

7.4 CONCLUSION

Artificial neural networks perform particularly well on classification and data fitting/regression problems. They can predict with greater accuracy than other techniques because of the networks' capability of fitting any continuous function. Their main drawback when applied to solve these problems is the lack of explanatory power in the trained networks due to their complex structure. In many applications, it is desirable to extract knowledge from trained neural networks for the users to gain better understanding of the problems at hand. The extracted knowledge is usually expressed as symbolic rules of the form

if *condition*, then *consequent*

The rule conditions describe the subregions of the input space, while the rule consequents are the predicted target values. For regression problems, the predictions can be expressed as linear equations.

In this chapter, we have described how such rules can be extracted from trained neural networks. Our approach to rule extraction is decompositional. The key step in this approach is the analysis of the network's hidden unit activation functions. For classification problems, an algorithm that discretizes the activation values is employed. The network predictions are first given in terms of the discretized hidden unit activation values. These values define the boundaries of the subspaces of the input data where all samples in a subspace are predicted to belong to the same class. For regression problems, the activation function at each of the hidden units is approximated by a simple three-piece linear function. Using this approximation, the input space of the data set is also segmented into subspaces, where predictions in a subspace are computed by a linear function. Examples that illustrate how the algorithms work in detail are presented. Extensive results from the experiments with the proposed methods can be found in our earlier works [6,8].

REFERENCES

1. S. Gallant. "Connectionist Expert Systems." *Comm. ACM*, vol. 31, no. 2, 152–169, 1988.
2. K. Saito and R. Nakano. "Medical Diagnosis Expert System Based on PDP Model." In *Proceedings of the IEEE International Conference on Neural Networks*, pp. I255–I266, IEEE Press, New York, 1988.
3. S. Thrun. "Extracting Rules from Artificial Neural Networks with Distributed Representation." *Adv. NIPS*, vol. 7, 1995.
4. R. Setiono and H. Liu. "Symbolic Representation of Neural Networks." *IEEE Computer*, no. 3, 71–77, 1996.
5. J. R. Quinlan. *C4.5: Programs for Machine Learning*, Morgan Kaufmann, San Mateo, CA, 1993.
6. R. Setiono and H. Liu. "NeuroLinear: From Neural Networks to Oblique Decision Rules." *Neurocomputing*, vol. 17, no. 1, 1–24, 1997.
7. L. Breiman, J. H. Friedman, R. A. Olshen, and C. J. Stone. *Classification and Regression Trees*. Wadsworth & Brooks/Cole, Belmont, CA, 1984.
8. R. Setiono, W. K. Leow, and J. Zurada. "Extraction of Rules from Artificial Neural Networks for Nonlinear Regression." *IEEE Trans. Neural Networks*, vol. 13, no. 1, 567–577, 2002.

9. J. Hertz, A. Krogh, and R. G. Palmer, *Introduction to the Theory of Neural Computation,* Addison Wesley, Redwood City, CA, 1991.
10. R. Setiono. "A Penalty Function Approach for Pruning Feedforward Neural Networks." *Neural Comput.*, vol. 9, no. 1, 185–204, 1997.
11. H. Liu and R. Setiono. "Chi2: Feature Selection and Discretization of Numeric Attributes." In *Proceedings of the 7th IEEE International Conference on Tools with AI*, 1995, pp. 388–391.
12. H. Liu and S. T. Tan, "X2R: A Fast Rule Generator." In *Proceedings of the IEEE International Conference on Systems, Man and Cybernetics*, IEEE Press, New York, 1995.
13. E. L. Altman. "Financial Ratios, Discriminant Analysis and the Prediction of Corporate Bankruptcy." *Finance*, vol. 23, no. 3, 589–609 (1968).
14. J. P. Ignizio and J. R. Soltys. "Simultaneous Design and Training of Ontogenic Neural Network Classifiers." *Comput. Oper. Res.*, vol. 23, no. 6, 535–546 (1996).
15. R. R. Trippi and E. Turban, (eds.). *Neural Networks in Finance and Investing,* Probus, Chicago, 1993.
16. P. Ein-Dor and J. Feldmesser, "Attributes of the Performance of Central Processing Units: A Relative Performance Prediction Model," *Commun. ACM*, vol. 30, no. 4, 308–3177, 1987.

CHAPTER 8

NEURAL NETWORKS FOR CONTROL: RESEARCH OPPORTUNITIES AND RECENT DEVELOPMENTS

PAUL J. WERBOS

8.1 THE CHALLENGE TO RESEARCHERS: CONTEXT AND MOTIVATION

From the view of a National Science Foundation (NSF) Program Director, neural-network control is, first and foremost, a crucial challenge to the research community. The ECS Division has long been seeking more proposals—especially cross-disciplinary proposals, well grounded in control theory—that can rise more effectively to this challenge.

Somehow or other, we know that the smallest mammal brain achieves a high degree of competence in learning to perform very complex, novel tasks in a highly nonlinear environment fraught with all kinds of uncertainties. It does so in a general-purpose way, without the use of formal symbolic logic (except in one or two species, in some situations). The effort to understand how this could be possible is one of the key challenges to basic mathematical science in this century.

Neuroscience is unlikely to answer these questions without some sort of cross-disciplinary collaborations. A well-known neuroscientist once stated: "I have asked myself what would have happened if we had used our methods to try to understand how a radio works. First we would pull out a capacitor, watch the radio whine, and publish a paper announcing the discovery of 'the whine center.' Then, on a new grant, we would buy a new radio, pull out a resistor, and announce 'the buzz center.' A thousand radios later, we would have a complete map of the functional centers of the radio . . .". Some of the more modern methods can be more like doing a spectral analysis of the radiation emitted by a central processing unit (CPU), when the PC is in various states, like boot-up, idle, word processing, and so on.

Computational Intelligence: The Experts Speak. Edited by D. B. Fogel and C. J. Robinson
ISBN 0-471-27454-2

Many neuroscientists have reached out to the system dynamics community or the physics community, in search of ideas to guide the development of mathematical models. There is growing interest in "complex adaptive systems," not only in biology, but in engineering areas of growing national attention, such as management of critical infrastructures and the "system of systems" in the wake of 9/11.

In the end, any effort to reverse-engineer or understand higher capabilities of the brain in serious mathematical terms requires some specification of what kind of capabilities we are looking for. We need an operational definition of what we are aiming at. With an appropriate definition, it should be obvious to many people in the control community both that the problem is very challenging, and that the control and decision community (CDC) has a critical role to play in meeting the challenge. The next section will propose an operational definition.

In general, the electrical engineering community faces major challenges in attracting and retaining the best graduate students, who (like Congress) need to be convinced that new work in this area can be exciting and of fundamental importance both to scientific understanding and to the emerging needs of humanity. Facing up to these challenges will be important to the health of the profession.

8.2 A SPECIFIC CHALLENGE AND ASSOCIATED ISSUES

There are many debates [1,2] about the exact nature of higher intelligence in the mammal brain. Those debates clearly go well beyond engineering. However, consider the following concept or challenge to engineering: to develop a family of control designs, such that any member of the family has a general-purpose ability to learn the "optimal" strategy of action in any "well-behaved" complex nonlinear stochastic environment, when the system is given only three specific pieces of information: (1) a vector of observations $\mathbf{y}(t)$ at each sampling time, t; (2) a vector of controls $\mathbf{u}(t)$ that it decides on itself; (3) the utility function $U(\mathbf{y})$ whose expected value of future time the system tries to maximize. The challenge is to achieve all this in a design that fits at least the major gross hardware constraint that we know the brain does meet: real-time operation implemented in a highly parallel distributed "computer" made up of billions of *relatively* simple, modular processing elements ("neurons").

Even though the brain is not an exact utility maximizer, it is clear that this does capture much of what we see in the higher levels of intelligence in the mammal brain [1,2]; the brain does have capabilities that are hard to believe, if one looks out from the perspective of today's technology, yet it proves that capabilities of this sort do exist.

Before discussing the strategy of how to reach this goal, we need to examine the goal itself in more detail. First, as a general matter, when I try to evaluate the potential impact of an effort in this area, I ask myself: "What *difference* would this particular work make to the expected delay time between now and the time when we really meet the full challenge?" The best effort will usually not be an effort aimed at reaching the final goal in one easy step. That is impossible. There are many parallel efforts possible, which represent *just one big step* beyond the present state of the art, providing pieces of what we will need to achieve the ultimate goal. Much of what we really need today is new general-purpose mathematics, applicable to nonlinear systems in general—including artificial neural networks (ANNs) as a special case, but not limited to them. Much of the best work in ANNs actually has been using neural networks as a context for developing that kind of more general mathematics. Indeed, backpropagation itself—the most widely used algorithm in the ANN field—is actually a more general mathematical algorithm [3].

Second, we need to think about the role of prior information and domain-dependent knowledge. There have been many extreme polarized debates, in the past, between people who believe in learning or data-driven approaches and those who believe in genetically determined ideas or prior knowledge. Both in engineering and in neuroscience, the extreme positions are untenable, in my view. In the most-challenging applications, the ideal strategy may be to look for a learning system as powerful as possible, a system able to converge to the optimal strategy without any prior knowledge at all, and then initialize *that* system to an initial strategy and model as close as possible to the most extensive prior knowledge we can find (see also [4, foreword]). Some research is needed to get the best possible results in learning "without cheating." In each application domain, research is also needed to find out how to "cheat" most effectively. The first kind of research is most important to fundamental scientific progress, but the second is also needed as part of the effort to deliver products that are important to the needs of society. In biology, many people have argued that cells to do edge-detection, for example, appear very early in the life of an organism; yet researchers have shown that cells in the lateral part of the brain can learn to take over as edge detectors, after damage to the usual visual areas. Powerful learning and prior information are both needed. But for higher intelligence, we are looking more for the ability to learn and adapt in a general-purpose way.

Third, we cannot expect the brain *or any other physical device* to guarantee an exact optimal strategy of action in the general case. That is too hard for any physically realizable system. We will probably never be able to build a device to play a perfect game of chess or a perfect game of Go. In computer science terms, those problems are all "nondeterministic polynomial (NP) hard." But in engineering and in biology, we do not need or ask for absolutely perfect solutions. We look for the best possible approximations, trying to be as exact as we can, but not giving up on the true nonlinear problems of real interest.

Fourth, the notion of "well behaved" is extremely subtle, and itself points toward one of the parallel strands of research that needs to be taken further. Decades ago, statisticians realized that it is impossible to learn very much from streams of time-series data, if there are billions of variables, and if one imposes the usual "flat priors" of maximum-likelihood statistics. Even simple ANNs are possible only because there are some implicit notions of "Occam's razor" priors that allow inference, both in brains and in ANNs. Almost all theorems about nonlinear function approximators make similar implicit assumptions about the "smoothness" of the function to be approximated; there are some control applications where the usual notions about smoothness break down, and the usual nonlinear function approximators perform very badly, compared to others that are less well known. Issues of this kind need to be explored further [3,4, Chap. 10].

Fifth, the issue of stability and safety is subsumed here into the choice of utility function, U, in this formulation. When the world is modeled, mathematically, as the truly uncertain place it really is, we can never give a 100% guarantee that bad events are absolutely impossible. The brain was evolved to *minimize* the probability of sudden death, in an environment where an absolute guarantee cannot be achieved. Many practical users of control systems would rather be certain that the probability of accidents is minimized, in a full-up stochastic simulation of the real world, rather than having ironclad guarantees that accidents could never happen if only the world were simple and linear. Stability theory will be an important tool in developing learning systems that can actually converge to strategies that minimize the probability of accidents, and it will be important to our ability to obtain and understand experience in using learning-based designs on complex real-world systems. But it is only one of several important strands of research, relevant to the larger goal. At higher levels of systems design and management, the president's Economic Adviser has recently urged engineers to place more weight on performance issues, and to address the trade-offs between performance and safety in a more balanced way, grounded in modern risk analysis (i.e., in the maximization of total expected utility [5]).

Sixth, I would agree with the classic artificial intelligence (AI) researchers who argue that the highest level of intelligence seen in brains on earth is intelligence based on *symbolic reasoning*, not the subsymbolic intelligence I am talking about here. But 99% of the human brain is identical in its underlying wiring and learning abilities to the brains of the smallest mouse. Before science is able to truly understand how symbolic reasoning works in the human brain, it must first develop a deeper understanding of the remaining 99% of the brain. From a larger viewpoint, it is a good thing that many people do research on symbolic reasoning, even before scientific closure is possible on those issues; however, research aimed at subsymbolic intelligence is clearly on the critical path to developing a deeper understanding of such higher levels of intelligence.

8.3 STRATEGIES, TASKS, AND TOOLS

Most CDC members will immediately see that the preceding challenge is a challenge in optimal control. It may seem, at first, that the challenge here is simply the old challenge of "solving the curse of dimensionality" in dynamic programming. But it is more than that. The challenge is also to learn the model of the environment and to concurrently solve the dynamic programming problem as accurately as possible. (Some computer scientists advocate a purely model-free approach, without any learning of how to predict or even do state estimation; this does not scale well to large problems, and is not consistent with what we know about brains or animal learning [2,4,6–8].)

It is also well known that the general nonlinear robust control problem is equivalent to the problem of solving a nonlinear Hamilton–Jacobi–Bellman equation as accurately as possible. If one allows off-line learning, then the challenge posed earlier is equivalent to the challenge of giving nonlinear robust control the tools that it needs to address the general nonlinear case as accurately as possible. Many of the near-term opportunities to achieve practical results with neural-network control involve a clever use of off-line learning, in part because of verification and validation issues [9,10]. We may be entering a period where the difference between nonlinear robust control and neural-network control may start to become more semantic and emotional rather than real and mathematical.

Adaptive control is relevant because of the need for systems based on learning or adaptation. Curiously enough, it now seems that methods derived from neural-network control may finally solve the old problem of universal stability in adaptive control for the linear multi-input multi-output (MIMO) case; however, even the preliminary theorems on those lines [7] make heavy use of quadratic stability concepts from the linear robust control world. Greater collaboration between experts in linear robust control and adaptive control may be necessary to grasp this new opportunity, close at hand as it is. Clearly, this is one of several very important open research opportunities.

The greater challenge here clearly depends on our ability to bring together the capabilities of all three of these communities more effectively.

The most important breakthrough that makes this a viable direction for research is the development of the field that some people now call neurodynamic programming [11] or, more recently, adaptive dynamic programming (ADP). ADP originated in three previously independent small strands of research led by Bernard Widrow ("adaptive critics"), Andrew Barron ("reinforcement learning"), and myself ("approximate dynamic programming" and "reinforcement learning") in the first major workshop on neural networks for control held back in 1990 [12]. (See [7] for a review of the history, and for mathematical details of new adaptation methods important to strong stability.) The 1981 international conference paper that first described backpropagation in detail as a method for adapting multilayer neural networks also gave the general form of the method, for arbitrary nonlinear systems, and described how to use it as part of a parallel distributed design for model-based ADP [13, chap. 7].

Since then, however, the various schools have drifted apart to some degree. Reinforcement learning methods have become amazingly popular in AI, where they are commonly regarded as "the answer" to higher-level decision-making and planning problems. Yet the simple model-free designs in general use do not really address continuous variable problems, and have difficulties in scaling up to large problems, as has been noted many times in engineering applications in the past [4,12,14]. Even their performance in game-playing applications has been somewhat overstated. In contrast, a researcher has achieved human expert-level performance in a difficult strategic game, based on learning without heavy prior knowledge, by using evolutionary computing to train the "critic" network in his system [15]. Clearly engineers have a critical role to play in developing designs that can scale up to handling larger problems, and can address the issue of partially observed systems, by combining learning-based system identification and ADP together. This has already begun, but considerably more work remains to be done.

A new book based on an NSF-sponsored workshop in 2002 [16] will review some of the recent progress in ADP work and the further research challenges important to areas like the control of complex network systems, such as power grids. Particularly notable is the recent success of Wunsch, Harley, and Venayagamoorthy in controlling a physical network of turbogenerators able to maintain robust operation in the face of disturbances much greater than the previous state of the art allowed; the success of Balakrishnan in benchmark evaluations of success in difficult missile interception problems; the success by Ferrari and Stengel in improving performance over well-tuned classical methods in aircraft control; and success by Lendaris' group at Portland State in tasks ranging from simulated vehicle skid control through to logistics control—all using model-based ADP methods. Major new results in stability have also been achieved, some by contributors of this book and some by the Hittle/Young/Anderson group at Colorado State (with application to improved energy efficiency in buildings), among others.

REFERENCES

1. K. H. Pribram, (ed.). *Brain and Values*, Erlbaum, Hillsdale, NJ, 1998.
2. K. Yasue, M. Jibu, and T. Della Senta (eds.). *No Matter, Never Mind: Proceedings of Toward a Science of Consciousness: Fundamental Approaches (Tokyo '99)*, Benjamin, New York, 2002.
3. P. Werbos, "Backpropagation: General Principles and Issues for Biology." In M. Arbib, (ed.), *Handbook of Brain Theory and Neural Networks*, 2nd ed., MIT Press, Cambridge, MA, 2002.
4. White and D. Sofge (eds.). *Handbook of Intelligent Control*, Van Nostrand, New York, 1992.
5. H. Raiffa. *Decision Analysis*, Addison-Wesley, Reading, MA, 1968.
6. wwwimacm.org
7. www.lanl.gov/abs/adap-org/9810001
8. P. Werbos, "Neurocontrollers." In J.Webster, (ed.). *Encyclopedia of Electrical and Electronics Engineering*, Wiley, New York, 1999.
9. J. S. Baras and N. S. Patel, "Information State for Robust Control of Set-Valued Discrete Time Systems." In *Proceedings of the 34th Conference on Decision and Control (CDC)*, IEEE, New York, p. 2302, 1995.
10. M. Motter (ed.). Special Session on Intelligent Flight Control. *ACC Conference Proceedings*, 2001.
11. D. P. Bertsekas and J. N. Tsisiklis. *Neuro-Dynamic Programming*, Athena Scientific, Belmont, MA, 1996.
12. W. T. Miller, R. Sutton, and P. Werbos, (eds.). *Neural Networks for Control*, MIT Press, Cambridge, MA, 1990.
13. P. Werbos. *The Roots of Backpropagation*, Wiley, New York, 1994. Contains complete reprints.
14. S. Haykin. *Neural Networks: A Comprehensive Foundation*, 2nd ed., Prentice-Hall, Upper Saddle River, NJ, 1998.
15. D. B. Fogel. *Blondie 24: Playing at the Edge of AI*, Morgan Kaufmann, San Francisco, 2002.
16. J. Si, A. Barto, W. Powell, and D. Wunsch, (eds.). *Handbook of Learning and Approximate Dynamic Programming*, forthcoming.

CHAPTER 9

INTELLIGENT LEARNING ROBOTIC SYSTEMS USING COMPUTATIONAL INTELLIGENCE

TOSHIO FUKUDA and NAOYUKI KUBOTA

9.1 INTRODUCTION

Intelligence and life itself have been discussed since ancient days. Until now, various theories and methodologies have been found and developed by analyzing human brains and by simulating human behaviors in order to build intelligent systems. To begin, we discuss intelligent systems from the viewpoint of traditional cybernetics [1–3].

Generally, cybernetics is considered to be the theoretical study of communication and control processes in biological, mechanical, and electronic systems. The traditions of cybernetics can be discussed from three different viewpoints: Wiener's cybernetics, Turing's cybernetics, and McCulloch's cybernetics [3]. Wiener's cybernetics is the study of control system based on the concept of feedback [1]. The computational model for a system is based on the functions, not symbolic representation and manipulation. Feedback analysis is used for discussing the stability of a system. Especially, homeostatis of an organism is discussed as the ability to maintain internal equilibrium or keep internal balance within suitable ranges by adjusting its physiological processes in a dynamic or open environment [2]. Therefore, ecological, biological, and social systems are also considered as homeostatic. In contrast, Turing's cybernetics is the study of the intelligence in calculations and machines based on computability [4]. A Turing machine is a theoretical model of a computer. Turing's original aim was to provide a method for evaluating whether or not a machine can think. McCulloch's cybernetics is the study of neuroscience. McCulloch and Pitts suggested a mathematical model of a single neuron as a binary device performing a simple threshold logic [5]. The brain is a network of neurons, and this is

Computational Intelligence: The Experts Speak. Edited by D. B. Fogel and C. J. Robinson
ISBN 0-471-27454-2

considered to be the first model of connectionism. Furthermore, McCulloch's tradition in cybernetics led to the development of second-order cybernetics [3]. Thus, cybernetics has influenced control theory, computer science, information theory, cognitive science, and artificial intelligence (AI). These studies have formed the basis of autonomous or intelligent systems.

Various methodologies concerning AI have been developed in order to describe and build intelligent agents that perceive an environment, make appropriate decisions, and take actions [6]. In a classic point of view, an intelligent agent was designed based on symbolic representation and manipulation of explicit knowledge. Recently, human intelligence has been discussed in cognitive science, soft computing, artificial life, and computational intelligence (CI) [6–13, 39]. Bezdek discussed intelligence from three levels: artificial, biological, and computational [7]. In the strictest sense, CI depends on numerical data and does not rely on explicit knowledge. Furthermore, Eberhart defined CI as a methodology involving computing [8]. We also summarized CI as follows: CI aims to construct intelligence from the viewpoints of biology, evolution, and self-organization. CI tries to construct intelligence using the bottom-up internal-description approach, while classic AI tries to construct intelligence from the top-down external (explicit) -description approach. Essentially, CI includes neural, fuzzy, and evolutionary computing as intelligent techniques. Neural computing and fuzzy computing are based on the mechanism of behavior of human brain. While neural computing simulates physiological features of human brain, fuzzy computing simulates psychological features of human brain [14].

With the progress of intelligent techniques, various robots have been developed for human assistance, welfare, amusement, and so forth. Here, a robot which can acquire and apply knowledge or skill is called intelligent. Many methodologies have been applied for intelligent capabilities such as learning, reasoning, predicting, communicating, and decision making. Particularly, world modeling, problem solving, and task planning have been discussed using symbolic representation and manipulation, mainly in classic AI, but frame problems and symbol grounding problems have been addressed [6]. To overcome the difficulty in modeling of the real world, the subsumption architecture was proposed as a new methodology by Brooks [15]. In the subsumption architecture, a robotic behavior is described directly as a coupling of sensory inputs and action outputs without generating its complete world model [15]. The agent design is decomposed into objective-based behaviors such as obstacle avoiding, photo tracing, and map building. This approach is called *behavior-based robotics*. Basically, behaviors are designed using finite-state machines, but neural networks and fuzzy systems also have been used for describing behavior rules. Furthermore, evolutionary optimization methods have been applied to robots as methods for acquiring behavior rules through interaction with their environment, and this research is called evolutionary robotics [16, 41–47]. In addition, reinforcement learning methods have been applied for obtaining the optimal policy that maximizes the expected return in an unknown environment [17]. In this way, behavior-based robotics and evolutionary robotics have been developed using fuzzy, neural, and evolutionary computing, as well as reinforcement learning, and others [14, 15, 17, 18, 19–25, 33–39].

This chapter presents several topics of motion planning and behavior acquisition of robots using intelligent techniques in unknown and dynamic environments. Section 9.2 presents the motion planning and behavior acquisition of robots as general issues. Section 9.3 presents recent topics of computational intelligence concerning robotics. Section 9.4 discusses computational intelligence for robotic systems from viewpoints of adaptation, learning, and evolution. Section 9.5 introduces structured intelligence for partner robots.

9.2 MOTION PLANNING AND BEHAVIOR ACQUISITION OF ROBOTS

In general, robots can be divided into mobile robots and arm robots (robot manipulator). The motion of a robot is constrained by its dynamics, kinematics, and environment. Because robots are controlled using joints and wheels, the motion of a robot results in the motion of the controllable degrees of freedom. The problems of robots can be divided into the two subproblems of motion planning and motion control. First, motion planning is solved given a geometric model. Next, motion control for a physical robot is accomplished according to a planned trajectory.

A robot receives a task from a human operator and performs the task in the workspace, which may include obstacles such as people, machining centers, and other robots. A robot should take into account collision avoidance with the obstacles. Furthermore, the robot should generate its motion, satisfying the spatial and temporal constraints for performing the task. The motion-planning problems for performing given tasks can be divided fundamentally into path-, trajectory-, and task-planning problems. Here, we define these planning problems as follows. The path-planning problem requires generating the shortest path for the robot from a given starting point to a target point, while satisfying spatial constraints. The trajectory-planning problem requires generating a trajectory that satisfies temporal constraints. The task-planning problem requires finding a sequence of primitive motion commands for solving a given task. In fact, each definition of these problems is differentiated conceptually from other planning problems, and therefore each planning problem shares some objectives of other planning problems.

On the other hand, autonomous robots also require intelligent capabilities such as learning, reasoning, predicting, communicating, and decision making in addition to motion-planning capabilities. Figure 9.1 shows the sequence of perception, decision making, and action of an intelligent robot from the functional point of view. Perception extracts perceptual information from sensed information. The robot makes decisions and takes actions based on perceptual information and its own internal states. In addition, the robot might learn by acquiring or perceiving feedback information concerning rewards or penalties. Thus, the robot repeats such perception, decision making, and action that are deeply dependent on information processing related to intelligence. Intelligence emerges from the synthesis of these system capabilities interacting with its environment. Therefore, the intelligence of a robot is related to the features of its environment that might be deterministic, dynamic, and/or

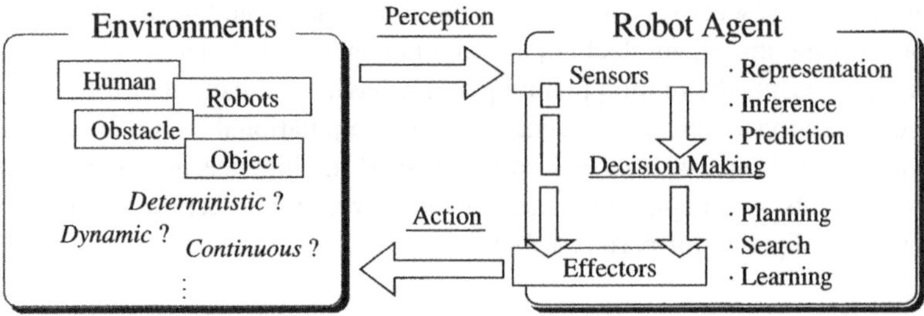

Figure 9.1 Perception, decision making, and action of an intelligent robot.

continuous. Furthermore, its environment might include human beings, obstacles, and other robots.

Figure 9.2 shows research categories of robotic systems: intelligent robotic systems, human-robot systems, and multiple robotic systems. Intelligent robotic systems aim mainly at realizing motion planning and behavior acquisition in unknown or dynamic environments. In these systems, optimization and adaptation of robotic behaviors are discussed. Human–robotic systems emphasize the importance of communication and cooperation between human and robots. Therefore, a robot requires the capabilities for human recognition, human intention recognition, and natural language processing. In multiple robotic systems, methods for knowledge sharing, distributed problem solving, and distributed control are discussed from the viewpoint of self-organization. Various methodologies are required to

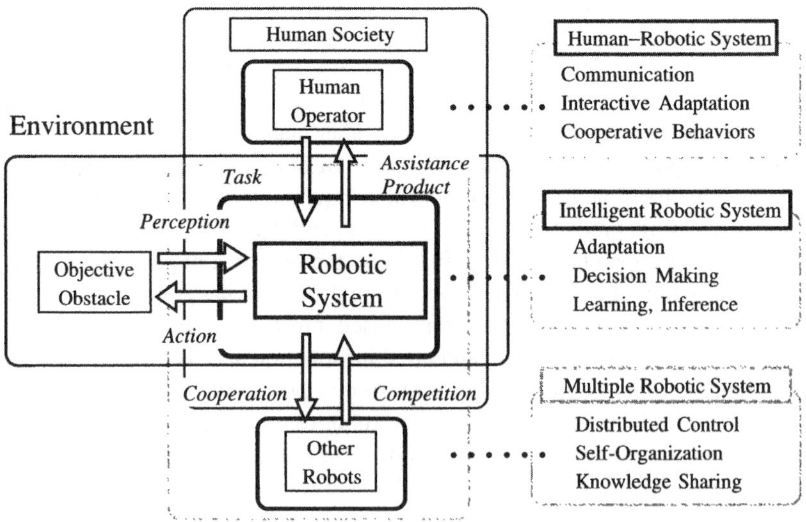

Figure 9.2 Research categories of robotic systems from the viewpoint of interaction.

realize these capabilities in robotic systems. In the following sections, we show some methodologies for intelligent robotic systems.

9.3 EMERGING SYNTHESIS OF COMPUTATIONAL INTELLIGENCE

A synthesis of various techniques is often required to build a highly intelligent system. Figure 9.3 shows the synthesis of neural, fuzzy, and evolutionary computing. Each technique plays a specific role in intelligent systems.

Neural networks are useful for recognizing patterns, classifying input, and adapting to dynamic environments by learning. However, the internal mapping structure of a neural network is considered to be a black box, and consequently the resulting behavior is often too difficult to explain. Fuzzy systems can cope easily with human knowledge and can be used to perform logical inference, but fuzzy systems do not fundamentally incorporate any learning mechanisms. Fuzzy neural networks have been developed to overcome this disadvantage [5–10]. In general, neural networks are used for learning, while fuzzy logic is used for representing knowledge. The learning is performed via an incremental learning, back propagation, or the delta rule based on error functions (e.g., a measure of misclassification). Evolutionary optimization methods can also tune neural networks and fuzzy systems [26]. Furthermore, evolutionary optimization methods have been used for optimizing the structure of neural networks and fuzzy systems [5–10].

Coevolutionary computation (CEC) has also been discussed in recent years [27,28]. CEC is generally composed of several species with different types of individuals, while standard evolutionary computation has a single population of individuals. In CEC, variation operators are performed only in a single "species," because a species is used as a group of interbreeding individuals not normally able to interbreed with other such groups. However, selection can be performed among individuals within a species and also among species.

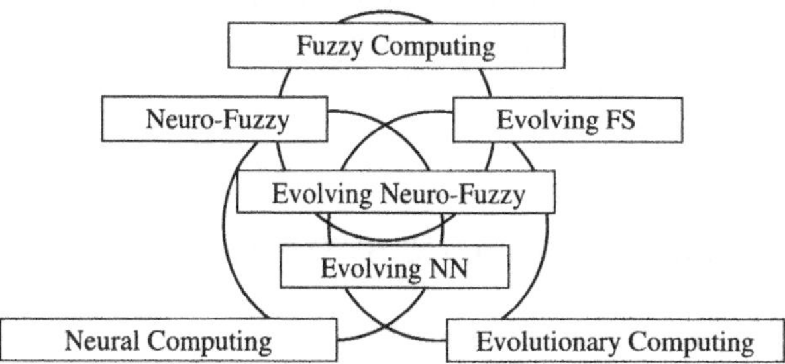

Figure 9.3 Emerging synthesis of neural, fuzzy, and evolutionary computing (NN: neural network, FS: fuzzy system).

TABLE 9.1 The Interaction Between Two Species *A* and *B*

		Influence of *B* to *A*		
		+ (benefit)	0	− (harm)
Influence of *A* to *B*	+	Mutualism	Commensalism	Parasitism
	0	Commensalism	Neutralism	Amensalism
	−	Parasitism	Amensalism	Competition

In general, there are various interactions in two or more species. These interactions depend on the influence of a species relevent to the other. To simplify the interaction, we consider two species: *A* and *B*. Table 9.1 shows the interaction between two species, and these terms are referred from biology as suitably as possible, except for neutralism. We first divide the relationship into *symbiosis* and *competition.* Furthermore, the symbiosis can be divided into three types: *mutualism*, *commensalism*, and *parasitism.* In CEC, these interactions are often described in terms of the influences concerning fitness between species. Each fitness value is defined as:

$$fit_A(x_i) = f_A(x_i, y_i) \tag{9.1}$$

$$fit_B(y_i) = f_B(x_i, y_i) \tag{9.2}$$

where x_i and y_i are individuals included in species *A* and *B*, respectively. Thus, each fitness value is evaluated by the combination of x_i and y_i. These fitness functions can be defined as two different functions, but the same fitness function might be used practically in both species, such as {minimization and maximization} and {positive evaluation and negative evaluation}. However, because the interaction between two species is quite complicated in general, it is difficult to define a fitness function according to the preceding discussion.

In the parasitism model, the same fitness function is often used with different objectives, such as minimization and maximization. This model is regarded as a predator–prey model. One species (predator) tries to maximize the fitness, while the other species (prey) tries to minimize the fitness. This model has often been applied to test-solution problems. One species searches for candidate solutions passing tests, and the other species searches for difficult tests against the candidate solutions.

9.4 INTELLIGENCE ON ROBOTIC SYSTEMS

9.4.1 Information and Representation

Knowledge, skills, and strategies for intelligent robots are expressed using systematic representations, such as natural languages, programming languages, structural memory, and inference rules. The functional processes obtaining necessary information can be classified mainly as logical inference and association. Representation methods for logical inference include production rules, fuzzy rules, and classifier systems. It is easy for people to understand the explicit representation using logical inference. On the other hand, the representation methods using association include neural networks and associative memories. Their inference structure is not clear, because spatiotemporal mapping based on many neurons is included in the structure, even though the role of a single neuron is very simple. Therefore, a method using association might be called *intuitive inference.*

An intelligent robot perceives its environment, using logical inference and association, makes decisions, and takes actions. Here we discuss three models of intelligent robots from the viewpoint of objective levels. The first one is the reaction-based robot. The reaction-based robot recognizes or classifies the state of its environment and takes reactive motions such as state–action pairs. Here, the reactive motions are designed as objective-based behaviors, that is, each given objective is assigned to each behavior. The next model is the model-based robot. The model-based robot constructs and maintains an internal representation or model of its environment, and takes actions based on the internal model. The final model is the objective-based robot, which is an extension model of the model-based robot. First, the objective-based robot constructs an internal model and finds objectives. But because the robot has no explicit objectives, the robot does not know how to take actions. The robot generates state-value or action-value functions, as in reinforcement learning, and tries to obtain the highest reward, not to achieve the objectives. Therefore, the objective-based robot must find or generate objectives in an environment, while the objectives of the robot are given in the model-based robot. To find objectives through the interaction with environments, the robot should generate evaluation functions for its behaviors autonomously.

As to the world modeling of a robot, representational and inferential frame problems are often pointed out under the condition that the robot must represent all properties of the environment as an internal model and must check all possible state-action pairs to make rational decisions [6]. This problem arises from generating an internal-world model completely and searching all possible actions in that model. To avoid the difficulty of world modeling, bounded rationality approaches have been proposed that try to reduce world modeling and action searching into a bounded amount of computation [6].

Behavior-based robotics uses a subsumption architecture in a quite different way from classic AI [15–17]. While a classic AI-based robot has an explicit central model based on information-processing modules using a world model, a behavior-based robot has no central model. In the subsumption architecture, the agent design is decomposed into objective-based behaviors (Figure 9.4). First, the zeroth behavior layer is designed as a basic competence, and a layer for improving the competence can be added incrementally. A higher level of behavior subsumes a lower level of behavior. Thus, the architecture does not try to reduce computation in the manner of classic AI, but starts with a small amount of computation. The subsumption architecture is based on the key concepts of location and embodiment, i.e., the robots are

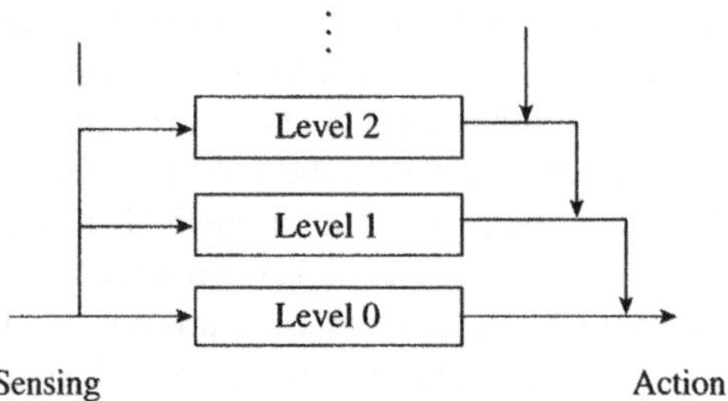

Figure 9.4 A control system based on the subsumption architecture.

situated in the world, and the robots have bodies and experience the world directly. Behavior-based robotics realizes a real-time control based on reactive motions in unknown or dynamic environments, but it is pointed out that the robot cannot perform sequential or complicated tasks [6].

9.4.2 Learning and Adaptation

The general objectives of learning and adaptation for intelligent robots are to identify an unknown or dynamic environment and also to acquire knowledge and behaviors. Learning methods can be classified into learning by discovery and learning from observation. Here, the learning by discovery might be categorized as evolution and search, because a robot does not use the perceptual information in an environment explicitly. On the other hand, learning from observation can be further classified into supervised learning, unsupervised learning, and reinforced learning, depending on the type of teacher. Supervised learning can use the correct teaching data, while reinforced learning can use only simple information of success or failure through interaction with an environment. In unsupervised learning, a robot receives no feedback signals from an environment, but the robot learns the relationship among perceptual information.

Adaptation is used for tuning internal parameters in the learning process [40]. For example, the learning rate or step size might be updated according to the average error, indicating the learning state. Furthermore, pruning and constructive algorithms might be applied to improve the architecture of neural networks. Basically, if the architecture of a neural network is suitable to the teaching data set, the neural network can learn them very well. However, too small a network would be unable to learn them well, while too large a network would result in overfitting. Therefore, the adaptation of network architecture plays an important role in learning. A pruning algorithm removes some hidden units or connections from a network. Pruning algorithms can be classified mainly into sensitivity calculation methods and penalty-term methods [29]. A sensitivity calculation method estimates the sensitivity of the error function to the removal of an element, i.e., the sensitivity is evaluated when a weight is set to zero. If the error increases too little, the weight is removed. A penalty-term method removes a weight that is nearly zero or is below a certain threshold during

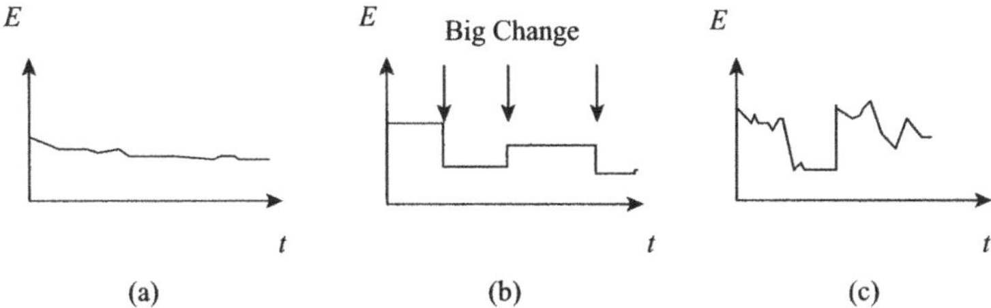

Figure 9.5 Spatial patterns of dynamic environments.

training. Such a weight is not likely to influence output much. On the other hand, a constructive algorithm adds some units or connections to a network [30]. First, the constructive algorithm starts with a small or minimal network and adds new layers, hidden units, and connections to the network until the required performance is obtained. Furthermore, after convergence using a constructive algorithm, some hidden units and connections might be removed from the network using a pruning algorithm. In this way, constructive and pruning algorithms can optimize network architecture and weights during training.

9.4.3 Search and Evolution

An intelligent robot should update or improve knowledge and behaviors, particularly if its environment is changing. We discuss the adaptability and optimality of robotic behaviors so it can deal with a changing environment. Robotic behaviors can be optimized if an environmental condition is fixed, but robotic behaviors should be adapted in real time if an environment is changing . The optimality and adaptability of robotic behaviors depend on the patterns of environmental changes. Figures 9.5 and 9.6 show some patterns of the changing environments, where E on the vertical axes is defined simply as a parameter corresponding to the environmental conditions. For our convenience, we designate the structures in the amount and speed of environmental change a spatial pattern and temporal pattern, respectively, but this categorization might not be exact in a general sense. The environments of Figures 9.5a and 9.6a include only small changes. These kinds of small changes

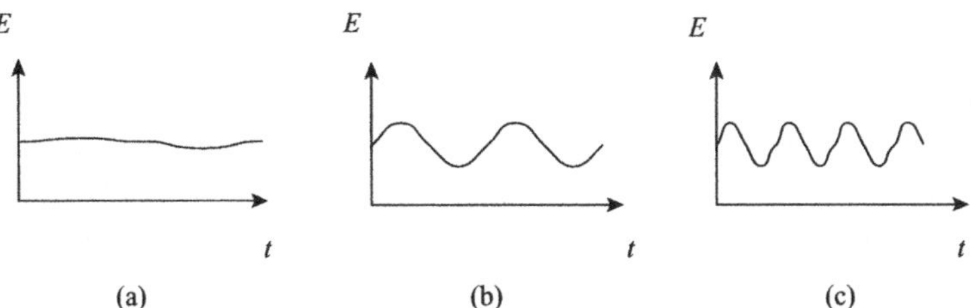

Figure 9.6 Temporal patterns of dynamic environments.

can be considered to be some sort of noise in a static environment. From the viewpoint of optimality, statistical approaches can be applied to obtain a behavior. The environment of Figure 9.5b includes big changes, but the environmental condition is static after a big change. For example, this kind of environmental change is a situation in which a human operator using a robotic system is replaced by another operator. In such a case, a robot can obtain the optimal behavior according to the current environment or the human operator. The environment of Figure 9.6b includes periodic environmental changes. If the robot has time enough to adapt to the environment, the robot should acquire several behaviors in different environmental conditions, and should select a behavior suitable to the environment. If a robot encounters a fast-changing environment (see Figure 9.6c) the robot cannot adapt to the environmental change in real time. Therefore, this kind of environment for the robot is considered to be something like noise. Finally, the environment in Figure 9.5c includes nonstationary changes. In this case, evolutionary computing methods that maintain behavioral diversity for search can be applied to obtain new behaviors in the changing environment [23].

The role of evolution in intelligent robots is to obtain behaviors while maintaining various candidate solutions, not a single candidate solution. In the concept of adaptation, the architecture is changed continuously and systematically, much like pruning and constructive algorithms for neural networks, while the architecture can be changed randomly and heuristically in the concept of evolution. In adaptation, the error or value function is calculated first, and then the architecture of robotic behavior is updated. This update is done systematically so as to reduce error or to increase value. Therefore, the update procedure is decided beforehand whenever error or value is calculated. In contrast, the error or fitness function in evolution is calculated after some changes in candidate solutions are performed heuristically according to the genetic information of candidate solutions. Here the correctness of the change cannot be judged beforehand. Consequently, maintaining diversity is very important for the global search. Accordingly, evolutionary methods might need much more time than adaptive methods, but evolutionary methods realize global search. To summarize, the systematic updating methods, such as delta rules, can be applied if the relationship between error and change is clear, while the heuristic update methods, such as evolutionary computing techniques, can be applied if the relationship between error and change is not clear.

9.5 STRUCTURED INTELLIGENCE FOR ROBOTIC SYSTEMS

A robotic system becomes increasingly complicated and large as intelligent capabilities are added gradually, while its behaviors depend largely on information processing related to intelligence. Therefore, we should consider the entire intelligence structure for processing information "flowing" over the hardware and software. We have proposed the concept of structured intelligence [14,23,24]. Structured intelligence emphasizes the importance of the close linkage among perception, decision making, and action. The concept of the structured intelligence

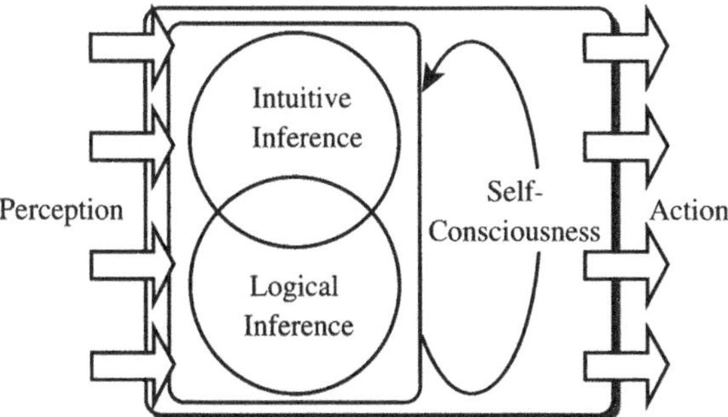

Figure 9.7 Structured intelligence for robotic systems.

includes three functions: intuitive inference, logical inference, and self-consciousness (Figure 9.7). Since it is difficult to define consciousness, we focus on the functional features of consciousness. Self-consciousness is consciousness toward a self, and this is regarded as a high level of consciousness. We can learn various behaviors unconsciously, whereas we can learn logical behaviors when the degree of self-consciousness is high. Furthermore, in our view, self-consciousness perceives the internal state, while consciousness perceives the external state. In this sense, consciousness can be used in the same role of perception. Furthermore, self-consciousness combines and selects the outputs from intuitive and logical inference. We consider that intuitive inference is realized by neural computing based on numerical processing, while logical inference is realized by production rules and fuzzy rules based on symbolic processing. In the following, we discuss logical inference and intuitive inference.

9.5.1 Logical Inference and Intuitive Inference

We have proposed multiobjective behavior coordination as a logical-inference model. A robot has a set of primitive objective-based behaviors written by fuzzy rules. A behavior weight is assigned to each behavior and the kth action output is calculated by

$$y_k = \frac{\sum_{h=1}^{B}\left(wgt_h(t)\sum_{i=1}^{R}\mu_{h,i}\cdot w_{h,i,k}\right)}{\sum_{h=1}^{B}\left(wgt_h(t)\sum_{i=1}^{R}\mu_{h,i}\right)} \tag{9.3}$$

where R and $\mu_{h,i}$ are the number of fuzzy rules and firing strength of the ith fuzzy rule, B, and $wgt_h(t)$ are the number of behaviors and a behavior weight of the hth behavior over the discrete time step, t, respectively. By updating the behavior weights, the robot can learn multiobjective behavior according to the time series of perceptual information. This method can be considered as a mixture of experts, if the behavior coordination mechanism is considered as a gating network.

A robot makes decisions using logical inference in unknown situations, and the behaviors of the robot are improved gradually and refined through learning. As a result, the robot learns actions using intuitive inference. This indicates that the robot acquires the specific perceptual systems and action systems suitable to facing environments using logical-inference models as behavioral knowledge. In general, the refined intuitive inference takes a little time, while logical inference based on the multiobjective behavior coordination takes considerable time. We have proposed modular neural networks (MNNs) as an intuitive-inference model related to consciousness. Each NN performs decision making and state prediction simultaneously. That is, inputs to NN are the current perceptual information and action output, and the outputs predict perceptual information, action outputs, and connectivity values to each NNs. The output of a neuron is calculated by

$$Y_p^l = S\left(\sum_{q=1}^{N_{l-1}} W_{p,q}^l \cdot Y_q^{l-1} - \theta_p^l\right) \tag{9.4}$$

where Y_p^l is an output of the pth neuron in the lth layer, S is a Sigmoid function, $W_{p,q}^l$, θ_p^l, and N_l are a weight parameter between pth neuron of the lth layer and qth neuron of the $(l-1)$th layer, threshold of the pth neuron, and the number of neurons of the lth layer, respectively. In general, self-consciousness is activated when the predicting perceptual information is different from actual perceptual information. When the predictive difference is high, the robot selects other NNs suitable to the other situation according to the connectivity values. The MNNs are trained using the outputs of the multiobjective behavior coordination through interaction with the environments. Consequently, the inference system of multiobjective behavior coordination is partially replaced by MNNs composed of compact NNs. To summarize, the robot using MNNs does not perform the inference of all possible behaviors, but performs only the inference of behaviors based on the predictive difference.

The robot must acquire behavior rules if the robot has no behavior knowledge applicable in an unknown environment. In such a case, the robot generates fuzzy rules by evolutionary computing techniques [23]. Futhermore, if the objective of the robot is not given beforehand, the robot autonomously generates its intention through interaction with its environment. Here, the generation of the intention can be considered to be the generation of evaluation functions. Therefore, the change in the intention means a change of evaluation functions. The selections of behavior knowledge and evaluation functions are preformed by self-consciousness according to the internal state of the robot.

9.5.2 Communication of Partner Robots

A robot might coexist with a human sharing the same environment. In such a case, the robot must form communication with the human through interaction with the environment [24]. Now, we discuss the communication between a human and a

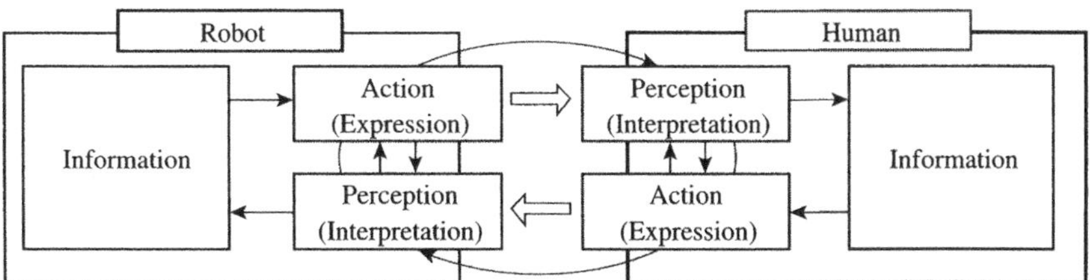

Figure 9.8 Communication between a human and a partner robot.

pet robot. For example, when a child begins to play with a pet robot, the child tries to have contact with the pet robot in various ways. And then the child searches for a causal relationship between the sensory inputs and motion outputs of the pet robot. The mechanism to enrich the relationship between a human and robot is not the architecture for realizing the given behavior patterns, but the architecture for learning the interrelation between the human and robot.

Figure 9.8 shows the communication between a human and a partner robot. If the structure of expression exists in the action patterns of the robot related to a human contacting pattern, the human can learn the structure. This indicates that the human gradually succeeds in finding the boundaries of the action patterns of the robot, if the robot can form the boundaries of action patterns. Then, we discuss the perceptual system and the action system used for a partner robot to generate specific action patterns related to human-specific contacting patterns. The perceptual system does not extract all of the object's features, but picks up the specific information of the object according to the spatiotemporal context of the other situation. Consequently, the perceptual system does not construct a complete world model, but makes ready beforehand for the next specific perception. That is, the perceptual system picks up the specific information from sensory inputs, using several functions based on the internal state. At the same time, the action system generates specific motion outputs using mapping functions based on the specific information related to the human contacting patterns. Furthermore, the motion outputs of the robot construct the spatiotemporal context for human-specific perception with the dynamics of the environment.

Figure 9.9 shows a mapping relation in the perceptual system and the action system. Here, the dimensions of the perception and action can be dynamic according to their interaction. Consequently, the robot using MNNs searches for a NN that is suitable for human contacting patterns, while the human tries to interpret the robotic action patterns. Therefore, if the robot can select a suitable NN so that the human can interpret the action patterns of the robot, the prediction of the robot is the same as that of the human. In this way, the interaction between a robot and human constructs their next interrelation, and that interrelation restricts their next interaction. We emphasize that the importance of social communication between a human and a partner robot lies in the mutual search of intentions through their interaction, not in the exact transmission of the intentions. That is to say, the intention of the robot

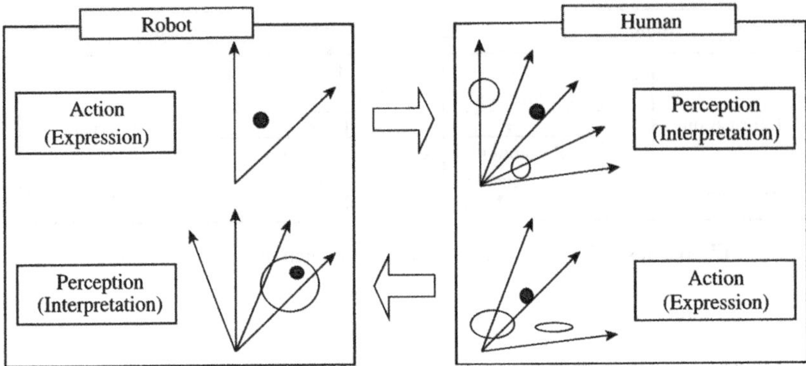

Figure 9.9 Perceptual system and action system of a robot through interaction with a human.

is not given beforehand, but is found through their interaction. Therefore, the concept of self-consciousness is required for the search of intention.

In the preceding discussion, the perceptual system and the action system restrict each other through interaction with the environment. In ecological psychology, this is called *perceiving-acting cycle* [31,32]. We have proposed the concept of perception-based robotics [23,24]. The perception-based robotics emphasizes the importance of a perceptual system for the perceiving–acting cycle. Figure 9.10 shows the coupling of a perceptual system and an action system in the perception-based robotics. Each module of a perception system or action system is a specific perception module or action module. The perception-based robotics is discussed from the viewpoint of information flow, while the structured intelligence is discussed from the viewpoints of algorithms and functions. When the perceiving–acting cycle forms a coherent relationship with the environment, the specific perceptual information generates the specific action outputs, like reactive motions. In this view, this approach includes the concept of behavior-based robotics, but the objective of each behavior is not

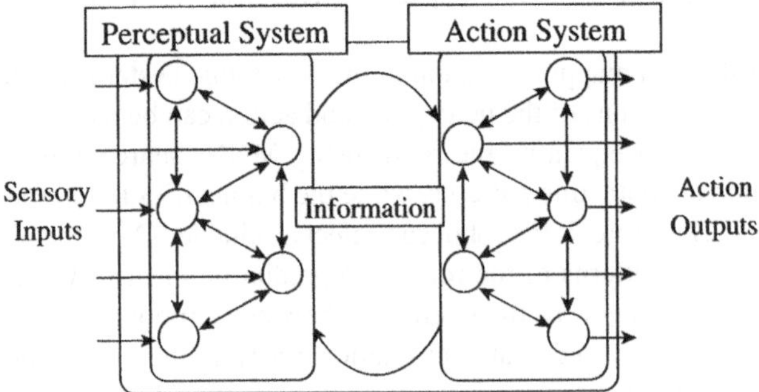

Figure 9.10 Interaction of the perceptual system and action system from the viewpoint of information flow.

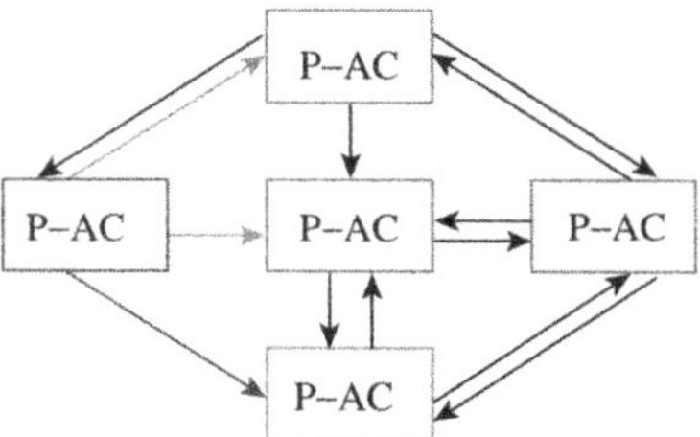

Figure 9.11 A phase transition of the perceiving–acting cycles.

given beforehand. The boundaries of the behaviors are formed through interaction with their environments. We consider the perceptual system and action system situated in the inverse environment as one phase of the perceiving–acting cycles (Figure 9.11). In a phase of the perceiving–acting cycle, the perceptual system picks up the specific information. To maintain the perceiving–acting cycle or to connect to another phase, the perceptual system prepares beforehand for a next specific perception. The self-consciousness searches the phase situated in the other environment, and updates the perceiving–acting cycles phase. Each phase corresponds to an NN of MNNs [35].

Next, we consider learning for the perceptual system and action system of a partner robot. The communication of a robot requires continuous interaction with the human, because the human tries to discover the relationship between the human approach and the robotic behavior; in addition, the human tries to find a more complicated relationship than the current relationships. Therefore, the robot needs to accumulate its perceptual system and action system through interaction with the human. This indicates that learning the perceptual system and action system is not a single task, but a kind of spiral learning (Figure 9.12). Consequently, the robot's perception and action are based on the current perceptual system and action system, while the learning of the perceptual system and action system is based on the current relationship of perception and action. Therefore, the learning structure for accumulating the perceptual system and action system is required.

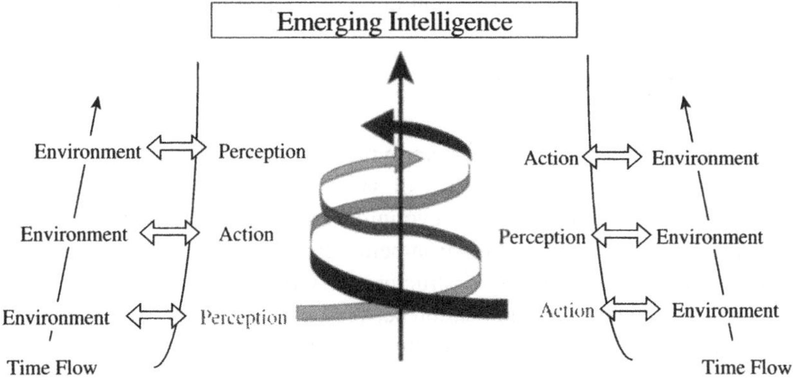

Figure 9.12 Spiral learning of the perceptual system and the action system.

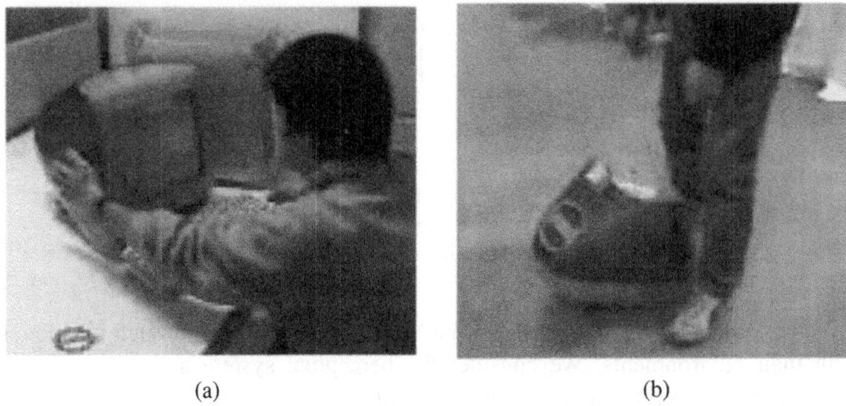

(a) (b)

Figure 9.13 Snapshots of experimental results in the communication of a partner robot.

We are developing partner robots. The partner robot uses the body of the all-in-one PC familiar to various people. Although we can use this robot as a standard PC, this robot also can be used as a pet robot. We aim to develop a mobile PC that we want to continue to use as a partner. Two CPUs are used as PC and robotic behaviors. The robot has two servomotors, a charge-coupled device (CCD) camera, four ultrasonic sensors, and four light sensors. Therefore, the robot can learn collision-avoiding, human-approaching, line-tracing behaviors, and others. In the experiments, the numbers of fuzzy rule sets and MNNs is four and five, respectively. Figure 9.13 shows some snapshots of experimental results of a partner robot. Figure 9.13a shows a snapshot of the partner robot on the desk. The robot finds the human, and the human is using the partner robot as a PC. The MNNs of the robot are trained gradually using the fuzzy rules selected as behavior knowledge. The human makes contact with the robot in various ways, and then the robot gradually learns some of the contacting patterns using MNNs. Figure 9.13b shows a snapshot of the partner robot taking a walk with the human in a passage way. The partner robot uses the NNs properly according to the situation through interaction with the humans.

9.6 CONCLUDING REMARKS

This chapter presented methods for applying intelligent techniques to intelligent robots from the methodological point of view. Furthermore, the chapter showed that the concepts of adaptation and evolution are essential to building intelligent robots in unknown or dynamic environments, from the conceptual point of view. Finally, it showed the concept of structured intelligence for building intelligent robots and discussed the communication between a partner robot and a human. However, to build really intelligent robots interacting with a human, more philosophical ideas and theories would be required, such as ecological psychology and second-order cybernetics [3,31,32].

REFERENCES

1. N. Wiener. *Cybernetics*, Wiley, New York, 1948.
2. W. R. Ashby. *An Introduction to Cybernetics*, Chapman & Hall, London, 1956 (Internet, 1999, http://pcp.vub.ac.be/books/IntroCyb.pdf.)
3. S. A. Umpleby and E. B. Dent. "The Origins and Purposes of Several Traditions in Systems Theory and Cybernetics." *Cybern. Syst.*, vol. 30, 79–103, 1999.
4. A. M. Turing. "Computing Machinery and Intelligence." *Mind*, vol. 59, 433–466, 1950.
5. J. A. Anderson and E. Rosenfeld. *Neurocomputing*, MIT Press, Cambridge, MA, 1988.
6. S. J. Russell and P. Norvig. *Artificial Intelligence*, Prentice Hall, Upper Saddle River, NJ, 1995.
7. J. M. Zurada, R. J. Marks II, and C. J. Robinson (eds.). *Computational Intelligence—Imitating Life*, IEEE Press, New York, 1994.
8. M. Palaniswami, Y. Attikiouzel, R. J. Marks II, D. Fogel, and T. Fukuda, (eds.). *Computational Intelligence—A Dynamic System Perspective*, IEEE Press, New York, 1995.
9. J.-S. R. Jang, C.-T. Sun, and E. Mizutani. *Neuro-Fuzzy and Soft Computing*, Prentice Hall, Upper Saddle River, NJ, 1997.
10. T. Fukuda and N. Kubota. "Fuzzy Control Methodology: Basics and State of Art." In H. N. Teodorescu, A. Kandel, and L. C. Jain, (eds.). *Soft Computing in Human-Related Sciences*, 1999, pp. 3–35.
11. S. V. Kartalopoulos. *Understanding Neural Networks and Fuzzy Logic*, IEEE Press, New York, 1996.
12. C. G. Langton. *Artificial Life—An Overview*, MIT Press, Cambridge, MA, 1995.
13. R. J. Marks II. "Intelligence: Computational Versus Artificial, *IEEE Trans. Neural Networks*, vol. 4, no. 5, 737–739, 1993.
14. T. Fukuda and N. Kubota. "An Intelligent Robotic System Based on A fuzzy approach," *Proc. IEEE*, vol. 87, no. 9, 1448–1470, 1999.
15. R. A. Brooks. *Cambrian Intelligence*, MIT Press, Cambridge, MA, 1999.
16. R. Pfeifer and C. Scheier. *Understanding Intelligence*, MIT Press, Cambridge, MA, 1999.
17. R. S. Sutton and A. G. Barto. *Reinforcement Learning*, MIT Press, Cambridge, MA, 1998.
18. R. C. Arkin. *Behavior-Based Robotics*, MIT Press, Cambridge, MA, 1998.
19. J. Xiao, Z. Michalewicz, L. Zhang, K. Trojanowski. "Adaptive Evolutionary Planner/Navigator for Mobile Robots." *IEEE Trans. Evol. Comput.*, vol. 1, no. 1, 18–28, 1998.
20. M. Colombetti, M. Dorigo, and G. Borghi. "Behavior Analysis and Training—A Methodology for Behavior Engineering," *IEEE Trans. Syst., Man, Cybern., Part B: Cybern.*, vol. 26, no. 3, 365–380, 1996.
21. J. Y. Donnart and J. A. Meyer. "Learning Reactive and Planning Rules in a Motivationally Autonomous Animat," *IEEE Trans. Syst., Man, Cybern., Part B: Cybern.*, vol. 26, no. 3, 381–395, 1996.
22. J. Tani. "Model–Based Learning for Mobile Robot Navigation from the Dynamical Systems Perspective," *IEEE Trans. Syst., Man, Cybern., Part B: Cybern.*, vol. 26, no. 3, 421–436, 1996.
23. N. Kubota, T. Morioka, F. Kojima, and T. Fukuda. "Learning of Mobile Robots Using Perception-Based Genetic Algorithm," *Measurement*, no. 29, 237–248, 2001.

24. N. Kubota, F. Kojima, and T. Fukuda. "Self-Consciousness and Emotion for A Pet Robot with Structured Intelligence," In *Proceedings of the Joint 9th IFSA World Congress and 20th NAFIPS International Conference*, 2001, pp. 2786–2791.
25. T. Fukuda, N. Kubota, and T. Arakawa. "GA Algorithms in Intelligent Robots. In *Fuzzy Evolutionary Computation*, Kluwer, Dordrecht, The Netherlands, 1997, pp. 81–105.
26. X. Yao. "Evolving Artificial Neural Networks." *Proc. IEEE*, vol. 87, no. 9, 1423–1447, 1999.
27. W. D. Hillis. "Co-Evolving Parasites Improve Simulated Evolution as an Optimization Procedure." In C. G. Langton, C. Taylor, J. D. Farmer, and S. Rasmussen (ed.), *Artificial Life II*, Addison Wesley, Reading, MA, 1991, pp. 313–324.
28. J. Paredis. "Coevolutionary Computation." *Artif. Life*, vol. 2, no. 4, 355–375, 1995.
29. R. Reed. "Pruning Algorithms—A Survey." *IEEE Trans. Neural Networks*, vol. 4, no. 5, 740–747, 1993.
30. T. Y. Kwok and D. Y. Yeung. "Constructive Algorithms for Structure Learning in Feedforward Neural Networks for Regression Problems." *IEEE Trans. Neural Networks*, vol. 7, no. 5, 1168–1183, 1996.
31. M. T. Turvey and R. E. Shaw. "Ecological Foundations of Cognition I. Symmetry and Specificity of Animal-Environment Systems." *J. Consciousness Stud.*, vol. 6, no. 11–12, 95–110, 1999.
32. R. E. Shaw and M. T. Turvey. "Ecological Foundations of Cognition II. Degree of Freedom and Conserved Quantities in Animal-Environment Systems." *J. Consciousness Stud.*, vol. 6, No. 11–12, 111–123, 1999.
33. L. A. Zadeh. "Fuzzy Sets." *Inf. Control*, vol. 8, 338–353, 1965.
34. C. C. Lee. "Fuzzy Logic in Control Systems: Fuzzy Logic Controller—Part I and Part II." *IEEE Trans. Syst. Man, Cybern.*, vol. 20, no. 2, 404–435, 1990.
35. T. Caelli, L. Guan, and W. Wen. "Modularity in Neural Computing." *Proc. IEEE*, vol. 87, no. 9, 1497–1518, 1999.
36. G. A. Carpenter and S. Grossberg. "The ART of Adaptive Pattern Recognition by a Self-Organizing Neural Network." *Computer*, vol. 21, 77–88, 1988.
37. T. Kohonen. *Self-Organization and Associative Memory.* Springer-Verlag, Berlin, 1984.
38. G. Hinton and T. J. Sejnowski. *Unsupervised Learning*, MIT Press, Cambridge, MA, 1999.
39. D. B. Fogel. *Evolutionary Computation*, IEEE Press, New York, 1995.
40. J. Holland. *Adaptation in Natural and Artificial Systems*, University of Michigan Press, Ann Arbor, 1975.
41. D. E. Goldberg. *Genetic Algorithms in Search, Optimization, and Machine Learning*, Addison-Welsey, Reading, MA, 1989.
42. G. Rudolph. "Convergence Analysis of Canonical Genetic Algorithm." *IEEE Trans. Neural Network*, vol. 5, no. 1, 61–101, 1994.
43. J. Koza. *Genetic Programming*, MIT Press, Cambridge, MA, 1992.
44. J. Koza. *Genetic Programming II*, MIT Press, Cambridge, MA, 1994.
45. W. T. Miller, R. S. Sutton and P. J. Werbos. *Neural Networks for Control*, MIT Press, Cambridge, MA, 1990.
46. J. N. Tsitsiklis and B. V. Roy. "An Analysis of Temporal-Difference Learning with Function Approximation." *IEEE Trans. Autom. Control*, vol. 42, no. 5, 674–690, 1997.
47. D. Whitley, T. Starkweather, and T. Bogart. "Genetic Algorithms and Neural Networks: Optimizing Connection and Connectivity." *Parallel Comput.*, vol. 14, 347–361, 1990.

CHAPTER 10

COMPUTATIONAL INTELLIGENCE IN LOGISTICS

HANS-JÜRGEN ZIMMERMANN

10.1 INTRODUCTION

There is no doubt that logistics is an area that has already demonstrated its importance and that will become even more important in the future. Even though information transfer is moving more and more from physical transportation (letters, etc.) to electronic transmittal in the framework of electronic business, electronic market places, etc., all goods that have been ordered electronically and all persons who want to get from one place to another will have to move or be moved physically.

Transportation logistics is a rather heterogeneous area. It includes public transportation, traffic management (i.e., the control and guidance of streams of individual drivers), fleet management, in-house-logistics (hubs, industrial companies, container and other harbors, hospitals), and other more specific areas. Problems in the different areas of logistics differ to various degrees from each other. They have, however, a number of common features: The standard (model) problems in transportation logistics, such as routing, dispatching, assignment, normally require the solution of large combinatorial problems; they are very often very complex and not perceived easily by human beings; they include considerable uncertainty and they differ from each other in the specific context, i.e., solutions to these problems have to satisfy various constraints, which are very often imposed by human requirements and are therefore not crisp but fuzzy and changing rapidly. In addition, many of these problems have to be solved almost on-line and therefore require very fast computations.

Computational intelligence, i.e., fuzzy technology, neural nets, and evolutionary computation, offers a number of features that, sometimes in combination with classic methods, are very well suited to solving problems of transportation logistics better than has been possible until now. In particular, these are:

Computational Intelligence: The Experts Speak. Edited by D. B. Fogel and C. J. Robinson
ISBN 0-471-27454-2

- *Uncertainty Modeling* Here fuzzy technology offers various ways to model uncertainties that are not random, but rather linguistic in character. These can be modeled in a more adequate way than using, for instance, probability theory.
- *Relaxation* Often problems are not dichotomous in character. Many traditional mathematical methods, however, (such as linear programming and cluster methods), rely on dual logic and therefore can only be applied properly to models with dichotomous elements (such as clusters and constraint solution spaces). Fuzzy technology has been used extensively to generalize optimization methods, so they can be applied to nondichotomous models, without losing their computational power.
- *Compactification* Due to the limited capacity of human short-term memory and the way human beings perceive reality, it is often not possible to either store all relevant data or to present masses of data to a human observer in such a way that he or she can perceive the information contained in these data. This very often leads to situations in which relevant information is "hidden" in these data without being available to the human observer. Fuzzy technology has been used to reduce the complexity of data to an acceptable degree, usually either via linguistic variables or via fuzzy data analysis. In this respect, neural nets can also be used, since they are particularly suited for pattern recognition, which is also a kind of complexity reduction.
- *Meaning Preserving Reasoning* Expert systems technology already has been used for three decades and has in many cases led to disappointment. One of the reasons for this might be that expert systems in their inference machines, if they are based on dual logic, perform symbol processing (they process truth values and not knowledge). Fuzzy set theory has been used to "expand" dual logic by "linking" the meanings to the statements and words in the rule. Then, of course, the inference engine also has to be able to process meanings rather than symbols. This way of modeling human reasoning is generally referred to as "approximate reasoning."
- *Optimization* Combinatorial optimization is known to be very demanding, and often heuristics have to be used rather than exact optimization methods, in order to determine good solutions to real problems in acceptable time. Here methods of evolutionary computation have proven to be very effective and flexible. They seem to be particularly suited when combinatorial problems have to be solved fast and dynamically, i.e., if problem structures change gradually and the search for a new solution can make use of good solutions that have been determined before. It even has been shown that unsupervised neural nets can be used to determine solutions for the traveling salesman problem (TSP).

It is beyond the scope of this chapter to describe all existing and potential applications of computational intelligence methods to transportation logistics problems. In the following it rather will be attempted to sketch major applications in the most important areas of logistics, to describe exemplarily some typical applications in more detail, and to point to several potential applications of computational intelligence (CI) in logistics that have not yet been tapped. Before considering the different areas, it might be useful to define what is meant by "application": application may mean the application of one theory to another. For instance, applying fuzzy set theory to linear programming yields fuzzy linear programming. It can also mean applying one theory to a model. For instance, applying fuzzy linear programming to an inventory model can also be called an application. Eventually application can mean the application of theories or models to real-world problems. In the rest of this chapter application, if not stated otherwise, always has the latter interpretation, i.e., real-world applications.

10.2 TRAFFIC MANAGEMENT

Four major fields of traffic management can be distinguished: (1) traffic supervision, traffic condition forecasting, and evaluation; (2) modeling of individual driving behavior; (3) choice of optimal routes; (4) traffic control.

1. *Traffic Supervision* There are hardly any publications in this area, but some systems exist and work. They collect information about the traffic flow (particularly on expressways), merge this information with other data, evaluate the traffic condition, and forecast traffic conditions in other parts of the traffic network. On the basis of these forecasts, either suggestions for route choices are broadcast to the traffic participants, or the speed limits posted (in central Europe, for instance, every kilometer) are set so as to avoid traffic jams and accidents. Fuzzy data analysis and neural nets are used for judging and evaluating traffic conditions. Fuzzy control is used to determine automatically the optimal maximum speeds posted. At least two companies also offer systems for optimal guidance to parking facilities in large cities (predicting the number of empty parking slots at the time of arrival of a car). In 1998 and 1999, two big projects were sponsored by German governmental agencies to compare classic systems with those based on fuzzy control. Both projects came to the conclusion that fuzzy systems were superior to classic ones, particularly in specific traffic conditions. Many potential applications in this area have not yet been tapped, presumably due to the current shortage of finances of public institutions.
2. *Modeling of Individual Driving Behavior* Some empirical research has been done on modeling individual driving behavior with fuzzy models. Results of this research have been entered as input into projects that tried to model traffic network models. However, no practical applications are known so far.
3. *Route Choice Behavior* Fuzzy approaches that have focused during the last three decades on this problem can be classified into cost-minimizing and ranking approaches. They have not yet had any important impact on existing systems.

4. *Traffic Control* This is certainly the most interesting and also most heterogeneous contribution that CI has made to traffic management. One of the problems considered most often is that of intersection control. Applications are based primarily either on simulation or knowledge-based fuzzy models, i.e., on fuzzy control models [1]. Landenfield and Cremer [2] compare conventional systems with fuzzy systems and conclude that the latter reduce traffic jams considerably in urban traffic networks. Another problem that is considered quite often (particularly in The Netherlands) is that of ramp metering control. These systems are either based on fuzzy control (see, for instance, [3]), or they use the difference between the capacity of the highway and the existing traffic flow to control the access to the highway [4]. Two conventional systems and one fuzzy system, all of them installed on Dutch superhighways, were compared by HEIDEMIJ Consultants. The fuzzy system was clearly superior to the conventional ones. More complex than these are systems that are designed to control entire traffic networks in a coordinated way (see, for instance, [5]). They normally include various fuzzy methods, neural nets, sometimes evolutionary algorithms, and other classic optimization and control algorithms. They are by far too complex to be described in this short chapter.

10.3 FLEET MANAGEMENT

Theoretically, fleet management means assigning schedules to vehicles or drivers. Since a fleet consists of many elements (trucks, ships, etc.), the locations that must be served by these elements need to be distributed to the elements (these are called *tours*), and for each element a sequence has to be determined according to which locations have to be visited. This is called a *route*. No matter whether a route-first–cluster-second or a cluster-first–route-second approach is used, the routing problem always constitutes a combinatorial problem. The best-known model for this type of problem is the so-called traveling salesman problem, of which many variants exist and for which a great many solution methods have been invented. One of these methods is genetic programming. It has even been shown that unsupervised neural nets can be used to solve this problem. Which of these methods is the best depends a great deal on the context. Particularly, time windows and other types of constraints imposed on the route greatly influence the suitability of the respective methods. Traditionally, it is assumed that in a TSP each location is only visited exactly once and that the mobile element arrives at the starting point at the end of its route. This, however, is not always true in practice. Other structures, in which, for instance, each location can be well and a sink at the same time happen frequently in in-house logistics, and will therefore be discussed in Section 10.4.

Here another type of fleet-management problem shall be described, in which fuzzy set theory was applied differently:

A big shipping company had 11 container ships sailing between different continents. Those ships carried normal containers and refrigerated containers. It usually happened

> that empty containers accumulated where they were not needed and there was a need for empty containers where they were not available. Frozen beef was, for instance, shipped in refrigerated containers from Australia to the west coast of the United States, but none of those containers was needed for shipments back to Australia. Since the shipment of empty containers caused only costs but no profits, captains were reluctant to accept empty containers as long as profitable full containers were available. Hence this fleet-management problem was actually an investment or inventory problem: The goal was to determine the number of empty and full containers (simple and refrigerated) of different sizes that should be loaded onto a specific container ship traveling between specific harbors at a specific time. The aim was to maximize profit and to take into consideration the dynamically changing demand for containers in all harbors, the dynamically changing inventories of containers in harbors, the capacities of the ships, and their travel schedules.

This problem was modeled as a mixed-integer linear program. For 10 routes, 20 periods, and 10 different types of containers the model had 21,000 variables and 15,000 constraints and upper bounds. By heuristic considerations, the model could be reduced to approximately 1,500 variables, 1,200 constraints, and 1,700 upper and lower bounds. The solution time on a mainframe turned out to be satisfactory (approximately 9.5 central processing unit (CPU) seconds). When running tests with real data of the past, however, it turned out that the model only generated infeasible schedules. The reason for this was that the capacities of the ships that were actually exactly defined were considered by the captains only as rough guidance. If there were profitable containers waiting at the quay, they were loaded onto the ship, even though they actually exceeded the official capacity. In addition, the travel times were uncertain and the demands could only be predicted approximately. As a consequence, the model was reformulated as a fuzzy linear-programming model in which the constraints were treated as soft constraints (fuzzy relations). Those constraints could be relaxed within tolerance intervals. In contrast to later versions of fuzzy linear programming [6], the relaxation of the constraints were, however, taken into consideration via penalties that were integrated into the objective function. The resulting linear-programming model could be solved as efficiently as normal linear programs and produced well-accepted and feasible schedules for the ships.

10.4 IN-HOUSE LOGISTICS

The last two sections considered logistic problems in a kind of macroscopic way. Logistic problems cause considerable costs inside of companies as well as other units. If one considers the production area in a factory, for instance, then usually each department has its own means of transportation (craddle carriers, fork lift trucks, etc.). These trucks are sent out to get material from other departments and also to bring finished goods to stores. Normally, the transportation capacity is empty one way, resulting in a capacity utilization of around 50%. This is due to the fact that the departments do not know of the transportation requirements of other departments. If control of all means of transportation were centralized, then two possible scenarios would exist: either the material flows are sufficiently steady (in direction and quantity) so that fixed routes can be established on which transportation is carried out regularly, or if this is not possible, in which case the control center faces a very serious problem. In contrast to the traditional TSP structure mentioned in Section 10.2, now each location (department) can be a well and a sink at the same time. In addition, demands for transportation occur irregularly and with different urgency, and the scheduling cannot be done in advance but has to be executed on line. Hence many assignment and scheduling problems have to be solved simultaneously and very fast.

With modern hard- and software, and using a combination of modified traditional operations research algorithms and heuristics, this task can be solved. It has turned out, however, that each application poses several specific demands due to physical conditions as well as context-dependent demands by the users. These demands are generally not crisp, but rather are approximate (as was the case with the ship capacities). Here, however, a closed formulation in the form of a fuzzy algorithmic model can hardly be achieved. Therefore knowledge-based modules that could accommodate necessary modifications of the results such that the additional constraints were satisfied were added to the crisp control system. Since the rules were modeled as fuzzy relations containing linguistic variables, the inference engine had to be able to perform meaning-preserving reasoning rather than only symbol processing.

Earlier, we called it factories. The same basic structure—and the same complications—can also be found in airport ground operations, in big hubs in which parcels have to be reloaded, and even in hospitals. In the latter case, additional (very often fuzzy) constraints have to be taken into consideration, since not only costs, but also the safety of the patients, legal constraints, and other criteria become very important.

The Swedish Medical Center in Seattle, for instance, could reduce the average transportation time for patients from 33 minutes to 22 minutes, reduce the number of mobile sickbeds, reduce space requirements, and safety stock, and at the same time increase the transparency of the system and the safety of the patients.

In order to give the reader an idea of the complexity of such systems, we shall describe one example in more detail: the control of the transport operations of a newly built container harbor. Figure 10.1 shows schematically the basic layout of such a container terminal.

The *real parameters* are: On the *land side* there are six rails (train length up to 2000 feet), 4 rail-mounted gantry (RMGs) Cranes, 200 chassis, and 20 tractors.

The *storage area* contains 22 blocks (each 10 lanes/37 bays/4–5 tiers) = 370 groundslots per block; 2 blocks for "out of gauge containers," and 1 block for empty containers. This amounts to 30,000 TEUs in total (where only 80–90% is used to improve shifting quality). The blocks are covered by 44 RMGs (one pair per block).

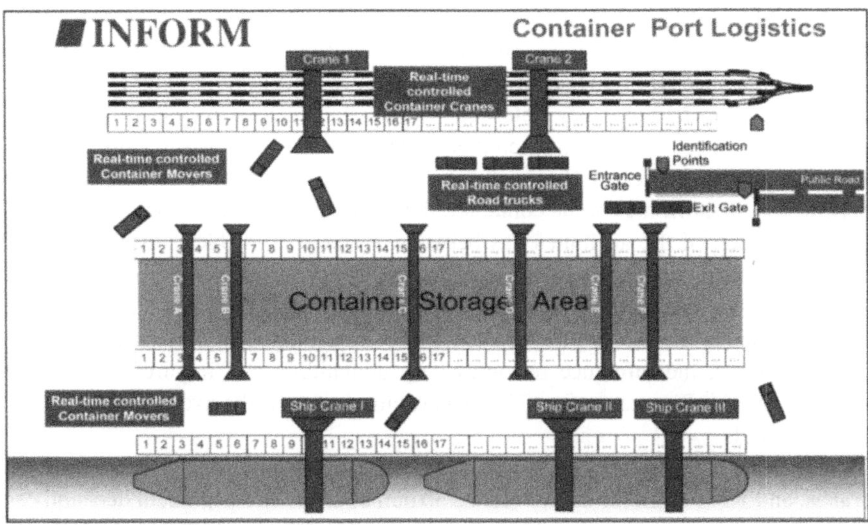

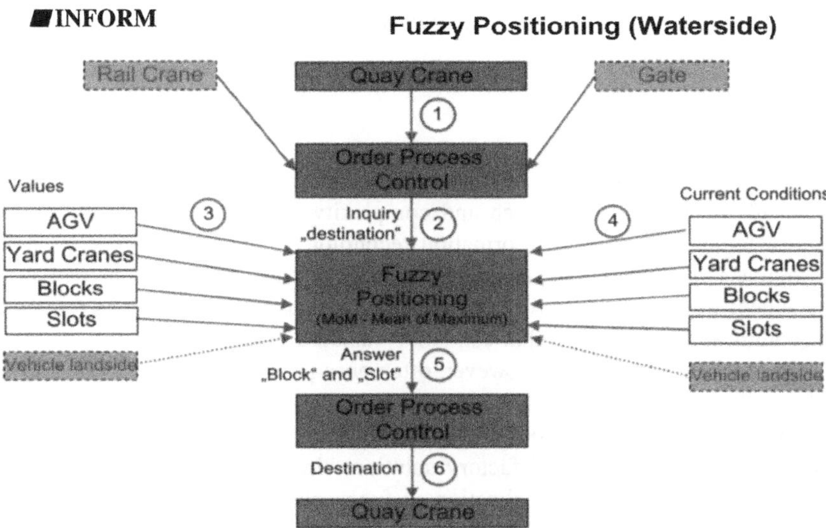

Figure 10.1 Layout of container terminal.

The *waterside* has 4 landing stations for container ships (quay length 4000 feet). Ships are loaded and unloaded by 14 container bridges, and the containers are carried between the container bridges and the blocks of the storage area by 60 automated guided vehicles (AGVs) with a speed up to 15 mph.

Before a container is loaded, for instance, from a container bridge onto an AGV, it has to be determined to which slot in the storage area this container has to be transported. Goals for this decision are to minimize the number of shifting operations (of other containers), to maximize the utilization of the storage space, and to minimize distances from the departure to the delivery location. The slot to which the container is moved obviously determines the distance. Strictly speaking, the distance, for instance, to the train when it is loaded on a train for further transportation, also has to be considered. Hence, the suitability of a slot for a certain container depends on the attributes of the container, the type of slot, and the types of neighboring slots. Each of the attributes has between 3 and 10 possible values, and those values are partly singletons and predominantly fuzzy in nature. Accordingly, they are considered as linguistic variables. On the one hand, this has the advantage that the respective rules are transparent and can be judged by human experts. On the other hand, the inference becomes very demanding and requires an efficient and structured inference engine. This is particularly true if the available time frame is considered.

There are 14 container bridges with cycle times between 45 and 60 seconds, 4 rail cranes, and 12 in-gates for trucks. Hence 30 demands for an assignment decision can arrive during a time interval of 45 seconds. This means that approximately 1 second is available for each decision. It would be very hard, if not impossible, to solve this type of problem with conventional types of algorithms. Approximate reasoning as well as evolutionary algorithms seem, however, to lead to acceptable solutions.

10.5 CONCLUSIONS

Transportation logistics for material as well as for personnel is an important area, and it will increase in importance and complexity in the future, in spite of, or even due to the advances in information technology. It is a heterogeneous field that stretches from traffic management via supply chain management and fleet management to in-house logistics. There exist, particularly in operations research, a large number of algorithms that can solve standard models of logistics, such as the TSP. Practical applications, however, often pose problems that cannot be solved satisfactorily with these methods.

It has been shown that methods of CI can contribute substantially to solving open problems or improving nonsatisfactory solutions. In this chapter, examples were described that reached from application of fuzzy clustering and neural networks in traffic management via fuzzy linear programming in fleet management to approximate reasoning in in-house logistics. It is hoped that those examples indicate the large potential for further scientific developments and for applications in this area.

REFERENCES

1. J. Nittymäki and M. Pursula. "Signal Group Control Using Fuzzy Logic." In *Proceedings of the 9th Mini Euro Conference on Fuzzy Sets in Traffic and Transportation Systems*, Budva, 1997.

2. M. Landenfield and M. Cremer. "Fuzzy Control Strategies for Oversaturated Urban Traffic Networks Using Queue Lengths and Origin Destination Information." In *Proceedings of the 1997 IST World Conference*, Berlin, 1997.

3. T. Sasaki and Akiyama. "Fuzzy On-Ramp Contro Model on Urban Expressway and Its Extension." In *Transportation and Traffic Theory*, Amsterdam, 1987, pp. 377–395.

4. F. Middekham. *Fuzzy Logik Demo*. (in Dutch). Rijkswaterstaat, AVV, Rotterdam, 1992.

5. O. Czogalla and R. Hoyer, "Simulation Based Design of Control Strategies for Urban Traffic Management and Control." In *Proceedings of the 1997 IST World Conference*, Berlin, 1997.

6. H.-J. Zimmerman. "Fuzzy Programming and Linear Programming with Several Objective Functions." *Fuzzy Sets Syst.*, vol. 1, 45–55, 1978.

6a. Heidemij. "Evaluation Toeritdosering met Fuzzy Logic." Research Rep. 672/CE 96/1275/12047 (in Dutch), 1996.

7. C.-K. Lin and G.-L. Chang. "Development of a Fuzzy Expert System for Incident Detection and Classification." *Math. Computer Modelling*, vol. 27, no. 9–11, 9–25, 1998.

8. N. Schretter and J. Hollatz. "A Fuzzy Logic Expert System for Determining the Required Waiting Period after Traffic Accidents." In *Proceedings of 1996 EUFIT*, Aachen, Germany, pp. 2164–2170, 1996.

9. H.-J. Zimmermann. *Fuzzy Set Theory and Its Applications*, 4th ed., Boston, 2001.

CHAPTER 11

TWO NEW CONVERGENCE RESULTS FOR ALTERNATING OPTIMIZATION

JAMES C. BEZDEK and RICHARD J. HATHAWAY

11.1 ITERATIVE OPTIMIZATION

We consider the alternating optimization (AO) method for computing minimizers of a real-valued scalar field $f : \Re^s \mapsto \Re$. We assume throughout that f is a *twice continuously differentiable* function of the vector variable x. Our discussion is restricted to minimization, but the theory is equally applicable to the maximization problem. Our presentation begins with a definition of the nonlinearly constrained optimization problem (NCOP):

$$\min_{x \in \Re^s} \{f(x)\} \qquad \text{(NCOP.1)}$$

subject to

$$c_i(x) = 0, \qquad i = 1, \ldots, k \qquad \text{(NCOP.2)}$$

and

$$c_i(x) \geq 0, \qquad i = k + 1, \ldots, m \qquad \text{(NCOP.3)}$$

The $\{c_i(x)\}$ are *constraint functions* and f is the *objective function* of NCOP; together these are called the *problem functions*. The set of points $\Psi \subseteq \Re^s$ that satisfy all of the constraints at (NCOP.2) and (NCOP.3) is the *feasible region* for NCOP. With Ψ specified, we can replace (NCOP.1–NCOP.3) with the more compact form

$$\min_{x \in \Psi \subseteq \Re^s} \{f(x)\} \qquad \text{(NCOP)}$$

Computational Intelligence: The Experts Speak. Edited by D. B. Fogel and C. J. Robinson
ISBN 0-471-27454-2

Only feasible points can be optimal, and the optimality of a solution x^* of NCOP depends on its relationship to its neighbors. The point x^* is called a *strong local minimizer* when $f(x^*) < f(x)$ for all $x \neq x^*$ in a neighborhood $N(x^*, \delta) \subset \Psi$. The local minimizer is weak when inequality is not strict. A strong or weak local minimizer is a *global* minimizer when the inequality holds for all $x \in \Psi$. Unless qualified otherwise, a "solution" of NCOP means a global solution. Generally, it is very difficult to find a global minimizer of f. However, local solutions of NCOP are usually satisfactory, and as we shall see, are often introduced as an artifact of building iterative optimization algorithms to solve NCOP from its first-order necessary conditions (FONCs).

The simple idea underlying AO is to replace the sometimes difficult joint optimization of f over all s variables with a sequence of easier optimizations involving grouped subsets of the variables. The AO approach begins with a partitioning of $x = (x_1, \ldots, x_s)^T \in \Re^s$ into t subsets of nonoverlapping variables as $x = (X_1, \ldots, X_t)^T$, with $X_i \in \Re^{p_i}$ for $i = 1, \ldots, t, \sum_{i=1}^{t} p_i = s$. For example suppose $s = 8$. The vector variable x might be partitioned into two subsets as $X_1 = (x_1, x_4, x_7)^T$, $X_2 = (x_2, x_3, x_5, x_6, x_8)^T$; or four subsets as $X_1 = (x_4, x_6)^T, X_2 = (x_1, x_2)^T, X_3 = (x_3, x_7)^T$, $X_4 = (x_5, x_8)^T$; and so on. For any reasonable value of s, there are a lot of ways to partition x, so the interesting question of how *best* to choose these subsets is an important issue.

We list a very few examples of alternating optimization that appear in the clustering and mixture decomposition literature: hard c-means [1]; the expectation-maximization algorithm for estimating the parameters in a mixture of normal distributions [2]; fuzzy c-means [3]; fuzzy c-varieties [4]; assignment-prototype (AP) clustering [5]; fuzzy c-shells [6]; fuzzy c-regression models [7]; possibilistic c-means [8]; and optimal completion strategy fuzzy c-means [9].

After a partitioning of x is chosen, AO attempts to minimize the function $f(x) = f(X_1, X_2, \ldots, X_t)$ jointly over all variables by alternating restricted minimizations over the individual sets of vector variables $X_1, \ldots, X_t$. Specifically, AO defines an iterate sequence $\{(X_1^{(r)}, X_2^{(r)}, \ldots, X_t^{(r)}) : r = 0, 1, \ldots\}$ that begins at an initial iterate $(X_1^{(0)}, X_2^{(0)}, \ldots, X_t^{(0)})$ via a sequence of restricted minimizations of the form, for $i = 1, \ldots, t$,

$$X_i^{(r+1)} = \underset{X_i \in \Psi_i \subset R^{p_i}}{\arg\min} \left\{ \begin{matrix} f(\not{X}_1^{(r+1)}, \ldots, \not{X}_{i-1}^{(r+1)} \\ X_i \\ \not{X}_{i+1}^{(r)}, \ldots, \not{X}_t^{(r)}) \end{matrix} \right\} \qquad \text{(AO)}$$

where $\{\Psi_i \subset \Re^{p_i}\}$ are the sets over which the (global) restricted optimizations are done.[1] The strikethrough notation ($\not{X}$) in AO indicates that these vectors are *fixed* with respect to the current subproblem at index i. Values of the variables $X_1, \ldots, X_t$

[1] We use NCOP and AO without parentheses as acronyms: (AO) and (NCOP) with parentheses stand for the equations shown here.

are updated successively via AO for each r as i runs from 1 to t until either a maximum number of iterations on r is reached or there is sufficiently little change between successive iterates. Notice that when $t = 1$, AO reduces to NCOP, and there are no subproblems as in AO. Hence, NCOP is the special case of AO with $t = 1$ where the optimization is done jointly (or directly) in the original variables.

If everything goes just right, a termination point $(X_1^*, X_2^*, \ldots, X_t^*) \in \Re^s$ of AO will be a solution of NCOP. Unfortunately, things can go wrong. To see this, let

$$S_{\text{NCOP}} = \{x^* \in \Re^s : x^* \text{ solves (NCOP)}\}$$

and

$$S_{\text{AO}} = \{x^* = (X_1^*, \ldots, X_t^*) \in \Re^s : x^* \text{ solves (AO)}\}$$

If we put $\Psi = \Psi_1 \times \cdots \times \Psi_t$, iteratively solving (for $r = 0, 1, \ldots$), the t subproblems in AO is sometimes simpler and equivalent in practice to solving NCOP directly. Our hope is, of course, that a termination point of AO solves NCOP, i.e., that $x^* = (X_1^*, \ldots, X_t^*)^T \in S_{\text{NCOP}}$. However, we make two sacrifices when we solve AO instead of NCOP: first, we may find purely local solutions to NCOP, and second, we may sacrifice joint optimality for a weaker result given by the global convergence theory of Section 11.7.

Any x in S_{NCOP} must also be in S_{AO}, but there could be points in S_{AO} that are not in S_{NCOP}. We illustrate this in Example 1, and then give a simple argument that establishes the general case.

Example 1 Consider the unconstrained minimization of $f(x, y) = x^2 - 3xy + y^2$ over $\Re^2$ by AO using the partitioning $X_1 = x$; $X_2 = y$. For this function, S_{NCOP} is empty. To see this, consider the restriction of $f(x, y)$ to the line $y = x$, which gives $g(x) = f(x, x) = -x^2$. Clearly, g has no minimizer, so neither does f. The function f does have a saddle point at $(0, 0)^T$, but this point is *not* in S_{NCOP}. On the other hand, $(0, 0)^T \in S_{\text{AO}}$, since the restricted (global) minimizer (over x) of $f(x, 0) = x^2 - 3x0 + 0^2 = x^2$ is $x = 0$, and the restricted (global) minimizer (over y) of $f(0, y) = 0^2 - 3(0)y + y^2 = y^2$ is also $y = 0$. Since S_{NCOP} is empty and S_{AO} is not, we have $S_{\text{NCOP}} \subset S_{\text{AO}}$ for this example.

To see that S_{NCOP} is *always* a subset of S_{AO}, we prove an even more general result, which answers the question: How does the partitioning of x affect the solution set for AO? Stated roughly, if partitioning $\hat{P}$ is obtained from partitioning P by splitting one or more (P partitioning) vector variables, then all solutions for partitioning P are inherited by partitioning $\hat{P}$, and $\hat{P}$ may have more solutions of its own.

THEOREM 1 Let t satisfy $1 \leq t \leq s$; let P denote a partitioning of $x \in \Re^s$ into $(X_1, \ldots, X_t)^T$; let $\hat{P}$ denote the refined partitioning of x into $(\hat{X}_1, \ldots, (\hat{X}_i, \hat{X}_k), \ldots, \hat{X}_t)$, obtained by splitting one vector variable, say X_i in P, into two parts, $X_i = (\hat{X}_i, \hat{X}_k)$. Now let S_{AO} and $\hat{S}_{AO}$ denote the sets of points in $\Re^s$ solving AO for the partitionings P and $\hat{P}$. Then

$$S_{AO} \subseteq \hat{S}_{AO} \tag{T1}$$

Proof Let $X_i^* = (\hat{X}_i^*, \hat{X}_k^*)$ for the solution $x^* = (\mathbf{X}_1^*, \ldots, \mathbf{X}_{i-1}^*, X_i^*, \mathbf{X}_{i+1}^*, \ldots, \mathbf{X}_t^*)$ $\in S_{AO}$, where k is an index inserted between i and $i+1$ in the original partitioning of x. Since

$$X_i^* = \underset{X_i \in \Psi_i \subset R^{p_i}}{\arg\min} \{f(\mathbf{X}_1^*, \ldots, \mathbf{X}_{i-1}^*, (\hat{X}_i^*, \hat{X}_k^*), \mathbf{X}_{i+1}^*, \ldots, \mathbf{X}_t^*)\}$$

it follows that

$$\text{(i)} \quad \hat{X}_i^* = \underset{\hat{X}_i \in \hat{\Psi}_i \subset R^{p_i}}{\arg\min} \{f(\hat{\mathbf{X}}_1^*, \ldots, \hat{\mathbf{X}}_{i-1}^*, \hat{X}_i, \hat{\mathbf{X}}_k^*, \hat{\mathbf{X}}_{i+1}^*, \ldots, \hat{\mathbf{X}}_t^*)\}$$

and

$$\text{(ii)} \quad \hat{X}_k^* = \underset{\hat{X}_k \in \hat{\Psi}_k \subset R^{p_k}}{\arg\min} \{f(\hat{\mathbf{X}}_1^*, \ldots, \hat{\mathbf{X}}_i^*, \hat{X}_k, \hat{\mathbf{X}}_{i+1}^*, \ldots, \hat{\mathbf{X}}_t^*)\}$$

for otherwise X_i could be altered from X_i^* to a different location so that one or both of conditions (i) and (ii) yield a smaller function value, contradicting the assumption that X_i^* is a global minimizer of the restricted function $f(\mathbf{X}_1^*, \ldots, \mathbf{X}_{i-1}^*, X_i, \mathbf{X}_{i+1}^*, \ldots, \mathbf{X}_t^*)$ over $X_i \in \Psi_i$. This is true for all i, which means that AO is satisfied, and hence that x^* is also in S_{AO}.

Theorem 1 shows that S_{NCOP} and S_{AO} are not necessarily equal. Comparing NCOP at $t = 1$ to AO with $t > 1$, (T1) immediately yields $S_{NCOP} \subseteq S_{AO}$. Since AO reduces to NCOP at $t = 1$, equality holds, at least in this case. It might be that the solution sets for NCOP and AO are equal when $t > 1$, but this must be verified case by case for specific instances. Next we turn to the questions: When are these sets empty? When are they singletons? When do they possess many solutions?

11.2 EXISTENCE AND UNIQUENESS

Perhaps the most important mathematical questions associated with NCOP and AO are *existence* (does any x^* exist?) and *uniqueness* (can more than one x^* exist?). It is impossible to resolve these two issues for a general instance of NCOP. Instead, our analysis will rely on an existence and uniqueness *assumption* for the subproblems comprising the general AO method. Specifically, the notation "=" used in AO implies a property of f, X_i, and Ψ_i for $i = 1, \ldots, t$ that we assume to be true in order to secure proofs of Theorems 2 and 3 stated in Sections 11.6 and 11.7.

EXISTENCE AND UNIQUENESS ASSUMPTION Let $\Psi_i \subseteq \Re^p_i$, $i = 1, \ldots, t$, and let $\Psi = \Psi_1 \times \cdots \times \Psi_t$. Partition $x = (X_1, \ldots, X_t)^T$, where $X_i \in \Re^{p_i}$ and for each $i = 1$ to t, let $g(X_i) = f(\not{X}_1, \ldots, \not{X}_{i-1}, X_i, \not{X}_{i+1}, \ldots, \not{X}_t)$. If $x \in \Psi$ then

$$g(X_i) \text{ has a unique (global) minimizer for } X_i \in \Psi_i \qquad \text{EU}$$

The existence and uniqueness (*EU*) assumption is pretty strong. On the other hand, most instances of NCOP that have been analyzed do possess it. In any case, without these two properties, there can be no convergence theory. Because of the difficulty of establishing EU, many practitioners skip these two questions and proceed directly to the main issue for NCOP, which is: how to find (any) x^*. Our specification of how to search for a solution using AO follows.

11.3 THE ALTERNATING OPTIMIZATION ALGORITHM

Here is a specification of the iteration procedure implied by AO.

AO-1 Let $\Psi_i \subseteq \Re^p_i$, for $i = 1, \ldots, t$, and let $\Psi = \Psi_1 \times \cdots \times \Psi_t$. Partition $x \in \Re^s$ as $x = (X_1, X_2, \ldots, X_t)^T$, with $X_i \in \Re^p_i$ for $i = 1, \ldots, t$, $\cup_{i=1}^t X_i = X$; $X_i \cap X_j = \emptyset$ for $i \neq j$; and $s = \sum_{i=1}^t p_i$. Pick an initial iterate $x^{(0)} = (X_1^{(0)}, X_2^{(0)}, \ldots, X_t^{(0)})^T \in \Psi = \Psi_1 \times \cdots \times \Psi_t$, a vector norm $\|\cdot\|$, termination threshold, ε, and iteration limit, L. Set $r = 0$.

AO-2 For $i = 1, \ldots, t$, compute the restricted minimizer

$$X_i^{(r+1)} = \underset{X_i \in \Psi_i \subset R^{p_i}}{\arg\min} \left\{ \begin{array}{l} f(\not{X}_1^{(r+1)}, \ldots, \not{X}_{i-1}^{(r+1)} \\ X_i \\ \not{X}_{i+1}^{(r)}, \ldots, \not{X}_t^{(r)}) \end{array} \right\} \tag{11.1}$$

AO-3 If $\|x^{(r+1)} - x^{(r)}\| \leq \varepsilon$ or $r > L$, then quit; otherwise, set $r = r + 1$ and go to AO-2.

The AO sequence is well defined if EU holds, which is typically true (but difficult to verify) in practice. When minimizers exist but are not unique, a simple tie-breaking strategy can be incorporated into (11.1) so that the AO sequence is still well defined. The heart of AO lies in finding the restricted minimizers at (11.1). We will discuss some strategies for solving these equations soon, but first, we give an example to illustrate the general idea.

Example 2 We illustrate the AO approach using a simple quadratic objective function. Let $f : \Re^4 \mapsto \Re$ be defined as $f(x) = x^T A x$,

$$f(x) = (x_1, x_2, x_3, x_4)^T \begin{pmatrix} 100 & 80 & 5 & 1 \\ 80 & 90 & 2 & 1 \\ 5 & 2 & 70 & 40 \\ 1 & 1 & 40 & 80 \end{pmatrix} \begin{pmatrix} x_1 \\ x_2 \\ x_3 \\ x_4 \end{pmatrix} \tag{11.2}$$

Table 11.1 AO of $f(X)$ in (11.2) Using $x^{(0)} = (1,1,1,1)^T, L = 100$, Euclidean norm $\|\cdot\|$, $\varepsilon = 0.001$

r	$X_1^{(r+1)}$	$X_2^{(r+1)}$	$\|x^{(r+1)} - x^{(r)}\|$
0	$(-0.1154, 0.0692)^T$	$(0.0083, -0.0036)^T$	2.0251
1	$(-0.0009, 0.0006)^T$	$(0.0000, -0.0000)^T$	0.1337
2	$(-0.0000, 0.0000)^T$	$(0.0000, -0.0000)^T$	0.0011
3	$(-0.0000, 0.0000)^T$	$(0.0000, -0.0000)^T$	0.0000

We want to minimize f over all of $\Psi = \Re^4$, so this is a case of unconstrained optimization. Suppose we choose $X_1 = (x_1, x_2)^T$ and $X_2 = (x_3, x_4)^T$ as the nonoverlapping partitioning of the variables, take $\Psi_1 = \Psi_2 = \Re^2$, and guess $x^{(0)} = (1,1,1,1)^T$ as the point of initialization. It is easily verified that the symmetric matrix in (11.2) is positive definite, which implies that f is strictly convex everywhere in the plane and has $(0,0,0,0)^T$ as its sole minimizer. The restricted minimizers in (11.1) can be found using calculus to find FONCs for each *subset* of variables. Setting the gradient $\nabla_{X_1} f(X_1, \not{X}_2^{(r)})$ to zero ($\in \Re^2$) and solving for X_1:

$$X_1^{(r+1)} = -\begin{pmatrix} 100 & 80 \\ 80 & 90 \end{pmatrix}^{-1} \begin{pmatrix} 5 & 1 \\ 2 & 1 \end{pmatrix} X_2^{(r)} \tag{11.3}$$

Similarly, rearranging $\nabla_{X_2} f(\not{X}_1^{(r+1)}, X_2) = 0 (\in \Re^2)$ gives

$$X_2^{(r+1)} = -\begin{pmatrix} 70 & 40 \\ 40 & 80 \end{pmatrix}^{-1} \begin{pmatrix} 5 & 2 \\ 1 & 1 \end{pmatrix} X_1^{(r+1)} \tag{11.4}$$

The results of iteratively minimizing $f(x)$ at (11.2) by alternately satisfying the FONCs for each subset of partitioned variables are given in Table 11.1, where the numerical results are truncated to four decimal places.

The AO scheme converges very quickly, requiring only four iterations to satisfy the stopping criterion $\|x^{(r+1)} - x^{(r)}\| < 0.001$. The speed of convergence depends on the chosen partitioning of the variables. In fact, every partitioning of the variables in (11.2) except the one used here yields an AO iterate sequence that terminates more slowly (by about an order of magnitude) than the termination seen in Table 11.1 [10].

The quadratic function in Example 2 is easily minimized directly in closed form (or in a single iteration of AO, where the partitioning groups the four variables together as a single subset, $t = 1$). So, Example 2 is not a situation where AO is a good alternative to the direct approach. What Example 2 provides us with is a first look at several important ingredients of the AO approach.

11.4 WHEN IS ALTERNATING OPTIMIZATION A GOOD CHOICE?

Alternating optimization is but one competitor in the race to solve NCOP. There are many, many other ways to look for x^*. Closed-form optimization via the calculus of scalar fields rarely admits a direct solution [11]. More typically, we resort to computational methods such as gradient-based descent in all variables [12–14], and gradient-based AO on subsets of the variables [15–17]. A relatively new set of interesting techniques that eschew the use of optimality conditions from calculus are based on evolutionary computation [18,19]. Finally, there are many data-driven approaches to solving NCOP, such as neural networks [20] and rule-based fuzzy systems [21], that require input–output pairs of *training data* (as opposed to derivative information) to search for solutions to NCOP. In a nutshell, the problems for which AO is worth considering are those for which the simultaneous optimization over all variables is much more difficult than the restricted optimizations of (11.1).

We offer five reasons why AO may be preferable to its competitors when considering a specific instance of NCOP. Some of our assertions are based on computational evidence, while others rest solely on our intuition about differences between NCOP and AO. We believe that AO should be considered:

1. When there is a natural division of variables into t subsets for which explicit partial minimizer formulas exist. This strong reason is exemplified many times in the pattern-recognition literature.
2. When there is a division of variables for which explicit partial minimizer formulas exist for *most* of the variables. This potentially greatly reduces the number of variables that require application of a numerical solution such as Newton's method during each iteration of the AO.
3. Because of savings in *run time*. Hu and Hathaway [22] found that for the fuzzy c-means (FCM) functional, AO in some examples is computationally cheaper (in time) than the best standard optimization routines applied to a reformulated version of the FCM function.
4. Because of savings in *development time*. When explicit formulas exist for AO, it may be easier to program the AO approach than to try to get a general approach written or adapted to the problem. Remember, AO comes with good convergence properties, so no time is wasted trying to pick a good global convergence strategy.
5. Because AO may be more adept at bypassing local minimizers than other approaches. Each restricted iteration of AO is typically global, and is therefore able to hop great distances through the reduced variable space in order to find an optimal iterate. On the other hand, Newton's method builds a model based on the current iterate, and in this sense is more trapped by local information about the function. For example, if the axes in Example 1 are rotated 45 degrees in the x-y plane, then $(0,0)^T$ would still be a saddle point of f, but it would no longer satisfy the AO conditions and would therefore not be "findable" using AO!

11.5 HOW DO WE SOLVE (11.1)?

The search for solutions to NCOP or AO is almost always made by an iterative algorithm. An *iteration function* $T : \Re^s \mapsto \Re^s$ generates an infinite sequence

$\{x^{(r+1)} = T(x)^{(r)}: r = 0, 1, \ldots, \}$ of approximations to x^*. The choice of T can be guided to some extent by classifying the problem functions and their derivatives. Gill et al. [13] itemize the following factors: number of variables, constraints on the variables, smoothness of the problem functions and their derivatives, highest level of derivatives that can be coded efficiently, sparseness of the Hessian and Jacobian matrices, number of general linear constraints compared to the number of variables, number of constraints likely to be active at a solution, and whether the problem functions can be evaluated outside the feasible region.

Most of the problems we see in practice can be usefully subdivided into five categories in a slightly different way, depending on whether the constraints are missing or not, linear or not, and equality or not. The easiest case is the unconstrained problem ($\Psi = \Re^s$). A pair of cases of intermediate difficulty occurs when there are (only) one or more equality constraints (linear or not); and the most difficult cases occur when there are one or more (linear or not) inequality constraints, as at (NCOP.3). The type of constraints will lead us to algorithms based on necessary conditions for the unconstrained theory, or to the Kuhn–Tucker conditions for any of the four constrained cases.

In all of these cases iterative algorithms are most often defined via optimality conditions associated with the first two derivatives of f. The first and second derivatives of f at a point $x \in \Re^s$ are represented by, respectively, the *gradient vector* $(\nabla f(x))$ and *Hessian matrix* $(H_f(x))$. Zeroing the gradient of f (or possibly its LaGrangian) at x^* provides FONCs for x^*. The necessary conditions provide equations on which to base iterative search algorithms that seek an $x^* \in \Psi$ to solve either NCOP or AO. The Hessian of f at x^* may also play a useful role in algorithmic development, and its eigenstructure is useful in determining the type of point found by an algorithm.

We used solutions of the FONCs for minimizing each of the restricted functions in Example 2 to define the steps of the AO illustrated by the iterate sequence in Table 11.1. Equations (11.3) and (11.4) capture the basic structure of almost all AO algorithms. Equation (11.3) gives $X_1^{(r+1)} = F_1(X_2^{(r)})$, and conversely, equation (11.4) gives $X_2^{(r+1)} = F_2(X_1^{(r+1)})$. The iteration function $T : \Re^s \mapsto \Re^s$ in this example is the vector field $T = (F_1, F_2)$.

The functions F_1 and F_2 are obtained by solving the FONCs for equations that are satisfied by any stationary point (point at which the gradient vanishes) of each restricted function. In Example 2, this strategy leads us to $X_1^{(r)}$ and $X_2^{(r)}$ as explicit functions of each other. Thus, given either estimate, we can compute the "other half" directly.

To illustrate this point, we exhibit the general situation for the easiest case, viz., unconstrained optimization, $\Psi = \Re^s$. We want to compute restricted minimizers

$$X_i^{(r+1)} = \underset{X_i \in \Psi_i \subset R^{p_i}}{\arg\min} \left\{ \begin{array}{l} f(\mathbf{X}_1^{(r+1)}, \ldots, \mathbf{X}_{i-1}^{(r+1)} \\ X_i \\ \mathbf{X}_{i+1}^{(r)}, \ldots, \mathbf{X}_t^{(r)}) \end{array} \right\}$$

for $i = 1, 2, \ldots, t$. The necessity for the gradients of these t restricted functions to vanish at any candidate solution leads to a set of t coupled equations:

$$\nabla f_{X_1}(X_1, \cancel{X}_2^{(r)}, \ldots, \cancel{X}_i^{(r)}, \ldots, \cancel{X}_t^{(r)}) = 0 \tag{11.5a}$$

$$\nabla f_{X_i}(\cancel{X}_1^{(r+1)}, \ldots, \cancel{X}_{i-1}^{(r+1)}, X_i, \cancel{X}_{i+1}^{(r)}, \ldots, \cancel{X}_t^{(r)}) = 0 \tag{11.5i}$$

$$\nabla f_{X_t}(\cancel{X}_1^{(r+1)}, \cancel{X}_2^{(r+1)}, \ldots, \cancel{X}_{t-1}^{(r+1)}, X_t) = 0 \tag{11.5t}$$

There are two possibilities for the system of equations at (11.5). When we can solve each equation explicitly for the active variables as functions of the remaining variables (this happens more often than you might suspect!), system (11.5) leads to

$$X_1^{(r+1)} = F_1(X_2^{(r)}, \ldots, X_i^{(r)}, \ldots, X_t^{(r)}) \tag{11.6a}$$

$$X_i^{(r+1)} = F_i(X_1^{(r+1)}, \ldots, X_{i-1}^{(r+1)}, X_{i+1}^{(r)}, \ldots, X_t^{(r)}) \tag{11.6i}$$

$$X_t^{(r+1)} = F_t(X_1^{(r+1)}, \ldots, X_i^{(r+1)}, \ldots, X_{t-1}^{(r+1)}) \tag{11.6t}$$

System (11.6) is the basis of *explicit* AO. Equations (6.11) allow us to immediately define the iteration function $T : \Re^s \mapsto \Re^s$ as the vector field $T = (F_1, F_2, \ldots, F_t)$, so that $x^{(r+1)} = T(x^{(r)}), r = 0, 1, \ldots$. Less cooperative problem functions yield a system at (11.5) that cannot be (completely) solved explicitly. We call this situation *Implicit* AO. In this case system (11.6) can look pretty intimidating, since one or more subsets of variables will appear on both sides of their subproblem equations. We suspect that some readers have arrived at a system like (11.5) in their research, but found it to be implicit, leading them to conclude that AO could not be used to solve their problem. AO in this harder case is still possible, but requires an additional level of effort, namely, *numerical solution* of each implicit necessary condition at each iteration. This sounds very bad, but sometimes it looks worse than it is. This harder type of alternating optimization is encountered, for example, in the fuzzy c-shells clustering algorithm [6]. But, each alternation through the implicit FONCs for this model requires but one iteration of Newton's method at each half step for maximum attainable convergence speed [23], so things may not be as bad as they seem.

Many, if not most, readers are automatically conditioned to think of AO in terms of iterative methods based on searching through the FONCs for the problem. When we zero gradients as in (11.5) to arrive at this stage, we get optimality conditions that identify all the stationary points of f, comprising its extrema (local minima and maxima), as well as its saddle points. While most examples in the literature define AO equations by zeroing gradients, the restricted AO minimizations are being done globally. This does not mean that AO will terminate at a global minimizer of f, but it does mean that points of convergence will *look like* global minimizers when viewed (with the blinders we put on when we partition x into t subsets) along the $X_1, \ldots, X_t$ coordinate directions. This is exactly how $(0,0)^T$ looks (like a global minimizer) for $f(x, y)$ in Example 1 if we look from $(0,0)^T$ in the $X_1 = x$ coordinate direction (by itself) and then look along the $X_2 = y$ coordinate direction (by itself).

Are the stationary points of f in AO and NCOP the same? To answer this question, let

$$E_{\text{NCOP}} = \{x^* \in \Re^s : \nabla f_x(x^*) = 0\} \qquad \text{and}$$
$$E_{\text{AO}} = \{x^* = (X_1^*, \ldots, X_t^*) \in \Re^s : \nabla f_{X_k}(x^*) = 0 \; \forall \; k\}$$

Points in E_{AO} are determined by choosing to break the bigger gradient given by the condition for membership in E_{NCOP} into smaller pieces. In both cases the sets consist of points in $\Re^s$ for which all partials of f with respect to $X_1, X_2, \ldots, X_t$ are 0. So these two sets are equal, $E_{\text{NCOP}} = E_{\text{AO}}$. In particular, any saddle point of f found by AO is certainly a saddle point of f. Moreover, there is not a saddle point or minimizer for AO other than a point that satisfies the conditions in AO. A tricky point in this regard is that f can have saddle points that can never be found by AO, because they do not look like a minimizer when viewed along the coordinate axis restrictions defined by the partitioning $X_1, \ldots, X_t$.

The problem of local solutions and saddle points for NCOP and AO is in some sense introduced by users who base their methods on FONCs, and hence, search for stationary points of f. This is not to say that, for example, a genetic algorithm approach to the solution of NCOP or AO, which eschews the FONCs in favor of a search based on other conditions, always avoids unwanted stationary points of f. But on the face of it, it is more likely that optimization of f using a method that is not guided by necessary conditions for a stationary point will not be so trapped.

11.6 LOCAL CONVERGENCE OF ALTERNATING OPTIMIZATION

A *local convergence result* is one that gives the properties of $\{x^{(r)}\}$ if the initial point $x^{(0)}$ is chosen sufficiently close to a solution. Often, local convergence theory also determines the "speed" with which $\{x^{(r)}\}$ converges. A sequence of vectors $\{x^{(r)}\}$ converges q-linearly to a limit point $x^* \Leftrightarrow \exists \; n_o \geq 0; \exists \; \rho \in [0, 1), \ni \forall \; k \geq n_o$,

$$\|x_{k+1} - x^*\| \leq \rho \, \|x_k - x^*\| \tag{11.7}$$

The q stands for "quotient," and is used to distinguish this type of convergence from the weaker notion of root (or r) orders of convergence. If an iterative algorithm converges to the correct answer at a certain rate when started close enough to the answer, the algorithm is *locally convergent* at that rate. Algorithms may be faster than q-linear; for example, q-superlinear, q-quadratic, q-cubic. Certainly "bragging rights" accrue to the iterative method with the fastest rate.

We are tempted to place more confidence in a method with a faster rate, on the presumption that we can get closer to a solution in a reasonable time than when a slower method is used. However, the theoretical conditions whereby an iterative method actually achieves its convergence rate can be very rare, and in almost all cases, the theory specifies "starting close enough" to a solution. This places a heavy burden on the initial guess, one that cannot often be verified in practice. It may be that most of the value in having convergence rates lies with the psychological reassurance they provide users (and, of course, the papers and grants they generate for the authors that secure the theory).

AO was shown to be locally, q-linearly convergent for the special case $t = 2$ by Bezdek et al. [24]. Hathaway and Bezdek [25] established that local q-linear convergence was maintained even if restricted minimizations for one of the vector variables was only done approximately, using a single iteration of Newton's method. Recently, the local theory was extended to the case $t = 3$ [26]. Our new result completes the local theory, by giving a proof of local convergence for an arbitrary partitioning of x, i.e., all values of t, $2 \leq t \leq s$. Reference [10] contains a full proof of Theorems 2 and 3; here we provide proofitos that should suffice to guide the interested reader toward the formal arguments.

THEOREM 2 (Local Convergence of AO) Let x^* be a local minimizer of $f : \Re^s \mapsto \Re$ for which $\nabla^2 f(x^*)$ is positive definite, and let N be an open neighborhood of x^* on which f is C^2 and strictly convex. If $y = (\not{X}_1, \ldots, \not{X}_{i-1}, Y_i, \not{X}_{i+1}, \ldots, \not{X}_t)^T \in N$, and Y_i^* locally minimizes $g_i(Y_i) = f(\not{X}_1, \ldots, \not{X}_{i-1}, Y_i, \not{X}_{i+1}, \ldots, \not{X}_t)$, then Y_i^* is also the unique global minimizer of g_i. Then there exists an open neighborhood N^* of x^* such that for any $x^{(0)} \in N^*$, the corresponding AO iterate sequence $\{x^{(r+1)} = T(x^{(r)})\} \to x^*$ q-linearly.

Proofito For notational convenience, let $x^* = 0 \in \Re^s$ and $\Psi_i = \Re^{p_i}$ for $i = 1, \ldots, t$. Let $M_i : \Psi_1 \times \cdots \times \Psi_{i-1} \times \Psi_{i+1} \cdots \times \Psi_t \mapsto \Psi_i$, for $1 \leq i \leq t$, be defined as

$$M_i(\not{X}_i) = M_i(X_1, \ldots, X_{i-1}, X_{i+1} \ldots, X_t) = \underset{X_i \in \Psi_i \subset \Re^{p_i}}{\arg\min} \{f(X_1, \ldots, X_i \ldots, X_t)\} \quad (11.8)$$

For each M_i in (11.8), define $C_i : \Psi \mapsto \Psi$ and $T : \Re^{p_1} \times \cdots \times \Re^{p_t} \mapsto \Re^{p_1} \times \cdots \times \Re^{p_t}$, for $1 \leq i \leq t$; (T corresponds to one complete outer iteration of AO) as

$$C_i(X_1, \ldots, X_t) = (X_1, \ldots, X_{i-1}, M_i(\not{X}_i), X_{i+1}, \ldots, X_t)^T \quad (11.9)$$

$$T(x) = T(X_1, \ldots, X_t) = C_t \circ C_{t-1} \circ \cdots \circ C_1(X_1, \ldots, X_t) \quad (11.10)$$

The assumptions and Mean Value Theorem imply the existence of $M : \Re^{p_2} \times \cdots \Re^{p_t} \mapsto \Re^{p_1}$, a continuously differentiable function, defined in a neighborhood of $(0, \ldots, 0)^T \in \Re^{p_2} \times \cdots \Re^{p_t}$, satisfying $M(0, \ldots, 0) \in \Re^{p_1}$, and $\nabla_{X_1} f(M(X_2, \ldots, X_t), X_2, \ldots, X_t) = 0 \in \Re^{p_1}$. Using the convexity of f and the uniqueness assumption stated in the theorem, it can be shown that M is in fact the AO function M_1 given in (11.8). The same argument establishes the existence of similar functions M_i in (11.8), and therefore C_i in (11.9), for $i = 1, \ldots, t$. It follows that the composition $T(x)$ in (11.10) exists, is continuously differentiable, and that $T(0) = 0$. Now, with some trouble, the gradient $\nabla T(0)$ can be calculated as $\nabla T(0) = B^{-1}C$, where, for $A_{ij} = f_{X_iX_j}(0)$,

$$B = \begin{pmatrix} A_{11} & 0 & \cdots & \cdots & 0 \\ \vdots & \ddots & \ddots & & \vdots \\ \vdots & & \ddots & \ddots & \vdots \\ \vdots & & & \ddots & 0 \\ A_{t1} & \cdots & \cdots & \cdots & A_{tt} \end{pmatrix} \qquad C = \begin{pmatrix} 0 & -A_{12} & \cdots & \cdots & -A_{1t} \\ \vdots & \ddots & \ddots & & \vdots \\ \vdots & & \ddots & \ddots & \vdots \\ \vdots & & & \ddots & -A_{t-1,t} \\ 0 & \cdots & \cdots & \cdots & 0 \end{pmatrix} \tag{11.11}$$

Theorem 7.1.9 in [12] can be applied to show that $\rho(\nabla T(0)) = \rho = \rho(B^{-1}C) < 1$ if $A = B - C$ is a P-regular splitting. By definition, $B - C$ is a P-regular splitting if B is nonsingular and $B + C$ is positive definite. It is easily shown that B is nonsingular and the symmetric part of $B + C$ is the block diagonal part of the Hessian matrix, $A = H_f(0)$, which is positive definite because A is positive definite. We apply Ostrowski's theorem ([12, Theorem 8.1.7]) to finish the proof. Pick $\delta > 0$ such that $\rho + 2\delta < 1$. There is a vector norm $\|\cdot\|_\delta$ on $\Re^s$ and number $\gamma > 0$ such that for all $x \in B_\gamma = \{x \in \Re^s : \|x\|_\delta < \gamma\}$, $\|T(x)\|_\delta \leq (\rho + 2\delta)\ \|x\|_\delta$. This establishes that for initialization of AO near x^*, the error is reduced by $\rho + 2\delta < 1$ at each iteration, which gives local q-linear convergence of $\{x^{(r)}\}$ to x^*.

The result in Theorem 2 is not specific to a particular choice of $2 \leq t \leq s$ and partitioning $(X_1, \ldots, X_t)$ of the input variables x. The actual speed of convergence depends on how much the error is reduced at each iteration, and this in turn depends on which partitioning is used [10]. In other words, Theorem 2 holds for all partitionings of x, but the particular value of ρ that can be used in (11.7) is dependent on the partitioning.

11.7 GLOBAL CONVERGENCE OF AO

Since $\{x^{(r+1)} = T(x^{(r)}) : r = 0, 1, \ldots\}$ is a sequence in $\Re^s$, numerical convergence to a limit point is well defined, $\{x^{(r)}\} \to x^* \Leftrightarrow \{x_i^{(r)}\} \to x_i^* = 1, 2, \ldots, s$. We hope that $\{x^{(r)}\}$ converges, and that it converges to the right thing, a solution of NCOP. In this section we state (with a proof sketch) a *global convergence result*, that is, a result that holds for an arbitrary initialization $x^{(0)} \in \Psi$. Note especially that the word "global" in the phrase "global convergence" refers to the domain of initialization, and does not imply convergence to a global minimum of the objective function.

Global results have been obtained for particular instances of AO, such as the FCM algorithm [27]. Our new convergence result is obtained by application of Zangwill's Convergence Theorem A [17, p. 91). We need iterates that lie in a compact set, and force this to happen by choosing $\Psi_1, \ldots, \Psi_t$ to be compact. While the assumption of compactness is strong, it is usually enforced during implementation, e.g., there are often bounds on the possible values of variables in an optimization routine. Here is the general global result, which holds for all partitionings of x and initializations $x^{(0)}$.

THEOREM 3 (Global Convergence of AO) Suppose that (EU) holds for $f : \Re^s \mapsto \Re$. Let $x = (X_1, \ldots, X_t)^T$, and $\Psi = \Psi_1 \times \cdots \times \Psi_t$, where Ψ_i is a compact subset of $\Re^{p_i}, i = 1, \ldots, t$. Let $T : \Psi \mapsto \Re$ be defined by (11.10) so that $\{x^{(r+1)} = T(x^{(r)} : r = 0, 1, \ldots\}$ denotes the AO iterate sequence begun at $x^{(0)} \in \Psi$. Denote the fixed points of T as

$$\Omega = \{x \in \Psi : x = T(x)\} \tag{11.12}$$

(i) If $x^* \in \Omega$, then $x^* = (X_1^*, \ldots, X_t^*)^T$ satisfies, for $i = 1, \ldots, t$,

$$X_i^* = \arg \min_{X_i \in \Psi_i \subset R^{p_i}} \{f(\mathbf{X}_1^*, \ldots, \mathbf{X}_{i-1}^*, X_i, \mathbf{X}_{i+1}^*, \ldots, \mathbf{X}_t^*)\} \tag{11.13}$$

(ii) $f(x^{(r+1)} \leq f(x^{(r)})$, with equality if and only if $x^{(r)} \in \Omega$;

(iii) Either: (a) $\exists x^* \in \Omega$ and $r_0 \in \Re$, so that $x^{(r)} = x^*$ for all $r \geq r_0$, or (b) the limit of every convergence subsequence of $\{x^{(r)}\}$ is in Ω.

Proofito First, we show (i). Let $x^* \in \Omega$. Since $x^* = (X_1^*, \ldots, X_t^*)^T$ is a fixed point of S, it follows from this and (11.8)–(11.10) that x^* is also a fixed point of C_i, for $i = 1, \ldots, t$, which implies that (11.13) holds. To show the inequality in (ii), we have, using the definition of $T(x)$ in (11.10), that

$$\begin{aligned}
f(x^{(r)}) &= f(X_1^{(r)}, X_2^{(r)}, \ldots, X_t^{(r)}) \geq \min_{X_1 \in \Psi_1} f(X_1, X_2^{(r)}, \ldots, X_t^{(r)}) \\
&= f(X_1^{(r+1)}, X_2^{(r)}, \ldots, X_t^{(r)}) \geq \min_{X_2 \in \Psi_2} f(X_1^{(r+1)}, X_2, X_3^{(r)}, \ldots, X_t^{(r)}) \\
&= f(X_1^{(r+1)}, X_2^{(r+1)}, X_3^{(r)}, \ldots, X_t^{(r)}) \geq \cdots \geq f(X_1^{(r+1)}, \ldots, X_t^{(r+1)}) \\
&= f(x^{(r+1)})
\end{aligned} \tag{11.14}$$

Furthermore, if $x^{(r)} \in \Omega$, then $x^{(r+1)} = x^{(r)}$ and equality must hold in all parts of (11.14). If $x^{(r)} \notin \Omega$, then for at least one value of i, we have $X_i^{(r+1)} \neq X_i^{(r)}$, and in this case, the uniqueness of solutions to arg $\min_{X_i \in \Psi_i} \{f(\mathbf{X}_1^{(r+1)}, \ldots, \mathbf{X}_{i-1}^{(r+1)}, X_i, \mathbf{X}_{i+1}^{(r)}, \ldots, \mathbf{X}_t^{(r)})\}$ implies there must be strictness in (11.14), since

$$f(X_1^{(r+1)}, \ldots, X_{i-1}^{(r+1)}, X_i^{(r)}, \ldots, X_t^{(r)}) > f(X_1^{(r+1)}, \ldots, X_i^{(r+1)}, X_{i+1}^{(r)}, \ldots, X_t^{(r)})$$

Part (iii) is exactly the conclusion of Convergence Theorem A of Zangwill [17, p. 91] applied to alternating optimization. Convergence Theorem A requires verification of three conditions, and we now sketch this verification. The first condition is that all iterates $\{x^{(r)}\}$ must lie in a compact subset, which is trivially true because of our assumption about each Ψ_i. The second condition follows directly from our result (ii). The third condition of Convergence Theorem A is that the iteration mapping, T, must be a closed point-to-set mapping. Since in our case T is a function (which is a special case of a point-to-set mapping), we can establish closedness by demonstrating that T is continuous. Continuity of T is demonstrated by showing that each of its compositional parts $C_1, \ldots, C_t$ is continuous, by adapting the argument in the proof of lemma 5.1 in Zangwill [17, p. 105].

Part (i) of Theorem 3 describes the set of points Ω to which convergence can occur. This set includes global minimizers of f, but it can also contain some purely local minimizers and a certain type of saddle point, viz., a point that behaves like a global minimizer when looking along the various grouped coordinate (X_1, X_2, etc.) directions (as in Example 1). While it is extremely difficult to find examples where convergence occurs to a saddle point rather than a minimizer, they do exist [27]. This potential for convergence to a saddle point is one price alluded to in Section 1 for swapping a difficult joint optimization for a sequence of easier ones involving subsets of the variables.

11.8 CONCLUSIONS

Alternating optimization is intuitively sound and works well in a surprising number of cases. Theorems 2 and 3 capture the fundamental global and local convergence properties of the general case of alternating optimization. Additional assumptions would enable cleaner results. For example, if $f(x)$ is a strictly convex function on $\Re^s$ that has a minimizer x^* at which $H_f(x^*)$ is continuous and positive definite, then AO (with $\Psi = \Re^s$) will converge q-linearly to the minimizer using *any* initialization.

Theorems 2 and 3 can also be applied in some important cases when variable constraints are present. For example, the constraints of subsets of variables summing to one, which are commonly found in clustering methods, can be handled by substituting out the last membership in each constraint. Then, the local theory given here can be applied to the reduced function and variables. The global result is much more flexible regarding constraints than the local; as long as the constraints are handled internal to the calculation of the partial minimizers so that the assumptions hold, then the global convergence result can be applied.

ACKNOWLEDGMENT

Research supported by ONR Grant 00014-96-1-0642.

REFERENCES

1. S. P. Lloyd. "Least Squares Quantization of PCM (originally an unpublished 1957 Bell Labs technical note). reprinted in *IEEE Trans. Inf. Theory*, vol. IT-28, 129–137, 1982.
2. J. H. Wolfe. "Pattern Clustering by Multivariate Mixture Analysis," *Multivar. Behav. Res.*, vol. 5, 329–350, 1970.

3. J. C. Bezdek. *Fuzzy Mathematics for Pattern Classification*, PhD Thesis, Cornell University, Ithaca, NY, 1973.

4. J. C. Bezdek, C. Coray, R. Gunderson, and J. Watson, "Detection and characterization of Cluster Substructure II. Fuzzy c-Varieties and Convex Combinations Thereof," *SIAM J. Appl. Math.*, vol. 40, no. 2, 358–372, 1981.

5. M. P. Windham. "Numerical Classification of Proximity Data with Assignment Measures," *J. Classif.*, vol. 2, 157–172, 1985.

6. R. N. Dave. "Fuzzy Shell-Clustering and Applications to Circle Detection in Digital Images." *Int. J. Gen. Syst.*, vol. 16, 343–355, 1990.

7. R. J. Hathaway and J. C. Bezdek. "Switching Regression Models and Fuzzy Clustering." *IEEE Trans. Fuzzy Syst.*, vol.1, no. 3, 195–204, 1993.

8. R. Krishnapuram and J. M. Keller. "A Possibilistic Approach to Clustering." *IEEE Trans. Fuzzy Syst.*, vol. 1, 98–110, 1993.

9. R. J. Hathaway and J. C. Bezdek. "Fuzzy *c*-Means Clustering of Incomplete Data." *IEEE Trans. Syst., Man, Cybern.*, vol. B31, no. 5, 735–744, 2001.

10. R. J. Hathaway and J. C. Bezdek. "Convergence of Alternating Optimization Algorithms." in review, *IEEE Trans. SMC*, 2003.

11. T. M. Apostol. *Calculus*, Blaisdell, Waltham, MA, 1969.

12. J. M. Ortega and W. C. Rheinboldt. *Iterative Solution of Nonlinear Equations in Several Variables*, Academic Press, New York, 1970.

13. P. E. Gill, W. Murray, and M. H. Wright. *Practical Optimization*, Academic Press, New York, 1981.

14. J. E. Dennis, Jr., and R. B. Schnabel. *Numerical Methods for Unconstrained Optimization and Nonlinear Equations*, Prentice Hall, Englewood Cliffs, NJ, 1983.

15. D. G. Luenberger, *Optimization by Vector Space Methods*, Wiley, New York, 1969.

16. D. G. Luenberger. *Linear and Nonlinear Programming*, 2nd ed., Addison-Wesley, Reading, MA, 1984.

17. W. Zangwill, *Nonlinear Programming: A Unified Approach*, Prentice Hall, Englewood Cliffs, NJ, 1969.

18. D. E. Goldberg. *Genetic Algorithms in Search, Optimization and Machine Learning*, Addison-Wesley, Reading, MA, 1989.

19. D. B. Fogel. *Evolutionary Computation*, IEEE Press, Piscataway, NJ, 1995.

20. R. M. Golden. *Mathematical Methods for Neural Network Analysis and Design*, Bradford Books, MIT Press, Cambridge, MA, 1996.

21. H. T. Nguyen and M. Sugeno (eds.). *Fuzzy Systems: Modeling and Control*, Kluwer, Norwell, MA, 1997.

22. Y. Hu and R. J. Hathaway. "On Efficiency of Optimization in Fuzzy *c*-Means." *Neural, Parallel Scientific Comp.*, vol. 10, no. 2, 141–155, 2002.

23. J. C. Bezdek and R. J. Hathaway. "Numerical Convergence and Interpretation of the Fuzzy *c*-Shells Clustering Algorithms." *IEEE Trans. Neural Networks*, vol. 3, 787–793, 1992.

24. J. C. Bezdek, R. J. Hathaway, R. E. Howard, C. A. Wilson, and M. P. Windham. "Local Convergence Analysis of a Grouped Variable Version of Coordinate Descent." *J. Optim. Theory Appl.*, vol. 54, 471–477, 1987.

25. R. J. Hathaway and J. C. Bezdek. "Grouped Coordinate Minimization Using Newton's Method for Inexact Minimization in One Vector Coordinate." *J. Optim. Theory Appl.*, vol. 71, 503–516, 1991.
26. R. J. Hathaway, Y. K. Hu, and J. C. Bezdek. "Local Convergence Analysis of Tri-Level Alternating Optimization." *Neural, Parallel, Sci. Comput.*, vol. 9, 19–28, 2001.
27. J. C. Bezdek, R. J. Hathaway, M. J. Sabin, and W. T. Tucker. "Convergence Theory for Fuzzy c-Means: Counterexamples and Repairs." *IEEE Trans. Syst., Man, Cybern.*, vol. SMC-17, 873–877, 1987.

CHAPTER 12

CONSTRUCTIVE DESIGN OF A DISCRETE-TIME FUZZY CONTROLLER BASED ON PIECEWISE-LYAPUNOV FUNCTIONS

GANG FENG, DONG SUN, and LOUIS WANG

12.1 INTRODUCTION

Fuzzy logical control (FLC) has recently proved to be a successful control approach for certain complex nonlinear systems; see [1–10], for example. FLC techniques usually decompose the complex system into several subsystems according to the human expert's understanding of the system and use a simple control law to emulate the human control strategy in each local operating region. The global control law is then constructed by combining all local control actions through fuzzy membership functions. Although the method has been practically successful, it has proved extremely difficult to develop a general analysis and design theory for conventional fuzzy control systems. The reason for this is believed to be due to the fact that no mathematical model is available from the conventional fuzzy control design.

Recently, a number of stability analysis and controller design results have appeared in the fuzzy control literature [11–17], where the Takagi–Sugeno (T-S) fuzzy models are used. The stability of the overall fuzzy system is determined by checking a Lyapunov equation or a linear matrix inequality (LMI). It is required that a common positive definite matrix, P, can be found to satisfy the Lyapunov equation or the LMI for all the local models. This is a difficult problem to solve, however, since such a matrix might not exist in many cases, especially for highly nonlinear complex systems. The controller designs are also based on a common positive definite matrix, P, and LMI techniques are used to facilitate the design process. Most recently, a stability result of fuzzy systems using a piecewise-quadratic-Lyapunov function has been reported [18]. It is also demonstrated in the paper that the piecewise-Lyapunov function is a much richer class of Lyapunov-function

Computational Intelligence: The Experts Speak. Edited by D. B. Fogel and C. J. Robinson
ISBN 0-471-27454-2

candidates than the common-Lyapunov-function candidates, and thus it is able to deal with a larger class of fuzzy dynamic systems. In fact, the common-Lyapunov function is a special case of the more general piecewise Lyapunov function.

During the last few years, a number of systematic controller design methods also have been proposed based on the so-called fuzzy dynamic model and a piecewise-continuous Lyapunov function [19–28]. However, for the methods based on the piecewise-Lyapunov function, certain restrictive boundary conditions have to be imposed.

Motivated by the results of piecewise-continuous Lyapunov functions in [18], a stability theorem is developed in this chapter for discrete-time fuzzy dynamic systems based on the piecewise-continuous Lyapunov function. And then one new constructive controller synthesis method is proposed for the fuzzy dynamic systems based on the stability theorem. It should be noted that with this kind of piecewise-Lyapunov function, the restrictive boundary condition existing in those controller designs in [19–28] can be removed and global stability of the resulting closed-loop system can be easily established. Moreover, the design procedure is to solve a set of LMIs that is numerically feasible with commercially available software.

The rest of the chapter is organized as follows. Section 12.2 introduces the discrete-time fuzzy dynamic model, and a new stability theorem is also presented that is crucial for the development of controller synthesis methods. Section 12.3 presents a controller synthesis method for fuzzy dynamic systems based on the new stability theorem. A numerical example is shown in Section 12.4. Finally, conclusions are given in Section 12.5.

12.2 FUZZY DYNAMIC MODEL AND ITS PIECEWISE-QUADRATIC STABILITY

The following fuzzy dynamic model, or the so-called T-S fuzzy model [14–28] can be used to represent a complex continuous-time system with both fuzzy inference rules and local analytic linear models as follows:

$$\begin{array}{lll} R^l: & \text{IF} & x_l \text{ is } F^l_l \text{ AND } \cdots x_n \text{ is } F^l_n \\ & \text{THEN} & x(t+1) = A_l x(t) + B_l u(t) \qquad l \in L := \{1, 2, \ldots, m\} \end{array} \tag{12.1}$$

where R^1 denotes the lth fuzzy inference rule, m the number of inference rules, $F^l_j (j = 1, 2, \ldots, n)$ are fuzzy sets, $x(t) \in \Re^n$ the system state variables, $u(t) \in \Re^p$ the system input variable, and (A_l, B_l) is the lth local model of the fuzzy system (12.1)

Let $\mu_l(x(t))$ be the normalized membership function of the inferred fuzzy set F^l where $F^l = \prod_{i=1}^n F^l_i$ and

$$\sum_{l=1}^{m} \mu_l = 1 \tag{12.2}$$

By using a center-average defuzzifier, product inference, and singleton fuzzifier [14–28], the dynamic fuzzy model (12.1) can be expressed by the following global model:

$$x(t+1) = A(\mu)x(t) + B(\mu)u(t) \tag{12.3}$$

where

$$A(\mu) = \sum_{l=1}^{m} \mu_l A_l, \qquad B(\mu) = \sum_{l=1}^{m} \mu_l B_l$$

$$\mu := \mu(x) := (\mu_1, \mu_2, \ldots, \mu_m)$$

Define m subspaces in the state space as follows,

$$\bar{S}_l = S_l \cup \partial S_l, \qquad l = 1, 2, \ldots, m \tag{12.4}$$

where

$$S_l = \{x | \mu_l(x) > \mu_i(x), \qquad i = 1, 2, \ldots, m, \quad i \neq l\} \tag{12.5}$$

and its boundary

$$\partial S_l = \{x | \mu_l(x) = \mu_i(x), \qquad i = 1, 2, \ldots, m, \quad i \neq l\} \tag{12.6}$$

Then the global model of the fuzzy dynamic system also can be expressed in each subspace as

$$x(t+1) = (A_l + \Delta A_l(\mu))x(t) + (B_l + \Delta B_l(\mu))u(t), \qquad x(t) \in \bar{S}_l \tag{12.7}$$

where

$$\Delta A_l(\mu) = \sum_{i=1, i\neq l}^{m_l} \bar{\mu}_i \Delta A_{li}, \qquad \Delta B_l(\mu) = \sum_{i=1, i\neq l}^{m_l} \bar{\mu}_i \Delta B_{li}$$

$$\Delta A_{li} = A_i - A_l, \qquad \Delta B_{li} = B_i - B_l, \qquad i = 1, 2, \ldots, m_l$$

$\bar{\mu}, \bar{\mu}_2, \ldots, \bar{\mu}_{m_l}$ are m_l membership functions that are not equal to zero when the lth subsystem plays a dominant role.

For convenience, the state space equation (12.7) on the lth subspace is called the lth subsystem. Here the lth subsystem is different from the fuzzy dynamic local model in (12.1) because it considers all interactions among the local models.

For the purpose of stability analysis and subsequent use, the following upper bounds are introduced for the uncertainty term of the fuzzy system (12.7):

$$[\Delta A_l(\mu)]^T [\Delta A_l(\mu)] \leq E_{lA}^T E_{lA} \tag{12.8a}$$

$$[\Delta B_l(\mu)]^T [\Delta B_l(\mu)] \leq E_{lB}^T E_{lB} \tag{12.8b}$$

It is noted that there are many ways to obtain these bounds. Interested readers can refer to [24–28] for details.

With such a state-space partition, the authors in [24–28] proposed a number of controller design methods based on a piecewise-Lyapunov function. The key idea is to design a local controller for each subspace based on the subsystem (12.7), and then to use the piecewise-Lyapunov function to establish the global stability of the resulting closed-loop fuzzy control system. Due to the discontinuity of the function across the boundaries of the subspace, certain boundary conditions are developed to ensure the stability of the system [24–28]. However, most of these boundary conditions are very restrictive in the sense that they are not checkable a priori or are very hard to check. Recently, the authors of [18] independently introduced a different kind of piecewise-Lyapunov function and developed a stability result based on this piecewise-Lyapunov function. The key idea is to make the piecewise-Lyapunov function continuous across the subspace boundaries, and thus avoid the boundary conditions that are encountered in those designs.

However, the state of the discrete-time system might never pass through the region boundaries; instead, the state most likely jumps from one region to another. In such a case, the boundary information, like the matrices F's in [18], cannot be used to characterize the state transition from one region to another, as they were in the case of continuous-time systems. More specifically, it may not be helpful to construct a piecewise-Lyapunov function that is continuous across boundaries for the discrete-time systems to analyze stability of the system as in [18] for the continuous time systems. Nevertheless, it may also be unnecessary to require the piecewise Lyapunov function to be continuous across boundaries for the discrete-time piecewise-linear systems, since the state of such systems might never pass through the boundaries. A novel piecewise-Lyapunov function is introduced in this chapter. This function is guaranteed to be decreasing when the state of the system jumps from one region to another.

THEOREM 1 Consider the fuzzy dynamic system (12.1) with $u \equiv 0$. If there exist a set of small constants $\varepsilon_l, l = 1, 2, \dots m$, a set of positive definite matrices $p_l, l = 1, 2, \dots, m$ such that the following LMIs are satisfied,

$$0 > \begin{bmatrix} -P_l & P_l A_l^T & P_l E_{lA}^T \\ A_l P_l & -(P_l - \varepsilon_l I) & 0 \\ E_{lA} P_l & 0 & -\varepsilon_l I \end{bmatrix}, \qquad l \in L \tag{12.9}$$

$$0 > \begin{bmatrix} -P_l & P_l A_l^T & P_l E_{lA}^T \\ A_l P_l & -(P_j - \varepsilon_l I) & 0 \\ E_{lA} P_l & 0 & -\varepsilon_l I \end{bmatrix}, \qquad l,j \in \Omega \cap L \tag{12.10}$$

where the set Ω represents all possible transitions from one region to another, that is,

$$\Omega := \{l,j | x(t) \in S_l, x(t+1) \in S_j, j \neq l\}$$

then the fuzzy dynamic system is globally exponentially stable, that is, $x(t)$ tends to zero exponentially for every continuous piecewise trajectory in the state space.

Proof Consider the following Lyapunov-function candidate, $V(t)$,

$$V(t) = x^T P_l^{-1} x, \qquad x \in \bar{S}_l, \qquad l \in L \tag{12.11}$$

It is obvious from (12.11) that there exists a constant $\beta > 0$ such that

$$V(t) \leq \beta \, \|x\|^2$$

Moreover,

$$0 < P_l^{-1}$$

which implies that there exists a constant $\alpha > 0$ such that

$$\alpha \, \|x\|^2 \leq x^T P_l^{-1} x$$

for $x \in \bar{S}_l$. Thus one has

$$\alpha \, \|x\|^2 \leq V(t) \leq \beta \, \|x\|^2 \tag{12.12}$$

In addition, using Schur complements, it follows from (12.9)–(12.10) that

$$P_l A_l^T (P_j - \varepsilon_l I)^{-1} A_l P_l - P_l + \frac{1}{\varepsilon_l} P_l E_{lA}^T E_{lA} P_l < 0 \tag{12.13}$$

Notice that

$$\begin{aligned}
&(A_l + \Delta A_l)^T P_j^{-1} (A_l + \Delta A_l) - P_l^{-1} \\
&\quad \leq A_l^T P_j^{-1} A_l - P_l^{-1} + A_l^T P_j^{-1} \Delta A_l + \Delta A_l^T P_j^{-1} A_l + \Delta A_l^T P_j^{-1} \Delta A_l \\
&\quad \leq A_l^T P_j^{-1} A_l - P_l^{-1} + A_l^T P_j^{-1} \left(\frac{1}{\varepsilon_l} I - P_j^{-1} \right)^{-1} P_j^{-1} A_l + \frac{1}{\varepsilon_l} \Delta A_l^T \Delta A_l \\
&\quad \leq A_l^T \left(P_j^{-1} + P_j^{-1} \left(\frac{1}{\varepsilon_l} I - P_j^{-1} \right)^{-1} P_j^{-1} \right) A_l - P_l^{-1} + \frac{1}{\varepsilon_l} E_{lA}^T E_{lA} \\
&\quad \leq A_l^T (P_j - \varepsilon_l I)^{-1} A_l - P_l^{-1} + \frac{1}{\varepsilon_l} E_{lA}^T E_{lA}
\end{aligned} \tag{12.14}$$

It then follows from (12.13) and (12.14) that there exists a constant $\rho > 0$ such that

$$(A_l + \Delta A_l)^T P_l^{-1}(A_l + \Delta A_l) - P_l^{-1} + \rho I < 0$$

where $j = l$ when x stays in the region $\bar{S}_l, l \in L; j \neq l$ when x transits from the region $\bar{S}_l$ to $\bar{S}_j$, with $l, j \in L \cap \Omega$.

Then along trajectories of the system, one has

$$\begin{aligned}\Delta V(t) &= V(t) - V(t-1) \\ &= x^T[(A_l + \Delta A_l)^T P_j^{-1}(A_l + \Delta A_l) - P_l^{-1}]x \\ &\leq x^T(-\rho I)x \\ &= -\rho \|x\|^2 \end{aligned} \tag{12.15}$$

Therefore, the desired result follows directly from (12.12) and (12.15) based on the standard Lyapunov theory.

Remark 1 The set Ω usually can be determined by all possible transitions of the state trajectories. If it is possible for the transitions to occur between all regions, then $\Omega = L^2$, which is defined as a set of $\{l, j \,|\, l, j \in L, j \neq l\}$.

12.3 CONTROLLER SYNTHESIS OF FUZZY DYNAMIC SYSTEMS

In this section, the controller synthesis problem will be addressed for the discrete-time fuzzy dynamic systems introduced in the last section. The proposed controller synthesis approach is based on the local subsystem defined in each subspace. However, the interactions from other subsystems must be accounted for in order to guarantee the stability of the global system. Consider the fuzzy-system model (12.7) on every subspace

$$x(t+1) = (A_l + \Delta A_l(\mu))x(t) + (B_l + \Delta B_l(\mu))u(t), \qquad x(t) \in \bar{S}_l \tag{12.16}$$

For the stabilization of the fuzzy system (12.3), or equivalently (12.16), consider the following piecewise-continuous controller as

$$u(t) = K(x)x = K_l x(t) \qquad x(t) \in \bar{S}_l, \qquad l \in L \tag{12.17}$$

With the control law (12.17), the global closed-loop system is obtained by combining the fuzzy system (12.3) and the controller (12.17), and can be described by the following equation:

$$x(t+1) = A_c(\mu)x(t) \tag{12.18}$$

where

$$A_c(\mu) = A(\mu) + B(\mu)K(x) \tag{12.19}$$

Equation (12.18) can also be expressed in each local subspace as,

$$x(t+1) = A_{cl}(\mu)x(t), \qquad x(t) \in \bar{S}_l \tag{12.20}$$

where

$$A_{cl}(\mu) = A_l + \Delta A_l(\mu) + (B_l + \Delta B_l(\mu))K_l$$

Then the following result can be obtained.

THEOREM 2 The system (12.18) is globally stable if there exist constants $\varepsilon_l > 0$, $l = 1, 2, \ldots, m$, a set of positive definite matrices $P_l, l \in L$, and a set of matrices $Q_l, l \in L$ such that the following LMIs are satisfied:

$$0 > \begin{bmatrix} -P_l & P_l A_l^T + Q_l^T B_l^T & P_l E_{lA}^T & Q_l^T E_{lB}^T \\ A_l P_l + B_l Q_l & -(P_l - \varepsilon_l I) & 0 & 0 \\ E_{lA} P_l & 0 & -\frac{1}{2}\varepsilon_l I & 0 \\ E_{lB} Q_l & 0 & 0 & -\frac{1}{2}\varepsilon_l I \end{bmatrix}, \qquad l \in L \tag{12.21}$$

$$0 > \begin{bmatrix} -P_l & P_l A_l^T + Q_l^T B_l^T & P_l E_{lA}^T & Q_l^T E_{lB}^T \\ A_l P_l + B_l Q_l & -(P_j - \varepsilon_l I) & 0 & 0 \\ E_{lA} P_l & 0 & -\frac{1}{2}\varepsilon_l I & 0 \\ E_{lB} Q_l & 0 & 0 & -\frac{1}{2}\varepsilon_l I \end{bmatrix}, \qquad l, j \in \Omega \cap L \tag{12.22}$$

Moreover, the controller gain for each local subsystem is given by

$$K_l = Q_l P_l^{-1}, \qquad l \in L \tag{12.23}$$

Proof Based on the result in Theorem 1 and its proof, one learns that the system (12.18) is globally stable if there exist positive definite matrices P_l satisfying the following inequalities:

$$0 > A_{cl}^T P_l^{-1} A_{cl} - P_l^{-1}, \qquad l \in L \tag{12.24}$$

$$0 > A_{cl}^T P_j^{-1} A_{cl} - P_l^{-1}, \qquad l, j \in \Omega \cap L \tag{12.25}$$

First we show that the inequality (12.21) implies (12.24). Using Lemma A.1 in the Appendix, the right-hand side of inequality (12.24) can be expressed as

$$
\begin{aligned}
RH &:= A_{cl}^T P_l^{-1} A_{cl} - P_l^{-1} \\
&= [A_l + \Delta A_l + (B_l + \Delta B_l)K_l]^T P_l^{-1} [A_l + \Delta A_l + (B_l + \Delta B_l)K_l] - P_l^{-1} \\
&= (A_l + B_l K_l)^T P_l^{-1} (A_l + B_l K_l) + (A_l + B_l K_l)^T P_l^{-1} (\Delta A_l + \Delta B_l K_l) \\
&\quad + (\Delta A_l + \Delta B_l K_l)^T P_l^{-1} (A_l + B_l K_l) + (\Delta A_l + \Delta B_l K_l)^T P_l^{-1} (\Delta A_l + \Delta B_l K_l) - P_l^{-1} \\
&\leq (A_l + B_l K_l)^T P_l^{-1} (A_l + B_l K_l) + (A_l + B_l K_l)^T P_l^{-1} \left(\frac{1}{\varepsilon_l} I - P_l^{-1} \right)^{-1} P_l^{-1} (A_l + B_l K_l) \\
&\quad + \frac{1}{\varepsilon} (\Delta A_l + \Delta B_l K_l)^T (\Delta A_l + \Delta B_l K_l) - P_l^{-1} \\
&\leq (A_l + B_l K_l)^T \left(P_l^{-1} + P_l^{-1} \left(\frac{1}{\varepsilon_1} I - P_l^{-1} \right)^{-1} P_l^{-1} \right) (A_l + B_l K_l) \\
&\quad + \frac{2}{\varepsilon_l} \Delta A_l^T \Delta A_l + \frac{2}{\varepsilon_l} K_l^T \Delta B_l^T \Delta B_l K_l - P_l^{-1} \\
&\leq (A_l + B_l K_l)^T (P_l - \varepsilon_l I)^{-1} (A_l + B_l K_l) + \frac{2}{\varepsilon_l} E_{lA}^T E_{lA} + \frac{2}{\varepsilon_l} K_l^T E_{lB}^T E_{lB} K_l - P_l^{-1}
\end{aligned}
\tag{12.26}
$$

It then can be easily seen that the following inequality:

$$
(A_l + B_l K_l)^T (P_l - \varepsilon_l I)^{-1} (A_l + B_l K_l) + \frac{2}{\varepsilon_l} E_{lA}^T E_{lA} + \frac{2}{\varepsilon_l} K_l^T E_{lB}^T E_{lB} K_l - P_l^{-1} < 0 \tag{12.27}
$$

is equivalent to

$$
\begin{aligned}
&P_l (A_l + B_l K_l)^T (P_l - \varepsilon_l I)^{-1} (A_l + B_l K_l) P_l + \frac{2}{\varepsilon_l} P_l E_{lA}^T E_{lA} P_l \\
&\quad + \frac{2}{\varepsilon_l} P_l K_l^T E_{lB}^T E_{lB} K_l P_l - P_l < 0
\end{aligned}
\tag{12.28}
$$

Let $Q_l = K_l P_l$, using Schur complement formulas, it is easily shown that inequality (12.28) is in turn equivalent to the linear matrix inequality (12.21). Thus, one has shown that the inequality (12.21) implies (12.24). Following the preceding procedure, it can also be shown that the inequality (12.22) implies the inequality (12.25). Therefore, it can be concluded that the closed-loop control system is globally stable, and thus the proof is completed.

Based on the preceding theorem, the following algorithm can be developed.

ALGORITHM 1

Step 1 Set $\varepsilon_l, l = 1, 2, \ldots, m$ to small constants, say $\varepsilon_l = 1, l = 1, 2, \ldots, m$.

Step 2 Solve the linear matrix inequalities (12.21) and (12.22) for a set of positive definite matrices $P_l, l \in L$, and a set of matrices $Q_l, l \in L$. This can be facilitated by using the Matlab *LMI Toolbox* [29].

Step 3 If the solutions are found, the controller parameters can be obtained by $K_l = Q_l P_l^{-1}, l \in L$, and then stop. Otherwise, set $\varepsilon_l = \varepsilon_l/2$, for those inequalities in (12.21) and (12.22) having no solution, and check whether $\varepsilon_l, l = 1, 2, \ldots, m$ are greater than some given threshold. If this is the case, then go back to Step 2. Otherwise, claim that the present controller design fails.

Remark 2 It should be noted that the conditions expressed in the theorem are only sufficient, and thus the closed-loop control system can still be stable even if the piecewise-Lyapunov function cannot be identified from the preceding controller synthesis Algorithm 1. Therefore, only failure of the present controller design is claimed in the algorithm.

12.4 SIMULATION EXAMPLES

To illustrate the controller synthesis approach, consider the following numerical examples.

Example 1 The fuzzy system is given below,

$$\begin{array}{lll} R^1: & \text{IF} & \text{abs}(x_1(t)) \text{ is greater than abs}(x_2(t)) \\ & \text{THEN} & x(t+1) = A_1 x(t) + B_1 u(t) \\ R^2: & \text{IF} & \text{abs}(x_2(t)) \text{ is greater than abs}(x_1(t)) \\ & \text{THEN} & x(t+1) = A_2 x(t) + B_2 u(t) \end{array} \tag{12.29}$$

where abs(.) denotes the absolute value, and

$$A_l = \begin{bmatrix} 1 & 0.4 \\ -0.5 & 1 \end{bmatrix}, \quad A_2 = \begin{bmatrix} 1 & 0.5 \\ -0.4 & 1 \end{bmatrix}, \quad B_1 = \begin{bmatrix} 0 \\ 1 \end{bmatrix}, \quad B_2 = \begin{bmatrix} 0 \\ 1 \end{bmatrix}$$

The following membership functions are used, if $x_1^2 + x_2^2 \neq 0$,

$$\mu_1 = \frac{x_1^2}{x_1^2 + x_2^2}, \qquad \mu_2 = \frac{x_2^2}{x_1^2 + x_2^2} \tag{12.30}$$

otherwise, $\mu_1 = \mu_2 = 0.5$.

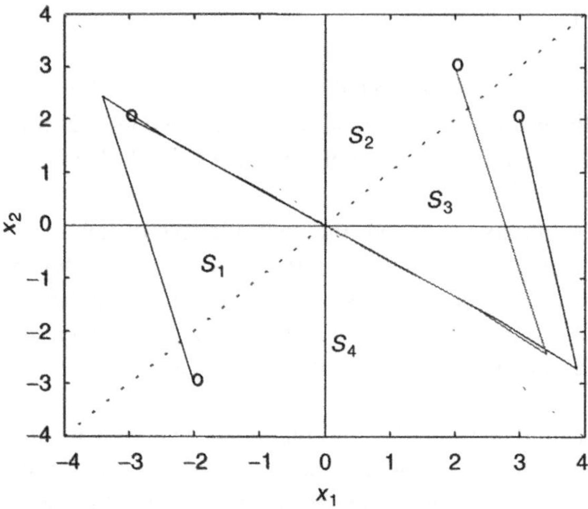

Figure 12.1 Responses of the closed-loop control system.

With the space partition defined in this chapter, the subspaces can be obtained as shown in Figure 12.1. It can also be found that the uncertainties for each subsystem are given as

$$E_{1A} = E_{2A} = 0.5\begin{bmatrix} 0 & 0.1 \\ 0.1 & 0 \end{bmatrix}, \qquad E_{1B} = E_{2B} = 0.5\begin{bmatrix} 0 \\ 0 \end{bmatrix}$$

Using the piecewise-Lyapunov-function approach proposed in this chapter, the following solution has been found for (12.21) and (12.22) LMIs when $\varepsilon_1 = \varepsilon_2 = 1$,

$$P_1 = \begin{bmatrix} 8.5874 & -4.9611 \\ -4.9611 & 9.0390 \end{bmatrix}, \qquad P_2 = \begin{bmatrix} 8.8562 & -5.1421 \\ -5.1421 & 8.6801 \end{bmatrix}$$

$$K_1 = \begin{bmatrix} -0.1905 & -1.2995 \end{bmatrix}, \qquad K_2 = \begin{bmatrix} -0.2945 & -1.3693 \end{bmatrix}$$

It thus follows from Theorem 2 that the stability of the closed-loop control system is guaranteed. The simulation result with a number of initial conditions is recorded in Fig. 12.1.

In order to demonstrate the advantage of the piecewise-Lyapunov-function-based approach proposed in this chapter over the normal common-Lyapunov-function-based approach, the following example will be considered.

Example 2 The following special fuzzy dynamic system is given with the membership functions chosen as either one or zero so that the system actually represents a piecewise-linear system,

$$
\begin{aligned}
R^1: \quad & \text{IF} && \text{abs}(x_1(t)) \text{ is greater than abs}(x_2(t)) \\
& \text{THEN} && x(t+1) = A_1 x(t) + B_1 u(t) \\
R^2: \quad & \text{IF} && \text{abs}(x_2(t)) \text{ is greater than abs}(x_1(t)) \\
& \text{THEN} && x(t+1) = A_2 x(t) + B_2 u(t)
\end{aligned}
\tag{12.31}
$$

where abs($\cdot$) denotes the absolute value, and

$$
A_1 = \begin{bmatrix} 1 & 0.4 \\ -0.5 & 1 \end{bmatrix}, \quad A_2 = \begin{bmatrix} 1 & 0.5 \\ -0.4 & 1 \end{bmatrix}, \quad B_1 = \begin{bmatrix} 0 \\ 1 \end{bmatrix}, \quad B_2 = \begin{bmatrix} 1 \\ 0 \end{bmatrix}
$$

In this case, similar space partitions can be obtained as shown in Figure 12.1. It is noted that in this example, different B's are chosen for the subsystems. It is also noted that there is no solution to the common-quadratic-Lyapunov-function approach. However, if using the piecewise-Lyapunov-function approach proposed in this chapter, then the following solution has been found for (12.21) and (12.22)

$$
\begin{aligned}
P_1 &= \begin{bmatrix} 1.9607 & -0.8576 \\ -0.8576 & 3.2186 \end{bmatrix}, & P_2 &= \begin{bmatrix} 3.2186 & 0.8576 \\ 0.8576 & 1.9607 \end{bmatrix} \\
K_1 &= [0.4038 \quad -1.0444], & K_2 &= [-1.0444 \quad -0.4038]
\end{aligned}
$$

It thus follows from Theorem 2 that the stability of the closed-loop control system is guaranteed. The simulation result with a number of initial conditions is recorded in Figure 12.2.

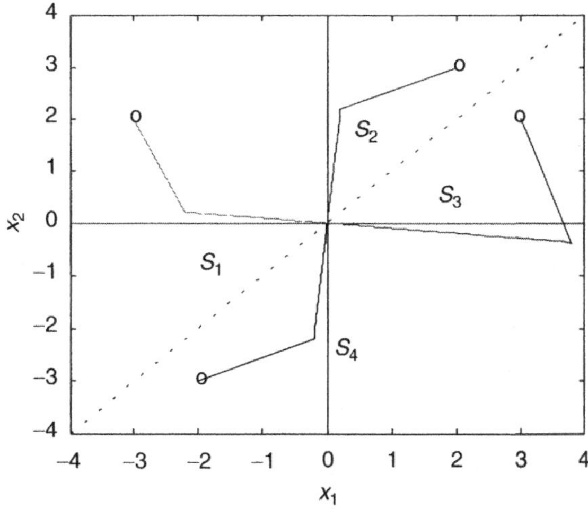

Figure 12.2 Responses of the closed-loop control system.

This example clearly demonstrates the advantage of the piecewise-Lyapunov-function approach to the common-Lyapunov-function approach.

12.5 CONCLUSIONS

In this chapter, a new method is developed to design stable controllers for discrete-time fuzzy dynamic systems based on a piecewise-Lyapunov function. A constructive controller design algorithm is also given based on LMI techniques. Simulation examples are presented to demonstrate the design procedure and the controller performance. It has also been demonstrated through examples that the piecewise-Lyapunov-function-based controller design approach is less conservative than the common-Lyapunov-function-based controller design approach, and thus leads to wider applications. This chapter only shows a simple stabilization control of a T-S fuzzy model. It is believed that the method can be extended to the more general controller design with various performance specifications requirements.

ACKNOWLEDGMENTS

The work described in this chapter was partially supported by a grant from the Research Grants Council of the Hong Kong Special Administrative Region, China [Project No. CityU 1085/01E) and a grant from City University of Hong Kong (Project No. 7001149).

REFERENCES

1. L. A. Zadeh. "Outline of a New Approach to the Analysis of Complex Systems and Decision Processes." *IEEE Trans. Syst., Man, Cybern.*, vol. SMC-3, 28–44, 1973.
2. E. H. Mamdani and S. Assilian. "Applications of Fuzzy Algorithms for Control of Simple Dynamic Plant." *IEE Proc. Part-D*, vol. 121, 1585–1588, 1974.
3. M. Sugeno. *Industrial Applications of Fuzzy Control*. Elsevier, New York, 1985.
4. M. Sugeno and G. T. Nishida. "Fuzzy Control of Model Car." *Fuzzy Sets Syst.*, vol. 16, 103–113, 1985.
5. W. J. Kickert and E. H. Mamdani. "Analysis of a Fuzzy Logic Controller." *Fuzzy Sets Syst.*, vol. 1, 29–44, 1978.
6. R. M. Tong. "A Control Engineering Review of Fuzzy Systems." *Automatica*, vol. 13, 559–568, 1977.
7. M. Sugeno and G. T. Kang. "Structure Identification of Fuzzy Model." *Fuzzy Sets Syst.*, vol. 28, 15–33, 1988.
8. T. Takagi and M. Sugeno. "Fuzzy Identification of Systems and Its Application to Modelling and Control." *IEEE Trans. Syst., Man, Cybern.*, vol. SMC-15, 116–132, 1985.
9. R. Langari and M. Tomizuka. "Analysis and Synthesis of Fuzzy Linguistic Control Systems." In *Proceedings of the 1990 ASME Winter Annual Meeting*, Dallas, Texas, 1990, 35–42.

10. R. Langari and M. Tomizuka. "Stability of Linguistic Control Systems." In *Proceedings of the 29th IEEE CDC*, Honolulu, 1990, pp. 2185–2190.
11. K. Tanaka and M. Sugeno. "Stability Analysis and Design of Fuzzy Control Systems." *Fuzzy Sets Syst.*, vol. 45, 135–156, 1992.
12. K. Tanaka and M. Sano. "A Robust Stabilization Problem of Fuzzy Control Systems and Its Application to Backing up Control of a Truck-Trailer." *IEEE Trans. Fuzzy Syst.*, vol. 2, 119–134, 1994.
13. L. X. Wang. "Stable Adaptive Fuzzy Control of Nonlinear Systems." *IEEE Trans. Fuzzy Syst.*, vol. 1, 146–155, 1993.
14. M. C. M. Teixeira and S. H. Zak. "Stabilizing Controller Design for Uncertain Nonlinear Systems Using Fuzzy Models." *IEEE Trans. Fuzzy Syst.*, vol. 7, 133–142, 1999.
15. H. Wang, K. Tanaka, and M. F. Griffin. "An Approach to Fuzzy Control of Nonlinear Systems: Stability and Design Issues." *IEEE Trans. Fuzzy Syst.*, vol. 4, 14–23, 1996.
16. X. Ma, Z. Sun, and Y. He. "Analysis and Design of Fuzzy Controller and Fuzzy Observer." *IEEE Trans. Fuzzy Syst.*, vol. 6, 41–51, 1998.
17. K. Tanaka, T. Ikeda, and H. Wang. "Fuzzy Regulators and Fuzzy Observers: Relaxed Stability Conditions and LMI Based Design." *IEEE Trans. Fuzzy Syst.*, vol. 6, 250–265, 1998.
18. M. Johansson, A. Tantzer, and K. Arzen. "Piecewise Quadratic Stability of Fuzzy Systems." *IEEE Trans. Fuzzy Syst.*, vol. 7, 713–722, 1999.
19. S. G. Cao, N. W. Rees, and G. Feng. "Analysis and Design for a Class of Complex Control Systems, Part I: Fuzzy Modeling and Identification." *Automatica*, vol. 33, 1017–1028, 1997.
20. S. G. Cao, N. W. Rees, and G. Feng. "Analysis and Design of Fuzzy Control Systems Using Dynamic Fuzzy Global Models." *Fuzzy Sets Syst.*, vol. 75, 47–62, 1995.
21. G. Feng, S. G. Cao, N. W. Rees, and C. K. Chak. "Design of Fuzzy Control Systems Based on State Feedback." *J. Intell. Fuzzy Syst.*, vol. 3, 295–304, 1995.
22. G. Feng, S. G. Cao, N. W. Rees, and C. K. Chak. "Design of Fuzzy Control Systems with Guaranteed Stability." *Fuzzy Sets Syst.*, vol. 85, 1–10, 1997.
23. G. Feng, S. G. Cao, and N. W. Rees. "An approach to H_∞ Control of a Class of Nonlinear Systems." *Automatica*, vol. 32, no. 10, 1469–1474, 1996.
24. S. G. Cao, N. W. Rees, and G. Feng. "Analysis and Design for a Class of Complex Control Systems, Part II: Fuzzy Controller Design." *Automatica*, vol. 33, 1029–1039, 1997.
25. S. G. Cao, N. W. Rees, and G. Feng. "Analysis and Design for a Class of Continuous-Time Fuzzy Control Systems." *Int. J. Control*, vol. 64, 1069–1087, 1996.
26. S. G. Cao, N. W. Rees, and G. Feng. "Quadratic Stability Analysis and Design of Continuous Time Fuzzy Control Systems." *Int. J. Syst. Sci.*, vol. 27, 193–203, 1996.
27. S. G. Cao, N. W. Rees, and G. Feng. "Further Results about Quadratic Stability of Continuous Time Fuzzy Control Systems." *Int. J. Syst. Sci.* vol. 28, 397–404, 1997.
28. S. G. Cao, N. W. Rees, and G. Feng. "Analysis and Design of Fuzzy Control Systems Using Dynamic Fuzzy State Space Models." *IEEE Trans. Fuzzy Syst.*, vol. 7, 192–200, 1999.
29. P. Gahinet, A. Nemirovski, A. Laub, and M. Chilali. *The LMI Control Toolbox*, The Mathworks, Natick, MA, 1995.

30. G. Garcia, J. Bernussou, and D. Arzelier. "Robust Stabilization of Discrete Time Linear Systems with Norm Bounded Time-Varying Uncertainty." *Syst. Control Lett.*, vol. 22, 327–339, 1994.

APPENDIX

LEMMA A.1 [30] Let A and E be matrices of appropriate dimensions, and P be a positive-definite symmetric matrix satisfying

$$\frac{1}{\varepsilon}I - P > 0, \qquad \varepsilon > 0$$

Then

$$A^T PE + E^T PA + E^T PE \leq A^T P\left(\frac{1}{\varepsilon}I - P\right)^{-1} PA + \frac{1}{\varepsilon}E^T E$$

CHAPTER 13

EVOLUTIONARY COMPUTATION AND COGNITIVE SCIENCE

JANET WILES and JENNIFER HALLINAN

13.1 COGNITIVE SCIENCE: WHAT'S ON YOUR MIND?

The human cognitive architecture is one of evolution's most intriguing products. With a few kilograms (pounds) of neural tissue, dextrous hands, and an ability to cooperate, the human species has invaded and affected every corner of the planet. *Cognitive architecture* is a specific term that refers to the built-in information-processing components of the mind, from neurons to systems, their design and organization. It includes not just the capacities that are shown by a brain at any one time, but also potential capacities, including abilities such as learning.

Homo sapiens is a recent development in evolutionary terms. Its ancestors diverged only about 7 million years ago from those of the other great apes, and evidence of a shared heritage remains in the genes. To build *Homo sapiens*, evolution invented no new neurons, neurotransmitters, or sensors. The major differences between common chimpanzees, bonobos, and humans lie not in their neural components, but rather in the way these components are assembled. Differences between the taxa include the ratio of brain to body size and the relative sizes of parts of the brain. In humans, a much expanded frontal lobe underpins dexterous motor control that permits an unmatched manipulation of tools and enhanced planning and reasoning capacities. In the back two-thirds of the brain, a larger proportion of the occipital, parietal, and temporal lobes in humans is devoted to secondary processing of sensory information.

However, the abilities that really distinguish *Homo sapiens* from even its closest relatives are language, creative symbolic thought, and some rather unusual social structures that allow groups to trade or fight over long distances, not just at individual or troop levels, but at hierarchies of cooperating and/or competing social groups. These consequences are all emergent by-products of the human mind, which

Computational Intelligence: The Experts Speak. Edited by D. B. Fogel and C. J. Robinson
ISBN 0-471-27454-2

itself arose via small changes to evolution's basic body plan and cognitive architecture.

Cognitive capacities are evolved capacities. However, evidence for the course of cognitive evolution is fragmentary. Most cognitive capacities, such as language, leave no fossils. Evidence of the existence of language can be inferred from the use of symbolic art, such as carved bones, cave paintings, and burial rituals, but many unanswered questions remain in the evolution of its components. Even the cognitive capacities that underpin our current linguistic competence are still controversial. Hence, the contribution from evolutionary theory to the current understanding of cognitive capacity is not based on direct evidence, as are disciplines such as cognitive neuroscience. Rather, evolutionary theory provides strong constraints on the potential designs for cognitive mechanisms. A major methodology for investigating the design of cognitive mechanisms is computational modeling. Evolutionary computation (EC) brings together the constraints of evolutionary design with the methodological power of computational modeling. Its application to cognitive science, in particular to the investigation of cognitive architecture, is still in its infancy, but is growing in strength.

There are several major theories of cognitive architecture. The first major paradigm was based on the analogy of information processing in the computer age. Later ones, such as connectionism and embodied cognition, developed in reaction to it. These multiple perspectives provide windows into the multifaceted discipline of cognitive science, each focusing attention on different human capacities. Like a series of maps that cover the same territory, they can differ in the scale and features they show. The tour begins with the symbolic part of human cognitive abilities—the classic view based on information processing—and then outlines the later approaches of connectionist and embodied cognition. At some points the perspectives are contradictory, at other points they complement one another. In particular, the classic and connectionist research agendas have challenged each other in ways that have deepened not just theories of cognitive capacities but also understanding of the phenomena themselves. The fourth approach described is evolutionary theory, which provides a perspective and set of constraints orthogonal to the classic, connectionist, and embodied approaches.

13.1.1 The Classic View of Cognitive Architecture: Symbolic Systems

The classic view of cognitive architecture is based on an information-processing paradigm. This approach is strongly reductionist. Using an organization analogous to that of computer systems, cognitive components are divided into several independent modules: inputs (the sensory systems), a central processor for high-level information processing tasks (e.g., thinking, reasoning, memory), and outputs (the motor system). The focus is typically placed on the high-level processes, and in early artificial intelligence research these were seen as the central challenge to understanding complex cognitive processing. The classic view makes no direct claims about the nature of the neural mechanisms that underpin these component parts, focusing on the functional modules, rather than their instantiation in the brain.

The key assumptions of the classic approach are that the central processor is a symbolic system and the modules function independently. Drawing on the theory of computation, a general-purpose computational processor is assumed to underlie human thinking (equivalent in computational power to a Turing machine). The sensory modules are assumed to be informationally encapsulated, meaning that their information processing is largely independent of processing in other components. For example, object recognition within the vision system delivers to the central processor information about the location and properties of objects, with minimal top-down communication. Language is viewed as a separate component to the central processor, one not acquired or processed using the mechanisms of the central processor. The language module communicates with, but is distinct from, other high-level functions. Human language has qualitatively different properties from the communication systems of other animals, including symbolic reference, compositional structure, and the systematic construction of meaning. These properties are assumed to arise from the special capabilities of a dedicated language processor, rather than from the generic learning properties of the central processing system.

The classic view set the original agenda for cognitive science, and its individual components are the domains of disciplines such as psychophysics (vision, auditory processing), cognitive psychology (human memory, analogical reasoning, problem solving), psycholinguistics (language use and language learning), and linguistics (language as a system in its own right).

13.1.2 The Connectionist View of Cognitive Architecture: Subsymbolic Computation

The connectionist view of cognitive architecture grew out of neural-network modeling approaches in cognitive psychology and linguistics and is based on subsymbolic models of cognitive processes. It developed in part as a reaction to the failure of the classic approach to account for the detailed properties of cognitive mechanisms. Cognitive computation does not reflect all the properties of symbolic computing, and the independence of symbols from their processing breaks down under detailed examination. The subsymbolic view seeks to model cognitive processes using distributed representations, without the strong theoretical assumptions of symbolic processes, such as encapsulated modules and universal computation.

Connectionist models are often designed as a bridge between thinking at the level of information processing over symbols and the physical substrate that constitutes the subject matter of neuroscience. The main assumptions of connectionism are that cognitive behavior emerges from distributed patterns over simple processing units operating in parallel (i.e., neural networks). Learning is an integral part of such models, and language learning and language processing are modeled using the same computational components as other aspects of perception, thinking, reasoning, or motor control.

13.1.3 The Embodied Cognition View of Cognitive Architecture

Both the classic and connectionist perspectives focus on cognition as a phenomenon of the brain itself. By contrast, embodied cognition takes the view that brain and behavior cannot be understood except by taking into account the body that houses the brain, and the environment within which it must function.

The embodied cognition approach has dominated the field of autonomous robotics, in which the "intelligent" behavior of a robot is intimately connected to the environment it must navigate, and to the types of sensors and motors that it can control. The cognitive functions in such a model are solely supportive of sensorimotor coordination, and a robotic agent and its environment are often considered as a coupled dynamic system. The embodied approach focuses attention on the sensory and motor systems, rather than thinking, reasoning, or memory per se. The inspiration for such systems often comes from sensorimotor control in insects, and the higher cognitive areas and language are relatively less important.

Language has been studied directly in the embodied framework in two areas, one using robots that evolve their own language to communicate concepts [1], and cognitive linguistics, in which metaphor systems are seen as the mechanism that enables abstract domains (such as time) to be understood in terms of more concrete ones [2] (for an introduction, see [3]).

13.1.4 The Evolutionary View of Cognitive Architecture

The evolutionary perspective on cognitive architecture is a complementary rather than alternative perspective to those just outlined. Evolutionary approaches are embraced by a wide range of researchers from the classic, connectionist, and embodied paradigms. The central idea is that the brain is an evolved system, and that the components of cognition can be viewed as independently adapted modules. This view draws on the idea that evolutionary theory provides critical constraints on what could, in principle, evolve. In biology, evolution is the theory that places myriad individual facts in a coherent context. Evolutionary cognitive scientists contend that it can also bring coherence to the diverse findings in cognitive science.

The brain accounts for 20% of the total oxygen requirement of the body. It could therefore be seen as an expensive luxury unless it has a selective value at least equivalent to its cost. The benefits of a having a large, active brain are indirect compared with those of the other systems of the body. The brain is not acquiring oxygen, as do the lungs, or nutrients in the manner of the digestive system; it is not essential to reproduction or the feeding of offspring; it does not have the sharpness of teeth and claws or the strength and speed of muscles. Just as internal organs can best be understood in terms of their individual functions, so the brain (from the evolutionary perspective) can be understood in terms of component modules, each adapted to a specific cognitive information-processing task. Examples include specific skills for living in social groups—the recognition of kin via face recognition—the phenomenon of joint attention used in learning from conspecifics, remembering the trading of favors, etc. In this view, strategic thinking as a general skill is less important than task-specific reasoning skills, such as detecting those who are cheating in social exchanges.

Additional constraints on cognitive architecture arise from considerations of the types of mechanisms that evolution can design. Evolution is a tinkerer, and an incremental optimizer. The evolutionary approach emphasizes that current functions evolved from precursor mechanisms that may have had quite different uses (a process termed *exaptation*). Examples include the use of feathers, which may have evolved for thermoregulation or for buoyancy in swimming, and the compositional structure of language, which may have evolved from sequential motor-control processes initially developed for tool use.

Another evolutionary constraint arises from the nature of the development of the brain. The detailed structure of the brain is not directly preprogrammed in the genome of any animal. There are too many neurons and connections to specify each connection individually, and if one part of the brain is damaged early in development, alternative developmental paths compensate for levels of damage that would cripple an adult. The structures of the neural circuits arise through growth processes, emerging during an organism's development as it interacts with its environment.

Just as the connectionist and embodied perspectives highlight aspects of cognitive architecture that were not central to the classic view, so the evolutionary approach has the potential to provide insight into areas that the other approaches do not see as central. Examples include the use of game theory to understand social interactions, and the use of modeling to investigate the evolution of language.

EC provides a methodology for studying not just the cognitive system as it is now but also the space of possible cognitive systems, constrained by the evolutionary processes that gave rise to them and the evolutionary tasks that face evolving agents.

13.1.5 The Role of Evolutionary Computation

EC has the potential to contribute to cognitive science in a number of areas, many of which are as yet relatively unexplored. These contributions include:

- *Development of New Explanations for Cognitive Phenomena* This is the most ambitious application of modeling and success is correspondingly rare. One example is an increased understanding of competition and cooperation in an evolutionary framework using tasks such as the iterated prisoner's dilemma [4,5]. A more modest approach is to use EC modeling to provide converging evidence for empirical studies. While the results of computational experiments do not provide hard evidence about the nature of human cognition, such results may be useful in conjunction with other sources of empirical evidence.
- *Testing the Internal Consistency and Completeness of Theories* This is the area where evolutionary modeling has the potential to play a major role in cognitive science. Computational models require the theorist to make all their assumptions explicit, and allow behavior to emerge directly from the hypothesized mechanisms. Inconsistent or incomplete theories can be exposed, modified, and retested.

- *Testing the Conditions Under Which Phenomena do or do not Occur* Complementing studies of the consistency and completeness of theories, modeling allows the exploration of initial conditions that result in different behavioral regimes.
- *Exploring the Emergent Properties of Systems of Agents in Which the Behavior of the System Cannot Be Deduced from the Behavior of a Single Agent* Complex systems are ubiquitous in cognitive science and are often intractable to mathematical analysis, leaving simulation modeling as the approach of choice.
- *Deepening our Understanding of What Is, Against a Background of What Might Have Been* Cohen and Stewart [6] argue that until we know the space of what is possible for life, we cannot understand the forces that shape the way life currently is. Cognitive phenomena are similar. EC models provide a method to evaluate what is known about cognitive structures in the light of what type of structure is evolutionarily feasible.

To illustrate the applications of EC to cognitive science, we now consider some of our recent work in this area, and the implications of EC for the future of cognitive science.

13.2 CASE STUDIES IN EVOLUTIONARY COMPUTATION AND COGNITIVE SCIENCE

I. Evolution and Learning: Strange Loops between Phenome and Genome

The Baldwin Effect In 1859 Darwin published his view of the theory of evolution [7]. At that time the mechanism of inheritance was not understood, and various explanations for the origins and persistence of genetic variability were considered plausible. These exceptions included "blending inheritance," in which offspring inherit characteristics that are a blend of those of their parents (an explanation favored by Darwin), and Lamarckian inheritance, in which characteristics acquired by individuals, for example, via use or disuse of limbs and organs, are passed on to their children. An obscure German monk named Gregor Mendel deduced the existence of genes in 1865, but his work remained unknown until 1900. Since the turn of the century, however, the Central Dogma of genetics, that information flows one way from genotype to phenotype, has become part of the received wisdom.

It appears, however, that under some circumstances characteristics that were originally acquired by a phenotype can become incorporated into the genome of a species; that is, learning by an individual can guide the evolution of an entire population. One situation in which the effect has been hypothesized to occur is the formation of calluses on the rear end of ostriches. Adult ostriches acquire calluses in this area from sitting on hot ground, and these calluses provide protection for the skin. However, calluses develop in ostrich chicks in the egg, before the individuals have ever experienced a desert environment. How can this arise?

One answer to this question was proposed in 1896 independently by Baldwin [8] and Morgan [9], and has come to be known as the Baldwin Effect. These authors suggested that phenotypic plasticity, whether behavioral or physical, permits acquisition of a desirable trait during the course of life of an individual. Individuals whose genotype permits them to acquire the trait quickly have an advantage over their less genetically fortunate fellows, which translates into a fitness advantage. The genes of individuals who acquire the trait quickly will therefore be overrepresented in the next generation, laying a foundation for further mutations that will enable the trait to be acquired even more quickly. Over time sufficient mutations accumulate so that the trait is genetically encoded rather than learned. Individual learning has guided the evolution of the population.

The Baldwin Effect was brought to the attention of the EC community when it was computationally demonstrated by [10]. They used a chromosome of 20 genes. Each allele could be either 1, 0, or ?. The target genome was a string of 20 1s, and could be achieved either by evolution or by "learning," where learning consisted of an individual "guessing" values of either 0 or 1 for those of its genes with a value of?. Individuals that guessed the correct genotype quickly achieved higher fitness values than those who took longer times. Hinton and Nowlan showed that given the right parameters and initial conditions, the Baldwin Effect occurs reliably *in silico* (in simulation): Over time the number of correct genes (1s) increases, the number of incorrect genes (0s) dwindles to nothing, and the number of guessable genes declines. In the 15 years since the publication of Hinton and Nowlan's results researchers have studied many facets of the Baldwin Effect (e.g., see the collection of papers in [11]. It has been shown to be highly sensitive to parameters such as the population size relative to the length of the chromosome, the type of selection operator (and thus the amount of selection pressure), the complexity of the problem, the amount of environmental variability, and many other factors.

The conditions under which the Baldwin Effect occurs were summarized by Mayley [12] in terms of the benefits and costs of learning over time, and the corresponding rise and fall in the value of learning to an individual. At the start of a simulation, a population has low average fitness and a high rate of learning is beneficial, as it enables individuals to explore their local fitness landscape. Over generations, genes for the high rate of learning spread and the entire population becomes fitter. The time taken to learn becomes the strongest selective pressure and individuals that are genetically closer to the target genome are favored [12].

The rise and fall of learning's contribution to fitness was not immediately obvious in Hinton and Nowlan's framework, as learning consisted solely of guessing the values of learnable alleles, which decreased over the course of the simulation. Using an alternative modeling framework based on neural networks with error correcting learning, Watson and Wiles [13] encoded the learning rate itself in the genome and allowed it to evolve in parallel with the weights of the neural networks over generations. The average learning rate of the population thus provided a direct indicator of the costs and benefits of learning over generations. Their simulations showed a clear rise and fall in the learning rate, with the rise in learning halting and then declining as the innate performance rose.

EC simulations of the Baldwin Effect have been of value to the cognitive science community not only by demonstrating that the effect is computationally consistent across a variety of frameworks, an outcome that is not easily demonstrated with real organisms, but also by providing an indication of the type of environment under which the effect may occur. Many researchers have concluded that it is a computationally plausible evolutionary process with the potential power to shape the fates of species. In particular, Pinker [14] has credited it with the power to evolve computational mechanisms for cognitive components that would appear to be very hard to evolve:

> The Baldwin effect probably played a large role in the evolution of brains.... If the ability to learn was in place in an early ancestor of the multicellular animals, it could have guided the evolution of nervous systems towards their specialized circuits, even when the circuits are so intricate that natural selection could not have found them on its own.

Note that EC techniques do not (cannot) provide evidence that the Baldwin Effect has operated in vivo in any given case. Simulations can, however, alert researchers to conditions under which the effect may or may not occur. The presence in a population of phenotypic plasticity does not in itself guarantee that the acquired behavior will become genetically encoded. A genetic encoding must first exist, and the conditions must be right for its discovery and assimilation. The Baldwin Effect is a transient dynamic in the strange loop between phenotype and genotype, and occurs because of differing benefits and costs of learning in populations that are poised on the brink of discovery.

II. A Second Strange Loop Between Phenome and Genome: Genetic Redistribution

As described in the preceding section, the Baldwin Effect has been hypothesised as a potential mechanism for evolving specific adaptations for linguistic and other modular cognitive capacities. Deacon [15], however, argues against such specificity. He contends that feedback from the phenotype to the genotype may shape evolution via a process we term here *genetic redistribution*. This phenomenon occurs when a trait that is initially genetically specified can also be duplicated by a combination of other abilities interacting with the environment. In this case, selection pressure is removed from the gene(s) specifying the trait and shifted to a suite of other genes that code for behaviors supportive of duplicating the trait. Deacon suggests that symbolic communication is just such a powerful masking agent. Its presence in an organism places selection pressure onto genes coding for a distributed suite of abilities supporting language, binding these genes into evolutionarily synchronized cognitive components.

The plausibility of this type of genetic redistribution has been explored by Wiles et al. [16], using a simpler task than that of symbolic communication, namely the synthesis of ascorbic acid (vitamin C). Humans are one of the few animal species that does not synthesize vitamin C, but rather acquires it from a diet of fruit and vegetables. There is evidence, however, that our ancestors did have the crucial gene for this pathway, homologous to those found in other mammals, but it is now mutated to such an extent that it no longer functions. A plausible scenario is that the adoption of a vitamin-C-rich diet removed selection pressure from the crucial gene for vitamin-C synthesis and transferred it to genes coding for such characteristics as color vision for the detection of fruit and a taste for sweet food, which would encourage the consumption of fruit.

Wiles et al. [16] simulated this process using a population of agents, each of which had the potential to acquire four separate abilities, designated A, B, C, and D. Ability A represents the ability to synthesize vitamin C, and abilities B–D represent abilities that have independent functions, such as color vision and taste preference. Following Hinton and Nowlan [10], an ability is of benefit to an individual only when its target phenotype is set correctly, either through evolution or learning. The fitness function is such that if abilities B, C, and D are all present and there is vitamin C in the environment, then the individual has an excess of vitamin C, which is discarded. Effectively, the endogenous synthesis of vitamin C is masked, and A no longer contributes to the individual's fitness. The agents evolved initially in an environment devoid of vitamin C, and quickly acquired all four abilities. Vitamin C was then introduced into the environment, at which point ability A was quickly lost, while abilities B, C, and D were retained. The cohesion of B, C, and D as a selective unit was demonstrated by reducing the amount of vitamin C in the environment, at which point improvement in these three abilities was correlated.

This simulation illustrates the core elements of the genetic redistribution theory: that masking can destroy an innate trait by removing the selection pressure that prevents deleterious mutations from accumulating, and that unmasking can bind together multiple genetically coded abilities.

As in simulations of the Baldwin Effect, the genetic redistribution simulation does not constitute evidence that either the vitamin C requirement or, by extension, symbolic language actually evolved in humans in this way. However, simulations such as these do demonstrate that hypotheses such as Deacon's [15] are computationally consistent, and they provide a means for exploring the conditions under which such phenomena may occur. In contrast to the Baldwin Effect, the strange loop from phenotype to genotype in genetic redistribution reduces genetic specificity for individual traits. The transient dynamic in this case is the result of an initial reduction in selection pressure for a genetically specified trait and transfer of the selection pressure to a distributed set of abilities.

III. Evolution of Language

Another area of cognitive science in which EC techniques have much to offer is the study of the evolution of language. Language is particularly difficult to study through the evolutionary record, since it leaves no fossils. Its evolutionary history must be deduced from observation of the system as it currently stands and from converging evidence from other methods. Languages across the world have common features such as phonology and syntax, a fact that implies that common mechanisms underlie such competences. The relative contribution of genes and environment to the dynamics of language is controversial. While genes are undoubtedly important in structuring the human cognitive architecture, there are also dynamics in the child's learning process and in the gradual change in languages themselves over time. EC methods cannot tell us what did happen in human evolution, but they allow us to explore how languages can change over time, and the space of what might have happened.

There are two main approaches to modeling language evolution, micromodeling and macromodeling. In the micromodeling approach, the learners are computational agents, a language is a set of utterances, and the global properties of the language are emergent. Either the language or the learners evolve. In contrast, under the macromodeling approach learners are bundles of parameters, a language is an abstract entity, and the global properties of the language are explicit parameters. In this case, the distribution of parameters evolves. Many aspects of language change have been studied using EC techniques, including phonology (e.g., the self-organization of sound systems), lexicon (e.g., learning concepts, grounding meaning, and the convergence of populations on word meanings), and syntax (e.g., the emergence of compositional structure from initially unstructured utterances).

One strong result from these studies has been to show that weak constraints on language learners can give rise to strong constraints on the form of languages themselves, locating causal factors for the shape and structure of language in the dynamics of its use over generations, not just in the cognitive capacities of an individual child. For a general review see Steels [17], and for recent studies in this area, see Tonkes et al. [18] and papers in Hurford et al. [19] and Wray [20].

13.3 SUMMARY

Evolutionary computation is promising to be an extremely useful tool for the study of cognitive science. EC is used primarily in cognitive science in one of two ways: to optimize parameters in cognitive models such as autonomous robots and symbolic models of language, and as a model of the evolutionary process itself. Considerable work has been done on the latter application, in areas of cognitive science as diverse as the evolution of altruism, the evolution of language, and the interaction between learning and evolution (for a summary of these areas, see Wiles and Hallinan [21]). EC provides a methodology for studying *in silico* the workings of the evolutionary processes that have shaped our brains and their cognitive architecture in vivo.

REFERENCES

1. L. Steels. *The Talking Heads Experiment* (Special preedition for Laboratorium), Antwerp, Belgium, 1999.
2. G. Lakoff. *Women, Fire and Dangerous Things: What Categories Reveal about the Mind*, University of Chicago Press, Chicago, 1987.
3. M. Tomasello. "Cognitive Linguistics." In W. Bechtel and G. Graham (eds.), *A Companion to Cognitive Science*, 1998, pp. 477–487.
4. R. Axelrod. *The Evolution of Cooperation*. Basic Books, New York, 1984.
5. R. Axelrod. "The Evolution of Strategies in the Iterated Prisoners Dilemma." In L. Davis (ed.), *Genetic Algorithms and Simulated Annealing*, Pitman, London, 1987, pp. 32–41.
6. J. Cohen and I. Stewart. *The Collapse of Chaos*, Penguin, London, 1994.
7. C. Darwin. *The Origin of Species by Means of Natural Selection*, Murray, London, 1859.
8. J. M. Baldwin. "A New Factor in Evolution." *Am. Nat.*, vol. 30, 441–451, 1896. (Reproduced in R. K. Belew and M. Mitchell, (eds.), *Adaptive Individuals in Evolving Populations*, Proceedings vol. XXVI, Santa Fe Institute Studies in the Sciences of Complexity, Addison-Wesley, Reading, MA.)
9. C. L. Morgan. "On Modification and Variation." *Science*, vol. 99, 733–740, 1896.
10. G. E. Hinton and S. J. Nowlan. "How Learning Can Guide Evolution." *Complex Syst.*, vol. 1, 495–502, 1987.
11. P. Turney, D. Whitley, and R. Anderson, (eds.). *Evolution, Learning and Instinct: 100 Years of the Baldwin Effect*, MIT Press, Cambridge, MA, 1996.
12. G. Mayley. "The Evolutionary Cost of Learning." In P. Maes, M. J. Mataric, J.-A. Meyer, J. Pollack, and S. W. Wilson, (eds.), *From Animals to Animats 4: Proceedings of the Fourth International Conference on Simulation of Adaptive Behavior.* MIT Press, Cambridge, MA, 1996, pp. 458–467.
13. J. Watson and J. Wiles. "The Rise and Fall of Learning: A Neural Network Model of the Genetic Assimilation of Acquired Traits." In *Proceedings of the World Congress on Computational Intelligence*, 2002.
14. S. Pinker. *How the Mind Works*, Penguin, London, 1997, p. 179.
15. T. Deacon. Paper presented at the Conference on Language, Brain and Culture, Sydney, Dec. 2001.
16. J. Wiles, J. Watson, B. Tonkes, and T. Deacon. "Strange Loops in Learning and Evolution." In *Proceedings of the International Conference on Complex Systems*, Nashua, NH, 2002.
17. L. Steels. "The Synthetic Modeling of Language Origins," *Evol. Commun.*, vol. 1, no. 1, 1–34, 1997.
18. B. Tonkes, A. Blair, and J. Wiles. "Evolving Learnable Languages." In S. A. Solla, T. K. Leen, and & K.-R. Muller, (eds.), *Advances in Neural Information Processing Systems 12*, MIT Press, Cambridge, MA, 2000, pp. 66–72.
19. J. R. Hurford, M. Studdert-Kennedy, and C. Knight. *Approaches to the Evolution of Language*, Cambridge University Press, Cambridge, 1998.
20. A. Wray, (ed.). *The Transition to Language*, Oxford University Press, Oxford, 2002.
21. J. Wiles and J. S. Hallinan, (eds.). *IEEE Trans. Evol. Comput. Spec. Issue EC Cognit. Sci.*, vol. 5, no. 2, 2001.
22. I. Harvey. "The Puzzle of the Persistent Question Marks: A Case Study of Genetic Drift." In S. Forrest, (ed.), *Proceedings of the Fifth International Conference on Genetic Algorithms*, Morgan Kaufmann, San Mateo, 1993.

CHAPTER 14

EVOLVABLE HARDWARE AND ITS APPLICATIONS

T. HIGUCHI, E. TAKAHASHI, Y. KASAI, T. ITATANI, M. IWATA, H. SAKANASHI, M. MURAKAWA, I. KAJITANI, and H. NOSATO

14.1 INTRODUCTION

Evolvable hardware (EHW) is a new concept in the development of on-line adaptive machines. In contrast to conventional hardware where the structure is irreversibly fixed in the design process, EHW is designed to adapt to changes in task requirements or changes in the environment through its ability to reconfigure its own hardware structure on-line (dynamically) and autonomously. This capacity for adaptation, achieved by evolutionary algorithms (such as genetic algorithms (GAs) [1,2]), has great potential for the development of innovative industrial applications.

Although the concept of EHW is relatively new, some EHW applications are already being commercialized. In this chapter, we introduce five EHW applications: a general-purpose EHW chip used in prosthetic hands, a data-compression EHW chip, an analog EHW chip for cellular phones, an EHW-based clock-timing architecture, and an evolvable optical system. Finally, we overview the current research on EHW.

14.2 MYOELECTRIC PROSTHETIC HAND CONTROLLER WITH EHW

14.2.1 Background

The myoelectric hand is operated by the signals generated with muscular movements (electromyography, EMG)[1]. However, it takes a long time, usually almost one month, before a person with a disability is able to control a multifunction prosthetic hand freely. During this period, the person with a disability has to

Computational Intelligence: The Experts Speak. Edited by D. B. Fogel and C. J. Robinson
ISBN 0-471-27454-2

undertake training to adapt to the myoelectric hand. We have reversed this situation by having the myoelectric hand adapt itself to the person with a disability and thus drastically reduce this training period.

The system using the EHW is suitable for this application, because of its compactness and high-speed adaptability. The adaptation speed with EHW is usually less than 10 minutes, which is a significant improvement as compared with other systems (e.g., one month).

14.2.2 The EHW Learning Method and Its Performance

The myoelectric hand used in this work is able to perform the six actions (Fig. 14.1), which are paired (open–grasp, supination–pronation, and flexion–extension), with a separate motor control for each pair. The task for the EHW controller is to synthesize pattern recognition hardware to map input patterns (i.e., feature vectors for two-channel electromyogram (EMG) signals) to the desired actions of the hand (i.e., one of the six actions).

However, because EMG signals vary greatly between individuals, it is impossible to design such a recognition circuit in advance. Furthermore, even for a particular person, the feature vectors of the EMG signals sometimes may change, even over short periods. Therefore, the control hardware circuit must be synthesized adaptively.

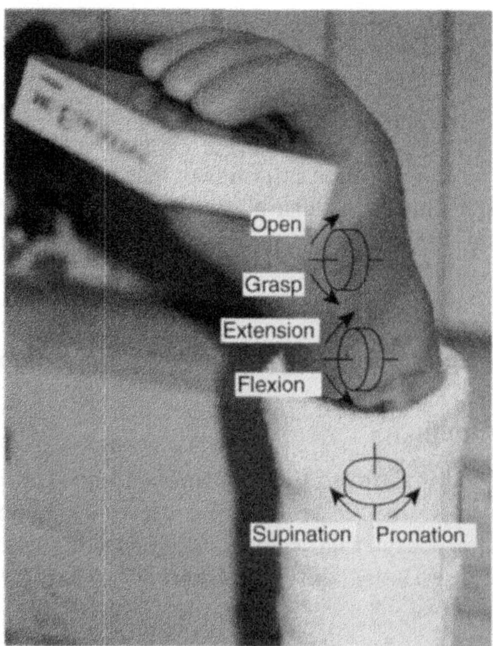

Figure 14.1 Myoelectric prosthetic hand.

TABLE 14.1 Output Pattern Rates of Synthesized Circuit

	Before Training Pattern Addition (%)	After Training Pattern Addition (%)
Supination	66	74
Pronation	49	72
Flecxion	67	88
Extension	84	95
Grasp	38	75
Open	36	84
Average	57	81

Note: These rates correspond to expected output patterns (averaged for three people).

The GA adaptively implements the circuit on the programmable logic array (PLA), which is a similar device to a programmable logic device (PLD) in the EHW controler. The number of the product term lines in the PLA is 32. The output and the input width are 6 bits and 8 bits, respectively.

The chromosome is 1024 bits long and the population size is 32. The GA used is called gene replacement genetic algorithm (GRGA), which accelerates adaptation speed. For details of the GRGA, refer to [2].

Table 14.1 shows the results of the learning after 5 minutes and 10 minutes. After 5 minutes, the average recognition rate over the six actions is 57%. After providing additional training patterns and further 5 minutes for GA execution, the average recognition rate is 81%.

14.2.3 General-Purpose EHW Chip for Gate-Level Hardware Evolution

This chip was developed in April 1998 to serve as an off-the-shelf device for gate-level hardware evolution (Figure 14.2). It was developed for an autonomous mobile robot and a myoelectric artificial hand.

In most research on EHW, GAs are executed with software on personal computers (PCs) or workstations. This makes it difficult to use EHW in situations that need circuits to be as small and light as possible. For example, a prosthetic hand should be of the same size as a human hand and weigh less than 700 grams. Similar restrictions exist for autonomous mobile robots with EHW controllers. One answer to these problems is to integrate both the GA hardware and the reconfigurable logic onto a single large-scale integration (LSI) chip.

This has been done with the digital EHW chip, which consists of three components: (1) a PLA, (2) the GA hardware with a 2K word chromosome memory and a 2K word training pattern memory, and (3) a 16-bit 33-MHz central processing unit (CPU) core (NEC V30; 8086 compatible). Arbitrary logic circuits can be reconfigured dynamically on the PLA component according to the chromosomes obtained by the GA hardware.

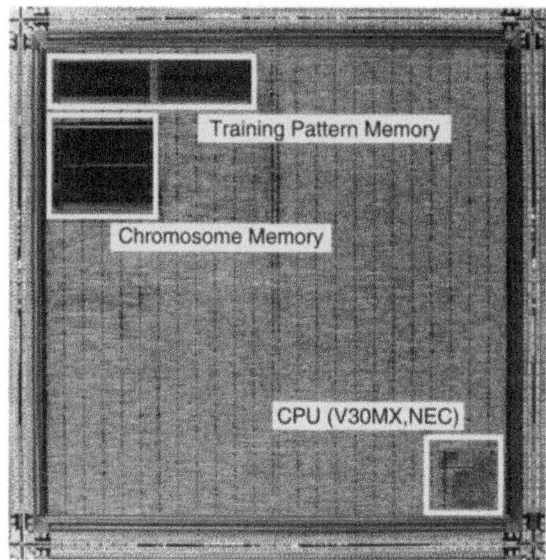

Figure 14.2 Gate-level EHW chip.

14.3 DATA-COMPRESSION CHIP FOR PRINTING IMAGE DATA

Because image data for printing are huge, an efficient data-compression method is very important in order to exchange printing contents via internets (e.g., on-demand publishing). An EHW-based data-compression method has outperformed current international standards of lossless data compression for bi-level image data. The data compression is now discussed at the International Standards Organization (ISO) SC29 committee for international standards.

14.3.1 Data Compression of Image Data

Traditional lossless data-compression techniques are insufficient both in terms of compression ratios and decompression speeds. The EHW data-compression chip can solve these two problems by a precise prediction mechanism using reconfigurable hardware [3]. Image data consists of the values for many pixels. Because the value of each pixel tends to be closely related to the values for neighboring pixels, it is possible to predict the value of a given pixel based on the values for its neighboring pixels. If the value can be predicted correctly, it is not necessary to store it separately, which represents a saving in the size of the image data. This means that compression ratios depend greatly on the precision of the predictions. In order to increase the compression ratio, it is necessary to continually reselect the most suitable prediction mechanism for the varying patterns within an image.

Table 14.2 Comparison of Data-Compression Ratio

	Printer Image	Fax Image
Lempel-Ziv	3.34	8.41
JBIG	3.35	14.67
EHW	6.52	19.82

14.3.2 Prediction of Pixel Values by EHW

GAs within the EHW can be used to determine which pixels to refer to at prediction. The pattern of locations for such reference pixels is called a template [4]. With the original image divided into a number of subimages, GAs search for a set of optimal templates for the subimages. Once a set of optimal templates has been discovered, the hardware prediction mechanism is reconfigured accordingly. This leads not only to improved compression ratios but also to higher decompression speeds, because decompression is also carried out by the EHW hardware.

A template consists of 10 pixel locations, and each location is selected from a 32×8 area (Figure 14.3). Each location is represented by 8 bits ($2^8 = 32 \times 8$), with 80 bits needed to indicate all 10 locations for the template. The chromosome population for the GAs represents templates that are used in data compression, where the size of data after compression is assigned back to the chromosome.

Table 14.2 shows a comparison with two major international standards for data compression: Lempel-Ziv ("compress" command of Unix) and joint bi-level image (JBIG) coding experts group) [5,6], both available on LSI chips. The EHW chip attained compression ratios for printer images almost twice those obtained by the international standards.

The data-compression EHW chip consists mainly of two parts: NEC V830 RISC processor (32 bit, 100 MHz) and the data compressor (Figure 14.4). The V830 controls the procedures in data compression, runs the GA calculations, and

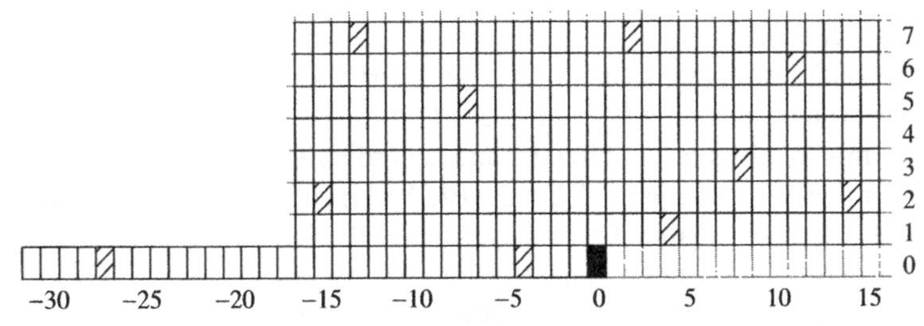

Figure 14.3 Template for pixel prediction.

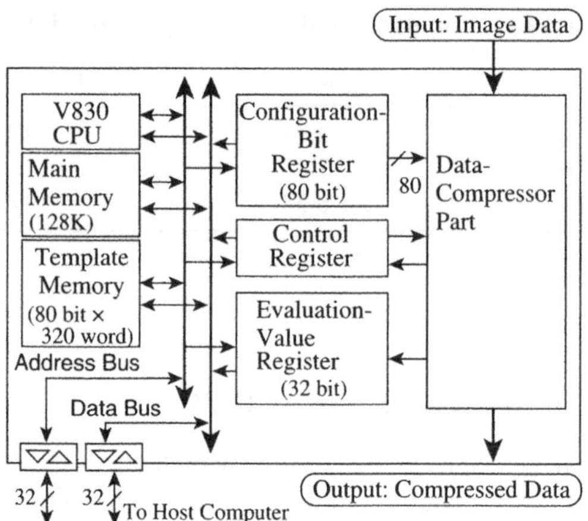

Figure 14.4 The organization of the data-compression EHW chip.

interfaces with the host computer. The data-compressor hardware receives the optimal template identified by the GA, compresses the input image, and returns the size of compressed data to the V830 for the GA evaluation.

14.4 ANALOG EHW CHIP FOR CELLULAR PHONE

14.4.1 Overview

An inherent problem in implementing analog circuits is that the values of the manufactured analog circuit components, such as resistors and capacitors, often differ from the precise design specifications. Such discrepancies cause serious problems for high-end analog-circuit applications. For example, in intermediate frequency (IF) filters [7], which are used widely in cellular phones, even a 1% discrepancy from the center frequency is unacceptable.

The analog EHW chip for IF filters can correct these variations in analog-circuit values by genetic algorithms [8]. Using this chip provides us with two advantages. The first is an improved yield rate. If an analog EHW chip is found not to satisfy the specifications, it can be corrected before shipping. This is done by executing the GA in the LSI tester at the factory to alter the defective analog-circuit components in line with the specifications.

The second advantage is smaller circuits. One way to increase the precision of component values in analog LSIs has been to use large-valued analog components. However, this involves larger circuits, and accordingly higher manufacturing costs and greater power consumption. With the EHW chip, however, the size of the analog circuits can be made smaller. Obviously, smaller IF filters are particularly welcome in cellular phones, but similar considerations exist in a wide variety of applications where analog circuits are used. The IF filter LSI has been used in the cellular phones since December 2001.

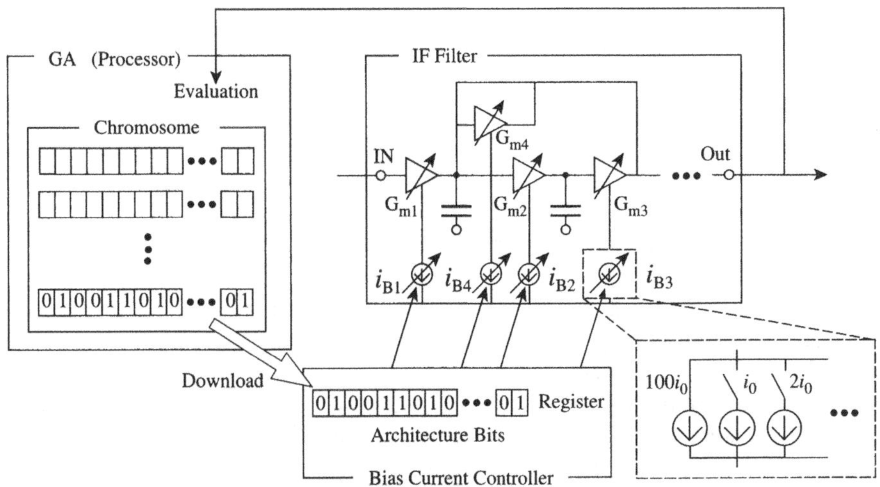

Figure 14.5 Adjustment using genetic algorithms.

14.4.2 The Chip Architecture and Yield Rate

Figure 14.5 illustrates the analog EHW chip, which is an integrated G_m-C IF filter. The filter chip is fabricated in a 0.8-μm complementary metal-oxide semiconduction (CMOS) process. The active area of the filter is 17 mm^2. The specifications are shown in Figure 14.6. The filter has a pass bandwidth of 21.0 kHz centered at 455 kHz, and stop bands specified at attenuations of 48 dB and 65 dB. Filter gain

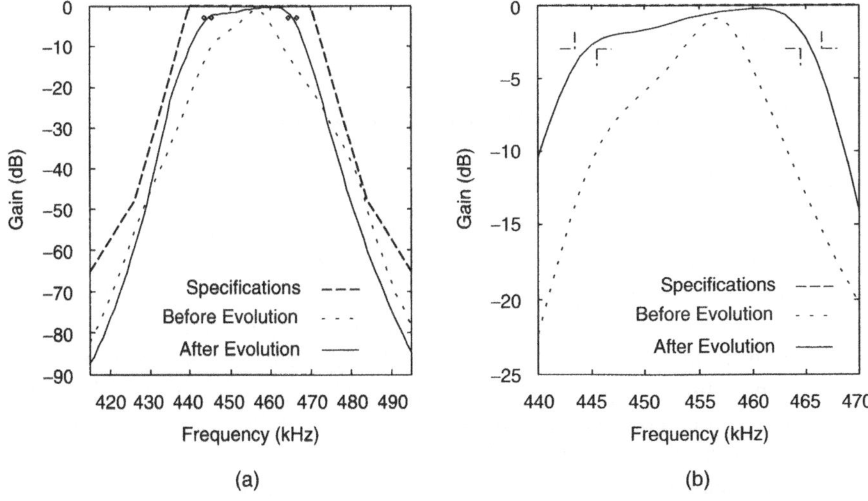

Figure 14.6 (a) Frequency responses; (b) magnification of (a).

should be within the dotted lines in the figures. The −3-dB points should be within $455 - 10.5 \pm 1$ kHz and $455 + 10.5 \pm 1$ kHz. These specifications are very hard to satisfy, because the −3-dB points will be outside these limits if the center frequency is shifted even by 1%.

This IF filter has 39 parameters in total: 16 of these are related to the center frequency, 16 for bandwidth, and 3 for filter gain. In the integrated circuit of the filter, these parameters correspond to the transconductance of the G_m amplifiers. Each transconductance can differ greatly from the target values, by up to as much as 20%.

To correct these variations, the value of the G_m amplifier can be set genetically. The values, which actually control the bias currents to the G_m amplifiers, are coded as configuration bits. The GA, which is executed on an external PC, determines the optimal configuration bits.

A chromosome for the GA consists of 39 genes that correspond to the filter parameters. Each gene has N bits that determine the transconductance. For example, if $N = 2$, there are four transconductance values for selection by the GAs. The genes 00, 01, 10, and 11 mean that the parameter is multiplied by $1.0 - 2 \times D$, $1.0 - D$, $1.0 + D$, and $1.0 + 2 \times D$, respectively, where D is a constant value. Fitness is the weighted sum of deviations between the ideal gain and the gain obtained by the EHW chip.

In simulations, each transconductance value in the circuit was assumed to vary from the target value by a Gaussian distribution of $\sigma = 5\%$. The parameters N, D were set to 2 and 0.025, respectively. We used a population of 50 individuals, each represented by a chromosome of length 78 bits. A run terminated after the 40th generation.

Figure 14.6 shows the frequency responses for the best chromosome in a run. After iteration, the best chromosome could satisfy the specifications, which the initial population was unable to meet. Out of 100 runs, 95% of the chips conformed to specifications. We have also tested 20 real chips, out of which 18 chips were evolved successfully to meet the specifications.

14.5 AN EHW-BASED CLOCK-TIMING ADJUSTING CHIP

14.5.1 Overview

The demand for high-speed LSIs such as Pentium IV is increasing. Unfortunately, the yield rates for such fast digital systems are rather poor. Typically, in the early stages of mass production, yield rates are lower than 10%. One of the reasons for the poor yield rates is that the timing delays between digital components often do not conform to the design specifications [9]. Such discrepancies arise from variations in the values of parasitic capacitances and resistors along the data lines between digital components, which can differ significantly depending on the LSI. Variations in clock timing are referred to as *clock skew*. LSIs that fail to satisfy design specifications because of clock skew are simply discarded, leading to poor yield rates.

In order to solve this problem, we propose an EHW-based clock-timing adjusting architecture for high-speed digital systems [10]. Instead of simply discarding chips that do not meet the specifications, we can genetically adjust the clock timings in the LSI in order to conform to the specifications.

We have developed an LSI, which is used in the high-speed memory tester, to show the advantages of this architecture. Simulation results show that the number of LSIs that can operate at 800 MHz increases from 2.9% to 51.1% after the clock-timing circuits have been evolved by the GA. This clock-timing adjusting architecture is, therefore, expected to become a basic LSI technology for gigahertz digital systems.

14.5.2 The Chip Architecture

The proposed architecture is depicted in Figure 14.7. The salient feature of this architecture is the introduction of a delay device, to genetically adjust the clock timing, which can easily be inserted within traditional architectures.

Figure 14.8 describes this clock-timing adjuster. It has quite a simple structure, consisting of a chromosome register and a delay generator. The bitwidth of the chromosome register depends on the degree of variation in delay time.

The delay generator includes a number of smaller delay devices, with set delays, such as one unit, two units, four units, and these delay devices are connected serially. Each bit of the chromosome register corresponds to one of the small delay devices, and the value of the bit determines whether the delay device is turned on or not.

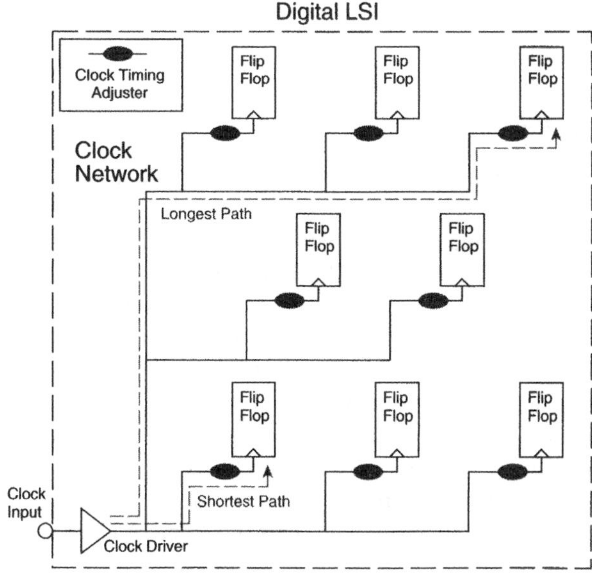

Figure 14.7 EHW-based clock-timing adjusting architecture.

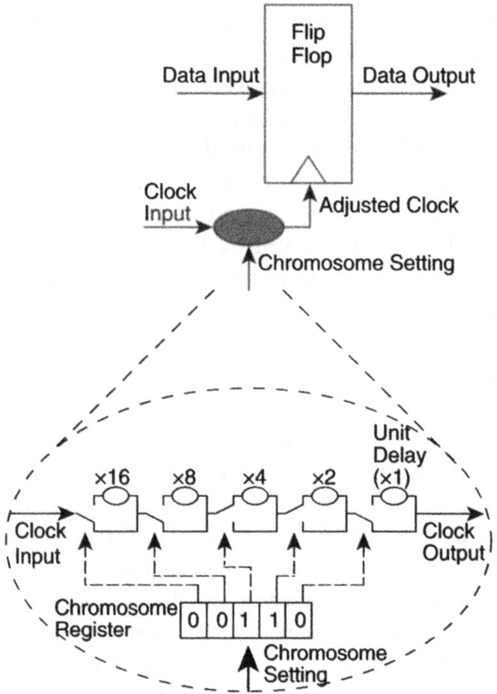

Figure 14.8 Clock-timing adjuster.

Taking the example depicted in Figure 14.8, when the delay has a value of 10 ps, the adjuster would generate a timing delay of 60 ps (10 ps $\times$ 4 + 10 ps $\times$ 2) in total.

14.5.3 Simulation Study

The simulation experiments conducted to adjust clock timing for a circuit are described next.

For the evaluation, a memory-test-pattern generator was selected, and converted to a simulation model for evaluation. This is a simple but quite important logic block for memory-testing devices. It is used to generate access patterns to test memory at speeds used when accessing real memory chips. For example, in testing memory modules for the Direct Rambus systems, the testing hardware should supply rather long test patterns at a speed of 800 MHz [11].

In the simulation, the number of sample chips was 1000, the population size was 50, and the number of generations was 20. Device parameters were assumed to vary according to a normal distribution. The results are depicted in Figure 14.9. The x-axis represents clock speed, with the percentage of chips that could operate at a given speed being plotted along the y-axis. The most significant result from these simulations was the finding that 50% of the chips designed with 500-MHz clocks

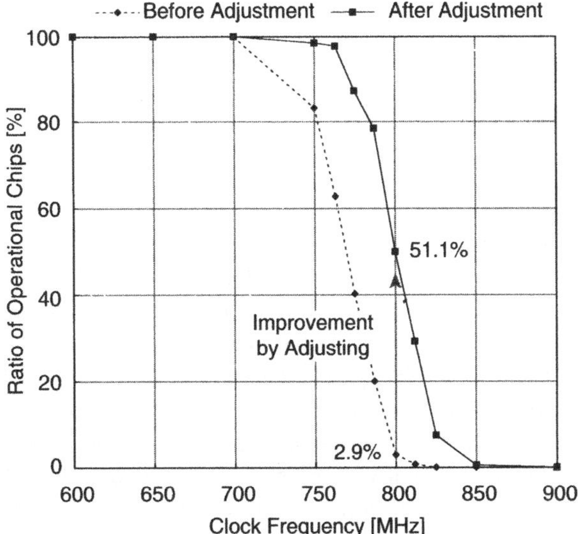

Figure 14.9 Simulation result (distribution function).

could be adjusted to operate at improved speeds of 800 MHz, whereas only 2.9% could operate at such speeds before adjustment. The LSI has been developed with bipolar technology, including 2000 gates.

14.6 EVOLVABLE OPTICAL SYSTEMS AND THEIR APPLICATION

In this chapter, we briefly introduce the third paradigm of evolvable hardware, the mechanical hardware evolution. As the typical examples of mechanical hardware evolution, three evolvable optical systems are introduced; fiber alignment, interferometer, and femtosecond laser.

14.6.1 Background

In recent years, the market for optical technology has been growing rapidly, particularly due to the advances in optical communication systems. In general, optical systems consist of many components, such as light sources, mirrors, lenses, prisms, semiconductor elements, and optical fibers. In order to obtain the optimal performance, it is necessary to align these optical components to the optimal positions with micrometer precision. Moreover, as shifts in the positioning of each component influences the alignment of the whole system, each component must be adjusted repeatedly until the optimal alignment is achieved. Since the number of experienced technicians is extremely limited, these difficulties increase the manufacturing times and the costs of optical systems.

14.6.2 Advantages of Evolvable Optical Systems

Although algorithms for automatic alignment have been devised, they are not suitable for systems where the parameters to be set optimally are numerous, where there are local optimum, and where the parameters are interdependent. We have proposed some methods of automatic alignment using GAs. These methods have the following four advantages:

1. *Automatic Adjustment for Maintenance-Free Systems* The performance of an optical system is affected by the temperature and the stability of the environment in which it is used. However, variations in performance can be adjusted automatically on-line by our algorithms. This means that the optical systems are maintenance-free, making them easy for nonexperts to use.
2. *Cost Reduction* Using less-expensive mechanical parts in optical systems unfortunately often leads to longer adjustment times, because the precision of these components is usually inferior. However, as our algorithms provide a quick and flexible way of adjusting performance, it is possible to use less-expensive mechanical parts in order to reduce the costs of the system.
3. *Compact Implementation* With automatic adjustment methods, it is possible to reduce the spaces between the components in an optical system, which is necessary when adjustments are made by technicians. Thus, it is possible to downsize optical systems.
4. *Realization of On-Site Optical Systems* Advantages 1 and 3 also make the realization of on-site optical systems possible. Compact and maintenance-free systems open up new application areas, such as portable on-site environment measurement systems, which is something that has been impossible to date, due to the difficulties of using high-performance lasers and spectrums outdoors.

14.6.3 Evolvable Optical Systems

Three optical systems using GA-based automatic-alignment algorithms are summarized below.

1. *Evolvable Fiber-Alignment System* The alignment of optical fibers according to five degrees of freedom can be completed within a few minutes, whereas it would take a human technician about half an hour.
2. *Evolvable Interferometer* The adjustment of plane mirrors in an interferometer is difficult for nonexperts. However, the automatic-adjustment method eliminates this problem, making it possible to use interferometers outdoors.
3. *Evolvable Femtosecond Laser* It often takes five days for experienced technicians to adjust the physical positioning of femtosecond laser components in order to achieve optimal performance. The GA-based adjustment can align the laser components automatically within 15 minutes.

14.7 CURRENT RESEARCH ON EHW

As a conclusion of this chapter, we briefly overview the current research on evolvable hardware. For the subject of the survey, we select the Fourth International Conference on Evolvable Systems (ICES2001). ICES was begun in 1996 as the first conference focused mainly on EHW. ICES includes all aspects of evolvable systems, that is, hardware, software, algorithms, and applications. Here we classify presented papers by sessions in ICES2001. All referred papers in this section are published in [12].

In the session "Evolutionary Design of Electronic Circuits," some new system architectures for evolving electronic circuits were presented. The important point is that some very large-scale integration (VLSIs) for EHW have been fabricated to test the new system architectures. Again referring to [12], Torresen proposed a new EHW architecture for pattern classification including incremental evolution. He showed that this method is applicable to a prosthetic hand controller. Iwata et al. developed an EHW chip by integrating the GA hardware and reconfigurable hardware loglc. They showed that the execution speed was about 40 times faster than with a GA program on a PC. Schemmel et al. presented a new analog neural-network architecture using weights determined by a GA and the VLSI implementation. Langenheine et al. fabricated a chip called field-programmable transistor array (FPTA). The chip is embedded in a hardware evolution system for intrinsic hardware evolution of analog electronic circuits.

Embryonic electronics (embryonics) is a research project attempting to draw inspiration from the biological process of ontogeny, to implement novel digital computing machines with better fault tolerance. In the session "Embryonic Electronics," some latest results showed that the learning algorithms and the applications are constantly in progress. Restrepo et al. presented a multicellular universal Turing machine implementation endowed with self-replication and self-repair capabilities. Jackson et al. proposed asynchronous embryonics with reconfiguration. Prodan et al. proposed artificial cells driven by artificial DNA. Stauffer et al. fabricated the self-repairing and self-healing electronic watch: the BioWatch. The system is based on an array of small processors.

In the session "Biological-Based Systems," some ideas for applying biological process to evolutionary systems were presented. Embryonics is also close to this session. The ideas from biology are fresh for researchers in engineering or information science. Haddow et al. presented the first case study using the mathematical formalism called L-systems and applied their principles to the development of digital circuits. Bradley et al. analyzed the body's approach to fault tolerance using the immune system and showed how such techniques can be applied to hardware fault tolerance.

In the session "Evolutionary Learning," some new ideas about a learning algorithm for EHW were discussed. The area deals with theoretical and fundamental study for the learning of EHW. Perez et al. showed a scheme based on case-based reasoning to extract design patterns from a GA used to optimize combinatorial circuits at the gate level. Leung et al. presented a method to balance samples distribution using a new GA fitness calculation method, called the dynamic samples weight (DSW). They showed that DSW could improve the successful rate and convergent speed of learning with GA. Sanchez et al. proposed a new approach for the automatic design of finite state machines using artificial evolution and learning techniques: the SOS-algorithm. They showed how to effectively use the evolution and learning of finite state machines to solve complex partially observable problems.

Genetic programming (GP) is a kind of learning algorithm that uses trees to construct circuits. Here we categorize papers related to GP because they were separated into some sessions in ICES2001. Some new learning algorithms for EHW using GP were presented. It seems that EHW using GP becomes more active. Yanal et al. depicted the emergence of the cooperative behavior for multiple robot agents by means of GP. Fernandez et al. presented a new method for placing and routing circuits on FPGAs by means of parallel and distributed GP.

Some new evolutionary learning algorithms for robots were presented in the session "Evolutionary Robotics." Robotics is a typical application of EHW. Kim et al. showed that the proposed GA guarantees a satisfactory smooth and stable walking, through the experiment on the real biped robot. Islam et al. applied an incremental approach, a two-stage evolutionary system, to develop the control system of an autonomous robot for a complex task.

In the session "Application," some new and practical applications for EHW were presented. The remarkable point is that some applications are practical enough to be used as industrial applications. A lossless data-compression method for bi-level images using EHW (see Section 14.3) and an evolvable optical system (see Section 14.6) were presented in this section. Stoica et al. introduced the concept of polymorphic electronics (polytronics), which is a new paradigm of circuits with superimposed multiple functionality. In polytronics, a function change does not require switches/reconfiguration as in traditional approaches. Instead, the change comes from modifications in the characteristics of devices involved in the circuit, such as temperature or power supply voltage. Keymeulen et al. presented the initial development of reconfigurable sensor adapted by evolution.

REFERENCES

1. M. Uchida, H. Ide, and S. P. Ninomiya. "Control of a Robot Arm by Myoelectric Potential." *J. Robotics Mechatronics*, vol. 5, no. 3, 259–265, 1993.
2. I. Kajitani, M. Iwata, H. Yokoi, D. Nishikawa, and T. Higuchi. "An Evolvable Hardware Chip and its Application as a Multi-Function Prosthetic Hand Controller." In *Proceedings of the 16th National Conference on Artificial Intelligence (AAAI-99)*. 1999, pp. V559–V564.
3. H. Sakanashi, M. Salami, M. Iwata, S. Nakaya, T. Yamauchi, T. Inuo, N. Kajihara, and T. Higuchi. "Evolvable Hardware Chip for High Precision Printer Image Compression." In *Proceedings of the 15th National Conference on Artificial Intelligence (AAAI-98)*, Madison, WI, 1998, pp. 486–491.

4. S. Forchhammer and K. Jansen. "Data Compression of Scanned Halftone Images." *IEEE Trans. Commun.*, vol. 42, no. 2, 1881–1893, 1994.

5. International Telegraph and Telephone Consultative Committee (CCITT). "Progressive Bi-level Image Compression." Recommendation T.82 (1993).

6. W. B. Pennebaker, J. L. Mitchell, G. G. Langdon, Jr., and R. B. Arps. "An Overview of the Basic Principles of the Q-Coder." *IBM J. Res. Dev.*, vol. 32, no. 6, 717–726, 1988.

7. T. Adachi, A. Ishikawa, K. Tomioka, S. Hara, K. Takasuka, H. Hisajima, and A. Barlow. "A Low Noise Integrated AMPS IF Filter." In *Proceedings of the IEEE 1994 Custom Integrated Circuits Conference*, 1994 pp. 159–162.

8. M. Murakawa, T. Yoshizawa, T. Adachi, S. Suzuki, K. Takasuka, D. Keymeulen, and T. Higuchi. "Analogue EHW Chip for Intermediate Frequency Filter." In *Evolvable Systems: From Biology to Hardware, Lecture Notes in Computer Science*, vol. 1478, Springer-Verlag, Berlin, 1998, pp. 134–143.

9. J. Rabeay. *Digital Integrated Circuits*, Prentice Hall, Englewood Cliffs, NJ, 1996.

10. E. Takahashi, M. Murakawa, K. Toda, and T. Higuchi. "An Evolvable-Hardware-Based Clock Timing Architecture Towards GigaHz Digital Systems." In *Proceedings of the Genetic and Evolutionary Computation Conference*, Morgan Kaufmann, San Francesco, 1999, pp. 1204–1210.

11. Rambus Inc. "Rambus Signaling Technology Overview." http://www.rambus.com/technology/technology_overview.html (HTML document on the WWW), 2001.

12. Y. Liu, K. Tanaka, M. Iwata, T. Higuchi, and M. Yasunaga (eds.). *Evolvable Systems: From Biology to Hardware, Lecture Notes in Computer Science*, Vol. 2210, Springer-Verlag, Berlin, 2001.

13. J. Holland. *Adaptation in Natural and Artificial Systems*, University of Michigan Press, Ann Arbor, MI, 1975.

14. D. E. Goldberg. *Genetic Algorithms in Search, Optimization, and Machine Learning*, Addison-Wesley, Reading, MA, 1989.

CHAPTER 15

HUMANIZED COMPUTATIONAL INTELLIGENCE WITH INTERACTIVE EVOLUTIONARY COMPUTATION

HIDEYUKI TAKAGI

15.1 INTRODUCTION

To view the future of computational intelligence research, first, let us take a general look at the course of computational intelligence over the past several decades.

All major seed technologies of computational intelligence were present around the 1960s. The basis of neural networks (NNs) was established by the perceptron model in 1958 following a neuron model of 1943. Fuzzy sets in 1965 became the basis of fuzzy systems (FS) and led to several FS applications following the first application of fuzzy control in 1973. Following the independent proposal of evolutionary programming (EP) (1960), evolutionary strategy (ES) (1964), and genetic algorithms (GAs) (1957 by Fraser, 1958 by Bremermann, 1975 by Holland), evolutionary computation (EC) came to form a group of useful techniques: EP, ES, GA, and genetic programming (GP).

Practical applications of each EC technology have become popular since the late 1980s. NN applications became popular following the Hopfield model in 1982 and a feedforward model with backpropagation algorithm in 1985. Applications of FS began from control of steam engines and cement kilns in 1973, and became popular especially in Japanese industry and consumer equipment following the second IFSA Congress in 1987.

Cooperative efforts to fuse technologies of NN, FS, and EC began in the late 1980s, and their applications spread to the real world in the 1990s. NNs and FS have different learning capabilities and explicit knowledge handling, respectively, but their essential structures to realize nonlinearity are the same [1]. EC can be used to design NNs and FS, which is easy to understand because EC searches nonlinear spaces; the characteristics of NNs and FS are changed by evolving synaptic

Computational Intelligence: The Experts Speak. Edited by D. B. Fogel and C. J. Robinson
ISBN 0-471-27454-2

weights and the antecedents and consequents of IF-THEN fuzzy rules. Since these technologies have different features, a cooperative technology whose new strong feature exceeds that of each original technology can be realized by combining the strong features of the NNs, FS, and EC. Neurofuzzy systems that have the capabilities of both learning and explicit knowledge representation are one such example. As a result, these fusion technologies have been used widely in our lives since the 1990s [1].

As we glance over the computational intelligence research of the last decades, we see that NNs, FS, and EC have played a large role, and their fusion technologies have become practical. How should the computational intelligence research expand now? We discuss this point and in Section 15.2 emphasize that the concept of *humanized computational intelligence* will be one of answers. Finally, in Section 15.3 we introduce an interactive evolutionary computation (IEC) as one of technologies realizing the concept.

15.2 HUMANIZED COMPUTATIONAL INTELLIGENCE

Computational intelligence (CI) in the twentieth century is characterized by the proposal of biologically inspired technologies and fusing these technologies. Major technologies include NNs, FS, and EC, and CI researchers who use hints from the immune system, DNA, virus, cell development, and so far in, to create new engineering models. NNs, FS, and EC each have become practical, have been fused, and have spread widely into the real world. From the practical perspective, we can say that the independent and cooperative use of NN, FS, and EC mostly characterized CI in the last century.

Then, what characterizes CI from this point forward? I believe that one of several research directions for this technology is to embed directly the capability of a human being or living thing into CI, instead of its model. We describe this type of technology as humanized CI. The background of this view includes: (1) any technology or system has advantages and disadvantages, and the combination of these advantages is expected to be more powerful than the original advantages; (2) humans can offer a performance that is superior to models of that performance; and (3) conventional CI cannot handle some real-world tasks that need human evaluation, such as visual or auditory inspection at the final manufacturing process or human preference.

The approach of conventional CI is analytical for human-related systems. Its approach to handling human capability is to analyze the capability, model it, and implement it in a computer. The major approach of optimization systems related to humans is to model knowledge expression, reasoning, associative memory, or preference and use the model as an evaluation system instead of the human. It is, of course, important to analyze the capability and functions of humans not only until now but also from now. Once we have such models, we can automate optimization systems with the model instead of a human, which is also important as a contribution of computational intelligence.

However, has the CI research not been biased toward this analytical approach too much? It is hard to believe that a perfect human model can really be realized, and the

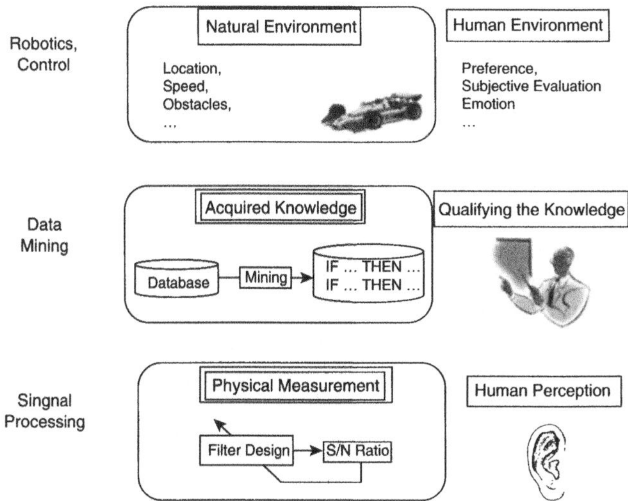

Figure 15.1 Humanized technology for conventional engineering tasks.

performance of a human itself is better than that of a human model in general. If the objective of our research or development is not to analyze human functions but to maximize the performance of a target system, it is a better idea to take a synthetic approach that directly embeds a human into a system, even if the human function is a black box. This approach is humanized CI, one area of the CI research, in which a methodology is developed wherein a human cooperates with CI technology to fully use his or her capability.

Let us look at the examples of a humanized technology shown in Figure 15.1.

A robot controller inputs a robot's position, speed, and distance to obstacles from its physical environment and uses them as control information. Unlike industrial robots, a natural behavior that matches human preference or lets humans feel safe and comfortable is required for consumer robots. To deal with such a human environment, a human must be involved in the robot control system.

Data mining is a technology for acquiring knowledge from numerical data. We can acquire rules automatically from data by using artificial intelligence (AI) tools, neurofuzzy systems, or EC-fuzzy systems. However, if the purpose is to consider the quality of rules and obtain better rules, a domain expert who can evaluate which rule is better and how it must be involved in the knowledge-acquisition systems.

If our reason for using signal-processing technology is to handle physical indexes such as the signal-to-noise ratio, we can use conventional mathematical-based signal-processing methods. But, if the reason is to make a signal auditorily or visually better, a human who finally judges should be involved in the signal-processing system rather than using perceptual-evaluation models.

Humans have two types of capabilities: one is a knowledge aspect, which deals with reasoning, knowledge expression, knowledge acquisition, associated memory, and learning, and the other is an aspect of *KANSEI*, which is a generic term of intuition, preference, subjective evaluation, feeling, and other psychological aspects. It is important for CI research to make both aspects cooperate to realize humanized CI, but the research on this topic so far has been too biased toward the knowledge aspect. Although it may be avoided due to the difficulty of psychological experiments, we need a methodology to deal with the *KANSEI* aspect from an engineering perspective.

Not only conventional engineering techniques but also human-related techniques, such as the methodology to handle aesthetic sense, experimental psychology, *KANSEI* engineering, human–machine interface, subjective tests, statistical tests, and others are necessary for humanized CI research. These techniques and methodologies have not been major subjects in engineering education, but they should be introduced more in the engineering field.

There are several possible approaches to realize humanized CI. IEC is one of them.

15.3 INTERACTIVE EVOLUTIONARY COMPUTATION

15.3.1 What Is IEC?

IEC is a system in which EC optimizes the characteristic of the target system based on human evaluation (see Figure 15.2). We can say that IEC is a system whose fitness function is replaced by a human. Since the characteristic of the target system can be optimized based on human evaluation, we can directly reflect our sense of value or *KANSEI* into system design.

Subjective evaluation is given by numerical values, and there is no need to linguistically express the evaluation. Imagine a montage system. It is difficult for us to describe which part of a given montage image is similar or dissimilar to a target suspect, but it is not so difficult to evaluate how the impression of the given montage images is close to that of the suspect in five evaluation levels from *very similar* to *very dissimilar*.

IEC research consists mainly of application-oriented research and interface research. In application-based research, the IEC has been applied to several types

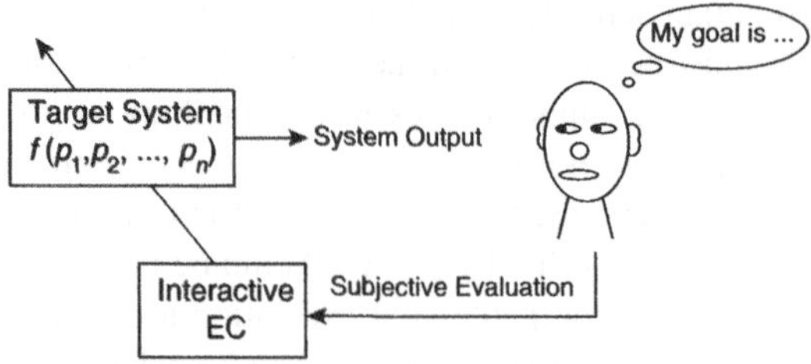

Figure 15.2 General IEC system: system optimization based on subjective evaluation.

of fields. In interface research, the fatigue problem that is a major drawback of the IEC has been given attention. Some IEC applications include graphic arts and animation; three-dimensional (3-D) computer graphics lighting; music; editorial design; industrial design; facial-image generation; speech processing and synthesis; hearing-aid fitting; virtual reality; media database retrieval; data mining; image processing; control and robotics; food industry; geophysics; education; entertainment; and social system [2]. IEC research on interfaces includes the input interface of subjective fitness fed back to the system; the interface of system output; the user's active intervention by visualizing a searching space; time sequential display for music, speech, or animation; and a prediction model of human evaluation [2].

We introduce some IEC research in major fields in the following sections. See [2] for a further detailed survey and discussion.

15.3.2 IEC-Based Computer Graphics

IEC research started with *biomorph* in 1986 [3]. The biomorph was intended to demonstrate the capability to create several varieties of insect-like 2-D computer graphics forms by iterating subjective selection of L-system outputs and the mutation of genes that express the number and angles of the L-system branches. Likewise, several computer graphics of plants and animals, abstract graphics, and computer graphics animations have been generated by using EC to optimize the parameters of L-system, math equations, and cellar automaton rules, or by using GP to generate mathematical equations.

Let us see how to create computer graphics with more concrete examples. First, a mathematical equation, $f(x, y)$, that has x and y at the terminal nodes is generated by the GP. Then, the numerical value of $f(x_i, y_j)$ is calculated for the pixel coordinate, (x_i, y_j). Two-dimensional computer graphics are generated by letting this value correspond to brightness and color at the coordinate and calculating all pixels. Graphic animations can also be generated by evolving $f(x, y, t)$, where t is a time variable. SBART is this type of 2-D computer graphics generator [4]. Instead of generating a math equation using GP, another type of computer graphics is generated by optimizing the coefficients of equations previously given using EC. The animation of not only abstract graphics but also a concrete body is available by setting a time variable in joint angles for arms and legs.

Drawing artistic graphics is not the only application of computer graphics. Computer graphics lighting design is also an IEC application for computer graphics design. Since 3-D computer graphics is a simulation of a photograph, a 3-D computer graphics impression is influenced deeply by lighting. Computer graphics or photography beginners do not have the knowledge and experience to design an appropriate computer graphics impression using multiple lights with different brightness and colors. IEC-based computer graphics lighting design system supports the beginners (see Figure 15.3) [5]. Industrial design is one computer graphics field. IEC has been applied to design the shapes of cars, knitwears, tools, a concrete arch dam, suspension bridges, buildings, and so on.

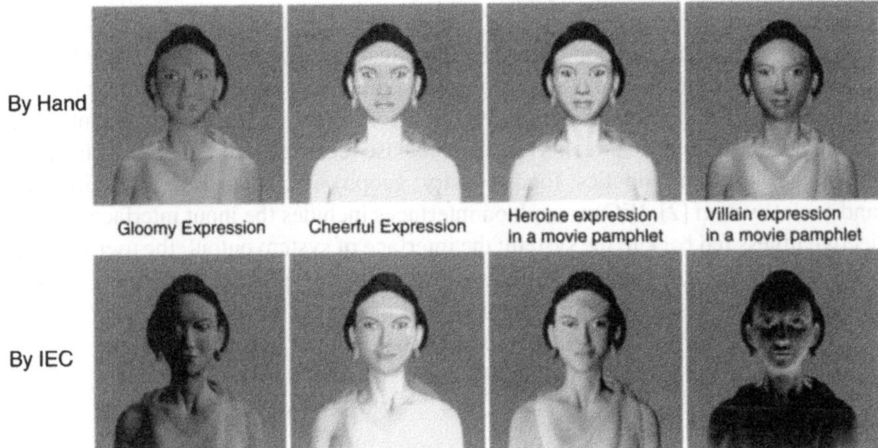

Figure 15.3 Lighting design examples by one computer graphics beginner for four given design motives by hand (upper) and IGA (lower). Color lights are used for the right two concepts.

15.3.3 IEC-Based Signal Processing

Signal processing has been based on mathematics and has progressed dramatically over several decades, and we receive the benefit of advanced signal processing in our daily lives. Because of advances in signal processing, cases where a signal-processing user is not a signal-processing expert, e.g., a medical doctor who uses medical image processing, have increased. It is difficult for the conventional signal-processing approach to close this gap.

Auditory-based or visual-based signal processing using IEC is a new approach to signal processing that can be conducted without *a priori* knowledge of the signal and signal processing, but with only domain knowledge or preference.

IEC Fitting is auditor-based signal processing applied to hearing-aid fitting [6–9]. The conventional approach is to fit a hearing aid based on measured partial auditory characteristics, the fitting expert's knowledge and experience, and the expert's interpretation of the user's oral description on how he or she hears. The IEC Fitting solves the essential problem, "fitting by others who cannot know how the user hears," and allows users to optimize their hearing aids based on their hearing in their daily environments with any sounds. Its framework is the same as other IEC tasks: users evaluate the processed sound based on articulation and their preference, and the EC optimizes the hearing-aid parameters based on the evaluation.

We developed Visualized IEC, which combines IEC and 2-D mapping from n-D EC searching space to accelerate IEC conversion [10], and implemented it into a personal digital assistant (PDA) to use the IEC Fitting anywhere and anytime. Now the IEC Fitting is in field evaluation.

Visual-based signal processing is used for the design of image-enhanced filters, feature extraction, and so on. Interactive GP (IGP) was applied to designing image

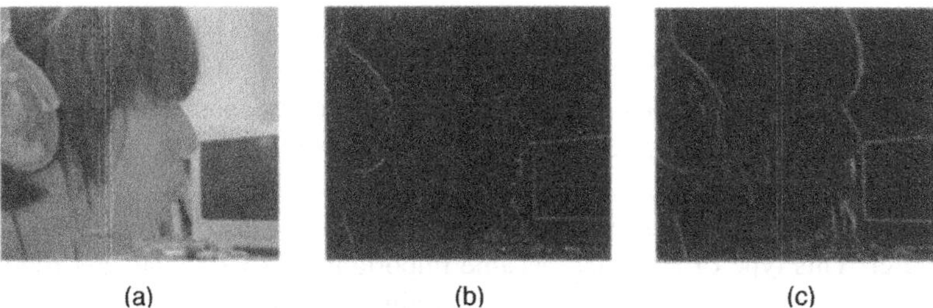

Figure 15.4 (a) Original image; (b) edge detection by a Laplacian filter; and (c) that by a IGP filter.

filters that enhance magnetic resonance image (MRI) and echocardiographic images [11]. The filters were visually designed to enhance each part of the MRI image by coloring and to show the difference between two echocardiographic images in one image.

We experimentally designed image filters based on our idea of investigating how the IEC-based approach can design filters whose characteristics are similar to those of a conventional filter that is expressed mathematically. The mathematical equations generated by the IGP input numerical values of 3×3 pixels and output a new value at the center pixel among the input pixels. Images enhanced by the math equations generated are displayed to an IGP user, and the user returns his or her evaluation to the GP. This process is iterated until the user discovers satisfactory images.

Figure 15.4b is an image processed by a conventional Laplacian filter using the original image of Figure 15.4a, and Figure 15.4c is an image processed by a filter designed visually based on the IGP approach without any *a priori* knowledge of edge detection. From the comparison of these detected edges, the edges detected by the IGP filter are smoother than those of the Laplacian filter, which implies the high potential of the IGP approach.

15.3.4 IEC-Based Control

Control tasks that need human evaluation have increased recently, though control has been regarded as a typical engineering technology that replaces a human for automation. Such typical control tasks include robotics control and virtual reality (VR). The first engineering application of the IEC was the GA control of human evaluation in 1992 [12].

The IEC was used to control a Lego robot to attain the interesting locomotion that children prefer. The connection weights of the NN that inputs robot sensor information and outputs locomotion control values are evolved according to the selection of better robot locomotion by children [13,14].

IEC was applied to generate humanlike movements of robots. One application involved planning a robot arm path so as not to frighten a human when a human and a robot do cooperative work, such as handing goods to a human [15]. While the evaluation measure for planning the arm path of industrial robots is efficiency, such as the shortest distance or time, the minimum energy, or the most stability, a different measure is needed for consumer robots. Humans tend to fear an approaching lump of iron, (i.e., robot arm). The objective of this research was to use IEC to determine the best tracking path and speed for the robot arm to minimize the frightened feeling of a robot user. This type of approach became important for care robots, pet robots, or other consumer robots in which human friendliness is preferred over efficiency.

When we design or acquire control rules, sometimes their intelligibility to other people has a higher priority than their best performance. IEC was applied to obtain such fuzzy control rules for car parking with the combination of a fitness function for objective evaluation of the control performance and human evaluation for the intelligibility of the obtained rules [16].

It was proposed that a user be allowed to indicate directly which control rules are better to increase the fitness during a normal fuzzy classifier system run. Their attempt to develop fuzzy logic rules that control a robot while it takes a flag and returns without colliding with other robots failed in their first simulation. Then, they found partially successful rules for reaching out to the flag in the 21st generation and told their classifier system to search in the neighborhood for the fired fuzzy control rules. This human intervention resulted in a successful determination of the robot control rules at the 23rd generation [17].

IEC is being applied to an arm-wrestling robot fighting against a human to obtain control rules that let the human fighter feel as if he or she was fighting against a human [18]. The only cue is how the human fighter feels fighting against the robot. IEC solves this task by optimizing the parameters of fuzzy control rules based on human evaluation, while classic and modern control theories cannot solve the problem. It is expected that VR factors in control can be found by analyzing the difference between the initial and obtained control rules.

Other IEC-based applications include (1) obtaining control rules that express the emotions of happiness, anger, or sadness in its movement [19]; (2) teaching a pet type of robot new tricks [20], (3) controlling an NN controller that inputs the throttle angle and vehicle speed and outputs the air–fuel ratio to determine the user's riding comfort preference [21], and (4) others.

15.3.5 IEC-Based Internet

Because the use of the Internet has increased dramatically, IEC has also been applied to disciplines related to the Internet.

IEC was applied to autodesign web banners [22]. EC optimizes the combination of design parts consisting of the banners according to the number of customer visits, i.e., the number of times the users click the banners. The appearance of the banners varies automatically to increase the number of customer visits.

IEC was applied to speech synthesis of a character agent. Instead of on-line manuals, personlike agents that advise users how to operate software has been made fit for practical use. IEC was applied to reflect human emotion in the behavior and

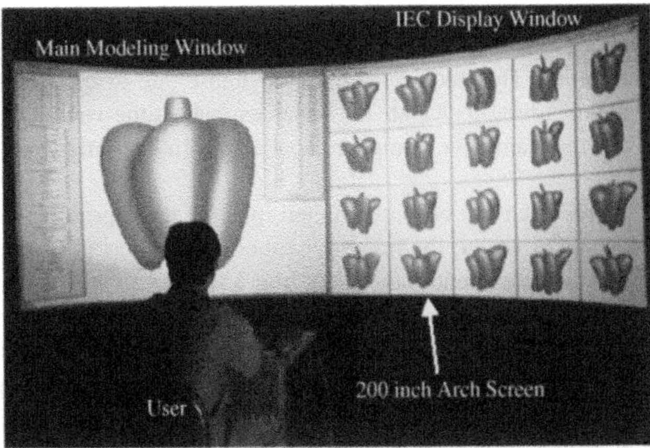

Figure 15.5 IEC-based 3-D CG modeling system for art education.

voice of Microsoft Agent by selecting one of 40 prepared kinds of behavior and voice parameters, such as pitch, amplitude, speed, and stress, based on the user's subjective evaluation [23].

IEC was applied to design home pages. The impression of a Web page depends on the combination of background color, type font, size, and color, font of the title level, link color, and so on. IEC is a good tool to optimize this combination visually and generate HTML-style sheets that match the user's preference [24].

Educational projects that use the Internet and IEC-based computer graphics systems are running. In orthodox art education, developing the capabilities of the artistic imagination is mainly conducted through artistic skill such as drawing, carving, or forming artistic works. In other words, the student's imagination, expressed in his or her artistic works, is filtered by the person's skill. The IEC-based computer graphics systems allow us to educate the students' artistic imagination with very little or no influence on their artistic skills.

Virtual aquarium is our project that allows unskilled computer graphics students to create imaginary fish shapes through the Internet and make the fish swim in a VR space. The 3-D fish are modeled by combining equations, and their coefficients are optimized by GA based on the students' evaluation of the created shape.

Our computer graphics figurative project lets unskilled students in computer graphics create general 3-D objects such as pots, cars, fruits, and so on (see Figure 15.5) [25]. The 3-D shape is modeled by a combination of hyperquadratic functions, and their coefficients are optimized by GAs based on the students' evaluation of the created shapes. We are also running an IEC-based educational project on computer graphics fireworks animation.

15.3.6 IEC Interface Research

IEC has some problems that normal EC does not have. The biggest problem remaining is human fatigue, which is caused by the IEC expectation that a human user cooperate with a tireless computer and evaluate EC individuals. The second problem is how to search for a goal with a smaller population size within a lower number of searching generations. This requirement is inevitable due to the fatigue problem. The third problem is how to let an IEC user evaluate time-variant tasks such as sounds or movies that cannot be compared spatially with less fatigue and less operation time.

IEC interface research has been conducted to solve these problems and to make IEC more practical. However, the number of these projects is not large because of the engineering education mentioned in Section 15.2.

The IEC interface research conducted so far includes a discrete fitness-value input method to reduce psychological fatigue, the prediction of fitness values that predict the characteristics of human evaluation to increase the real number of individuals for the EC (not for the user) and support human evaluation, IEC interface for time-sequential display tasks such as sounds or movies, EC acceleration, especially in early generations, and active intervention that allow users to join the EC search, plus subjective evaluation in order to reduce the user's psychological fatigue. See [2] for details about this interface research.

15.4 CONCLUSION

The future direction of computational intelligence has been discussed through a survey of past research and emphasizing that the concept of humanized CI is one of keywords to pilot the future of CI. IEC is one of the key technologies for developing this concept. As seen in this chapter, several new approaches based on IEC show the high potential of IEC, and have started by combining human capabilities. We hope that the concept emphasized in this chapter becomes a good guideline for those who work in this field.

REFERENCES

1. H. Takagi. "Fusion Technology of Neural Networks and Fuzzy Systems: A Chronicled Progression from the Laboratory to Our Daily Lives." *Int. J. Appl. Math. Comput. Sci.*, vol. 10, no. 4, 647–673, 2000.
2. H. Takagi. "Interactive Evolutionary Computation: Fusion of the Capacities of EC Optimization and Human Evaluation." *Proc. IEEE*, vol. 89, no. 9, 1275–1296, 2001.
3. R. Dawkins. *The Blind Watchmaker*, Longman, Essex, UK, 1986.
4. T. Unemi. "SBART2.4: Breeding 2D CG Images and Movies, and Creating a Type of Collage." In *Proceedings of the 3rd International Conference on Knowledge-Based Intelligent Information Engineering Systems* (*KES799*), Adelaide, Australia, Aug./Sept. 1999, pp. 288–291.
5. K. Aoki and H. Takagi. "3-D CG Lighting with an Interactive GA," In *Proceedings of the 1st International Conference on Conventional and Knowledge-Based Intelligent Electronic Systems (KES'97)*, Adelaide, Australia, May 1997, pp. 296–301.

6. M. Ohsaki and H. Takagi. "Application of Interactive Evolutionary Computation to Optimal Tuning of Digital Hearing Aids." In *Proceedings of the International Conference on Soft Computing (IIZUKA'98)*, Iizuka, Japan, Oct. 1998, pp. 849–852.
7. M. Ohsaki and H. Takagi. "Design and Development of an IEC-based Hearing Aids Fitting System." In *Proceedings of the 4th Asia Fuzzy System Symposium (AFSS'00)*, Tsukuba, Japan, June 2000, pp. 543–548.
8. H. Takagi, S. Kamohara, and T. Takeda. "Introduction of Soft Computing Techniques to Welfare Devices." In *Proceedings of the IEEE Midnight-Sun Workshop on Soft Computing Methods in Industrial Applications (SMCia/99)*, Kuusamo, Finland, June 1999, pp. 116–121.
9. H. Takagi and M. Ohsaki. "IEC-based Hearing Aids Fitting." In *Proceedings of the IEEE International Conference on System, Man, and Cybernetics (SMC'99)*, Tokyo, Japan, Oct. 1999, pp. 657–662.
10. N. Hayashida and H. Takagi. "Acceleration of EC Convergence with Landscape Visualization and Human Intervention." *Applied Soft Computing*, vol. 1, no. 4F, 245–246, 2002.
11. R. Poli and S. Cagnoni. "Genetic Programming with User-Driven Selection: Experiments on the Evolution of Algorithms for Image Enhancement." In *Proceedings of the 2nd Annual Conference on Genetic Programming*, Stanford, CA, July 1997, pp. 269–277.
12. M. A. Lewis, A. H. Fagg, and A. Solidum. "Genetic Programming Approach to the Construction of a Neural Network for Control of a Walking Robot." In *Proceedings of the IEEE International Conference on Robotics and Automation*, vol. 3, Nice, France, May 1992, pp. 2618–2623.
13. H. H. Lund and O. Miglino. "Evolving and Breeding Robots." In *Proceedings of the 1st European Workshop on Evolutionary Robotics (EboRobot98)*, Berlin, Germany, Apr. 1998, pp. 192–210.
14. H. H. Lund, O. Miglino, L. Pagliarini, A. Billard, and A. Ijspeert. "Evolutionary Robotics—A Children's Game." In *Proceedings of the IEEE International Conference on Evolutionary Computation (ICEC'98)*, Anchorage, AK, May 1998, pp. 154–158.
15. N. Kubota, K. Watanabe, and F. Kojima. "Interactive Genetic Algorithm for Trajectory Generation of Human Friendly Robots." vol. 1, no. 4F, 245–256, *Trans. Jpn. Soc. Mech. Eng.*, Series C, (in Japanese), vol. 66, no. 647, 2274–2279, 2000.
16. T. Onisawa and T. Anzai. "Acquisition of Intelligible Fuzzy Rules." In *Proceedings of the IEEE International Conference on Systems, Man, and Cybernetics (SMC'99)*, vol. 5, Tokyo, Japan, Oct. 1999, pp. 268–273.
17. M. Fujii and T. Furuhashi. "A Study of Interactive Between Humans and Systems Using Fuzzy Classifier System." In *Proceedings of the Workshop on Interactive Evolutionary Computation (in Japanese)*, Fukuoka, Japan, Mar. 1998, pp. 37–41.
18. S. Kamohara, H. Takagi, and T. Takeda. "Control Rule Acquisition for an Arm Wrestling Robot." In *Proceedings of the IEEE International Conference on System, Man, Cybernetics (SMC'97)*, vol. 5, Orlando, FL, Oct. 1997, pp. 4227–4231.
19. Y. Katurada and Y. Maeda. "Support System for Automatically Emotional Generation Using Interactive EC." In *Proceedings of the 16th Fuzzy System Symposium* (in Japanese), Akita, Japan, Sept. 2000, pp. 297–300.
20. N. Kubota, Y. Nojima, N. Baba, F. Kojima, and T. Fukuda. "Evolving Pet Robot with Emotional Model." In *Proceedings of the Congress on Evolutionary Computation (CEC00)*, La Jolla, CA, July 2000, pp. 1231–1237.

21. I. Kamihira, M. Yamaguchi, and H. Kita. "Online Adaptation of Vehicles by Means of an Evolutionary Control System." In *Proceeding of the IEEE International Conference on Systems, Man, and Cybernetics* (*SMC'99*), Tokyo, Japan, Oct. 1999, pp. 553–558.

22. R. Gatarski. "Breed Better Banners Design Automation Through Online Interaction." *J. Interact. Mark.*, vol. 16, no. 1, 2–13, 2001.

23. T. Morita, H. Iba, and M. Ishizuka. "Generating Emotional Voice and Behavior Expression by Interactive Evolutionary Computation." In *Proceedings of the 62nd Annual Meeting of Japan Society for Information Processing* (in Japanese), Yokohama, Japan, Mar. 2001, pp. 45–46.

24. N. Monmarché, G. Nocent, M. Slimane, G. Venturini, and P. Santini. "Imagine: A Tool for Generating HTML Style Sheets with an Interactive Genetic Algorithm Based on Genes Frequencies." In *Proceedings of the IEEE International Conference on System, Man, and Cybernetics* (*SMC'99*), vol. 3, Tokyo, Japan, Oct. 1999, pp. 640–645.

25. H. Nishino, H. Takagi, S.-B. Cho, and K. Utsumiya, "A 3D Modeling System for Creative Design." In *Proceedings of the 15th International Conference on Information Networking* (*ICOIN-15*), Beppu, Japan, Jan./Feb. 2001, pp. 479–486.

CHAPTER 16

UNSUPERVISED LEARNING BY ARTIFICIAL NEURAL NETWORKS

HAROLD SZU

16.1 A NEW CHALLENGE: SPACE-VARIANT UNSUPERVISED CLASSIFICATIONS

What does remote satellite sensing for rain forest deforestation [1,2] and camouflaged enemy ground vehicles have to do with breast cancer diagnosis [3,4]? Both require space-variant unsupervised classification. The major difference in application depends on the number of independent sources and the number of spectral components needed. In breast imaging, the measurement data vector has a minimum of two components of two spectral bands (e.g., a long 8–12-μ and 3–5-μ middle-wavelength infrared breast imaging for benign or malignant tumors). By comparison, there are seven spectral bands in the earth satellite (Landsat [5] in this chapter), and 200 spectral components on board U2 airplanes for hyperspectral measurements [6]. The medium transfer (Green's) function (MTF) is by definition composed of spectral feature templates that vary diurnally and seasonally so much that they cannot be classified accurately by a closed-set library approach. Such a spatiotemporal-varying MTF from pixel to pixel must be considered to be unknown, and the unknown classification radiation sources is referred to as *unsupervised classification*.

The traditional approach to solving for unknown mixtures of unknown sources is also known as *blind source separation* (BSS) or *independent components analyses* (ICA), which overcomes the underdeterminacy of an unknown MTF by computing the neighborhood pixel ensemble for the entropy contrast function, cf. Bell and Sejnowski [7], Amari et al. [8], or by the use of higher-order statistics, e.g., references in three annual ICA BSS IEEE conferences. Unfortunately, medical imaging and remote sensing tasks present space-variant MTFs for unknown point targets and tumors. The traditional neighborhood pixel ensemble approach to ICA BSS, which assumes implicitly an invariant MTF, will suffer from point-source blurring. In such cases, the information needed to resolve the ambiguity should not be derived

Computational Intelligence: The Experts Speak. Edited by D. B. Fogel and C. J. Robinson
ISBN 0-471-27454-2

spatially from the neighborhood (because each individual pixel may have a different MTF over the landscape); rather, spectral vector per pixel data are required. This chapter has derived a space-variant unsupervised classification algorithm, pixel by pixel independently, using the minimization of the thermodynamics free energy per pixel to reduce the redundancy of spectral components.

When more than one spectral camera is used, the corresponding pixel data become a vector **X** per pixel, and the space-variant MTF becomes a blind matrix $[A]$ per pixel. We wish to invert, per pixel, the matrix ($\mathbf{X} = [A]\mathbf{S}$) for the unknown heat-sources vector **S** ($\mathbf{S} = [A]^{-1}\mathbf{X}$) without knowing what the mixing matrix is. The main finding is that automatic target recognition (ATR) with space-variant MTFs can be resolved unambiguously per pixel provided that (1) vector spectral data per pixel have more than one independent spectral measurement, and (2) a pertinent physics constraint is the thermodynamics free energy that can generalize Shannon's entropy theory to an open information-processing system, the Earth and the breast, involving an arbitrary flux of energy.

16.2 POWER OF PAIRS: VECTOR VERSUS SCALAR DATA

Having more measurements conceivably narrows the arbitrariness inherited in one component of measurement. For example, if we had only one infrared camera to take a thermal-image measurement, then, per pixel, we might obtain an arbitrary gray-scale intensity value

$$30 = 2 \times 15 = 3 \times 10 = 5 \times 6 = 6 \times 5 \tag{16.1}$$

which has several possible equally valid multiplicative (deconvoluted) solutions. To resolve them, the traditional classifier would impose a priori knowledge upon a library of matched filters using an arbitrary decision threshold to determine the nearest-neighborhood class features. However, we have departed from the traditional library approach, because it is more reasonable in an information-theoretical sense to gather further direct evidence, so that more independent spectral measurement data become a multiple-component vector per pixel that could enjoy the "power of pairs."

In the cases of remote satellite sensing, the number of independent spectral components per pixel could be anywhere between 5 and 200. This vector data per pixel approach is proposed in order to take advantage of a question often posed when dealing with the biomimetics of human sensory systems (HSS): "Why is it that, for every emitter, there always exists at least a pair of receptors (e.g., eyes, ears, nostrils, taste buds, and hands)?" Multiple-choice answers to this question include the following: (1) fault tolerance; (2) stereo perception; (3) unsupervised learning; (4) all of the above. A common mistake, as pointed out by David Marr [9], is that two eyes alone could achieve stereovision, because light rays (like sound waves) are passive and do not carry distance information. In fact, a two-eyed viewer cannot tell (in the dark) whether three points of light come from a horizontal row or a column in depth (see Fig. 16.1).

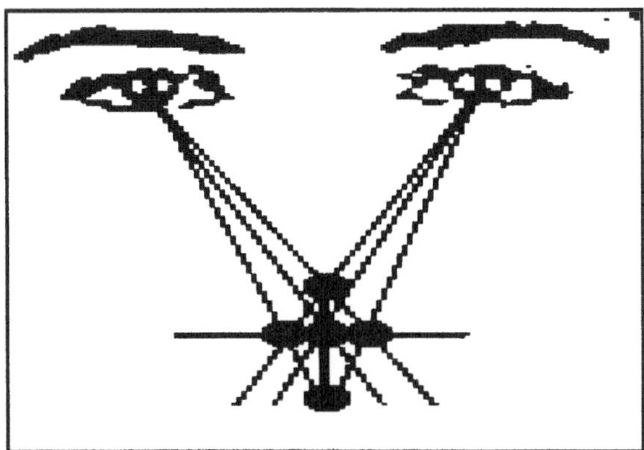

Figure 16.1 Two eyes alone cannot discern whether three points of light are in a row or a column. If two eyes are not intended for stereovision, then the question remains, Why do we have two eyes? The answer: intravenously unsupervised sensor fusion.

In a benchmark optics ICA experiment [10–13], we examined "parallax" to give a vector time series $\mathbf{X}(t)$, the equivalence of four eyes or six eyes with memory delays. From these delays, the relative movement of point sources with respect to the range and local integration smoothness in the neighborhood give depth information, but not from two eyes alone. Thus, the question remains: Why two eyes? The answer is that they provide vector data for unsupervised processing.

Barlow [14] summarized the HSS lesson succinctly: he suggested that two eyes with excessive excitation from 260-million rods and cones should experience signal decay to conserve energy. This prompted us to determine what would happen during such a redundancy reduction. We showed that it is only required to replenish the instantaneous common excitations of the noisy pair of images, such as the common Hubel–Wiesel edges maps [9], that ultimately reveal the clear image of the face image presented in "De-mixed image 1" of a dominant eye (see Fig. 16.2); the left-over noise is left to "De-mixed image 2" of Figure 16.2.

The essence of a pair's power is further illustrated by a game we like to call "name that tone number," which is somewhat reminiscent of a popular TV show in which contestants would guess the name of a piece of music from a few notes. In this case, the entity we are trying to guess after "hearing" a few "notes" is first distorted through a bad player of unknown MTF. We measured a two-component vector, e.g. $\mathbf{X} = (41,61)$, of the middle- and the long-wavelength infrared radiation generated by hot-blood heat sources, e.g., $\mathbf{S} = (5,3)$, representing the unknown benign and malignant tumor in units of hundred photons and being propagated through the unknown breast tissue MTF, whose effect mixes the sources to produce the two-component vector data:

$$\begin{aligned} 41 &= 4 \times 5 + 7 \times 3 \\ 61 &= 8 \times 5 + 7 \times 3 \end{aligned} \tag{16.2}$$

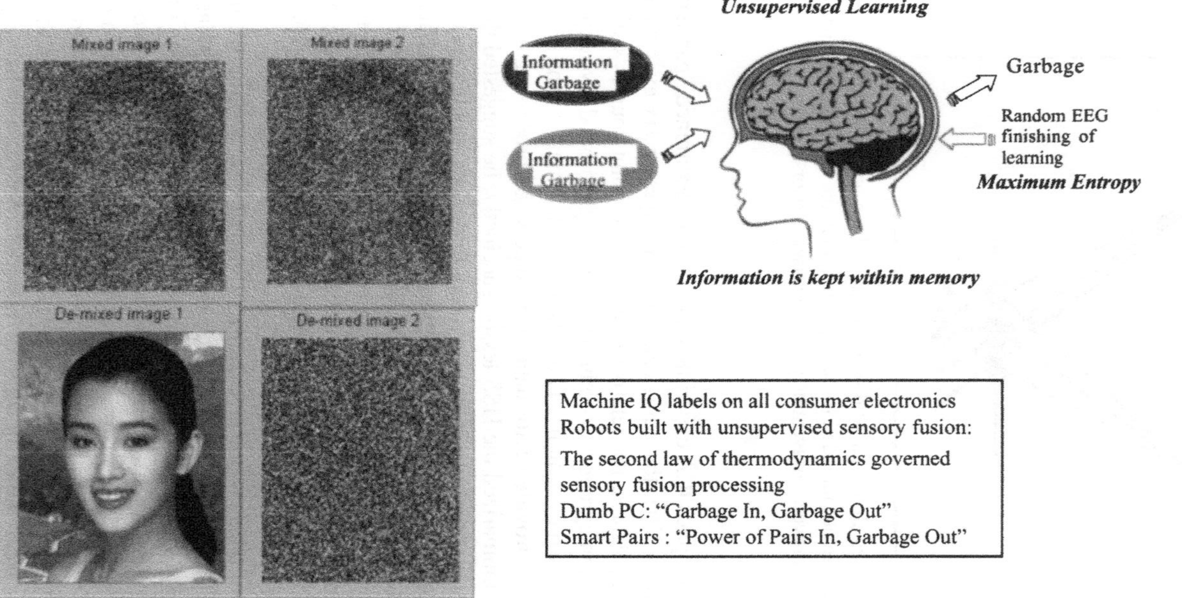

Figure 16.2 Two robot eyes equipped with unsupervised learning neural networks can have a machine IQ label beyond 50% of the average human being. While the dominant left eye picks out the agreed-upon signal per pixel, the less dominant right eye keeps the other's leftover noise.

To demonstrate the arbitrary and unknown MTF explicitly, we rewrote the pair of equations in matrix form:

$$\begin{bmatrix} \frac{1}{\sqrt{5}} & \frac{1}{\sqrt{2}} \\ \frac{2}{\sqrt{5}} & \frac{1}{\sqrt{2}} \end{bmatrix} \begin{pmatrix} 5 \\ 3 \end{pmatrix} = \begin{bmatrix} 0.447 & 0.707 \\ 0.894 & 0.707 \end{bmatrix} \begin{pmatrix} 5 \\ 3 \end{pmatrix} = \begin{bmatrix} \cos\theta & \cos\varphi \\ \sin\theta & \sin\varphi \end{bmatrix} \begin{pmatrix} 5 \\ 3 \end{pmatrix}$$
$$= 8\left[\frac{5}{8}\begin{pmatrix} 1 \\ 2 \end{pmatrix}\left(\frac{1}{\sqrt{5}}\right) + \frac{3}{8}\begin{pmatrix} 1 \\ 1 \end{pmatrix}\left(\frac{1}{\sqrt{2}}\right)\right] \cong \begin{pmatrix} 4.3 \\ 6.6 \end{pmatrix} \tag{16.3}$$

in units of thousands of photons. The 2×2 matrix indicated two degrees of freedom in the unknown MTF, [**A**], which had two column vectors called mixing feature vectors, **a**, **b**. This was multiplied by two heat source components and gave rise to the radiation spectral data:

$$[\mathbf{A}]\mathbf{S} \equiv [\mathbf{A}]N\mathbf{S} = N\left(s'_x\mathbf{a} + s'_y\mathbf{b}\right) = \mathbf{X} \tag{16.4}$$

At the limit of weak radiation intensity, we should have assumed a conservative propagation medium, such that, once the normalized mixing matrix[A] was determined, the total source strength would be given subsequently by a single unknown constant $\mathbf{N} = 5 + 3$ and $\mathbf{S}' = (s'_x, s'_y)^1$, where $s'_x = s_x/N$ denotes a normalized source component. It is the relative strength between two spectral components that determines the tumor physiology and the angles of the unit-mixing feature vectors **a**, **b** at $\theta = 63.5° = 64°$ and $\varphi = 45°$. The challenge for the unsupervised classifier nevertheless remains to find four unknowns: both the unknown MTF unit mixing feature vectors **a**, **b** and the unknown heat sources. The classifier must accomplish this given only two spectral data vectors, as shown in Figure 16.3.

To appreciate such a blind ATR, one must understand the general strategies of supervised versus unsupervised classification. If the MTF features are known a priori, it would be efficient to match one of the mixing-feature vectors of MTF, as in the case of supervised classification. If the MTF is unknown, one should try to apply the "divide and conquer" rule to reduce the degrees of freedom, as in the case of unsupervised classification. In the two infrared spectral breast-imaging cases, two degrees of freedom implied that two mixing-feature vectors **a**, **b** are located within the positive-energy quadrant of a total span of 90° within the first quadrant of the Cartesian coordinates in Figure 16.3. Although a perfect matching filter at one coordinate would result in cross matching with the other—because these positive-feature vectors cannot be orthogonal to each other—a perfect killing filter nevertheless ensures complete elimination, namely killing, of any one of the degrees of freedom [15,16]. Therefore, while supervised classifiers still require an ambiguously arbitrary threshold of local maximum after matching, unsupervised classifiers require a vector subspace to search uniquely the killing vector at a local minimum of a suitable contrast function. This turns out to be the thermodynamics free energy of radiation photons. The latter would be better than the former, given a greater number of independent and simultaneous measurements.

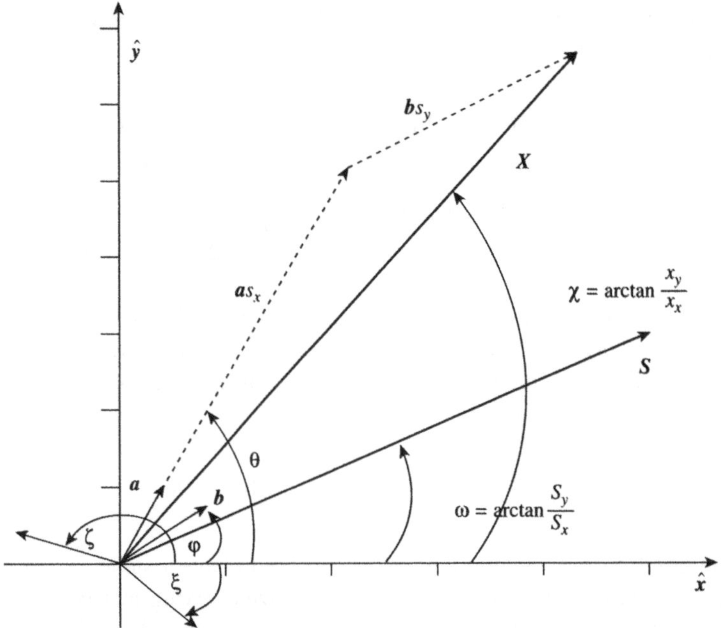

Figure 16.3 Unsupervised determination of the unknown MTF composed of mixing feature vectors; **a** and **b**, is accomplished by an exhaustive subspace search, simulated annealing, or gradient descents in order to find two killing vectors that by definition are orthogonal to the unknown feature vectors **a** and **b**, in order to eliminate completely either one of two degrees of freedom. The thermodynamics free energy is the first-order contrast function based on physics for a way of finding such local minima.

In general, every pixel-pair data can have had its own MTF mixing matrix represented by different propagation media surrounding different features of radiation sources. In the case of a very large tumor that has a large number of pixels on target (POT), the neighborhood pixel data could share a similar or identical MTF. However, this cannot help us resolve the underdeterminacy condition rigorously, except in the sense of statistical ensemble average. Every new pair of data images is associated with a new pair of unknown sources, thus, the number of known sources gained is always equal to the number of unknown ones lost, even if all neighborhood pixels have an identical MTF, except in the approximated sense of generating high-order statistical moments. Thus, an identical MTF for large tumors permits the use of the pixel ensemble average used in the statistical ICA methodology [7]. However, it is the other interesting limit of a single and subpixel tumor that gives the earliest possible precancer warning to the patients tracking the angiogenesis phase transition longitudinally in time without the danger of exposure to radiation.

There are two reasons for doing the magic pixel-by-pixel independently: (1) the power of pairs permits a divide-and-conquer subspace search of the angle of the killing weight vector to the data that generated the local minima of an appropriate contrast function, and (2) it turns out that the uncertainty is resolved adequately by the minimization of a thermodynamics free energy for a general open system, which involves the balance between the minimization of estimation error energy and the maximization of the entropy of independent sources.

16.3 GENERALIZATION OF SHANNON'S ENTROPY INFORMATION THEORY TO OPEN SYSTEMS

An appropriate contrast formula supplied by the second law of thermodynamics—"as the (estimation error) energy diffuses, the (independence) entropy increases"—is, according to the Helmholtz free energy, $H = U - T_0S$. The estimated-error energy, $U = \boldsymbol{\mu}^T \{[\mathbf{W}]\mathbf{X} - \mathbf{S}\}$, was by definition a scalar, which should be multiplied by a vector Lagrange multiplier $\boldsymbol{\mu}^T$ to be self-consistently determined at a constant reservoir temperature T_0, at which the Boltzmann entropy $\mathbf{S}$ (the definition of which Boltzmann had engraved on his gravestone) approached a local maximum. The Boltzmann entropy was defined for a total number $N = R + G + B$ of red (R), green (G), and blue (B) color photons (in units of hundreds) $V_N = (N!/R!G!B!)$; this gave the equivalent combinatorial degrees of freedom, which yielded an indication of intrinsic wandering space. Applying Shannon's logarithmic measure in Stirling's approximation ($\log N! = N \log N - N$), we obtain Boltzmann entropy as S:

$$S = K_B \log V_I = K_B \log\left(\frac{N!}{R!G!B!}\right) = -K_B N \sum_i s'_i \log s'_i \tag{16.5}$$

The normalization

$$\frac{R}{N} + \frac{G}{N} + \frac{B}{N} = \sum_i s'_i = 1 \tag{16.6}$$

yielded the unit probability constraint s'_i, which should be augmented by a scalar Lagrange multiplier for free energy, μ_0, in order to make the partial differentiations independent from one another. The weight matrix $[\mathbf{W}]$ had, as each row vector, a killing vector eliminating one of the mixing vectors of $[\mathbf{A}]$ by being orthogonal to it, and thus could reduce the absolute value of the Helmholtz free-energy operator H to a local minimum value μ_0:

$$\begin{aligned} H = U - T_0 S = \boldsymbol{\mu}^T([\mathbf{W}]\,\mathbf{X} - N\,\mathbf{S}') + NK_BT_0 \sum_{j=x,y} s'_j \log s'_j \\ + (N\mu_0 - NK_BT_0)\left(\sum_{j=x,y} s'_j - 1\right) \end{aligned} \tag{16.7}$$

The *ab initio* model is defined by statistical mechanics (16.7), which needs no more assumption for both the feedforward redundancy reduction and the feedback associative recall of image data from the source, $U = \boldsymbol{\lambda}^{\mathbf{T}}(\mathbf{X} - [\mathbf{A}]\mathbf{S}) = \boldsymbol{\mu}^T([\mathbf{W}]\,\mathbf{X} - \mathbf{S}')$, of a new class of unsupervised artificial neural networks (ANN) defined by Fig. 16.4 and four theorems as follows.

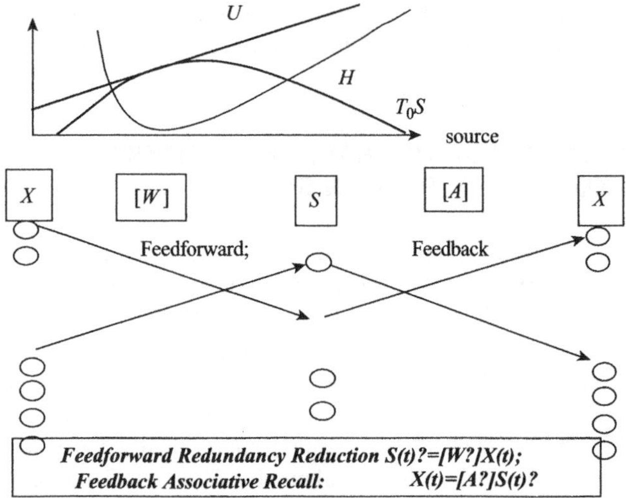

Figure 16.4 Helmholtz free energy is defined as $H = U - T_0S$; (16.7). The internal energy U could be modeled in two forms: the feedforward redundancy reduction for sensory fusion and the feedback for associative recalls. Both are useful for two unsupervised neural networks that also can be coupled together to determine whether a proper registration and segmentation can reproduce the original data set.

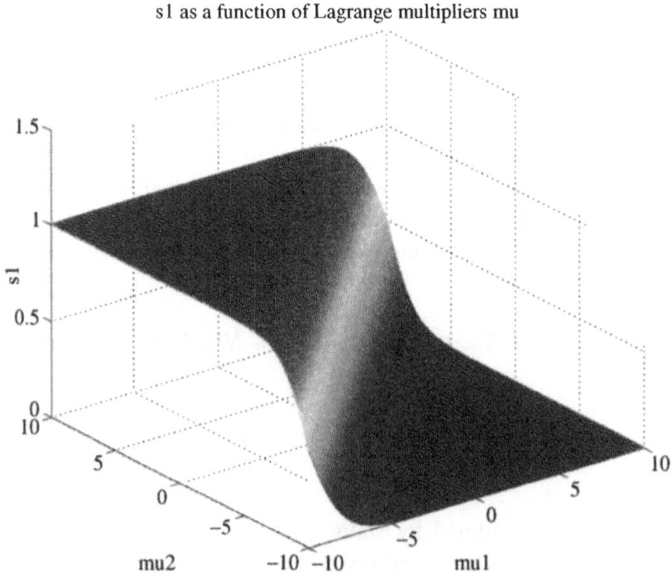

Figure 16.5 Sigmoid threshold is derived from Helmholtz free-energy minimization and its partition function.

THEOREM 1 The equilibrium partition function of Helmholtz free energy yields the McCulloch–Pitts sigmoid threshold: (Fig. 16.5)

$$s'_j = \frac{1}{1 + \exp\left(\frac{1}{K_B T_0}(\mu_k - \mu_j)\right)} = \sigma(\mu_k, \mu_j) \tag{16.8}$$

Proof We differentiated the Helmholtz free energy, set it to zero to solve for the source probability, and summed it to one to give the partition function:

$$\frac{\partial H(s_x, s_y)}{\partial s'_j} = -\mu_j N + N K_B T_0 \left(\log s'_j\right) + N\mu_0 = 0; \qquad s'_j = \exp\left(\frac{\mu_j - \mu_0}{K_B T_0}\right)$$

Imposing the constraint of the probability normalization condition, $\sum_{j=x,y} s'_j = 1$, we obtained the partition function of the canonical ensemble in statistical mechanics:

$$\exp\left(\frac{\mu_0}{K_B T_0}\right) = \sum_{i=x,y} \exp\left(\frac{\mu_i}{K_B T_0}\right) \equiv Z$$

Eliminating the free energy μ_0, we get the sigmoid threshold of the normalized source component s'_j.

We can simply replace the partition-function identity by $\boldsymbol{\mu} = [\mathbf{A}]^T \boldsymbol{\lambda}^T$ for the feedback associative recall ANN.

THEOREM 2 The virtual Lagrange constraint forces, μ_k, with respect to the virtual sources displacement gives the thermodynamic free-energy value μ_0.

Proof Differentiating the free energy μ_0, we verified

$$\frac{\partial \mu_0}{\partial \mu_j} = s'_j \tag{16.9}$$

which, after partial integration, yields

$$\mu_0^{(k+1)} = s_x'^{(k)} \mu_x^{(k+1)} + s_y'^{(k)} \mu_y^{(k+1)} + C; \qquad C \equiv \mu_0^k - s_x'^{(k)} \mu_x^{(k)} - s_y'^{(k)} \mu_y^{(k)}$$

THEOREM 3 The learning rule of Lagrange forces represents the dendrite ion-channel current.

Proof Using the perturbation theory, $\Delta\mu_j = (\partial\mu_j / \partial s_\alpha)\Delta s_\alpha$, the stability update rule for the Lagrange multipliers with respect to k iteration index data for two spectral components $i, j \in \{x, y\}$

$$\mu_j^{(k+1)} = \mu_j^{(k)} + \left(\frac{K_B T_0}{N s_j'^{(k)}} + \frac{\mu_i^{(k)}}{N}\right)\left(w_j^{(k+1)} X - s_j^{(k)}\right) + \frac{\mu_i^{(k)}}{N}\left(w_i^{(k+1)} X - s_i^{(k)}\right) \tag{16.10}$$

The minimum number of two components of vector data is given here, while interested readers should be able to generalize both Theorems 3 and 4 to multispectral cases beyond two. The novel aspects of ANN models will now be postulated as follows.

THEOREM 4 The killing vectors of the unknown mixing matrix MTF can be determined independently of Boltzmann entropy.

Proof Because the Boltzamnn–Shannon entropy, S, is a simple convex function that does not depend on the killing angles, we can add it to (16.6), yielding

$$\min_{[W]}|H + T_0 S| = \min_{[W]}|H| = \min_{[W]}|U| = \sqrt{\sum_{i=x,y} (\mu_i(w_i X - Ns'_i))^2} \qquad (16.11)$$

Applying the Holder triangle-inequality identity, one can show that the local minimum of linear first-order free energy can determine identical values of the killing angles weight matrix $[W]$ in the modified Helmholtz free energy, $\mathrm{H} + \mathrm{T_0 S} = U$, and the internal energy, U.

Note that the free parameters of (16.11) are the killing angles and the successive estimation of the sources must be derived consistently from (16.12)–(16.14), based on the full Helmholtz free energy. The search for killing angles began at the initial conditions at maximum entropy with zero Lagrange constraint forces: $s_x'^{(0)} = s_y'^{(0)} = \frac{1}{2}$; $\mu_x^0 = \mu_y^0 = 0$. Using the partition function, we computed the free energy at iteration $k + 1$:

$$\mu_0^{(k+1)} = K_B T_0 \ln\left(\exp\left(\frac{\mu_x^{(k+1)}}{K_B T_0}\right) + \exp\left(\frac{\mu_y^{(k+1)}}{K_B T_0}\right)\right) \qquad (16.12)$$

Similarly, the equilibrium sigmoid solution estimated the source at iteration $k + 1$:

$$\hat{s}_j'^{(k+1)} = \exp\left(\frac{\mu_j^{(k+1)} - \mu_0^{(k+1)}}{K_B T_0}\right) \qquad (16.13)$$

The unknown scaling constant $N = s_x + s_y$ was estimated from data vector $\mathbf{X}$, based on the triangle inequality $||\vec{X}||_2 \leq Ns'_x||\vec{a}||_2 + Ns'_y||\vec{b}_2 = N(s'_x + s'_y) = N,$ which gave

$$N = \mathrm{ceil}\left(||X'||_2\right) \qquad (16.14)$$

where *ceil* denotes positive integer roundoff.

16.4 BENCHMARKS OF SPACE-VARIANT UNSUPERVISED CLASSIFICATION

Exhaustive search in the angular support domain is one way to find the killing angles. Because the estimation error energy function had local minima, gradient algorithms became stuck in some of them. A more efficient way to find the killing angles is to use a simulated annealing algorithm to solve combinatorial optimization problems [17,18]. A 2-D plot of the minimum Helmholtz free energy with respect to the killing angles, (16.13), is shown in Figure 16.6. Plot 16.6a is the error function (16.12) in the linear scale, while plot 16.6c is the inverse of the error function (16.13) in the logarithmic scale. The solution is at the global minimum of the error function at the angles $\zeta^* = 90° + 64° = 154°, \xi^* = 45° - 90° = -45°$. Since the value of the error at the global minimum was extremely small ($|U| < 10^{-16}$), this point could not be seen in the linear scale. One solution was to use an inverse of it so that minima became maxima.

Lacking accurate ground truth for real-world experiments, the Lagrange constraint neural networks (LCNN) have been benchmarked with synthetic blind demixing in Figure 16.7 and 16.8.

16.5 MULTISPECTRAL MEDICAL IMAGING

The conclusion of these derivations invites discussion of an application of unsupervised learning that is very important; not only to researchers but also to current and future breast-cancer patients: multispectral breast imaging. To supplement traditional X-ray mammography for early tumor detection [4], which is usually less than a pixel, e.g., microcalcifications as remnants of cells destroyed by cancer after the fact, we propose a nonintrusive, private, passive imaging approach that utilizes high-precision multispectral infrared cameras and can be conducted at a comfortable room temperature. This approach allows a patient to be tracked as frequently as necessary to detect the hemodynamics of angiogenesis—the ramping up of precancerous tumor demands for blood supply—or to follow a patient's progress during postcancer treatment.

The challenge was that there existed no reliable lookup template library for supervised classification because breast tissue variability produces an inhomogeneous and nonisotropic propagation medium through which the blood vessel and tumor locations generate a variety of heat-distribution functions (e.g., normal Gaussian thermal diffusion heat versus abnormal Laplacian singular heat concentration). We applied precision instrumentation developed recently for remote sensing to a patient's breasts: This instrumentation processes a spectrum similar to blackbody radiation, and thus enjoys an operating range "from tanks to tumors." Fortunately, the issue of buried-tumor depth turned out to be less sensitive than first expected: Just as the hot engine of a tank can appear in an arbitrary location, the detectable heat diffusion one measures comes from surface body temperature, underneath which passes any capillary heat sources rerouted by the angiogenesis process. However, the breast imaging

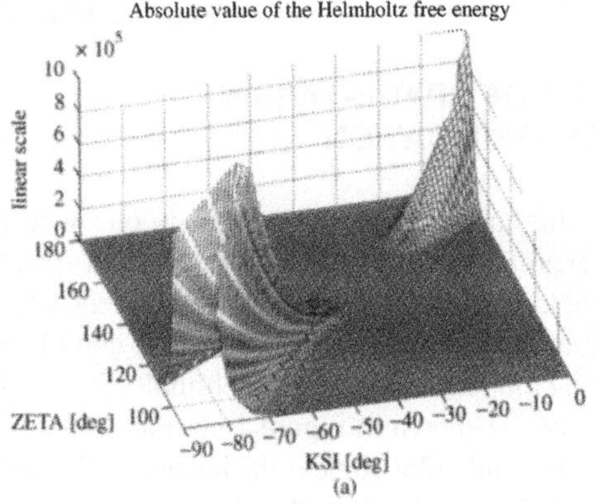

(a)

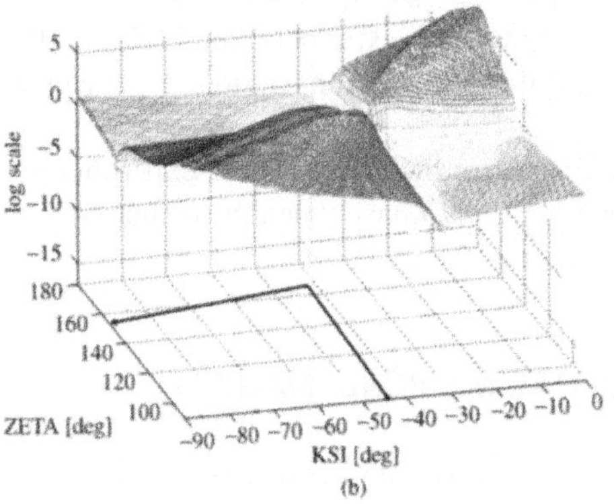

(b)

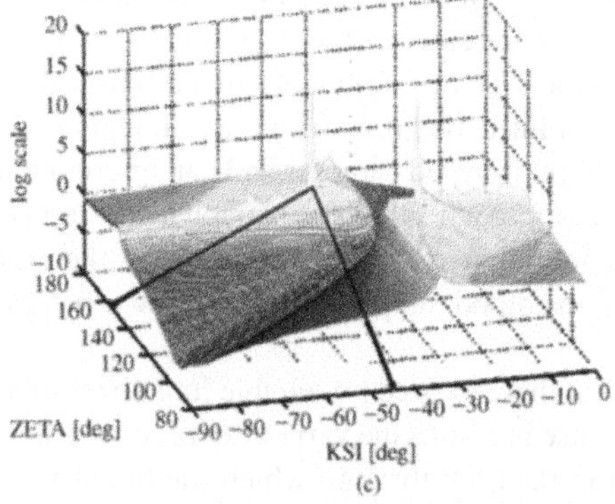

(c)

Figure 16.6 2-D plot of the absolute value of the absolute value of Helmholtz free energy as an error function. (a) The error function (16.11) in the linear scale; (b) the error function (16.11) in the logarithmic scale; (c) the inverse of the error function (16.11) in the logarithmic scale. The solution is at the global minimum of the error function at angles $\zeta^* = 90° + 64° = 154°$, $\xi^* = 45° - 90° = -45°$. Unfortunately, since the value of the error at the global minimum is extremely small ($|U| < 10^{-16}$), this point cannot be seen in the linear scale. The solution is either to use the log function, which acts as amplifier (b), or to use the inverse of the error function in the logarithmic scale (a).

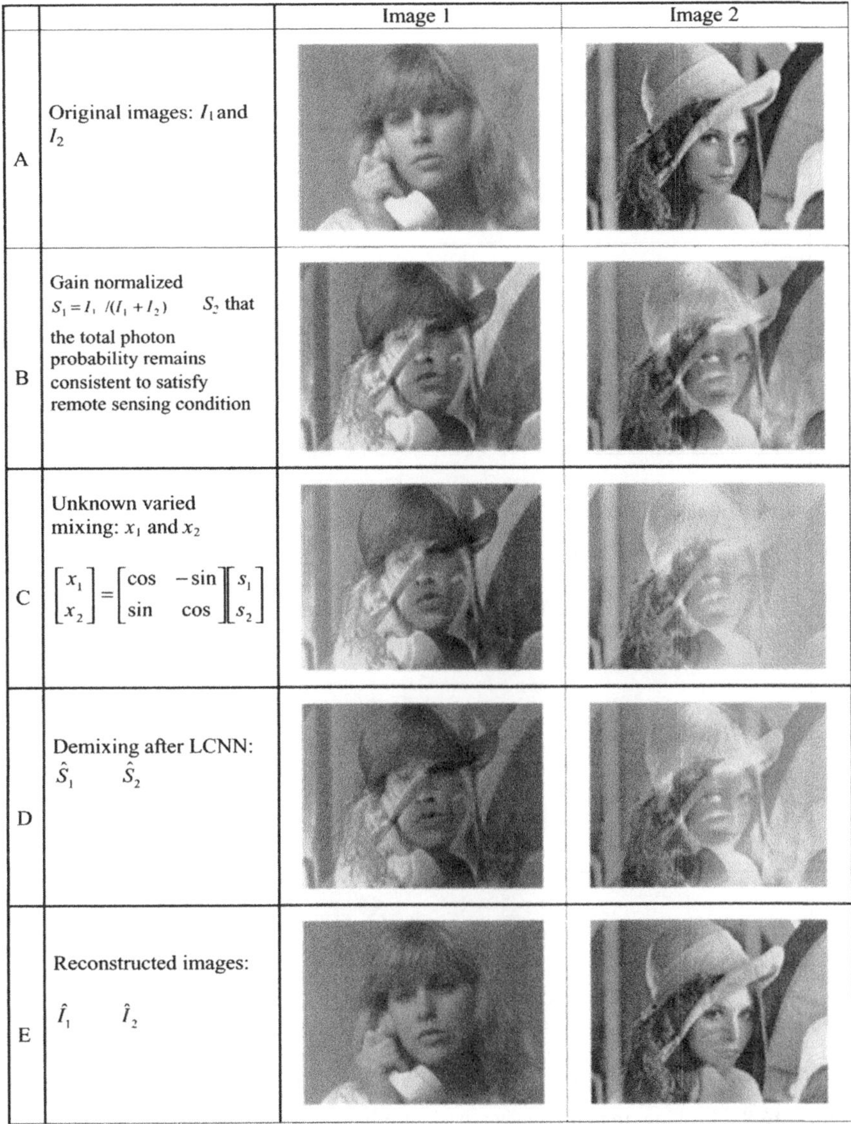

Figure 16.7 Lacking remote sensing ground truth, we tested the LCNN algorithm with spatially varying angle mixture, as evident from the changing shade.

experiments required a much refined minimum resolvable temperature difference (MRTD) at 10 milli-Kelvin degrees, covering two different spectral bands at 3–5 μ and 9–12 μ wavelengths (Mid IR: InSb Cincinnati Elec. 3–5 Micrometer wavelength, and Long IR: Platinum Selicide ICC 9–12 Micrometer wavelength). The key innovative ingredient that made this diagnosis possible was an unsupervised

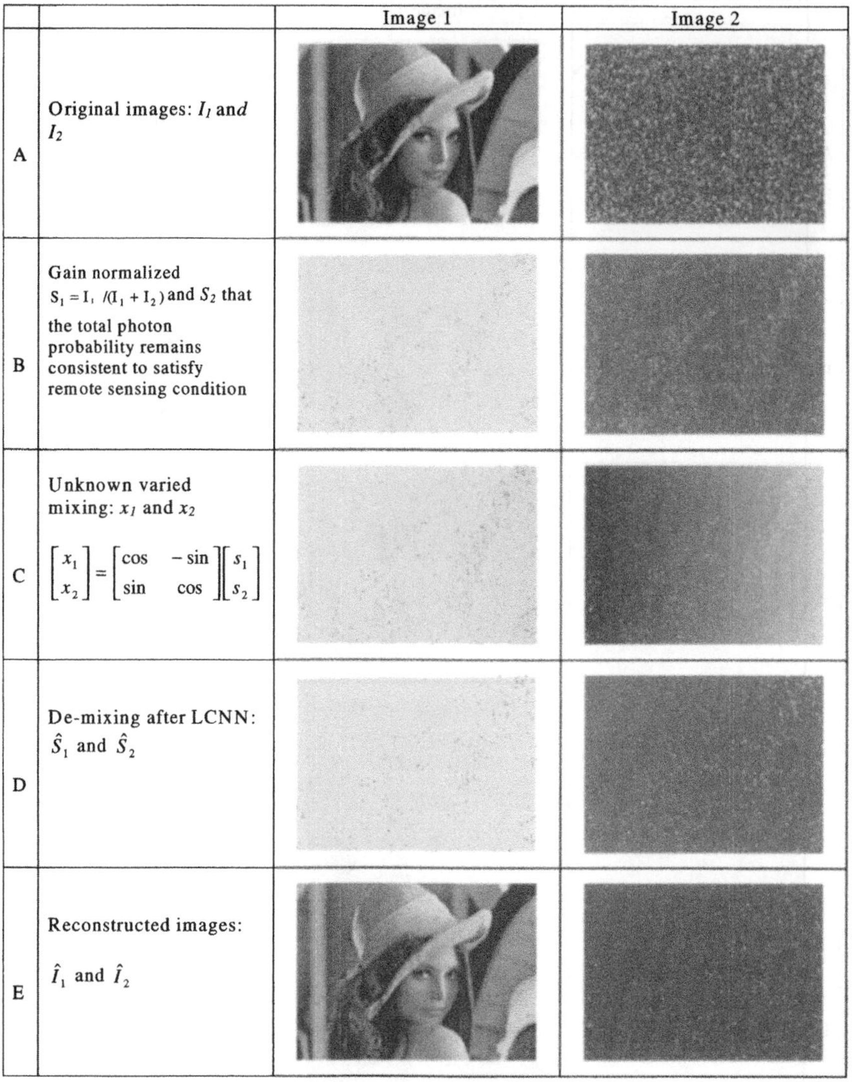

		Image 1	Image 2
A	Original images: I_1 and I_2		
B	Gain normalized $S_1 = I_1/(I_1 + I_2)$ and S_2 that the total photon probability remains consistent to satisfy remote sensing condition		
C	Unknown varied mixing: x_1 and x_2 $\begin{bmatrix} x_1 \\ x_2 \end{bmatrix} = \begin{bmatrix} \cos & -\sin \\ \sin & \cos \end{bmatrix} \begin{bmatrix} s_1 \\ s_2 \end{bmatrix}$		
D	De-mixing after LCNN: $\hat{S}_1$ and $\hat{S}_2$		
E	Reconstructed images: $\hat{I}_1$ and $\hat{I}_2$		

Figure 16.8 Lacking remote sensing basic truth, we tested the LCNN algorithm for de Cauchy noise with spatially varying angle mixture, as is evident from the changing shade.

classification algorithm derived now in this chapter. Simulation examples were provided in Figures 16.7 and 16.8 to verify the algorithm with known ground truth.

Here, we showed the results of the same algorithm applied to unsupervised classification of the multispectral IR breast images for early breast-cancer detection and tracking. The performance with single-color breast imaging is shown in Figure 16.9 for healthy breast tissue and Figure 16.10 for pathological tissue. Two recordings per session were necessary: the first recording was made one minute after the patient undressed, and the second was made 10 minutes later. In Figure 16.10, it can be

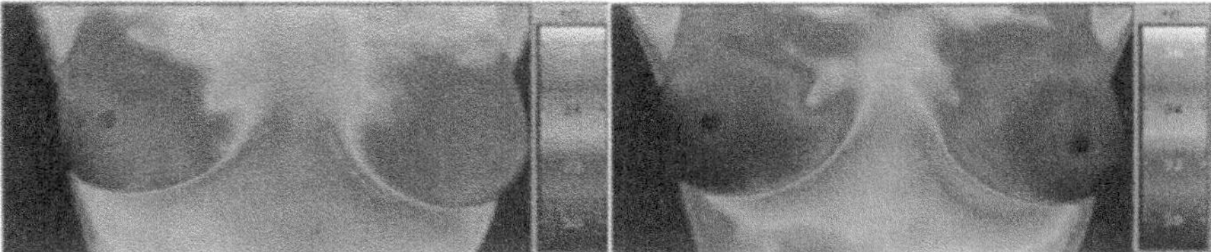

Figure 16.9 A single infrared camera took two images of healthy woman in a room cooled to 21°C. After 10 minutes, the image on the right shows most heat has dissipated, and no abnormal heat emission within either breast is visible.

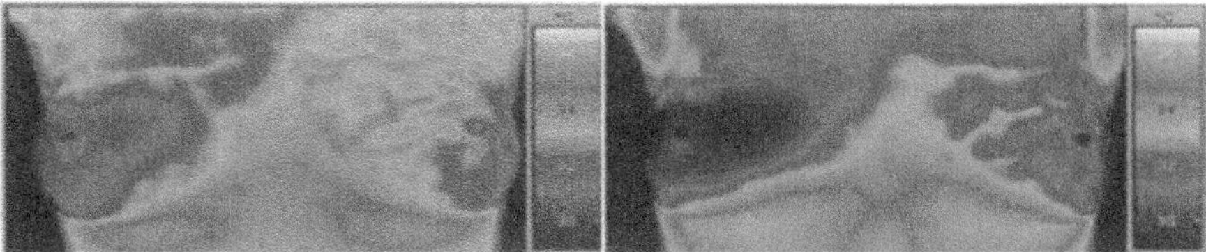

Figure 16.10 A single infrared camera took images of a breast cancer patient in a room cooled to 21°C. After 10 minutes, the image on the right shows active cancer cells (angiogenesis) emitting abnormal heat, while the surrounding tissue has cooled.

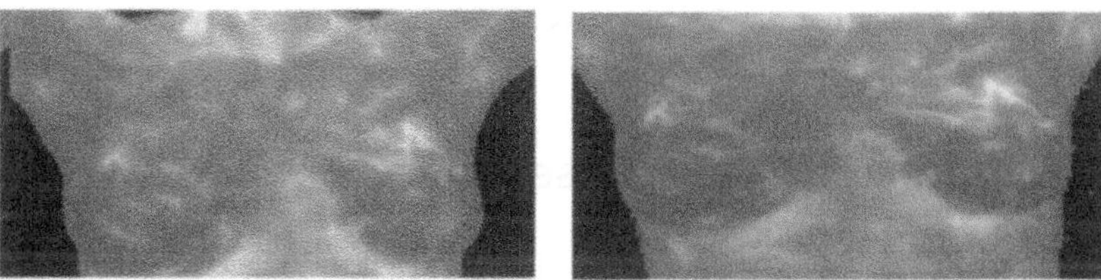

Figure 16.11 (Double-Blind Test Result): Two-camera multispectral infrared breast image. Left figure is medium-wavelength IR and right figure is long-wavelength IR breast imagery. The neural-network-unsupervised classification algorithm can do detection from one set of imagery without a library.

readily seen that the right breast continued to emanate heat even after body temperature decreased in a cold room. This illustrates the nutrition coming from the warm blood vessels necessary to feed the tumor. In Figure 16.11, we show the mid- and long-IR images of the pathological breast. Unlike to the single-camera IR method, our method required only one recording. Figure 16.12 shows two independent classes when the unsupervised classification algorithm (Theorem 1) had been applied to the image of the left breast: two independent classes in terms of a variable probability between zero and one. The classification results for the right breast are shown in Figure 16.13. The marked area on the right breast indicates the existence of a ductal carcinoma in situ (DCIS) of stage #0 (confined) to stage #1(local spread). We thus recommend supplementing traditional X-ray mammography with this bispectral IR imaging in order to track patients' angiogenesis phase transitions or postcancer treatment progress without increasing patients' radiation exposure.

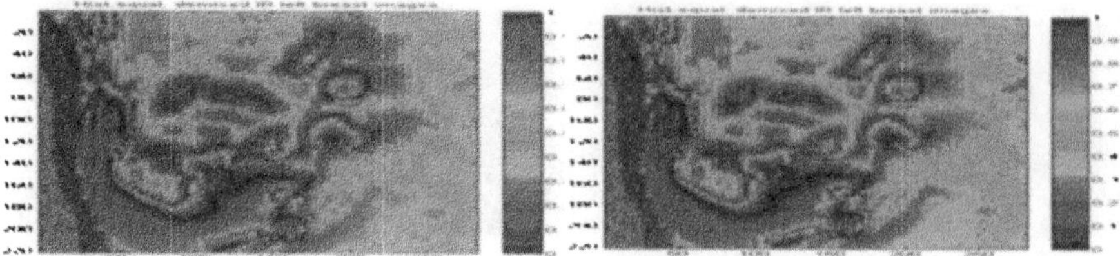

Figure 16.12 (Blind Test Result): Unsupervised classification images of the left breast. Here the color scheme indicates the probability of normal heat source versus the abnormal heat source class.

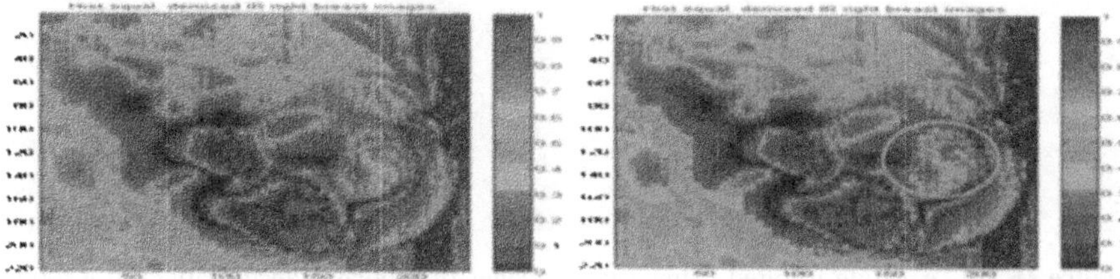

Figure 16.13 (Blind Test Result): Unsupervised classification images of the right breast. The left image shows normal heat distribution generated by the blood vessels. The right image indicates abnormal heat distribution, as shown by the double circled area near the breast nipple. According to the medical diagnosis, it is ductal carcinoma in situ (DCIS) cancer stage zero.

16.6 MULTISPECTRAL REMOTE SENSING

Applications in multispectral remote sensing on Landsat 7 spectral band images have already been demonstrated [5, 6, 19, 20]. The unsupervised classification method described in Theorem 1 has been demonstrated to be capable of discovering small man-made objects located sparsely in a desert when the objects exhibited similarly shaped spectral intensities, as they would if located in a city area. We reviewed Landsat remote sensing for monitoring Amazon deforestation [9]. To elucidate the challenge, we constructed in the 3-D spectral feature space (Figure 16.14). Given data $\boldsymbol{x} = [3\ 2\ 1]^T$, we construct three possible solutions: (1) a sparse solution, (2) a perturbation solution, and (3) a trivial solution at the maximum entropy (no more knowledge):

$$\begin{aligned}
\boldsymbol{x} = \begin{bmatrix} 3 \\ 2 \\ 1 \end{bmatrix} &= \begin{bmatrix} 3 & a' & a \\ 2 & a' & a \\ 1 & a' & a \end{bmatrix} \begin{bmatrix} 1 \\ 0 \\ 0 \end{bmatrix} \cong \begin{bmatrix} 3+\ddot{a}' & 3-\ddot{a}' & a \\ 2+\ddot{a}'' & 2-\ddot{a}'' & a \\ 1+\ddot{a}''' & 1-\ddot{a}''' & a \end{bmatrix} \begin{bmatrix} 1/2+\mathring{a} \\ 1/2-\mathring{a} \\ 0 \end{bmatrix} \\
&= \begin{bmatrix} 3 & 3 & 3 \\ 2 & 2 & 2 \\ 1 & 1 & 1 \end{bmatrix} \begin{bmatrix} 1/3 \\ 1/3 \\ 1/3 \end{bmatrix}
\end{aligned} \tag{16.15}$$

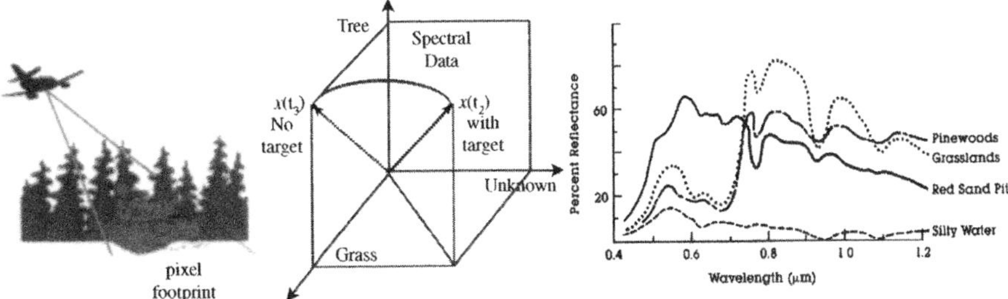

Figure 16.14 The spectral feature domain required real-time tracking for novelty detection of a moving tank in time beyond the measured spectrum of the background tree and grass materials shown in the middle and other known material at the right-hand side, so-called "blackbody radiation as displaced/distorted Maxwell distributions" library, which, unfortunately, changes constantly by looks, hours, and seasons.

Figure 16.15 shows the original 7-band Landsat images, while Figure 16.16 shows the LCNN pixel-by-pixel approach to blind demixing of the 7-band Landsat images. In Figure 16.15, fine details in the beach, the band-6 images, and desert area were clearly visible. These two images showed the "city" class. It also can be seen in the Figure 16.16 that band-2 and band-7 images contain the "desert" class that is complementary to the "city" class contained in the band-6 image. This emphasized the basic feature of the LCNN method to demix original images into new sets of independent classes pixel by pixel without neighborhood pixel ensemble averages. Moreover, from the band-6 image we saw that same city class also existed on a few locations in the desert area, suggesting the possible existence of man-made objects. Furthermore, the spectral vectors at the city and the man-made points in the desert were determined by LCNN to be similar, and are shown in Figure 16.16.

We gave the experimental results obtained after applying the LCNN algorithm on a set of 7-band Landsat images (from the blue-green visible to the near, middle and long infrared) over the Mediteranean Sea, a typical city and a desert, that were the training set for supervised Landsat classification by spectral features (Figure 16.17).

16.7 BIOLOGICAL RELEVANCE

This unsupervised learning model involves no arbitrary learning rate and stopping criterion, and involves both the ionic-channel coincidence input preprocessing of the biologically massive dendrite tree and the coaxial axon output postprocessing. By the physics dimensionality argument, if the data vector $\dot{\mathbf{X}}$ was the evoked potential 0.1 volts, as measured first by 1952 Nobel laureates Hodgkin and Huxley at the axon synaptic junction, then we speculated that the Lagrange multipliers $\overset{r}{i}' \equiv [\mathbf{A}]^T \ddot{\mathbf{e}}^T$ could represent electrical current in pico-amperes, measured first by 1991 Nobel laureates Neher and Sakmann at dendrite ion channels.

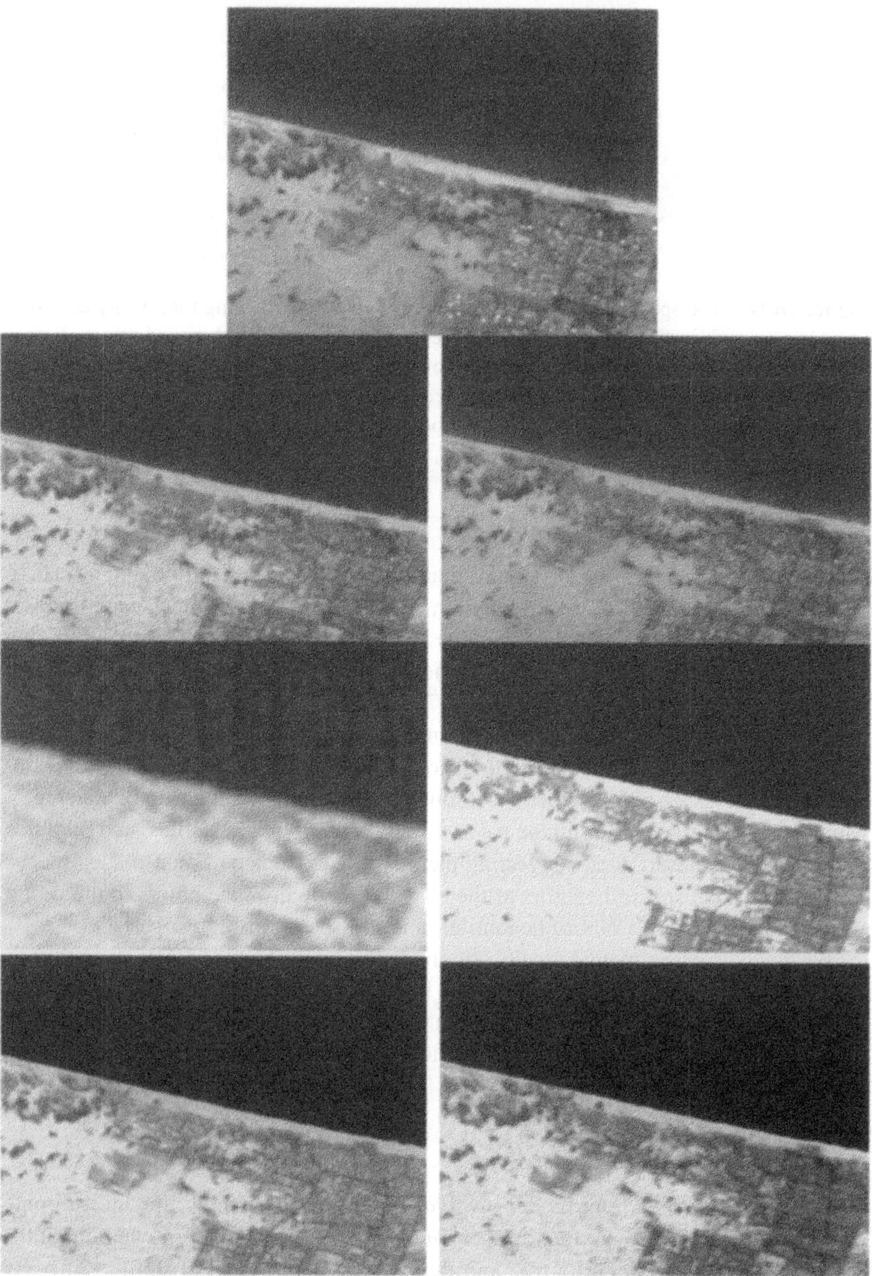

Figure 16.15 Original Landsat imageries from 1-micrometer visible, to 12-micrometer thermal imaging. Display reveals vertical sensory stripped clutters (due to nonequilibrium of thermal cooling effect) after the Matlab standard histogram equalization. Their original histograms are enclosed in the lower right-hand side.

Figure 16.16 The Lagrange constraint neural network (LCNN) blindly demixed 7-band Landsat images. The not-yet-cooled sensor noise can be seen in all the images. The thin line representing beach has the same color value as the desert area, implying the same class (sand) in both areas. On the band-6 image on a few locations in the desert area, the existence of the same objects as in the city class can be observed, suggesting the possibility of man-made objects.

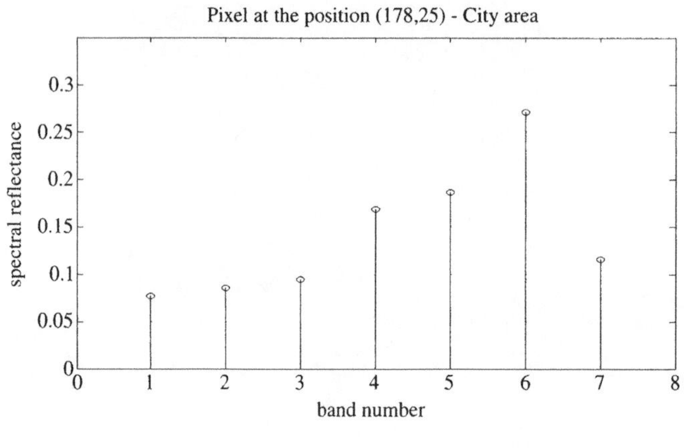

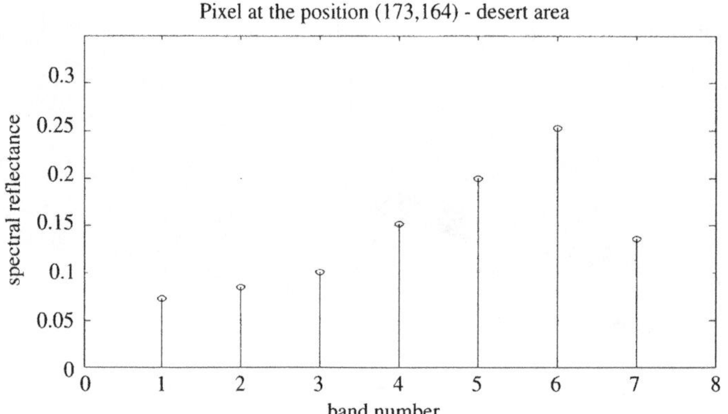

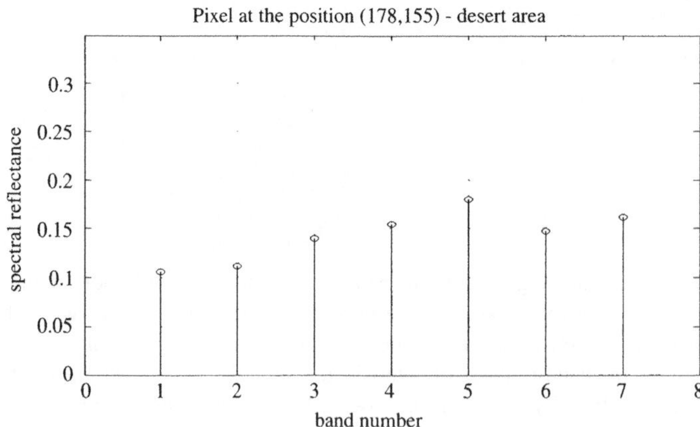

Figure 16.17 (a) Spectral reflectance of the corresponding pixel (178,25) in the city area. (b) Spectral reflectance of the pixel (173,164) suspected to be "man-made" object. (c) Spectral reflectance of the pixel (178,155) that is "typical" for desert area.

Figure 16.18 Psychological fact of learning to discriminate between a dog and a big cat with/without a teacher.

When your parents taught you about what a dog or a cat is (Fig. 16.18), did they ever give you the definitions? Seldom! Yet, you effortlessly reduced the overwhelming and costly redundancy sensory and motor data vector $\mathbf{X}_{\text{dog}}$ into a semiotic fuzzy but mathematically sharp ICA feature set S for efficient storage and retrieval.

We expect unsupervised learning to achieve the blind demixing of the data vector $\mathbf{X}_{\text{dog}} \rightarrow \mathbf{S}_{\text{dog}}$ toward the independent knowledge-source vector for efficient and robust storage. Learning shall be both supervised and unsupervised, of which the learning with a teacher is conjectured to be a fuzzy subscript to label the knowledge source vector. Learning without a teacher is the vector component called the independent component:

$$\mathbf{S}_{\text{dog}} \equiv (s_1, s_2, \text{sensory IC without teacher})_{\text{fuzzy label by supervision}}$$

Acceptance of the new theory, LCNN, depended on its ability to make predictions. The natural reaction of the thermodynamics entropy was to balance the action of Lagrange constraint estimation-error energy by means of an LCNN unsupervised algorithm. On the other hand, there were those emotional intelligence quotient measures (e-IQ) for timing, rhythm, gut feeling, body temperature, etc., that were known to be like Newton's law of physics, "action and reaction," that influences our thought processes known as "thinking through feeling." How could we substantiate such a novel capability with the ANN model?

The LCNN can accomplish that, because it predicts that something else other than the neurons themselves must become involved in the unsupervised learning. Without the external tutor, Lagrange constraints from the environmental heat reservoir λ' provided the necessary reaction forces to balance the diffusion of neuron excitation energy generated by input data, $\mathbf{x}$, and associative entropy increase. Brain anatomy revealed billions of neurons (defined by the binding between pair firing rates for the Hebbian synaptic memory) and billions of housekeeping glial cells. The active roles of these glial cells in information processing were suspected, but have not been verified explicitly yet.

We predicted that the role of glial cells had to do more than the housekeeping of brain activity, but also to be Lagrange multipliers (having the same number as neurons) in maintaining their dynamic balance, which was required for unsupervised learning and the equilibrium of the thermal reservoir. Thus, both the neurons' actions and the housekeeping glial cells' reactions were simultaneously present in this LCNN model of ANN. The Lagrange constraints represented the internal housekeeping tutor for unsupervised learning truly without an outside teacher. While there were hundreds of types of neurons, only three classes of glial cells existed to keep the thermodynamic balance: (1) astrocytes glial cells provided "the so-to-speak glue" of the blood vessels to the neurons; (2) oligodendroglia/cytes provided the myelin sheath wrapped around the central nervous system like a link of sausages, forming an expressway; (3) Schwann cells wrapped around the peripheral nervous system other than the brain and the spinal cord. Any direct or indirect evidence in biological and neuropsychological experiments would be timely. Lacking biomimetic evidence, it still makes sense to equip robots with the unsupervised learning capability in outer space, deep ocean, and nuclear reactor, where human beings could not be as the tutors.

We have shown, using the definition of thermodynamic Helmholtz free energy, that a constant cybernetic temperature, T, allows simultaneous minimization of the internal energy for supervised categorization and the maximization of the entropy for unsupervised component analysis. In this sense, warm-blooded homeostasic animals were proved by the author (in 1999; using the Lyapunov convergence based on thermodynamics Helmholtz free energy in the Conclusion section) to be more capable of learning with and without a concurrent teacher. The conjecture about the homeostasis theory of learning seems to agree with the hypothalamus that sits above the pituitary gland, the so-called "third eye" in the animal kingdom, which is located at the center of the brain to regulate many functions of brain and body. The body was kept at a fixed temperature (36°C for most humans), in order to maintain the proper kinetic diffusion activity of the immune system and the enzymes catalytic reaction rate, which balanced the chemical reaction by a negative feedback system. This was done by means of the hormonal pathway via organic molecules, e.g., antidiuretic hormone (ADH) regulated through the membranes, the intracellular (thyroxin to mitochondria), and the blood stream (e.g., adrenal, an enlarged ganglion, secrete adrenalin versus the almond-shaped gateway to the limbic system—amygdale generating emotional fear and the depression serotonin versus neurotransmitter). The feedback balance was further controlled by the limbic (C-shaped inner loop circuit) system connecting the cerebral cortex with the hypothalamus and the pituitary gland to translate complex emotion and drive into actions that in turn guide the motion perception and learning experience. The coupling among these intricate parts might be mathematically understood from the viewpoint of the second law of thermodynamics as the necessary action–reaction principle among the synaptic matrix [**A**] coupling among information-processing sensory neurons, $\check{x}(t)$, and the counterflow of "where and what" knowledge representation neurons, $\check{s}(t)$, together with the indispensable housekeeping reactionary glial cells, λ, in the unsupervised learning methodology.

16.8 CONCLUSION

According to the definition of "unsupervised classification," the information required must be learned and derived directly and solely from the data alone, which is consistent with the classic definition of "unlabeled data" ATR in the Duda/Hart book.

There are three major approaches and two major applications: (1) the spatially pixel-ensemble averaging for the source-density factorization, e.g., Bell–Sejnowski–Amari–Oja (BSAO) space-invariant ICA, and the kernel by Jorden and SVD by Vapnik approaches; (2) the spectral ensemble factorization per pixel for space-variant blind sources separation, e.g., derived by Szu from the statistical-mechanics the per-pixel truly unsupervised classifications for remote sensing and breast imaging due to a space-variant imaging where the neighborhood spatial information is not there; instead, the spectral information per pixel is there; (3) temporal ensemble factorization, e.g., Szu optical flow in WaveNet video. So far there are two major applications: (4) nonlinear and nonstationary blind-mixing intelligent systems, e.g., in digital watermarking and authenticity intellectual property right protection; and (5) applications defining machine IQ organized by the National Institute of Science and Technology for the last three summers.

This per-pixel unsupervised algorithm is based on the fact that brainlike smart sensing requires the "power of pairs" brainlike receptors to follow the vector and physics constraints of thermodynamics free-energy minimization in order to reveal hidden features contained in a single pixel image data vector $\mathbf{X} = [\mathbf{A}]\mathbf{S}$, without knowing the breast-medium heat-transfer matrix $[\mathbf{A}]$ and the heat source $\mathbf{S}$. While this unique algorithm has achieved subpixel accuracy, the other statistical methodologies experience pixel-ensemble averaging blurring effects. This is because the so-called joint-pdf density factorization by ICA must average over all neighborhood pixels by assuming an identical $[\mathbf{A}]$, which was only true in cases of a very large tumor without the need for ATR.

We conclude the chapter with the Lyapunov convergence proof that a mammal's simultaneous (supervised and unsupervised) learning capability is achieved by means of the minimization of Helmholtz thermodynamic energy at a constant cybernetic temperature, namely, the so-called homeostasis warm-blood animal theory.

THEOREM OF HOMEOSTASIS LEARNING (Szu, 1999)

1. Assume brain nonlinear neurodynamics governed by the second law of thermodynamics in terms of the Helmholtz free energy:

$$H(s_1, \ldots, s_n; w_1, \ldots, w_n) = Energy\ (s_1, \ldots, s_n) - TEntropy\ (w_1, \ldots, w_n)$$

   where the cybernetic temperature T is the r.m.s. synaptic vesicles' transport fluctuation assumed for mammals to be homeostasis at a constant (adrenalin versus amygdale fear and the depression serotonin versus neurotransmitter).

2. Assume scalable local gradient dynamics:

$$\frac{du_i}{dt} = -\frac{\partial\, Energy}{\partial v_i} \text{(minimum LMS energy)}$$

a la Hopfield–Grossberg–Kohonen like;

$$d[W]/dt = \left\langle \frac{dEntropy}{d[W]}[W]^T[W] \right\rangle_{\text{pixel}} \quad \text{(a posteriori maximum entropy)}$$

a la Bell–Sejnowski and Amari, Oja MaxEnt postprocessing algorithms. Then, both supervised and unsupervised learning happen concurrently and effortlessly at the Lyapunov equilibrium:

$$\frac{dH}{dt} = \frac{dEnergy}{dt} - T\frac{dEntropy}{dt} \leq 0$$

Proof

$$\begin{aligned} dE/dt &= \Sigma_i(dEnergy/dv_i)(dv_i/du_i)(du_i/dt) \\ &\cong -\Sigma_i(dEnergy/dv_i)^2(dv_i/du_i) \leq 0 \end{aligned}$$

$$\begin{aligned} \frac{dEntropy}{dt} &= \left\langle \frac{dEntropy}{d[W]}[W]^T[W] \right\rangle_{\text{pixel}} (d[W]/dt) \\ &= \left(\left\langle \frac{dEntropy}{d[W]}[W]^T[W] \right\rangle_{\text{pixel}} \right)^2 \geq 0 \end{aligned}$$

Guaranteed to be real positive! Together

$$\frac{dH}{dt} = \frac{dEnergy}{dt} - T\frac{dEntropy}{dt} \leq 0$$

These unsupervised methods are inspired by biology but based on the thermodynamic physics of statistical (molecular photon) mechanics. On the one hand, it generalizes the Shannon entropy information theory to open systems with energy flux. On the other hand, it has consequently combined Neher–Sakemann ion-channel dendrite preprocessing with housekeeping glial cells and the Hodgkin Huxley axonic synaptic modification that has generalized the Hebb rule, becoming a truly unsupervised learning between data and internal dynamic variables (representing glial cells and/or coincident events of dendrite ion channels).

ACKNOWLEDGMENTS

We thank Mr. James Buss of ONR for support, Dr. Philip Hoekstra, Thermal Scan Inc., Michigan, for providing us with the two spectral IR breast images necessary for performing the unsupervised classification test. We thank Ivica Kopriva and Charles Hsu for helping coding.

REFERENCES

1. H. Szu. "Thermodynamics Energy for Both Supervised and Unsupervised Learning Neural Nets at a Constant Temperature." *Int. J. Neural Syst.*, vol. 9, 175–186, 1999.
2. H. Szu and C. Hsu. "Landsat Spectral Unmixing à la Superresolution of Blind Matrix Inversion by Constraint MaxEnt Neural Nets." *Proc. SPIE*, vol. 3078, 147–160, 1997.
3. J. R. Keyserlink, P. D. Ahlgren, E. Yu, N. Belliveau, and M. Yassa. "Functional Infrared Imaging of the Breast." *J. IEEE Eng. Med. Biol.*, vol. 19, 30–41, 2000.
4. Ch. Gorman. "Rethinking Breast Cancer." *Time*, 50–58, Feb. 18, 2002.
5. NASA's Landsat web site: http://geo.arc.nasa.gov/sge/landsat/.
6. H. Szu and I. Kopriva. "Constrained Equal A Priori Entropy for Unsupervised Remote Sensing." IEEE Trans. Geosci. Remote Sensing, to appear, 2003.
7. A. J. Bell and T. J. Sejnowski. "An Information-Maximization Approach to Blind Separation and Blind Deconvolution." *Neural Comput.* vol. 7, 1129–1159, 1995.
8. S. Amari. "Natural Gradient Works Efficiently in Learning." *Neural Comput.* vol. 10, 251–276, 1998.
9. D. Marr. *Vision*, Freeman, San Francisco, 1982.
10. S. Noel and H. Szu. "Multimedia Authenticity with ICA Watermarks." In *Wavelet Applications VII, SPIE Proceedings*, vol. 4056, Apr. 2000, pp. 175–184.
11. H. H. Szu, I. Kopriva, and A. Persin. "Independent Component Analysis Approach to Resolve the Multi-Source Limitation of the Nutating Rising-Sun Reticle Based Optical Trackers." *Opt. Commun.*, vol. 176, no. 1–3, 77–89, 2000.
12. I. Kopriva, H. Szu, and A. Persin. "Optical Reticle Trackers with Multi-Source Discrimination Capability by Using Independent Component Analysis." Accepted for *Opt. Commun.*, 2002.
13. H. Szu and I. Kopriva. "Artificial Neural Networks for Noisy Image Super-Resolution." *Opt. Commun.*, vol. 198, no. 1–3, 71–81, 2001.
14. H. B. Barlow. "Possible Principles Underlying the Transformation of Sensory Messages." In W. A. Rosenblith (ed.), *Sensory Communication*, MIT Press, Cambridge, MA, 1961, pp. 217–234.
15. H. Szu. "Progresses in Unsupervised Artificial Neural Networks of Blind Image Demixing." *IEEE Ind. Electron Soc. Newslett.*, 7–12, June 1999.
16. H. Szu. "ICA—An Enabling Tech For Intelligent Sensory Processing." *IEEE Circuits Syst. Newslett. Mag.*, 14–41, Dec. 1999.
17. H. Szu and R. Hartley. "Fast Simulated Annealing." *Phys. Lett. A*, vol. 122, no. 3, 157–162, 1987.
18. H. Szu and R. Hartley. "Nonconvex Optimization by Simulated Annealing." *Proc. IEEE*, vol. 75, no. 11, 1538–1540, 1987.

19. H. Szu and I. Kopriva. "Comparison of Lagrange Neural Network of Unsupervised Remote Sensing with Other Traditional ICA." In *Proceedings of the IEEE WCCI* Hawaii, 2002.
20. H. Szu and I. Kopriva. "Constrained Equal A Priori Entropy for Unsupervised Remote Sensing." *IEEE Trans. Geosci. Remote Sens.*, 2002.
21. K. Huang. *Statistical Mechanics*, Wiley, New York, 1970.
22. A. N. Diakides and M. Diakides. "International Activities in IR Imaging for Medicine." In *Proceedings of the Tanks to Tumor Workshop*, Arlington, VA, Dec. 2001.

CHAPTER 17

COLLECTIVE INTELLIGENCE

DAVID H. WOLPERT

17.1 MOTIVATION AND BACKGROUND

17.1.1 Collectives

Many systems of self-interested agents have an associated performance criterion that rates the dynamic behavior of the overall system. This chapter presents an introduction to the science of such systems. Formally, **collectives** are defined as any system having the following two characteristics: First, the system must contain one or more agents each of which we view as trying to maximize an associated *private utility*; second, the system must have an associated *world utility* function that rates the possible behaviors of that overall system [1–5]. In practice, collectives are often very large, distributed, and support little, if any, centralized communication and control, although those characteristics are not part of their formal definition.

A naturally occurring example of a collective is a human economy. One can identify the agents and their private utilities as the human individuals in the economy and the associated personal rewards they are each trying to maximize. One could then identify the world utility as the time average of the gross domestic product. ("World utility" per se is not a construction internal to a human economy, but rather something defined from the outside.) To achieve high world utility it is necessary to avoid having the agents work at cross-purposes lest phenomena like liquidity traps or the Tragedy of the Commons (TOC) occur, in which agents' individually pursuing their private utilities lowers world utility [6]. The obvious way to avoid such phenomena is by modifying the agents' utility functions to be "aligned" with the world utility. This can be done via punitive legislation. A real-world example of an attempt to do this was the creation of antitrust regulations designed to prevent monopolistic practices.[1]

[1] In conventional economics, imposing governmental regulations is viewed as a change in the dynamical laws of the variables constituting the world (e.g., if you perform the proscribed action *A* you now go to jail, whereas that wasn't the case before). Here instead it is abstracted to be a direct change in the mapping

(*continued...*)

Computational Intelligence: The Experts Speak. Edited by D. B. Fogel and C. J. Robinson
ISBN 0-471-27454-2

We do not insist that the agents in a collective really are "trying"to maximize their private utilities, in some teleological sense. We require only that they can be *viewed* that way. This allows us to circumvent the fraught exercise of formulating a definition of what an arbitrary component of some physical system is "trying to do." This is illustrated with another naturally occurring example of a collective: a spin glass. One can take the agents in such a glass to be the individual spins. Each spin's "private utility" is (the negative of) its local Hamiltonian (which is determined only by the states of the other spins to which it is coupled). The "world utility" is (the negative of) the Hamiltonian of the entire system. In this example, both the world utility and all of the private utilities are at (local) maxima at equilibrium. This is what allows us to view the spins *as though* they were agents trying to maximize their private utilities.

In addition to such naturally occurring examples, many current artificial systems can be viewed as collectives. For example, the routers in a terrestrial telecommunications network can be viewed as agents in a collective consisting of the entire network. Real-world routers can reasonably be viewed as "trying to maximize" the quality of service accorded to the traffic that crosses them. Hence they can be taken to be the collective's agents. World utility in this example can then be set to aggregate quality of service of the entire network.

With the advent of ubiquitous cheap computing in the near future, the number of artificial control systems that are collectives should explode. Two obvious examples here are a user's constellation of multiple wearable computers, and "computational clouds" of computationally enabled household devices. If such distributed systems are not to be extremely brittle, then absent centralized communication and control, the individual components of the system will need to be both autonomous and adaptive. Almost by definition, this means that those components will be using statistical and machine learning techniques of some sort to modify their behavior to try to meet a goal, i.e., to maximize their private utility.[2] Moreover, in both of these examples, there is an obvious choice of world utility: the satisfaction level of the user(s) of the system.

Other more prosaic examples of artificial collectives will be dynamic job migration and/or data migration across heterogenous networks of computers. World utility here will be aggregate satisfaction of the network's users, suitably quantified. As with our previous examples, with centralized control being impractical, for the system to be robust there will have to be adaptive "agents" in the system that can be viewed as trying to maximize associated private utilities. As examples, the individual agents could be the computers in the network, or even the jobs and/or sets of data themselves. Similarly, as soon as associated computational control devices are

---

between the state of the world and the agent's utility value, without any change in underlying dynamical laws. (To continue with the example, in this alternative there is no direct introduction of a new variable having to do with some physical jail—rather your utility function is directly changed so that now if you do A, your utility value is smaller than if you do not do A.)

[2] When used for this purpose, such techniques are either explicitly or implicitly related to the field Reinforcement Learning (RL) [7–15].

distributed across such systems, many aspects of the management of supply chain, of electric power grid management, of automobile traffic control and automated control of constellations of deployable autonomous vehicles will constitute collectives.

Another broad class of artificial collectives is essentially every system that will involve copious amounts of nanotechnology where many of the nano-scale components in the system have nontrivial associated computational capabilities. This may include everything from continuously deformable wings to smart paint to nano-scale information storage and retrieval systems.

Finally, consider search algorithms that try to find the value of a high-dimensional variable $\vec{z}$ for which a prespecified function f has a large value. Examples of such algorithms are gradient ascent, simulated annealing, evolutionary algorithms, etc. Say we take the final value of f achieved by such an algorithm to be the "world utility" of the entire system's dynamic history. Assuming each individual component of $\vec{z}$ evolves with the "goal" of maximizing that final value of $f(\vec{z})$, we can view each such component as an agent, with private utility given by the final value of f. (Note that the private utility of an agent depends on variables not directly under the agent's control, in general.) In this way any search algorithm can be viewed as a collective. However, conventionally, such algorithms use very "dumb" agents (e.g., semi-random agents rather than reinforcement learning [RL]-based agents). They also don't consider possible modifications to the underlying system, e.g., to the choice of private utilities, that might result in a better value of final value of f. (The design problem of how best to set private utilities is discussed in the next section.) Constructing search algorithms that use techniques of this nature—intuitively, "agentizing" the individual variables of a search problem by providing them with adaptive intelligence—would provide a search algorithm that is immediately parallelizable. Owing to their use of"smart" variables, such algorithms might also lead to substantially better final values of f than conventional search algorithms.

17.1.2 The Design of Collectives

The "forward problem" in the science of collectives is how the precise configuration of the system—including in particular the private utilities of the agents—affects the ensuing behavior, and therefore affects the value of the world utility. In light of the examples above, however, there is another problem that is at least as rich scientifically, but as a practical matter is of more immediate concern. This is the inverse problem: *How should one initialize/update the private utility functions of the individual agents so that the ensuing behavior of the entire collective achieves large values of the provided world utility?* In particular, since in truly large systems detailed modeling of the system is usually impossible, how can we solve this problem in a way that avoids such modeling? Can we somehow solve it if we leverage only the simple assumption that our agents' learning algorithms are individually fairly good at what they do?

This design problem is related to work in many other fields, including multi-agent systems (MASs), computational economics, mechanism design, reinforcement learning, statistical mechanics, computational ecologies, (partially observable)

Markov decision processes, and game theory. However none of these fields is both applicable in large problems, and directly addresses the *general* inverse problem, rather than a special instance of it. (See [16] for a detailed discussion of the relationship between these fields, involving hundreds of references.)

For example, the subfield of game-theory known as mechanism design might, at first glance, appear to provide techniques for solving the inverse problem. However, mechanism design is almost exclusively concerned with collectives that are at (a suitable refinement of) Nash equilibrium [17–19]. That means that every agent is assumed to be performing *as well as is theoretically possible*, given the behavior of the rest of the system. In setting private utilities and the like on this basis, mechanism design ignores completely the issue of how to design the system so that each of the agents can achieve a good value of its private utility (given the behavior of the rest of the system). In particular it ignores all statistical issues related to how well the agents can be expected to perform for various candidate private utilities. Such issues become crucial as one moves to large systems, where each agent is confronted implicitly with a very high-dimensional RL task.

There are many other issues that arise in bounded rational situations that are not considered by mechanism design since they do not arise when there is full rationality. For example, it is often the case that by "stabilizing" the sequence of actions of some agent ρ, the other agents, being in a more predictable environment, are able to perform better. Conversely, such enforced stabilization of its actions will often hurt the performance of agent ρ. Mechanism design almost completely ignores the associated issues of how best to trade off the performance of one agent against that of other agents, or more generally of how best to trade off the degree of rationality of one agent against that of another agent. (Indeed, mechanism design does not even possess a broadly applicable model-independent measure of "degree of rationality.")

In addition to these problems, many of the techniques derived in mechanism design cannot be applied in numerous application domains, since those techniques are tailored largely to collectives of human beings. In particular, many of those techniques are tailored to the idiosyncracy of such collectives that their members have hidden variables whose values they do not want to reveal. This idiosyncracy is reflected in restrictions on the allowed form of the private utilities and the world utility and communication structures among the agents. Indeed, if there were no such restriction, then given the Nash equilibrium presumption of mechanism design, how best to set the private utilities would be a trivial problem: To have the maximum of world utility be a Nash equilibrium, simply set each such private utility to equal the world utility, in a so-called "team game" or an "exact potential game" [20]. To have the analysis be nontrivial, restrictions such as those that apply to the private utilities of human beings are needed.

Not only are the techniques of mechanism design not relevant to many domains because those domains do not have the restrictions assumed in mechanism design, but in addition there are many issues that loom large in such domains about which mechanism design is mute. For example, in computational domains, where the agents are computer programs each controlling a set of certain variables, we often have some freedom to change how the set of all variables being controlled is partitioned among the agents, and even change the number of such agents. Needless to say, with its focus on human agents, mechanism design has little advice to provide on such issues of how best to define the agents in the first place.

Perhaps the most striking illustration of the shortncoming of mechanism design is the fact that it does not allow for run-time adaptive redesign. For real-world bounded rational agents, the initial design of the system necessarily makes assumptions that invariably are at least partially at variance with reality. To address this, adaptive techniques are employed (e.g., statistical estimation) on the running system to refine initial assumptions, and then modify the design accordingly. Yet almost all of mechanism design has no room for addressing such macro-learning.

There is other previous work that does consider the inverse problem in its broadest sense, and even has each agent explicitly use RL techniques, so that no formal assumption is made in the associated theory that the system is at Nash equilibrium. Despite this use of RL though, in general, in that work the private utilities are set as in a team game. So again, there is no concern for how well the agents can discern how best to act to maximize their utilities. Unfortunately, as intimated previously (and expounded in the following text), ignoring this issue means that the approach scales extremely poorly to large problems. Intuitively, the difficulty is that each agent will have ahard time discerning the echo of its behavior on its private utility when the system is large if that private utility is the world utility; each agent has a horrible "signal-to-noise" problem in such a situation.[3]

Intuitively, in designing the private utilities of a collective we want them to be aligned with the world utility, in that modifications an agent might make that would increase its private utility also must increase world utility. Fortunately, the equivalence class of such private utilities extends well beyond team-game utilities. In particular, it extends to include utilities that have far better signal-to-noise properties. By using those utilities one can get far better values of world utility than would otherwise be possible. The mathematical theory for how to generate such alternative private utilities is presented in the next section. The following, last section of this chapter then summarizes many experiments that demonstrate that by using those alternative private utilities one can improve performance by up to orders of magnitude, and that the gain in performance grows as the system gets larger.

17.2 THE MATHEMATICS OF DESIGNING COLLECTIVES

In this chapter, attention is restricted to collectives in which the individual agents are pre-fixed, being the players in multistage noncooperative games, with their moves at any single stage in no a priori way restricted by their moves at other times or by the

[3] To help see this, consider the example of a collective provided by the human economy. A team game in that example would mean that every human gets U.S. GDP as its reward signal, and tries to discern how best to act to maximize that reward signal. At the risk of understatement, this would provide the individual members of the economy with a difficult reinforcement learning task.

moves of the other players. Some techniques for the design of the private utilities in such games are known as the "COllective INtelligence (COIN)" framework [1]. This section presents some of the mathematics necessary to understand that framework. It should be emphasized, however, that the full mathematics of how to design collectives extends significantly beyond what is needed to address such games.[4]

The restricted version of that full mathematics needed to present the COIN framework starts with an arbitrary vector space Z whose elements ζ give the joint move of all players in the collective in some stage. We wish to search for the ζ that maximizes the provided world utility $G(\zeta)$. In addition to G, we are concerned with private utility functions $\{g_\eta\}$, one such function for each variable/player η. We use the notation $\hat{\eta}$ to refer to all players other than η.

We will need to have a way to standardize utility functions so that the numeric value they assign to a ζ only reflects their ranking of ζ relative to certain other elements of Z. We call such a standardization of some arbitrary utility U for player η the *intelligence* for η at ζ with respect to U. Here we will use intelligences that are equivalent to percentiles:

$$\epsilon_{\eta,U}(\zeta) \equiv \int d\mu_{\zeta_{\hat{\eta}}}(\zeta')\Theta[U(\zeta) - U(\zeta')] \tag{17.1}$$

where the Heaviside function Θ is defined to equal 1 when its argument is greater than or equal to 0, and to equal 0 otherwise, and where the subscript on the (normalized) measure $d\mu$ indicates it is restricted to ζ' sharing the same non-η components as ζ.[5] Intelligence values are always between 0 and 1.

Our uncertainty concerning the behavior of the system is reflected in a probability distribution over Z. Our ability to control the system consists of setting the value of some characteristic of the collective, e.g., setting the private utility functions of the players. Indicating that value of the *global coordinate* by s, our analysis revolves around the following *central equation* for $P(G \mid s)$, which follows from Bayes' theorem:

$$P(G \mid s) = \int d\vec{\epsilon}_G P(G \mid \vec{\epsilon}_G, s) \int d\vec{\epsilon}_g P(\vec{\epsilon}_G \mid \vec{\epsilon}_g, s) P(\vec{\epsilon}_g \mid s) \tag{17.2}$$

where $\vec{\epsilon}_g \equiv (\epsilon_{\eta_1,g_{\eta_1}}(\zeta), \epsilon_{\eta_2,g_{\eta_2}}(\zeta), \cdots)$ is the vector of the intelligences of the players with respect to their associated private utility functions, and $\vec{\epsilon}_G \equiv (\epsilon_{\eta_1,G}(\zeta), \epsilon_{\eta_2,G}(\zeta), \cdots)$ is the vector of the intelligences of the players with respect to G.

[4] That framework encompasses, for example, arbitrary dynamic redefinitions of the "players" (i.e., dynamic reassignments of how the various subsets of the variables comprising the collective across all space and time are assigned to players), as well as modification of the players' information sets (i.e., modification of interplayer communication). See [21].

[5] The measure must reflect the type of system at hand, e.g., whether Z is countable or not, and if not, what coordinate system is being used. Other than that, any convenient choice of measure may be used and the theorems will still hold.

Note that $\epsilon_{\eta,g_\eta}(\zeta) = 1$ means that player η is fully rational at ζ, in that its move maximizes the value of its utility, given the moves of the players. In other words, a point ζ where $\epsilon_{\eta,g_\eta}(\zeta) = 1$ for all players η is one that meets the definition of a game-theory Nash equilibrium.[6] On the other hand, a ζ at which all components of $\vec{\epsilon}_G = 1$ is a local maximum of G (or more precisely, a critical point of the $G(\zeta)$ surface). So if we can get these two vectors to be identical, then if the agents do well enough at maximizing their private utilities we are assured we will be near a local maximum of G.

To formalize this, consider our decomposition of $P(G \mid s)$. If we can choose s so that the third conditional probability in the integrand is peaked around vectors $\vec{\epsilon}_g$ all of whose components are close to 1, then we have likely induced large (private utility function) intelligences. If we can also have the second term be peaked about $\vec{\epsilon}_G$ equal to $\vec{\epsilon}_g$, then $\vec{\epsilon}_G$ will also be large. Finally, if the first term in the integrand is peaked about high G when $\vec{\epsilon}_G$ is large, then our choice of s will likely result in high G, as desired.

Intuitively, the requirement that private utility functions have high signal-to-noise arises in the third term. It is in the second term that the requirement that the private utility functions be aligned with G arises. In this chapter we concentrate on these two terms, and show how to simultaneously set them to have the desired form.[7]

Details of the stochastic environment in which the collective operates, together with details of the learning algorithms of the players, are all bundled into the distribution $P(\zeta)$ which underlies the distributions appearing in Eq. 17.2. Note though that *independent of these considerations*, our desired form for the second term in Eq. 17.2 is assured if we have chosen private utilities such that $\vec{\epsilon}_g$ equals $\vec{\epsilon}_G$ exactly for all ζ. Such a system is said to be *factored.* In game-theory parlance, the Nash equilibria of a factored collective are local maxima of G. In addition to this desirable equilibrium behavior, factored collectives also automatically provide appropriate off-equilibrium incentives to the players (an issue rarely considered in the game theory/mechanism design literature).

As a trivial example, any team game in which all the private utility functions equal G is factored [20, 24]. However, team games often have very poor forms for term 3 in Eq. 17.2, forms that get progressively worse as the size of the collective grows. This is because for such private utility functions each player η will usually confront a very poor signal-to-noise ratio in trying to discern how its actions affect

[6] See [12]. Note that consideration of points ζ at which *not* all intelligences equal 1 provides the basis for a model-independent formalization of bounded rationality game theory. This formalization contains variants of many of th theorems of conventional full-rationality game theory. See [22].

[7] Search algorithms that do not involve game theory (e.g., simulated annealing) can be viewed as addressing how to have term 1 possess the desired form. They do this by trying to ensure that the particular local maximum they find of the function they are searching has a high value of that function. This is the essence of why such algorithms trade off exploration and exploitation. One can combine such term-1-based techniques with the techniques presented in this paper. Intuitively, this amounts to "wrapping" a system using the private utilities derived below in an outer loop that trades off exploration and exploitation. The resultant hybrid algorithm, addressing all three terms, outperforms simulated annealing by over two orders of magnitude [23].

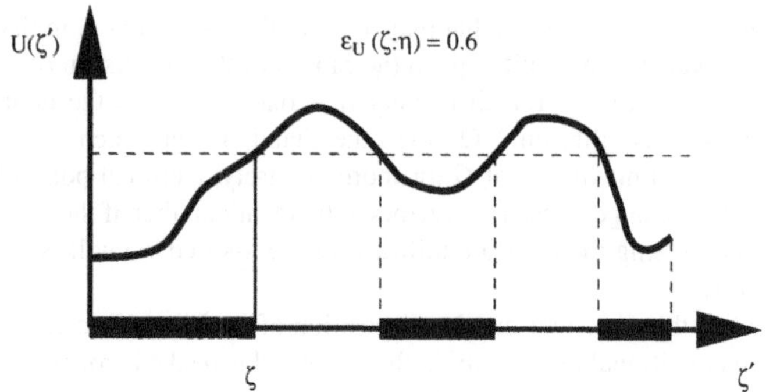

Figure 17.1 Intelligence of agent η for utility U for the actual joint move at hand, ζ. The x-axis shows agent η's alternative possible moves (all states ζ' having ζ's values for the moves of all players other than η.). The thick sections of the x-axis show the alternative moves that η could have made that would have given η a worse value of the utility U. The fraction of the full set of η's possible moves that lies in those thick sections (which is 0.6 in this example) is the intelligence of agent η at ζ for utility U, denoted by $\epsilon_{\eta,U}(\zeta)$.

its utility $g_\eta = G$, since so many other player's actions also affect G and therefore dilute η's effect on its own private utility function.

We now focus on algorithms based on private utility functions $\{g_\eta\}$ that optimize the signal/noise ratio reflected in the third term, subject to the requirement that the system be factored. To understand how these algorithms work, say we are given an arbitrary function $f(\zeta_\eta)$ over player η's moves, two such moves $\zeta_\eta{}^1$ and $\zeta_\eta{}^2$, a utility U, a value s of the global coordinate, and a move by all players other than η, $\zeta_{\hat{\eta}}$. Define the associated *learnability* by

$$\Lambda_f(U;\zeta_{\hat{\eta}},s,\zeta_\eta{}^1,\zeta_\eta{}^2) \equiv \sqrt{\frac{[E(U;\zeta_{\hat{\eta}},\zeta_\eta{}^1) - E(U;\zeta_{\hat{\eta}},\zeta_\eta{}^2)]^2}{\int d\zeta_\eta[f(\zeta_\eta)Var(U;\zeta_{\hat{\eta}},\zeta_\eta)]}} \tag{17.3}$$

The expectation values in the numerator are formed by averaging over the training set of the learning algorithm used by agent η, n_η. Those two averages are evaluated according to the two distributions $P(U|n_\eta)P(n_\eta|\zeta_{\hat{\eta}},\zeta_\eta{}^1)$ and $P(U|n_\eta)P(n_\eta|\zeta_{\hat{\eta}},\zeta_\eta{}^2)$, respectively. (That is the meaning of the semicolon notation.) Similarly the variance being averaged in the denominator is over n_η according to the distribution $P(U|n_\eta)P(n_\eta|\zeta_{\hat{\eta}},\zeta_\eta)$.

The denominator in Eq. 17.3 reflects how sensitive $U(\zeta)$ is to changing $\zeta_{\hat{\eta}}$. In contrast, the numerator reflects how sensitive $U(\zeta)$ is to changing ζ_η. So the greater the learnability of a private utility function g_η, the more $g_\eta(\zeta)$ depends only on the move of player η, i.e., the better the associated signal-to-noise ratio for η. Intuitively then, so long as it does not come at the expense of decreasing the signal, increasing the signal-to-noise ratio specified in the learnability will make it easier for η to achieve a large value of its intelligence. This can be established formally: If scaled, appropriately g'_η will result in better expected intelligence for agent η than will g_η whenever $\Lambda_f(g'_\eta; \zeta_{\hat{\eta}}, s, {\zeta_\eta}^1, {\zeta_\eta}^2) > \Lambda_f(g_\eta; \zeta_{\hat{\eta}}, s, {\zeta_\eta}^1, {\zeta_\eta}^2)$ for all pairs of moves ${\zeta_\eta}^1, {\zeta_\eta}^2$ [21].[8]

It is possible to solve for the set of all private utilities that are factored with respect to a particular world utility. Unfortunately, in general it is not possible for a collective both to be factored and to have infinite learnability for all of its players. However, consider *difference* utilities, which are of the form

$$U(\zeta) = \beta[G(\zeta) - \Gamma(\zeta_{\hat{\eta}})] \tag{17.4}$$

Any difference utility is factored [21]. In addition, under usually benign approximations, $\Lambda_f(U; \zeta_{\hat{\eta}}, s, {\zeta_\eta}^1, {\zeta_\eta}^2)$ is maximized over the of difference utilities for all pairs ${\zeta_\eta}^1, {\zeta_\eta}^2$ by choosing

$$\Gamma(\zeta_{\hat{\eta}}) = E_f(G(\zeta) \mid \zeta_{\hat{\eta}}, s) \tag{17.5}$$

up to an overall additive constant, where the expectation value is over ζ_η. We call the resultant difference utility the *Aristocrat* utility (AU), loosely reflecting the fact that it measures the difference between a player's actual action and the average action. If each player η uses an appropriately rescaled version of the associated AU as its private utility function, then we have ensured good form for both terms 2 and 3 in Eq. 17.2.

Using AU in practice is sometimes difficult, due to the need to evaluate the expectation value. Fortunately there are other utility functions that, while being easier to evaluate than AU, still are both factored and possess superior learnability to the team game utility, $g_\eta = G$. One such private utility function is the *Wonderful Life* Utility (WLU). The WLU for player η is parameterized by a prefixed *clamping parameter* CL_η chosen from among η's possible moves:

$$WLU_\eta \equiv G(\zeta) - G(\zeta_{\hat{\eta}}, CL_\eta) \tag{17.6}$$

WLU is factored no matter what the choice of clamping parameter. Furthermore, while not matching the high learnability of AU, WLU usually has far better learnability than does a team game, and therefore (when scaled appropriately) results in better expected intelligence [2, 5, 16, 25].

Figure 17.2 provides an example of clamping. As in that example, in many circumstances there is a particular choice of clamping parameter for player η that is a "null" move for that player, equivalent to removing that player from the system.

[8] In many RL algorithms, changing the scale of the utility is exactly equivalent to changing a temperature parameter of the algorithm. Such temperatures have to usually be set via a search process. The result presented here establishes that so long as g'_η has higher learnability than does g_η, the expected intelligence of g'_η at the associated optimal temperature will be higher than that of g_η at its optimal temperature.

$$\begin{array}{c} \eta_1\\ \eta_2\\ \eta_3\\ \eta_4 \end{array} \overset{\zeta}{\begin{bmatrix}1&0&0\\0&0&1\\1&0&0\\0&1&0\end{bmatrix}} \quad \underset{\text{to ``null''}}{\overset{\Longrightarrow}{\text{Clamp } \eta_2}} \quad \overset{(\zeta_{\hat{\eta}_2},\vec{0})}{\begin{bmatrix}1&0&0\\0&0&0\\1&0&0\\0&1&0\end{bmatrix}} \quad \underset{\text{to ``average''}}{\overset{\Longrightarrow}{\text{Clamp } \eta_2}} \quad \overset{(\zeta_{\hat{\eta}_2},\vec{a})}{\begin{bmatrix}1&0&0\\.33&.33&.33\\1&0&0\\0&1&0\end{bmatrix}}$$

Figure 17.2 This example shows the impact of the clamping operation on the joint state of a four-player system where each player has three possible moves, each such move represented by a three-dimensional unary vector. The first matrix represents the joint state of the system ζ where player 1 has selected action 1, player 2 has selected action 3, player 3 has selected action 1 and player 4 has selected move 2. The second matrix displays the effect of clamping player 2's action to the "null" vector (i.e., replacing ζ_{η_2} with $\vec{0}$). The third matrix shows the effect of instead clamping player 2's move to the "average" action vector $\vec{a} = \{.33, .33, .33\}$, which amounts to replacing that player's move with the illegal move of fractionally taking each possible move ($\zeta_{\eta_2} = \vec{a}$).

(Hence the name of this private utility function—cf. the Frank Capra movie.) For such a clamping parameter, assigning the associated WLU to η as its private utility function is closely related to the economics technique of "endogenizing a player's externalities," for example with the Groves mechanism [9, 17, 19, 26].

However it is usually the case that using WLU with a clamping parameter that is as close as possible to the expected move defining AU results in far higher learnability than does clamping to the null move. Such a WLU is roughly akin to a mean-field approximation to AU.[9] For example, in Fig. 17.2, if the probabilities of player 2 making each of its possible moves were $1/3$, then one would expect that a clamping parameter of $\vec{a}$ would be close to optimal. Accordingly, inpractice use of such an alternative WLU derived as a mean-field approximation to AU almost always results in far better values of G than does the "endogenizing" WLU.

Intuitively, collectives having factored and highly learnable private utilities like AU and WLU can be viewed as akin to well-run human companies. G is the bottom line of the company, the players η are identified with the employees of that company, and the associated g_η given by the employees' performance-based compensation packages. For example, for a factored company, each employee's compensation package contains incentives designed such that the better the bottom line of the corporation, the greater the employee's compensation. As an example, the CEO of a company wishing to have the private utilities of the employees be factored with G may give stock options to the employees. The net effect of this action is to ensure that what is good for the employee is also good for the company. In addition, if the compensation packages are highly learnable, the employees will have a relatively easy time discerning the relationship between their behavior and their

[9] Formally, our approximation is exact only if the expected value of G equals G evaluated at the expected joint move (both expectations being conditioned on given moved by all players other than η). In general though, for relatively smooth G, we would expect such a mean-field approximation to AU, to give good results, even if the approximation does not hold exactly.

compensation. In such a case the employees will both have the incentive to help the company and be able to determine how best to do so. Note that inpractice, providing stock options is usually more effective in small companies than in large ones. This makes perfect sense in terms of the formalism summarized above, since such options generally have higher learnability in small companies than they do in large companies, in which each employee has a hard time seeing how his/her moves effect the company's stock price.

17.3 TESTS OF THE MATHEMATICS

As a test of the preceding mathematics, in some of our previous work we used the WLU for distributed control of network packet routing [2]. Conventional approaches to packet routing have each router run a Shortest Path Algorithm (SPA), i.e., each router routes its packets in the way that it expects will get those packets to their destinations most quickly. Unlike with a WLU-based collective, with SPA-based routing the routers have no concern for the possible deleterious side-effects of their routing decisions on the global goal (e.g., they have no concern for whether they induce bottlenecks). We ran simulations that demonstrated that a WLU-based collective has substantially better throughputs than does the best possible SPA-based system [2], even though that SPA-based system has information denied the agents in the WLU-based collective.

In related work, we have shown that use of the WLU automatically avoids the infamous Braess' paradox, in which adding new links can actually decrease throughput—a situation that readily ensnares SPAs [5, 27].

In yet other work we have applied the WLU to the problem of controlling communication across a constellation of satellites so as minimize the importance-weighted loss of scientific data flowing across that constellation [28]. Due to the novelty of this problem domain, we first had to design a baseline distributed control algorithm, one that involves no learning. To minimize the number of confounding distinctions between that baseline algorithm and the collective-based algorithm we investigated, we had that collective "run on top" of the baseline algorithm. The action of each agent in the collective was the determination of fictitious "ghost traffic" that is presented to the baseline algorithm, thereby (hopefully) inducing that baseline algorithm to achieve an even better value of the world utility. (Note that this idea can be applied with most any baseline algorithm and most any distributed RL algorithm.) Again, we achieved a significant increase in performance, in this case relative to the baseline algorithm.

We have also successfully applied the COIN techniques to problems that are explicitly cast as search. These include setting the states of the spins in a spin glass to minimize energy; the conventional bin-packing problem of computer science, and a model of human agents connected ina small-world network who have to synchronize their purchase decisions. We have also successfully applied COIN techniques to the problem of coordinating a set of autonomous rovers so as to maximize the importance-weighted value of a set of locations they visit [29].

Finally, it is worth going into some detail our investigations on variants of congestion games [1, 3, 25], in particular of a more challenging variant of Arthur's El Farol bar attendance problem [30], sometimes also known as the minority game [31]. In this problem the individual processes making up the collective are explicitly viewed as 'players' involved in a noncooperative game. Each player has to determine which night in the week to attend a bar. The problem is set up so that if either too few people attend (boring evening) or too many people attend (crowded evening), the total enjoyment of the attending players drops. Our goal is to design the private utility functions of the players so that the total enjoyment across all nights is maximized. In this previous work we showed that use of the WLU can result in performance *orders of magnitude* superior to that of team game utilities.

Arthur's bar problem [30] can be viewed as a problem in designing collectives. Loosely speaking, in this problem at each time step each player η decides whether to attend a bar by predicting, based on its previous experience, whether the bar will be too crowded to be "rewarding" at that time, as quantified by a utility function G. The selfish nature of the players frustrates the global goal of maximizing G. This is because if most players think the attendance will be low (and therefore choose to attend), the attendance will actually be high, and vice-versa.

The variants of the bar problem we investigated were all of the following type: There are N players, each picking one out of seven moves every week. Each variant of the game is parameterized by $\ell \in \{1, 2, 3, 4, 5, 6\}$. In a given variant, each move of an agent corresponds to attending the bar on some particular subset of ℓ out of the seven nights of the current week (i.e., given ℓ, each possible move is an 'attendance profile' vertex of the 7-dimensional unit hypercube having ℓ 1's). In each week every player chooses amove. Then the associated private utility values for each player are communicated to that player, and the process is repeated. For simplicity, for each ℓ we chose the seven possible attendance profiles so that if the moves are selected randomly uniformly, the expected resultant attendance profile across all seven nights is also uniform. (For example, or $\ell = 2$, those profiles are (1, 1, 0, 0, 0, 0, 0), (0, 1, 1, 0, 0, 0, 0), etc.)

More formally, the world utility in any particular week is:

$$G(\zeta) \equiv \sum_{k=1}^{7} \phi(x_k(\zeta)) \tag{17.7}$$

where $x_k(\zeta)$ is the total attendance on night k; ζ_η is η's move in that week; $\phi(y) \equiv y \exp(-y/c)$; and c is a real-valued parameter. Our choice of $\phi(.)$ means that when either too few or too many players attend some night, in some week, world utility G is low.

Since we wished to concentrate on the effects of the utilities rather than on the RL algorithms that use them, we used (very) simple RL algorithms.[10] We would

[10] On the other hand to use algorithms so patently deficient that they have never even been considered in the RL community—like the algorithms used in most of the bar problem literature—would seriously interfere with our ability to interpret our experiments.

expect that even marginally more sophisticated RL algorithms would give better performance. In our algorithm each player η had a 7-dimensional vector giving its estimates of the utility it would receive for taking each possible move. At the beginning of each week, each η picked the night to attend randomly, using a Boltzmann distribution over the seven components of η's estimated utilities vector. For simplicity, temperature did not decay in time. However, to reflect the fact that each player operated in a nonstationary environment, utility estimates were formed using exponentially aged data: in any week t, the estimate η makes for the utility for attending night i was a weighted average of all the utilities it has received previously when it attended that night, with the weights given by an exponential function of how long ago each such utility was. To form the players' initial training set, we had an initial period in which all moves by all players were chosen uniformly randomly, with no learning.

In these experiments we found once again that use of highly learnable factored private utilities resulted in vastly better performance than use of team game private utilities. Also as usual, we found that the gain in performance grew as the problem grew, reaching orders of magnitude once the system grew to consist of thousands of agents. We always found that AU performed at least as well as WLU with clamping to 0, which is essentially identical to the economics technique of endogenizing externalities. In addition though, for some choices of ℓ, we found that AU performed substantially better than did this alternative, as would be expected based on the formalism presented above.

Finally, the central equation makes numerous other predictions that preliminary experiments seem to bear out. Some of these predictions concern ways to modify the behavior of the collective to try to optimize term 1 as well as terms 2 and 3. (The work in [28] can be viewed as an initial investigation of this issue.) Other predictions are on how to modify a factored private utility so that it is *not* perfectly factored any more, but has undergone such a large gain in learnability that (as quantified in the central equation) overall performance improves [31]. It is worth emphasizing that such beneficial modifications to private utilities are prohibited by the starting premise of the field of mechanism design, that the private utilities must exhibit incentive compatibility.

17.4 CONCLUSION

A collective is any multi-agent system in which each agent adaptively tries to maximize its own private utility, while at the same time there is an overall world utility rating the behavior of the entire system. Collectives are quite common in the natural world, the canonical example being any human organization. In addition, as computing becomes ubiquitous in artificial systems, the number of such systems that constitute collectives will explode.

Associated with any collective is a design problem, of how to configure the system—and in particular how to set the private utilities of the agents—to optimize the world utility. This paper cursorily synopsizes some of the mathematical theory underpinning this design problem. That theory has now been tested in many different experiments. As summarized above, those tests of the theory have clearly validated it, often resulting in performance up to orders of magnitude superior to traditional techniques from the fields of multi-agent systems and economics/mechanism design. Intuitively, that superiority lies in the fact that these alternative approaches completely ignore the issue of how an agent's ability to maximize a candidate private utility will vary with changes in that private utility. This issue is especially crucial in large systems, in which each agent will face an extremely difficult "signal-to-noise" term in discerning the effects of its actions on its utility unless that utility is crafted carefully.

REFERENCES

1. D. H. Wolpert and K. Tumer. "Optimal Payoff Functions for Members of Collectives." *Advances Complex Systems*, vol. 4, no. 2/3, 265–279, 2001.
2. D. H. Wolpert, K. Tumer, and J. Frank. "Using Collective Intelligence to Route Internet Traffic." In *Advances in Neural Information Processing Systems—11*, pages 952–958. MIT Press, 1999.
3. D. H. Wolpert, K. Wheeler, and K. Tumer. "General Principles of Learning-Based Multi-Agent Systems." In *Proceedings Third International Conference of Autonomous Agents*, pages 77–83, 1999.
4. D. H. Wolpert and K. Tumer. An Introduction to Collective Intelligence. Technical Report NASA-ARC-IC-99-63, NASA Ames Research Center, 1999. URL:http://ic.arc.nasa.gov/ic/projects/coin_pubs.html. To appear in *Handbook of Agent Technology*, J. M. Bradshaw, (ed.) AAAI/MIT Press.
5. K. Tumer and D. H. Wolpert. "Collective Intelligence and Braess' Paradox." In *Proceedings of the 17th National Conference on Artificial Intelligence*, pages 104–109, Austin, TX, 2000.
6. G. Hardin. "The Tragedy of the Commons." *Science*, vol. 162, 1243–1248, 1968.
7. L. P. Kaelbing, M. L. Littman, and A. W. Moore. "Reinforcement Learning: A Survey." *J. Artificial Intelligence Res.*, vol. 4, 237–285, 1996.
8. R. S. Sutton and A. G. Barto. *Reinforcement Learning: An Introduction.* MIT Press, Cambridge, MA, 1998.
9. R. S. Sutton. "Learning to Predict by the Methods of Temporal Differences." *Machine Learning*, vol. 3, 9–44, 1988.
10. C. Watkins and P. Dayan. "Q-Learning." *Machine Learning*, vol. 8, no. 314, 279–292, 1992.
11. C. Boutilier. " Multiagent Systems: Challenges and Opportunities for Decision Theoretic Planning." *AI Mag.*, vol. 20, no. 35, 35–43, 1999.
12. C. Claus and C. Boutilier. "The Dynamics of Reinforcement Learning Cooperative Multiagent Systems." In *Proceedings of 15th National Conference on Artificial Intelligence*, pages 746–752, Madison, WI, June 1998.
13. J. Hu and M. P. Wellman. "Multiagent Reinforcement Learning: Theoretical Framework and an Algorithm." In *Proceedings Fifteenth International Conference on Machine Learning*, pages 242–250, June 1998.

14. M. L. Littman."Markov Games as a Framework for Multi-Agent Reinforcement Learning." In *Proceedings of the 11th International Conference on Machine Learning*, pages 157–163, 1994.
15. T. Sandholm and R. Crites. "Multiagent Reinforcement Learning in the Iterated Prisoner's Dilemma." *Biosystems*, vol. 37 147–166, 1995.
16. D. H. Wolpert and K. Tumer. An Introduction to Collective Intelligence. Technical Report NASA-ARC-IC-99-63, NASA Ames Research Center, 1999. URL:http://ic.arc.nasa.gov/ic/projects/coin_pubs.html. To appear in *Handbook of Agent Technology*, J. M. Bradshaw, (ed.) AAAI/MIT Press.
17. D. Fudenberg and J. Tirole. *Game Theory*. MIT Press, Cambridge, MA, 1991.
18. D. C. Parkes. *Iterative Combinatorial Auctions: Theory and Practice*. Ph.D. thesis, University of Pennsylvania, 2001.
19. N. Nisan and A. Ronen. "Algorithmic Mechanism Design." *Games Economic Behavior*, vol. 35, 166–196, 2001.
20. R. H. Crites and A. G. Barto. "Improving Elevator Performance Using Reinforcement Learning." In D. S. Touretzky, M. C. Mozer, and M. E. Hasselmo (eds.), *Advances in Neural Information Processing Systems—8*, pages 1017–1023. MIT Press, 1996.
21. D. H. Wolpert. Theory of design of collectives. pre-print, 2002.
22. D. H. Wolpert. Bounded-rationality game theory. pre-print, 2001.
23. D. H. Wolpert, E. Bandari, and K. Tumer. Improving simulated annealing by recasting it as a non-cooperative game. 2001. Submitted.
24. D. Monderer and L. S. Sharpley. "Potential Games." *Games Economic Behavior*, vol. 14, 124–143, 1996.
25. D. H. Wolpert, K. Wheeler, and K. Tumer. "Collective Intelligence for Control of Distributed Dynamical Systems." *Europhysics Lett.*, vol. 49, no. 6, March 2000.
26. W. Nicholson. *Microeconomic Theory*, Seventh Edition, The Dryden Press, 1998.
27. D. H. Wolpert and K. Tumer. Collective Intelligence, Data Routing and Braess' paradox. *J. Artificial Intelligence Res.* 1995. To appear.
28. D. H. Wolpert, J. Sill, and K. Tumer. "Reinforcement Learning in Distributed Domains: Beyond Team Games." In *Proceedings of the Seventeenth International Joint Conference on Artificial Intelligence*, pages 819–824, Seattle, WA, 2001.
29. K. Tumer, A. Agogino, and D. Wolpert. "Learning Sequences of Actions in Collectives of Autonomous Agents." In *Proceedings First International Joint Conference on Autonomous Agents Multi-Agent Systems*, Bologna, Italy, July 2002.
30. W. B. Arthur. "Complexity in Economic Theory: Inductive Reasoning and Bounded Rationality." *Amer. Econ. Rev.*, vol. 84, no. 2, 406–411, May 1994.
31. D. Challet and Y. C. Zhang. "On the Minority Game: Analytical and Numerical Studies." *Physica A*, vol. 256 514, 1998.

BIBLIOGRAPHY

C. Boutilier, Y. Shoham, and M. P. Wellman. "Editorial: Economic Principles of Multi-Agent Systems." *Artificial Intelligence J.*, vol. 94, 1–6, 1997.

J. M. Bradshaw, (ed.), *Software Agents*. MIT Press, 1997.

G. Caldarelli, M. Marsili, and Y. C. Zhang. "A Prototype Model of Stock Exchange." *Europhysics Let.*, vol. 40, 479–484, 1997.

B. A. Huberman and T. Hogg. "The Behavior of Computational Ecologies." In *The Ecology of Computation*, pages 77–115. North-Holland, 1988.

N. R. Jennings, K. Sycara, and M. Wooldridge. A Roadmap of Agent Research and Development. *Autonomous Agents Multi-Agent Sys.*, vol. 1, 7–38, 1998.

N. F. Johnson, S. Jarvis, R. Jonson, P. Cheung, Y. R. Kwong, and P. M. Hui. "Volatility and Agent Adaptability in a Self-Organizing Market." preprint cond-mat/9802177, February 1998.

T. Sandholm, K. Larson, M. Anderson, O. Shehory, and F. Tohme. "Anytime Coalition Structure Generation with Worst Case Guarantees." In *Proceedings of the Fifteenth National Conference on Artificial Intelligence*, pages 46–53, 1998.

S. Sen. *Multi-Agent Learning: Papers from the 1997 AAAI Workshop (Technical Report WS-97-03*. AAAI Press, Menlo Park, CA, 1997.

K. Sycara. "Multiagent Systems." *AI Magazine*, vol. 19, no. 2, 79–92, 1998.

M. P. Wellman. "A Market-Oriented Programming Environment and Its Application to Distributed Multicommodity Flow Problems." In *J. Art. Intel. Res.*, 1993.

D. Wolpert and J. Lawson. "Designing Agent Collectives for Systems with Markovian Dynamics." In *Proceedings of the First International Joint Conference on Autonomous Agents and Multi-Agent Systems*, Bologna, Italy, July 2002.

Y. C. Zhang. "Modeling Market Mechanism with Evolutionary Games." *Europhysics Let.*, March/April 1998.

CHAPTER 18

BACKPROPAGATION: GENERAL PRINCIPLES AND ISSUES FOR BIOLOGY

PAUL J. WERBOS

18.1 INTRODUCTION

Like reinforcement learning, backpropagation is a large collection of methods, mathematics and research areas which has become very fragmented as back propagation has been propagated, popularized, interpreted, enhanced and implemented in different ways across a wide variety of application domains. There are two relatively standard definitions of backpropagation [1]:

- Backpropagation is a procedure for *efficiently* calculating the derivatives of some function of the outputs of any nonlinear differentiable system, with respect to all inputs and parameters of that system, through calculations proceeding *backwards* from outputs to inputs. It permits "local" implementation on parallel hardware (or wetware).
- Backpropagation is any technique for adapting the weights or parameters of a nonlinear system by using such derivatives or the equivalent.

One family of backpropagation methods, called vanilla backpropagation, accounts for most applications of artificial neural networks (ANNs) published in journals today. Yet in many challenging engineering applications—applications where computational intelligence is especially important to success—more advanced and powerful forms of backpropagation are essential; if applications in the pipeline are weighted by economic value added, rather than words published, these are probably more important than vanilla backpropagation. Finally, one may argue that some form of backpropagation would be essential to replicating (or understanding) some of the high-level information-processing capabilities of the

Computational Intelligence: The Experts Speak. Edited by D. B. Fogel and C. J. Robinson
ISBN 0-471-27454-2

mammalian brain [2,3]. Yet neuroscientists have rightly pointed out that vanilla backpropagation is too simple to be plausible even as one part of a model of functional circuit-level computation in the brain.

Backpropagation has been used to perform at least five different types of tasks, in computational intelligence. Suppose that $\mathbf{Y} = \mathbf{f}(\mathbf{X}, W)$ denotes any nonlinear input–output mapping, such as an ANN, which inputs a vector, $\mathbf{X}$, outputs a vector, $\mathbf{Y}$ and contains a set of tunable weights or parameters, W.
Backpropagation has been used to perform:

1. Supervised learning, in which the system is given a *training set* of pairs of values for $\mathbf{X}(t)$ and $\mathbf{Y}^*(t)$, and tunes W so as to make $\mathbf{Y}(t)$ a good predictor of $\mathbf{X}(t)$. In some variations of this task, the pairs are presented one-at-a-time, while in others there is a fixed database.
2. Gradient learning, in which the system is given a training set of pairs of values for $\mathbf{X}(t)$ and $\nabla_Y U(\mathbf{Y}(t))$ where U is some (unknown) function, and W is tuned so as to maximize or minimize U over time.
3. Neuroidentification, which is like supervised learning, except that the nonlinear system to be adapted can be described as a system which outputs two vectors at each time t:

$$\mathbf{Y}(t) = \mathbf{f}_Y(\mathbf{X}(t), W, \mathbf{R}(t-1)) \tag{18.1a}$$

$$\mathbf{R}(t) = \mathbf{f}_R(\mathbf{X}(\mathbf{t}), \mathbf{W}, \mathbf{R}(t-1)) \tag{18.1b}$$

4. Probability distribution learning, which is like 1 or 3, except that the task is to accurately represent a probability distribution. This can be done by outputting $\mathbf{Y} = \mathbf{f}(\mathbf{X}, W, \mathbf{u})$, where $\mathbf{u}$ is a vector of random numbers, and seeking $\Pr(\mathbf{Y}^*|\mathbf{X}) = \Pr(\mathbf{Y}|\mathbf{X})$.
5. Pass-through of derivatives, as in "backpropagation through a model," where $\nabla_Y U(\mathbf{Y}(t), t)$ is given and the task is to output $\nabla_X U(\mathbf{Y}(t), t)$

This list is only slightly oversimplified. It is important to note that supervised learning is only one of five ways to use backpropagation. The design choices and trade-offs, in performance and in software, vary greatly from area to area. Vanilla backpropagation, in turn, is only one of the many forms of backpropagation used in supervised learning.

Intelligent control systems, like biological brains, are not static input–output devices. Sophisticated decision-making capabilities over time require components which perform some of the tasks in 2–5 above [4,5; also, www.iamcm.org.] Supervised learning can be useful as a research testbed, in developing tools which could be extended to tasks 2–5. It has major value as a present market for ANNs. (See www.hnc.com and www.neuralware.com and www.nd.com, for examples involving areas such as pattern recognition for OCR systems, financial risk assessment systems, and airport screening systems in the wake of September 11th, to pick just a few.) But its importance within the larger scheme of backpropagation and basic science should not be overstated.

This chapter first reviews the chain rule for ordered derivatives, the original mathematical foundation for the use of backpropagation in all five areas. Next it reviews backpropagation for supervised learning, including vanilla backpropagation. Unfortunately, the introductory nature of this text prohibits discussion of the four other tasks, despite their greater importance both to engineering and to cognitive neuroscience; see the references and web pages cited herein for discussions of those larger tasks.

18.2 THE CHAIN RULE FOR ORDERED DERIVATIVES

The chain rule for ordered derivatives addresses the following task: given a nonlinear, distributed system which computes some output result $R(\mathbf{Y})$, where $\mathbf{Y} = \mathbf{f}(\mathbf{X}, W)$ (or $\mathbf{Y} = \mathbf{f}(\mathbf{X}, W, \mathbf{u})$), how can we efficiently compute *all* the derivatives of R with respect to all components of the inputs vector $\mathbf{X}$ and the weights in W?

There are two cases which commonly arise.

When there is a finite bound on the time it takes to compute $\mathbf{Y}$, then in principle we can always represent the sequence as an ordered, "feedforward" sequence of computations of the form:

$$R = f_{N+1}(f_N, \ldots, f_0) \qquad (18.2a)$$

$$Y_n = f_N(f_{N-1}, \ldots, f_0) \qquad (18.2b)$$

$$\ldots$$

$$f_k = X_k \qquad (18.2c)$$

$$\ldots$$

$$f_0 = 1 \qquad (18.2d)$$

where the initial nodes in the network just "load in" or register the inputs, $\mathbf{X}$ and W (and $\mathbf{u}$), where each intermediate node is allowed to be *any* function of preceding nodes, where the last block of nodes but one represent the output vector, and where the result is treated as if it were a node in the network. (When the distributed system is partially ordered, there are typically many equivalent representations of this form.) My 1974 Harvard Ph.D. thesis [3] proved that one may simply compute, recursively:

$$\frac{\partial^+ R}{\partial f_i} = \sum_{k=i+1}^{n} \frac{\partial^+ R}{\partial f_k} \cdot \frac{\partial f_k}{\partial f_i}, \qquad (18.3)$$

where the partial derivative on the far right represents the *direct* impact of f_i on f_k in that equation (in Eqs. 18.2) which determines f_k, and where the ordered derivatives (the derivatives with a "+" superscript) represent the *total* impact of a change in f_i on the result R. This system may be initialized by using the fact that $\partial^+ R/\partial R = 1$; however, we usually just assume that the terms $\partial^+ R/\partial Y_i$ are available as a starting point. The ordered derivatives of R with respect to the inputs are what we need for the five tasks outlined previously.

This chain rule was published in several papers between 1977 and 1983, particularly in a major conference paper [reprinted 3] which elaborated on the applications to layered neural networks, intelligent control, and various forms of sensitivity analysis. It also discussed forwards propagation or conventional perturbation, a method which is neither biologically plausible nor useful in large-scale engineering applications where computational cost is important. (Forwards propagation has been reinvented under different names many times.) Anderson and Rosenfeld [6] published some of the history of backpropagation. See Werbos [3] and White and Sofge [4] for many examples and intuitive explanations of this chain rule. Rumelhart and McClelland [7] played a central role in popularizing vanilla backpropagation and reviving the neural network field in general.

Note that the calculation of derivatives through a stochastic system is achieved most efficiently and most simply by representing $\mathbf{u}$ as another set of exogenous inputs. Complex papers have described the use of complicated sampling methods as an alternative; however, from a statistician's viewpoint, the former is like a paired comparison test, while the latter is like an unpaired comparison.

In social science, biology and engineering, one often encounters nonlinear systems defined implicitly, as a system of simultaneous equations. These can be written as:

$$\mathbf{Y} = \mathbf{f}_Y(\mathbf{X}, W, \mathbf{y}) \tag{18.4a}$$

$$\mathbf{y} = \mathbf{f}_y(\mathbf{X}, W, \mathbf{y}), \tag{18.4b}$$

where $\mathbf{f}$ itself is a feedforward system which outputs both $\mathbf{Y}$ and $\mathbf{y}$. Eqs. 18.4 define a simultaneous recurrent network (SRN). (Unfortunately, later authors used "SRN" to denote a "Simple Recurrent Network," a related but distinct concept.) To calculate the derivatives of $R(\mathbf{Y})$ with respect to $\mathbf{X}$ and W one must use a numerical estimation or iterative method. Several choices exist, all requiring use of backpropagation through $\mathbf{f}$ as part of the larger calculations.

Simultaneous backpropagation is an efficient forwards-time method to calculate these derivatives in the general case. In 1987, I proved that simultaneous backpropagation converges to the correct derivatives, at least as quickly as the original system in Eqs. 18.4 converges, *if* $\mathbf{y}$ exactly solves Eqs. 18.4. [4, Chapter 3, gives algorithm and citations.] It was first applied in 1981, to calculate the sensitivities of a Department of Energy model of the natural gas industry used in a major deregulation study. The methods of Pineda and Almeida are special cases of this earlier general method.

Some psychologists use *simple truncation* to estimate derivatives of SRNs. (Indeed, they sometimes define simple recurrent networks as networks adapted on that basis.) They perform one pass of backpropagation , and implicitly treat values of

y from the next-to-last iteration as if they were external constants. This does not yield correct derivatives. In training cellular SRNs to assist in maze navigation, Pang and I found that simple truncation led to useless results, while *backpropagation through time (BTT)*—though slow in our crude implementation—worked well. [See 8 and www.lanl.gov/abs/adap-org/9806001.] BTT gives *exact* derivatives, and requires only the same computational time required to converge the original system; therefore, it was better in guaranteeing performance in a computational experiment, even though it is not a plausible model of brain computation.

Because BTT is not biologically plausible, a forwards-time consistent approximator—the error critic (EC) (also discussed in adap-org 9806001)—merits further research. Preliminary empirical work by Danil Prokhorov at Ford suggests that the EC might have superior performance in some control applications. Neither BTT nor the EC require starting from a fully converged value of **y**.

18.3 BACKPROPAGATION FOR SUPERVISED LEARNING

18.3.1 Basic and Vanilla Backpropagation: Principles

Backpropagation, in our general formulation, can be used in almost any nonlinear regression or statistical estimation. From a statistician's viewpoint, the supervised learning task over a fixed database, or training set, is the same as the task of nonlinear regression, for which an enormous literature already existed when the ANN field was reborn in 1987, at the IEEE International Conference on Neural Networks. But the traditional literature from statistics asked the user to pick a function **f** specifically based on prior information about the process which generates $\mathbf{Y}^*$. The neural network field seeks to develop and use general-purpose functions **f** which can learn to approximate any well-defined nonlinear function and can be implemented as distributed systems made up of common, modular components ("neurons"). Computational speed and convergence were challenges in traditional nonlinear regression packages, even more than with ANNs.

Basic backpropagation uses a combination of backpropagation, steepest descent and least squares error to adapt a specific choice of **f**—the Generalized Multilayer Perceptron (GMLP). The GMLP may be defined by:

$$x_0 = 1 \qquad (18.5a)$$

$$x_i = X_i \qquad (i = 1 \text{ to } m) \qquad (18.5b)$$

$$\left.\begin{aligned} v_j &= \textstyle\sum_{k=0}^{j-1} W_{jk}\, x_k \\ x_j &= s(v_j) \end{aligned}\right\} \qquad (k = m+1 \text{ to } N+n) \qquad (18.5c)$$

$$Y_i = x_{i+N} \qquad (i = 1 \text{ to } n) \qquad (18.5d)$$

where the components of the vectors **X** and **Y** are usually restricted to the interval from -1 to $+1$, and where the squashing or sigmoidal function s is normally chosen to be the hyperbolic tangent, tanh. The variables "x_i" are thought of as the scaled frequency output of a model neuron, and "v_j" is thought of as the voltage stimulating that neuron. The number of "hidden neurons," N-m, must be chosen by the user; however, the weights W_{jk} can be adapted in a totally automatic way in principle. (Of course, when there is prior knowledge telling us that we should zero out certain weights, it is easy enough to do so.)

Vanilla backpropagation is that special case of basic backpropagation where there are "three layers"—the input layer (x_i for $i \leq m$), the output layer (x_i for $i > N$), and the hidden layer (all neurons in-between)—and where all the weights are zeroed out apriori except for the weights connecting the input layer to the hidden layer, and the hidden layer to the output layer. Most papers published using backpropagation today use vanilla backpropagation, with intuitive modifications to steepest descent and least squares error as required to get decent learning performance. In vanilla backpropagation, as in basic backpropagation, the user only needs to decide how many hidden neurons to use, in order to invoke the system. The user must also develop the training set of **X** and **Y** pairs; this is essentially the same as the problem of choosing independent and dependent variables in a classical linear regression analysis. Companies which make money using vanilla backpropagation often say that 90 percent of their effort usually lies in constructing a good database. The use of vanilla backpropagation is similar to the use of linear regression, except that nonlinear relationships can be learned, and a larger training set is needed to make that really work.

Some researchers have explored an intermediate case, between GMLP and the 3-layer network, where the hidden neurons are divided into L sequential strings of neurons, called intermediate layers. Sontag, for example, proved that a 2-hidden-layer network can approximate certain nonlinear mappings encountered in direct inverse control more reliably than the vanilla design. DeFiguerido has published papers on research issues and methods for choosing L. Nauta's description of the cerebellar system sounds similar to a multilayer feedforward design, but he discusses important additional loops in the system, like time-delayed recurrence in the Purkinje layer important to shaping action over time [9].

In applying the chain rule for ordered derivatives to Eq. 18.5, basic and vanilla backpropagation try to minimize the usual square error function well-known from statistics:

$$E(\underline{Y}^*(t), \underline{Y}(t)) = \frac{1}{2}\sum_{i=1}^{n}(Y_i^*(t) - Y_i(t))^2 \tag{18.6}$$

To calculate the derivatives, we begin by doing a simple calculation and introducing a short-hand abbreviation for the ordered derivatives of interest:

$$F\_Y_i(t) = \frac{\partial^+ E}{\partial Y_i} = Y_i(t) - Y_i^*(t) \qquad i = 1 \text{ to } n \tag{18.7}$$

The prefix "$F\_$" may be thought of as "derivative Feedback back to . . .". The chain rule for ordered derivatives yields the recurrence relations:

$$\left.\begin{aligned} F\_x_i(t) &= F\_Y_{i-N}(t) + \textstyle\sum_{j=i+1}^{N+n} W_{ji} F\_v_j(t) \\ F\_v_i(t) &= s'(v_i)^* F\_x_i(t) \end{aligned}\right\} i = N+n, \ldots, m+1 \text{ or } 1 \tag{18.8}$$

$$F\_W_{ij}(t) = F\_v_i(t)^* x_j(t) \qquad \text{all adapted weights } ij \tag{18.9}$$

The asterisk signifies multiplication just in the last two equations, for clarity. F_Y_{i-N} is taken as zero for $i \leq N$. In Eq. 18.8, we only need to do recurrence back to $m+1$ when we only need to know F_W_{ij}. When we need to know the derivatives back to the inputs, F_X_i, we take the recurrence back to 1.

When adaptation is done one-observation-at-a-time, each weight W_{ij} is changed by $-\lambda^* F\_W_{ij}$ at each time, where λ is a positive parameter called "the learning rate." When adaptation is done in "batch" mode, over an entire database, F_W_{ij} is calculated by adding $F\_W_{ij}(t)$ over all observations t, and one usually uses a more powerful gradient based optimization method to adapt the weights. See [3] for some pseudocode.

18.3.2 Performance Issues for Today's User

A brief article cannot do full justice to the enormous literature on performance issues across all the many application domains. It could not even give full citations to all the texts considered definitive within their particular application domain or school of thought. The diverse literature suggests that no single individual could properly critique the whole set of these texts in detail.

The user who wishes to use existing software might begin by downloading the SNNS shareware, from one of the many links listed in the pages of the Neural Network Society under www.ieee.org. The commercial websites cited here are also worth visiting.

Performance tradeoffs in data mining applications have been discussed in numerous papers in the Proceedings of the IEEE conference on Knowledge Discovery and Datamining (KDD). Mark Embrechts, for example, has done extensive studies on financial databases and drug-discovery types of databases.

In pattern recognition, Richard Duda, co-author of the earlier classic text on pattern recognition, has updated his text to include various ANN designs and tradeoffs. In the early 1990s, the U.S. Postal Service funded extensive studies and evaluations of competing methods (neural and nonneural) for automated recognition of ZIP code digits. Recipients of such grants often announced that they had achieved the "best reported performance" (usually within the methods they tried), but Jay Lee of the Postal Service reported that two systems using MLPs (one from AT&T) did best overall. ZIP code segmentation, not digit recognition, is now the barrier to automation, and many believe that some sort of recurrent network is needed to overcome that barrier. Certainly MLPs and local networks and classic AI have not achieved adequate or human-like performance.

In chemical engineering, Chapter 10 of [4] discussed many applications and tricks then used, which are not so different from what is used today.

In engineering as a whole, the bulk of supervised learning applications use MLPs or "local networks"—usually, radial basis functions (RBFs), self-organizing maps (SOMs), CMAC, or even adaptive resonance theory (ART) or modified ART. Naive, unmodified steepest descent with unscaled data can easily be used to achieve slow learning in all these systems, but modern software applied to reasonable databases generally does much better. With the best software, accuracy of learning and generalization is generally better with the MLP, when there is ample training data and more than a handful of inputs, but learning speed is generally better with local networks. Local networks also work better than naive MLPs in some diagnostic applications when there are few "bad cases" in the training set; however, more comprehensive diagnostic systems usually require a hybrid of approaches combined with time-series data. See www.iamcm.org for more discussion of applications and tradeoffs in engineering applications.

On the theoretical side, numerous theorems were proved long ago, showing that a host of nonlinear systems, ranging from fuzzy logic and Taylor series to all types of ANN, are universal approximations of well-behaved nonlinear functions. Barron of Yale University and Sontag of Rutgers University initiated a new stream of results in the 1990s, with larger practical applications. This Chapter cannot review that entire literature, but one of Barron's results was a particular watershed. He proved that the number of parameters required for a given level of approximation accuracy for smooth functions grows exponentially, with respect to the number of inputs, for ALL fixed linear basis networks, including Taylor series and local networks and traditional fuzzy logic. With MLPs, by contrast, the number of required parameters grows in a gentle polynomial fashion. Sontag showed that ratio-based approximators (not so useful in practical many-input networks) also have good approximation properties, and I would speculate that elastic fuzzy logic does also. But for now, MLPs clearly have the edge.

Standard texts by Haykin, Wasserman, Principe and others have been strongly recommended by various users for general applications. Fiesler and Beale [10] provide extensive details on various approaches to MLPs.

18.4 DISCUSSION AND FUTURE RESEARCH

None of the existing systems used in supervised learning (ANN or other) replicates the brain's ability to combine one-trial learning and powerful generalization. Good theoretical approaches exist which should be able to close that gap, but more research is needed, especially cross-disciplinary research, developing designs which *combine* the strengths of different approaches. Among the many relevant sources are books by Vapnik, Roychowdhury et al., Tikhonov, Trafalis, Chapter 10 of White and Sofge [4] and even chapters of Pribram [2] discuss the interplay of short-term and long-term memory in memory-based learning. Recent work by Sejnowski on cortical learning is important to the latter. Also, Phatak has studied error functions with penalty functions that provide fault-tolerance and brain-like redundancy in addition to addressing learning speed and generalization.

Equally important to many engineering applications (i.e., diagnostic analysis and decision-making for large networks) is the use of supervised learning when the inputs or outputs form relational networks rather than vectors. See the discussion of ObjectNets in www.iamcm.org. Cellular SRNs are a special case of ObjectNets, relevant to tasks like image segmentation, maze navigation and the classification of connectedness, a classical challenge posed by Minsky and Papert [11] which cannot be met by MLPs. Chua's cellular neural net chips, fabricated in several countries, may well provide many times more throughput than any other general-purpose electronic chip.

REFERENCES

1. Michael A. Arbib, (ed.), *The Handbook of Brain Theory and Neural Networks*, MIT Press, Cambridge, MA, 1995.
2. Karl H. Pribram, (ed.), *Brain and Values*, Erlbaum, Hillsdale, NJ, 1998.
3. P. Werbos, *The Roots of Backpropagation: From Ordered Derivatives to Neural Networks and Political Forecasting*, Wiley, New York, 1994.
4. D. White, and D. Sofge (eds.), *Handbook of Intelligent Control*, Van Nostrand, 1992.
5. K. Narendra, and F. Lewis, (eds.), "Special Issue on Neural Network Feedback Control," *Automatica*, vol. 37, no. 8, August 2001.
6. J. Anderson and E. Rosenfeld, (eds.), *Talking Nets*, MIT Press, Cambridge, MA, 1998.
7. D. Rumelhart and J. McClelland, *Parallel Distributed Processing*. MIT Press, Cambridge, MA, 1986.
8. T. Yang and L. O. Chua, "Implementing Back-Propagation-Through-Time Learning Algorithm Using Cellular Neural Networks," *Int'l J. Bifurcation and Chaos*, vol. 9, 1041–1074, 1999.
9. W. Nauta and M. Feirtag, *Fundamental Neuro-anatomy*, W. H. Freeman, New York, 1986.
10. E. Fiesler and R. Beale (eds.), *Handbook of Neural Computation*, Oxford University Press, New York, 1997.
11. M. Minsky and S. Papert, *Perceptrons: An Introduction to Computational Geometry*, M MIT Press, Cambridge, MA, 1969.

INDEX

ABOUT THE EDITORS

Dr. David B. Fogel is chief executive officer of Natural Selection, Inc., a small high-tech company in La Jolla, California that applies methods of computational intelligence to challenging problems in industry, medicine, and defense. Dr. Fogel has published more than 200 articles in technical literature with the majority addressing the science and application of evolutionary computation and neural networks. He is the author of six books, including *Blondie24: Playing at the Edge of AI* (Morgan Kaufmann, 2002), *Evolutionary Computation: Toward a New Philosophy of Machine Intelligence, Second Edition* (IEEE Press, 2000), *How to Solve It: Modern Heuristics* (co-authored with Zbigniew Michalewicz, Springer, 2000), and *Evolutionary Computation: The Fossil Record* (IEEE Press, 1998). Dr. Fogel was the founding editor-in-chief of the *IEEE Transactions on Evolutionary Computation* (1996–2002), and is the current vice president for publications of the IEEE Neural Network Society. He was the founding president of the Evolutionary Programming Society (1991–1993) and was elected a Fellow of the IEEE in 1999. He also serves as editor-in-chief of *BioSystems*, and is on the editorial boards of several other technical journals, including the Proceedings of the IEEE. Dr. Fogel served as the general chairman for the 2002 IEEE World Congress on Computational Intelligence, held in Honolulu, Hawaii, May 2002.

Charles J. Robinson, D.Sc., P.E., is the Max and Robbie L. Watson Eminent Scholar Chair in Biomedical Engineering and Micromanufacturing, and director of the University Center for Biomedical Engineering and Rehabilitation Science (CyBERS), at Louisiana Tech University in Ruston, Louisiana, and a senior rehabilitation research career scientist at the Overton Brooks VA Medical Center in Shreveport, Louisiana. Dr. Robinson was the director general of the first World Congress on Computational Intelligence in 1994 and co-edited an IEEE Press book on the symposium from that Congress: *Computational Intelligence: Imitating Life,* which is the predecessor to this book. Robinson has been active as a volunteer within the Institute of Electrical and Electronics Engineers and has traveled and lectured throughout the world on its behalf. He was elected as a corporate director of the Institute representing the Systems and Control Division (Division X) during 1993 and 1994. Dr. Robinson previously served 2 terms as president of the IEEE Engineering in Medicine and Biology Society. He was the founding editor of the

IEEE Transactions on Rehabilitation Engineering, which is sponsored by that society, and was an associate editor for the *IEEE Transactions on Biomedical Engineering*. Robinson is internationally known for his research and leadership efforts in biomedical engineering and rehabilitation science. Dr. Robinson has been a registered Professional Engineer in Ohio since 1974 and Louisiana since 2000. Dr. Robinson is a Fellow of the IEEE and a Founding Fellow of the American Institute for Medical and Biological Engineering. In 1995, Dr. Robinson received the Purkynje Medal from the Czech Association of Medical Sciences (the highest scientific honor in the medical and related fields that can be given a noncitizen), and honorary membership in the Czech Society of Biomedical Engineering and Medical Informatics. He is an IEEE Millennium Medallist. He was awarded the 2001 IEEE Richard M. Emberson Award for "outstanding sustained contributions to the Institute's technical objectives through innovative enhancements in society and corporate leadership, technical publications, conferences, membership development and transnational outreach."

Printed and bound by CPI Group (UK) Ltd, Croydon, CR0 4YY

27/10/2024

14580256-0001